D1625864

ADVANCES IN GLOBAL LEADERSHIP

ADVANCES IN GLOBAL LEADERSHIP

Series Editor: William H. Mobley

Volume 1:   Executive Editor: William H. Mobley;
                Co-Editors: M. Joycelyne Gessner and Val Arnold

ADVANCES IN GLOBAL LEADERSHIP

EDITED BY

WILLIAM H. MOBLEY

PDI Global Research Consortia Ltd, Hong Kong

MORGAN W. McCALL, JR

Marshall School of Business,
University of Southern California,
Los Angeles, USA

2001

JAI
An Imprint of Elsevier Science

Amsterdam – London – New York – Oxford – Paris – Shannon – Tokyo

ELSEVIER SCIENCE Ltd
The Boulevard, Langford Lane
Kidlington, Oxford OX5 1GB, UK

First edition 2001

Library of Congress Cataloging in Publication Data
A catalog record from the Library of Congress has been applied for.

British Library Cataloguing in Publication Data
A catalogue record from the British Library has been applied for.

ISBN: 0-7623-0723-4

∞ The paper used in this publication meets the requirements of ANSI/NISO Z39.48-1992 (Permanence of Paper).
Printed in The Netherlands.

CONTENTS

PREFACE

Welcome to Volume II of *Advances in Global Leadership*. As documented in Volume I of this series and in multiple other forums, the accelerating globalization of business and the relative dearth of leadership talent requires better developed models, definitions, measures, processes and tools for understanding and developing leaders in the global economy. This deeper understanding of multinational and global leadership requires, among other things:

- Understanding the interplay among country and company cultures, corporate strategy, stage of company and business unit development, as well as individual differences;
- Evaluating the generalizability of models from Western cultures;
- Addressing the virtual/distance leadership of multinational organizations and teams and how new technologies bear on leading across multiple boarders;
- Understanding of multicultural and global leadership across national boundaries in non-traditional organizational structures, e.g. alliances and JV's;
- Encouraging greater communication among executives, leadership development professionals, consultants and academics dealing with global leadership;
- "Giving voice" to authors from, or working, in non-Western as well as Western cultures, from emerging as well as mature markets.

This biennial series of high quality, original papers seeks to address each of these issues by advancing the definition, conceptualization, measurement, and development of multinational and global leaders.

Our intent is to provide a series that will be of interest and value to:

- Those leading or aspiring to lead in multinational settings;
- Academics teaching and researching in areas related to multinational and global leadership;
- Those responsible for developing multinational and global leaders.

Based on the feedback from Volume I, we are reaching these multiple audiences and we believe Volume II will continue to do so. The risk of our broad and eclectic approach is that there will be something of interest for everyone but not everything will interest everyone. Our hope is that the selection of manuscripts will stimulate, pollinate and challenge among and across practitioners and academics, Westerners and non-Westerners, students and leaders. We encourage you to read and reflect on the chapters that are out of your current comfort zone.

It is an honor and pleasure to join with Morgan W. McCall, Jr. in co-editing Volume II. Morgan has been a sustained contributor to the leadership dialogue from his days at the Center for Creative Leadership to his current professorial position at the Marshall School of Business at the University of Southern California. Among his five books, with others on the way, Morgan McCall's *Lessons of Experience* (with Lombardo and Morrison) and *High-Flyers: Developing the Next Generation of Leaders* are benchmarks for lucid, stimulating and useful contributions to understanding leadership. Morgan is a rare boundary spanner in his ability to communicate clearly among the halls of ivy and the bastions of free enterprise. His insights, network and commitment to quality and candor have contributed immeasurably to this volume. In addition he is fun to work with, whether walking and talking on the beach near his Southern California home or sharing time at SIOP or participating at Global Research Consortia (GRC) meetings in Singapore or Hangzhou, China. Morgan has raised the bar on this series in lucid and enjoyable fashion.

The biographical summaries of the Volume II contributing authors are included in a subsequent section. Our special thanks to each of these authors for contributing their insights, time and energy to this still young series. Our deep appreciation also to Kim Canon for her editing and coordination among the authors, editors and publisher. Kim did a superb job on Volume II, as she did with Volume I. Thanks also to Maureen Bayless, GRC Coordinator of Member Relations and Special Projects, for her communication and coordination efforts, always with patience and good grace. We appreciate the support of Roger Dunn, former Managing Director at JAI Press and Diane Cogan, Senior Publisher, Social Sciences at Elsevier Science who has handled smoothly the transition of this series after Elsevier Science purchased JAI Press.

With authors from three continents, teaming with Kim Canon in Houston, Texas, Maureen Bayless in Dallas, Texas, Diane Cogan in Oxford, England, Morgan McCall in Los Angeles, California and myself in Hong Kong, we have together advanced our own learning about virtual teaming. We read with particular interest, as we know that you will, the two chapters in this volume on distance leadership and teaming. Finally, thanks to the leadership of PDI, Lowell Hellervik and Ken Hedberg, and to the charter corporate members of the PDI Global Research Consortia (GRC) for their support of this project. Agilent, Air Products, BP-AMOCO, Caltex, Coca-Cola, Dow, Eli Lilly,

Hewlett-Packard, Honeywell, IBM, Mandarin Oriental Hotel Group, Motorola, PDI, PPG, Shell, and MCI Worldcom continue to demonstrate leadership in multiple ways.

Planning for Volume III is underway. Suggestions, comments and manuscript ideas will be welcomed. BillM@pdi-corp.com

William H. Mobley
Executive Editor
Hong Kong
November 2000

INTRODUCTION

William H. Mobley and Morgan W. McCall, Jr.

Anyone can steer the ship when the sea is calm
Publilius Syrus

Rather than beginning with another recantation of why "the sea is not calm," of the multiple forces driving globalization and the increased urgency about better understanding global leadership and developing global leaders, we will begin with several situations we have observed in the past year. The names are fictitious, but the situations and the "conditions of the sea" are real. We take the liberty of organizing these vignettes into the three general categories that serve as the organizational basis of the subsequent chapters in this volume: I. International perspectives on leadership; II. Leading international teams and alliances; and III. Developing global leaders. Many of the vignettes cut across multiple categories.

I. INTERNATIONAL PERSPECTIVES ON LEADERSHIP

- The Global Strategy Task Force of a major global manufacturing firm is calling into question the very fabric of organizational hierarchy, control and leadership. They are arguing for a far *flatter, empowered, networked and accountable organization where regional teams are close to the customer and able to move with high speed, within broad corporate values, financial parameters and controls.* Senior corporate leadership is resisting.
- William Li, a 20-year veteran of a global manufacturing company with experience in U.S., Europe and Taiwan, is the CEO of a new *joint venture* in

Advances in Global Leadership, Volume 2, pages 1–5.
ISBN: 0-7623-0723-4

China that involves a newly privatized PRC state enterprise and two newly merged western firms. He is searching for insights on *JV leadership effectiveness in China and emerging markets.*

- Steve Shepard, COO for a global manufacturing firm based in the U.S., is increasingly concerned about headquarters staff visits and communications to his Southeast Asia facilities that reflect *blatant cultural insensitivity* and are undercutting his regional team's progress in *building a "hybrid third-culture."*

- Professor Andre Jason is having trouble finding reviewers for his Western-based journal on international leadership who can *cogently and fairly review and critique international leadership manuscripts* from international authors. Concurrently, Professor Kim at a major Korean University has stopped submitting manuscripts to Western journals because of perceived ethno-centric reviews. Concurrently, Professor Kathy Quinn, a leading global leadership scholar, is having trouble getting travel grants from her state university because travel for *international research is considered susceptible to legislative criticism as a boondoggle.*

II. LEADING INTERNATIONAL TEAMS AND ALLIANCES

- Vice President Karen Decker has been given the assignment by her global automotive firm of *leading an alliance* of automotive manufacturers in implementing *a consortium for e-commerce based global sourcing.*

- Alex Mogumbo, Vice President for Human Resources for a global electronics company has been given the responsibility for leading a global team in developing and rolling out within the year a global internet-based HR support system for the 64 countries where the firm operates. He is searching for insights on *leading an effective global project team* in double time.

- Carlos Ortiz, South America Managing Director of a global consulting firm, has just received a biting e-mail from his corporate headquarters criticizing him for proceeding with a major regional project requested by the regional office of a client. This client has a global client manager in the consulting firm's New York office, and that office is protesting Carlos' proceeding without *communicating and aligning* with the New York client manager (who wants the business development credit for her bonus calculation).

- Robert Cooke is CEO of a major financial services firm based in Europe that has just merged with a major New York-based financial services firm. Michael is well aware of the challenges of meeting post-merger and acquisition (M & A) expectations, let alone driving a *multi-country post-M & A alignment* to high performance.

III. DEVELOPING GLOBAL LEADERS

- Pat Blakovich, CEO of a leading global pharmaceutical firm, has established a global leadership talent task force. Included in his charge to the task force: define *global leadership in the context of our strategy; what competencies, experiences and attributes are needed for global leadership; how do we most effectively recruit, develop and retain global leaders; how many global leaders do we need now and in the future; how many and how effective are our pools of current and potential global leaders; what is our go forward plan?*
- Kerry Cooper, the head of Asia Pacific HR for a global financial services firm, is seeking innovative solutions for slowing down the resurgence of *attrition of critical skill talent* to "new economy" start-ups with their lure of stock options, flexibility and responsibility. The firm's A/P strategy is at risk.
- Michael Griffin, CEO of a global computer and technology firm, is alarmed at the high rate of *derailment of previously successful domestic executives when given international assignments.* She is questioning the *competency model* the company has been using for the past 10 years.

As these real time questions, issues and challenges illustrate, the multinational and global leadership seas are anything but calm. Understanding leadership and executing effective leadership have always been an enigma, a puzzle within a puzzle. At the dawn of the 21st century, multinational and *global* leadership is even more so. The vignettes above illustrate some of the challenge. How do we define a global firm and global leaders? What aspects of cultural differences are relevant to effective business leadership? What cultural and other contingencies are relevant to effective multinational and global leadership? Should we focus more on leadership behavior than on formal leaders? How to effectively lead and team at a distance on a global scale? How does one lead post-merger and acquisition (M & A), joint venture (JV), and alliance organizations across multiple national and cultural boundaries on multiple continents? How can leaders and academics escape their own ethnocentric filters? How does one blend new economy and old economy technologies and corporate cultures across national and cultural boundaries? How does one best align strategy, structure and leadership across multiple geographic and cultural boundaries? What are the leadership knowledge, skills and attitudes and the knowledge, skill and attitude building *experiences* that contribute to leadership effectiveness in multinational and global settings? Are there universal principals and relationships? How can we develop and retain effective multinational and global leaders? An enigma indeed!

In Volume II of *Advances in Global Leadership*, we have invited submissions that will illuminate parts of this puzzle. The chapters are divided into three major sections: I. International Perspectives on Leadership; II. Leading International Teams and Alliances; and III. Developing Global Leaders. Within each section, there are chapters by academics and practitioners; empirical as well as conceptual, descriptive, prescriptive and critical chapters; and even a bit of humor in places. Each section will be introduced by a preface by one of the co-editors, and as a last chapter we will offer our conclusions and directions for multinational and global leadership research and development.

Section I. includes several reviews; George Hollenbeck guides us in engaging style through the global leadership literature while Dickson, Hanges and Lord develop a taxonomy for aiding in finding generalizations, trends, developments and gaps in the cross-cultural leadership research. Howard Crabtree provides a futuristic, challenging and provocative analysis of leadership. Xiao Ping Chen and Jing-Lih Farh examine the effects of transformational and transactional leadership in Taiwan and the PRC and discuss the implications for contingent leadership. Tjosvold and Hui provide an integration and interpretation of the literature on leadership and relationship building in China, challenging some stereotypes along the way. Pearce, Ramirez and Branyiczki use the globalization effects on the transformation of the political and economic system in Hungary to illuminate the role of status in leaders' willingness to drive change.

Section II focuses on leading international teams and alliances and captures some of the implications of rapidly changing information and communication technology on global leadership and teaming. Laree Kiely presents a lucid examination of the challenges facing international virtual executive teams and suggests approaches to dealing with these challenges. Isabella and Spekman document the growth in strategic alliances and argue that the new kinds of leadership and the attributes of effective alliance managers are the characteristics required of global leaders of the future. Gibson, Conger and Cooper examine the effects of perceptual distance, power distance and collectivism on team processes and outcomes across cultures. Alison Eyring takes a practical look from Asia at challenges faced in distance leadership, including effective communications, building alignment around business strategy and fostering individual and group learning.

Section III focuses on developing multinational and global leaders. Charles Corace, a seasoned leadership development executive, documents the shortage of business leadership talent and inadequate human capital investment. He then presents an approach and the critical success factors in creating an effective supply of leadership talent. Hall, Zhu and Yan examine the development of multinational and global leaders and argue that firms are not managing the international assignments well, and need to clearly define success in international assignments. They examine the paradox of loading international assignments with challenge, utilization, and development (thus enhancing mobility), which can enhance performance and retention. Adler, Brody and Oswald use a significant organizational change initiative led by the CEO at Best Foods (now Unilever) to illustrate how a global firm can address the leadership talent challenge by moving women from around the world into senior executive positions. Data from this project also illuminate similarities and differences between and among male and female career development strategies and barriers.

As we will note in our section introductions and conclusions, there is emerging consensus on some of the questions framed above. However, some old questions remain and some new questions are framed. At a minimum, the chapters that follow will sharpen some of the enigma's pathways and cul-de-sacs in the continuing quest for understanding global leadership. Morgan McCall has suggested that the search for understanding multinational and global leadership is much like searching for a clear view of a leopard moving through the dense jungle. The chapters that follow provide valuable guidance in this search. Paraphrasing lead chapter author George Hollenbeck, let the sojourn begin, and may it be a rewarding one.

PART I

INTERNATIONAL PERSPECTIVES ON LEADERSHIP

INTRODUCTION: INTERNATIONAL PERSPECTIVES ON LEADERSHIP: A LEOPARD IN THE DARK WOODS

Morgan W. McCall, Jr.

What is a global leader anyway? As we tire of seeing the litany of reasons why even a small Kansas merchant is part of the grand global competition, and as it becomes increasingly obvious that effective global leaders are critical to international success, we still puzzle at what exactly a global leader is and how to find or develop one. This puzzlement is not for lack of exploration – indeed, the intensity of inquiry into the nature of international leadership has kept pace with the increasing interest in it. As reflected in the chapters in this section, the exploration is as diverse as it is determined. This variety should be expected, as the domain to be traversed is global rather than limited, and agreement on what leadership is was never fully reached even when the scope of the search was restricted to domestic venues.

What "global leadership" and "global leader" mean is not a purely academic question, although academics pursue it with vigor. From their academic perch at Harvard, for example, Bartlett and Ghoshal in their classic series have defined the playing field of global leadership, segmenting global leaders into a variety of types – country managers, business managers, and the like (Bartlett & Ghoshal, 1990). From the equally lofty perch of CEO, Percy Barnevik, formerly head of ABB, also described global leadership as multi-dimensional. In his now-classic interview in the *Harvard Business Review*, European leadership legend Barnevik asserted that ". . . a global company does not need

Advances in Global Leadership, Volume 2, pages 9–14.
2001 by Elsevier Science Ltd.
ISBN: 0-7623-0723-4

thousands of global managers. We need maybe 500 or so out of 15,000 managers to make ABB work well – not more. I have no interest in making managers more 'global' than they have to be" (Taylor, 1991, 94). He went on to define the qualities he thought the global leader should have, which included being open minded, respecting differences, incisiveness, willingness to "push the limits of the culture," generosity, patience, and English fluency. If it begins to sound a little like the "competency" models that have come to dominate thinking and practice about leadership, it is because the myth of the quintessential global leader is as active in the world of practice as it has been in academia. This, even when it is acknowledged that different types of global leaders exist.

The chapters in this section will not resolve the debate or end the search. A leopard in a dark wood is still hard to see. However, this section certainly will advance the debate, and its chapters expose us to the some of the many possible paths that the search might take. It begins with overviews from three different perspectives. George Hollenbeck takes the broadest look ("A Serendipitous Sojourn through the Global Leadership Literature"), approaching the topic, as his eclectic background as an HR executive, consultant, and researcher would suggest, by taking a "sojourn" through a variety of topics that in one way or another are connected with global leadership. Following him along these trails in the woods we get fascinating glimpses of the same animal from six different perspectives: strategy, cross-cultural research, expatriation, competencies, leadership, and adult development. At the end of his wanderings he finds that the literature related to global leadership is vast and scattered, but that common themes do emerge, as does a core set of references that serve as touchstones for those interested in the topic. Despite its popularity, he concludes that seeking the quintessential global leader in the literature of global competencies is ultimately a futile effort, but that the idea of a "global mindset" provides a convenient way to capture the critical competencies of global leaders.

The second overview chapter ("Take me to your Leader") also reflects the lens of its author. Howard Crabtree has spent his career in multinational corporations trying to identify and develop the global leaders that others only study. In spite of his position on the firing line, he looks at the phenomenon from the greatest distance, taking the perspective of the proverbial alien visitor coming to earth for enlightenment. His light-hearted chapter makes a serious point and ends up taking a strong and controversial stance. After considering several different approaches to the practice of international leadership, Crabtree concludes that the effectiveness of the different styles depends very much on the developmental stage of the organization. Not so controversial yet, though it does undermine the idea of a single set of competencies. But he goes on to suggest that these stages of organizational evolution are ultimately more important than cultural differences – that the world of global business is undergoing an homogenization that is inevitably eroding the cultural differences that many have focused on so intently.

The third overview is a state-of-the-art review of the traditional leadership approach applied across cultures ("Trends, Developments, and Gaps in Cross-cultural Research on Leadership"). Dickson, Hanges and Lord have been intimately involved with the awesome Project GLOBE, ". . . a network of 170 social scientists and management scholars from 62 cultures throughout the world, working in a coordinated long-term effort to examine the interrelation-ships between societal culture, organizational culture and practices, and organizational leadership" (Mobley, Gessner & Arnold, 1999, 171). Shaped by the approaches and methods of this undertaking, unparalleled in scope and ambition, these authors provide a systematic review of the vast and rapidly expanding academic literature on cross-cultural leadership. They provide a sophisticated framework for sorting out the complex array of findings, in the process clarifying some seeming contradictions in the data. By directly taking on the view of cross-cultural leadership as a dichotomy between universal and particularistic, they provide both a frame of reference for interpreting the data and an empirical base for identifying which cultural dimensions matter under what circumstances. They conclude by pointing out the gaps in our knowledge, reflecting that progress often takes the form that the more we learn, the more we see how much there is to know.

After the peek in the woods through the three overview chapters, this section moves to specific examples of selected approaches to cross-cultural leadership. There are two chapters on leadership in China – one by Chen and Farh (Transformational and Transactional Leader Behavior in Chinese Organiza-tions") and the other by Tjosvold and Hui ("Leadership in China") – that illustrate some key issues raised by the overviews. These scholars apply different frames and methods to the same issue, leadership in China, and, like the blind men and the elephant, paint equally valid but tauntingly different pictures. The former is an empirical study that applies the academic model of transformational and transactional leadership via survey methods in the PRC and Taiwan; the latter is a conceptual tour d'force that uses Deutch's theory of cooperation and competition to explain differences in Eastern and Western relationships. Between them, the two chapters on China provide examples of most of the key distinctions raised by the three overviews, including the relationships between culture and leadership, changes in culture over time, differences in methodologies and conceptual perspectives, and practical implications.

The final chapter by Pearce, Ramiriz & Branyiczki ("Leadership and the Pursuit of Status") takes us to yet another part of the world – Hungary – and to a different level of analysis – the impact of the transformation of political and economic systems on a leader's status. Using case studies of different leaders coping with the vast implications of post-communist Hungary, these authors examine how global forces result in dramatic changes in social standing that in turn affect how leaders behave.

The six chapters in this section never find the leopard in the woods. But they do provide some enticing glimpses into what is out there. Perhaps their cumulative photograph can be seen as six observations that in some way frame central issues in the continuing search for truth.

(1) We continue to grow more sophisticated in our approach to global leadership. We are moving from the simplistic universal-versus-culturally-specific notions of leadership to deeper looks beneath these surface differences. Whether it is Crabtree suggesting that cultural differences are dwarfed by the developmental stage of the global organization, two different approaches to leadership in China ending up at the same point, or Dickson et al. providing a sophisticated framework for understanding seemingly contradictory empirical relationships, all point to the conclusion that a deeper level of understanding is needed of cross-cultural leadership.

(2) As global research and practice grow more sophisticated, they raise much more interesting questions about what aspects of leadership should be influenced by cultural differences. We find that transformational leadership behavior is effective across at least some cultures, that new variables emerge as explanatory candidates in different cultures (for example, Confucian work dynamism in China and changed leader status in Hungary), that information processing has re-emerged as a promising approach to understanding global leadership – and so on. We may not yet fully understand the relationship between leadership and culture, but we are at once eliminating sacred cows, creating new ones and sniffing out new trails that someday may lead to answers.

(3) A variety of methodologies, many of which are represented in these chapters, have been brought to bear in trying to understand global leadership. From practitioner personal experience to case studies to massive surveys, from eclectic literature reviews to focused literature reviews to conceptual logic, the chapters in this section are nothing if not diverse. But each one reveals something that the others don't, proving once again that applying different methods and perspectives to the same topic both enriches and obscures. But somehow the diversity of approach stands

a better chance of revealing what we are looking for than any one method. And, as always, the best method is the one that best addresses what one is interested in. Different questions call for different approaches. At least for now, it's all okay.

(4) How important is culture, relatively speaking, to leadership? Putting aside for the moment that even the meaning of culture is ambiguous (e.g. geography versus shared beliefs), where does it fit in the grand sweep of the economic, political, technological and social changes that are shaping and reshaping the world? Could it not be argued that these larger forces are so powerful that they are changing cultures, and that focusing minutely on cultural differences and dimensions might keep us from seeing the real context of global leadership? Taking the example of the Cultural Revolution in China or the fall of communism in Eastern Europe, we see that global leadership can be viewed from a very broad perspective indeed.

(5) Perhaps one reason for confusion about global leadership is that with so many potential variables to look at, we sometimes fail to take into account hierarchical level. Perhaps relationships between culture and leadership depend on where one sits in the hierarchy and the scope of the job. At the face to face level, lower in the corporate structure, it is not surprising that people are strongly influenced by the specific culture in which they are embedded and that leadership can be viewed in terms of a small group of followers (even dyads) and local situational variables. This level of inquiry leads to intriguing questions about people – for example, are people basically the same wherever you are in the world? Are there common hopes, needs and values that cross cultural lines and language barriers? On the other hand, at the top of the organizational pyramid a different set of circumstances exists. To be sure, leaders still have face-to-face relationships with followers, but here we somehow have to take into account leading across multiple cultures, English as the common language of business, strategic alliances and other forms of virtual organization (see Chapter 8 by Isabella & Spekman in the next section), and global perspectives on economics, capital, and resources. Is this by any stretch of the imagination the same leadership?

(6) Finally, these chapters raise an issue of leaders' willingness to change, not others, but themselves. Considering leadership from all these different perspectives highlight just how many ways a leader may face a need to adapt. To mention only a few, a leader may be moved from one culture to another, new technologies can fundamentally change the nature and scope of a business, a promotion or reorganization can shift responsibility from

one perspective (say a country manager) to another (say a global business), a new boss may come from a wholly different culture, globalization can change the nature of competition over night – the list goes on. In the international sphere, a critical question becomes, "Can a leader change?" What makes a leader willing to try to change, and once trying, successful at it?

In conclusion, the six chapters that begin Volume II are representative of the state of the art. They do not cover all of the perspectives – indeed, the scope of this domain (as captured by Hollenbeck's review) is so broad that no volume could possibly include it all. There are many ways to cut this pie, many countries that could be the focus of research. However, we do see here the varying perspectives of academics and practitioners, of diverse methodologies, of within culture and across culture approaches. In that respect they represent the ongoing progress in bringing many resources to bear on answering the question, "what is a global leader?" But it may be that what we eventually discover is that we are asking the wrong question; that like finding that leopard in the dark wood, sometimes all we see is spots – the reality has once again slipped away.

REFERENCES

Bartlett, C. A., & Ghoshal, S. (1990). What is a Global Manager? *Harvard Business Review, 70*(5), 124–132.

Mobley, W. H. (Executive Editor), Gessner, M., & Arnold, V. (Co-Editors) (1999). *Advances in Global Leadership. Volume I.* Stamford, CT: JAI Press.

Taylor, W. (1991). The Logic of Global Business: An Interview with ABB's Percy Barnevik. *Harvard Business Review, 69* (Mar-Apr.), 91–105.

A SERENDIPITOUS SOJOURN THROUGH THE GLOBAL LEADERSHIP LITERATURE

George P. Hollenbeck

ABSTRACT

In a search for the meaning of global leadership, we use the metaphor of a sojourn. We travel into six areas of the literature: strategy, cross-cultural research, expatriation, competencies, leadership and adult learning. We draw from our visit to each literature its perspective on global leadership and then step back to reflect on the lessons of our sojourn – what we learned about the literature of global leadership and what we learned about global leadership itself. We learned that the literature is vast and ever expanding and too often uses a single methodology. However, common themes emerge. With a few exceptions, the literature is engaging, and tempts one to take side trips and explore back roads. We found many answers to the riddle of global leadership, both in definitions and in competencies, and we gained an appreciation for the complexity and ambiguity of international work. We answer the "favorite place" question and conclude, after all, that the mystery of global leadership remains unsolved.

INTRODUCTION

Global interests are an acquired taste. Most people left to themselves would indeed do that – stick with themselves and their kind. Throughout history there

Advances in Global Leadership, Volume 2, pages 15–47.
2001 by Elsevier Science Ltd.
ISBN: 0-7623-0723-4

have been explorers who gave up the home and hearth for the highs and hardships of a different land, but most people stay close to home. It should not have been a surprise that when we asked a group of Boston area 30-something MBA students enrolled in a leadership course, "How many would be willing to relocate to Hong Kong?" not one volunteered. Describing their own experiences in the Preface to Volume I of this series, Gessner, Arnold and Mobley write: "The most universal experience we have had is the variations on this theme: 'I don't know about you, but I'm normal. If you don't look, act, value as I do, then there must be something wrong with *you*'" (p. xv).

However, once bitten by the global bug our interest is likely to be intense. This chapter describes our sojourn – a sojourn being a temporary stay and implying more than just flying over or traveling through – into the literature of global leadership. Our interest began with global leadership specifically, rather than the broader field, but, as we will see, our stay would have been short indeed had we not included the broader literature that informs about global leadership and its context. Although we sampled a wide range, we selected that which we judged to contribute, underpin or serve as the basis for defining and developing global leaders.

Our intention here is to serve the purposes of a travelogue rather than a formal literature review. We offer glimpses of a world out there as yet unseen by some readers; or, if one has indeed been there, we hope to provide that satisfactory feeling of revisiting the familiar, nodding agreement (and disagreement) with our observations.

Our method is as modern as our times. We began with an Internet search rather than a search of a university library. Our Web search followed the links of Amazon.com to "customers who bought this book also bought . . ." rather than related topics in a Library of Congress catalog. We networked from reference to reference, often finding the most valuable part of a publication to be a nugget or two in its reference list rather than the content per se, and we networked from person to person – "What are you reading in the global area, what are your favorites?"

The result is as idiosyncratic as our method. The chapter won't be of universal interest, but we are aiming for what Dickson, Hanges and Lord (this volume) describe as "variform universality," where the level of one's interest depends on what the reader brings to and seeks from the reading.

Where did we go? We begin describing our efforts to define the "global leader" and how that leader develops. In our search we were informed by the worlds of strategy and cross-cultural research. We visited the expatriate compound, competency country, the leadership literature and the field of adult learning.

We continue by sharing our conclusions from our sojourn – our reflections about global leadership, about the literature of global leadership, and we share our unanswered questions and continuing interests. What was our favorite place? We save that for our closing.

Despite our efforts to take the perspective of other cultures, our origins – both by birth and culture – inevitably produce a certain U.S.-centricity to our views. And, regrettably we only speak, write and read English (or some would say, American!).

Language is important, however, so a word about our usage. Like it or not, judging from the literature we sampled, the term "leader" has overtaken the field. New books promise the secrets of leaders and leadership, not of executives and management. In keeping with that, we use leader, executive and manager interchangeably. Also, today's world is more "global" than "international," and we will use global to include international unless specifically focusing on the distinction. And in the interest of diversity neutrality, we will knowingly and without guilt use the pronoun "they" as singular.

Defining Global Leadership: Breaking the Code – What IS Global Leadership?

Leadership has a long history as a concept that is difficult to define and easy to misinterpret: "Leadership has an elusive, mysterious quality about it. It is easy to recognize, hard to describe . . . perhaps no other topic has attracted as much attention from observers, participants and philosophers – with so little agreement as to basic facts." (Campbell, 1984) And the misinterpretations are not U.S.-centric: "It is equally misunderstood in Africa, Asia, South America, Europe and the Middle East" (Avolio, B., p. 65, in Church, 1998).

With this history, perhaps it should come as no surprise that defining "global" leadership is equally, if not more, difficult. Like leadership, global leadership is even more mysterious, with something about the term that beckons interested writers and researchers to offer their own definitions. There is a temptation to dance on the head of the definitional pin.

We will avoid that, however, in two ways. First, as our beginning point we accept the definition of "leadership" in Volume I of this series (p. xv) (Gessner & Arnold, 1999): ". . . leadership involves people in business settings whose job or role it is to influence the thoughts and actions of others to achieve some finite set of business goals . . . usually displayed in large, multicultural contexts; that is, not just from one's native perspective." This definition is not intended to limit global leadership to some specific number of cultures. Second, we avoid a head-on confrontation. We will instead approach the beast indirectly, looking at the various literatures of global leadership as different perspectives on what global leadership is, does, requires and means. Our divisions into the six areas – strategy, cross-cultural research, expatriates, competencies, leadership and adult learning – will be used to help us make sense of our travels. The boundaries are sometimes arbitrary and often overlapping, but each provides a perspective that enlightens. We begin with the perspective from the literature of strategy.

From the Strategy Perspective

Prior to the mid-1980s, "global leadership" was not a common term – "international" or "cross-cultural" leadership sufficed. But in the 1980s corporate strategists described a new organizational imperative driven by the changing business environment. The best known chronicle of that new organization (whether first or not: note 1) is Bartlett and Ghoshal's (1989) *Managing Across Borders*, now in its second edition. We had initially intended to summarize their thinking, but as we traveled further, we found summaries and annotations so widespread (e.g. London & Sessa, 1999) that we offer here only the basics: the transnational organization builds global efficiencies and national responsiveness while leveraging learning across markets in order to cope with the increasing competitive demands of a global world.

The organizational structure of the resulting triple matrix – country x business x function – is difficult to understand, much less to implement and manage within. Bartlett and Ghoshal addressed these difficulties in a 1990 article titled "Matrix Management: Not a Structure, a Frame of Mind:" "Over the past 20 years, strategic thinking has far outdistanced organizational capabilities." (p. 128); and, "The problem is that their companies are organizationally incapable of carrying out the sophisticated strategies they have developed." More difficult to put in practice than just setting up an organizational structure, the transnational organization is a "mindset," not an organizational chart. And so was born the notion of the "global mindset" that, as we will see, has pervaded the literature.

Continuing their thinking, Bartlett and Ghoshal (1992) answered the question – "What is a global manager?" as: ". . . there is no such thing as a universal global manager. Rather, there are three groups of specialists: business managers, country managers, and function managers." Managing these three groups is a smaller group of corporate leaders, transnationals, ". . . who manage the complex interactions of the three," negotiate among them, establish a corporate vision and identify and develop the talent to fill these positions (p. 125). Consistent with the strategy field's emphasis on responsibilities and tasks,

Bartlett and Ghoshal define the three leaders' roles in terms of what must be done. Just why this fourth category, transnational corporate manager, is not THE global manager we seek is not clear, but their point is to emphasize the varieties of global work, not the similarities.

Our link-to-link search method led us to realize that the Bartlett and Ghoshal work, intentionally or not, was part of a related stream coming out of Harvard University in the late 1980s and early 1990s. Kanter was also exploring the world of global business, dividing the new world-class executives of the information economy into cosmopolitans and locals (see Kanter, 1995, both for the discussion and references to other works and cases developed during the time). Her cosmopolitans, not unlike Bartlett and Ghoshal's "transnational leaders," are defined ". . . not so much by their travel as their mindsets . . ." of world class concepts, competencies and connections. Robert Reich, in two articles titled "Who is us?" (1990) and "Who is Them?" (1991), addressed similar issues of what is a global company and what it takes to compete, describing the new global manager's job as ". . . to exploit the opportunities created by . . . new worldwide communication technologies and deregulation of national controls over capital flows." Both of these articles are notable to us for their descriptions of the political and economic forces shaping the competitiveness for U.S. corporations, as well as the broader world.

With these descriptions of corporate globalization, the stage was set for a much-referenced article by Adler and Bartholomew (1992), which takes the theme of the evolving domestic/international/multinational/global organization and frames the issue in terms of the different leader competencies required at each stage. Bartlett and Ghoshal had laid the foundation, but their work is not an easy read for a non-strategist, and they didn't make explicit the links of strategy/structure/executive skill that was done so well by Adler and Bartholomew.

Adler and Bartholomew's six transnational skills, still a mixture of responsibilities and attributes, are Global Perspective, Local Responsiveness, Synergistic Learning, Transition and Adaptation, Cross-cultural Interaction, Collaboration and Foreign Experience (p. 54). The key distinction between traditional international and transnationally competent managers is the cross-border nature of their tasks and skills. Rather than focus on a single country, they have a global perspective. Rather than becoming an expert in one culture, they learn and work with people from many cultures simultaneously. Although Adler and Bartholomew called both international and transnational strategies "global business strategies," "global leader" was defined as the executive who executed global strategies across, rather than within, borders of time and geography, nation, function and product.

Adler and Bartholomew accept the premises, as have most writers on global business, that the external forces (information technology et al.) driving toward a global economy are inevitable, and that the globally competent manager is essential for implementing the resulting strategies. We would be remiss if we did not acknowledge that there is another point of view. The transnational difficulties are not just the result of a faulty "mindset," according to this view, but are the result of strong cultural forces inhibiting globalization. Exploring this territory takes us too far afield, however, and we refer the interested traveler to the convincing case presented by Doremus, Keller, Pauly and Reich (1998) and the excellent review of their book by Kogut (1999). And a global world is not an unmixed blessing in the eyes, at least, of a very vocal few – see Krugman (2000) for a description and critique of the "extremist" anti-global views of Ralph Nader.

Our brief discussion illustrates the strategy perspective: strategy defines the global leader in terms of what they do and what tasks are carried out in achieving the corporate strategy. The essence of global leadership is that those tasks require working across boundaries – across geography, culture, function and business and product units simultaneously. Across cultures, our next area, is one of the major crosses.

Bartlett and Ghoshal's 1989 book (now in its 2nd edition) is truly a monument in the global strategy/organization/leadership area. Almost every discussion of those topics references it, and we use it as the touchstone of the strategy view of leadership. The great virtue of this view, we believe, is its focus on doing business. The view ultimately frustrates, however, because it leaves to others to get from business to leadership.

From the Cross-Cultural Perspective

Cross-cultural research has a history and an extensive literature quite separate from that of management and leadership. Dickson, Hanges and Lord (this volume) reference this literature, describing how over the past 25 years the two literatures have begun to come together. Drawn from several of the social sciences – social psychology, communications, sociology, anthropology – cross-cultural researchers were, for the most part, a world apart from the world of business. Their writings often seemed more idealistic, their interests "agenda driven." Gessner and Arnold (Volume I of this series, p. 3) describe the contributions from Volume I authors who ". . . view global leadership as an opportunity to tackle the challenges of creating an ideal global community characterized by tolerance and hope." Despite, or because of, these one-world ideals, cross-cultural research has laid the groundwork for much of our understanding of how people relate across cultures. And, as viewed from the perspective of the strategist, the trans-cultural aspect of the work in all its facets (nation, function, business or product) is the essence of global leadership.

One tactic for travelers in such a large and diverse literature is to find secondary sources that provide perspective. We found such a source in Smith and Bond (1998), a cross-cultural social psychology text written with the expressed purpose of presenting a less "U.S./Euro-centric" review. As neophytes to the area ourselves, a virtue of this book for us was the summary of literature and critiques that guide our thinking, as well as introductions to terms like "etic" and "emic," which we don't ordinarily come across. (For the uninitiated, etic and emic refer to analyses that focus on how things are alike (etic) or how they are different (emic)).

Gudykunst (1998) provided much the same function in the communication area, overlapping many topics with Smith and Bond. Originally a text, now in its third edition and using a "how to" focus to seek a broader audience, Gudykunst is a veritable source book of cross-cultural communication, the impact of culture, group differences, social attribution processes, conflict resolution and relationship development. Much of the book is organized around the dynamics of communicating with strangers. The notion of "the stranger" is an engaging one, with a history dating back to 1908 in the sociology of Georg Simmel (1950).

Especially interesting to us are Gudykunst's discussion of stereotypes (pp. 122–138) and their uses for good and ill, a topic of U.S.-centric sensitivity. Lewis (1996), a British linguist, gives more detailed coverage for understanding and making use of cultural differences in "getting to know" other people, providing detailed descriptions of the "generally accepted" characteristics of a variety of cultures and accompanying management, leadership and organization styles.

Another broad-based guide is Adler's (1997) classic text on how culture impacts organizational behavior. We would not ordinarily have classified Adler in the cross-cultural research area, but the overlap in coverage (communication across cultures, leadership, negotiation and cross-cultural transitions) with others such as Smith and Bond and Gudykunst is so great that it fits here as well as in other areas. Like other survey books, Adler's strength – its broad coverage of a wide range of topics – is its weakness, also. Often only the surface is touched. The extensive reference list illustrates just how big this literature is. Unfortunately, the list also indicates how badly outdated this third edition has become – our quick tally of 60-plus references in one chapter found twice as many from the 1960s and 1970s as that from the 1990s. And most were from the early 1980s. It is not that we view old ideas as necessarily bad ideas, but that, for example, studies of attitudes of mid-1980s MBA students seem unlikely to represent the views of 21st century students. And the book is decidedly American.

A prominent theme in all of these books is cultural differences, and all roads lead to Hofstede. Our casual observation is that *Cultures and organizations: software of the mind* (Hofstede, 1991) is the most frequently referenced of Hofstede's work, with the earliest Hofstede a 1979 chapter. Nowhere else in our sojourn did we find a source so dominant, so widely referenced, (and so thoroughly criticized) as Hofstede's conceptualization of the dimensions of culture. Annotated and referenced so widely that we will forego the temptation to do our own summary (see Dickson et al., this volume), the Hofstede work has become a touchstone of leadership's attempt to go global, with its dimensions or some variant serving as the organizing principle for writing, research studies and training programs.

Trompenaars and Hampden-Turner (we read the second edition, 1998) is also devoted to dimensions of cultural differences and understanding global business. Trompenaars came to our attention both in other books (Fulkerson & Tucker, 1999) and in a business press listing of fashionable consulting gurus. First published in 1993, this second edition presents questionnaire data from over 30,000 participants of training programs. The book ". . . is about cultural differences and how they affect the process of doing business and managing. It is not about how to understand the people of different nationalities. It is our belief that you can never understand other cultures" (p. 1). Continuing in this provocative style, Trompenaars and Hampden-Turner describe seven dimensions of cultural difference [see Note 2] and provide tips for recognizing the differences and doing business in cultures with dimensional differences. A central feature of the book is charts that display differences among 40 countries' responses to questionnaire items about the dimensions – about organizations, leadership and values. Staking out a strong belief that management theories are U.S.-centric and do not apply elsewhere, Trompenaars and Hampden-Turner use these country differences to illustrate the need for diversity of views.

We found the Trompenaars and Hampden-Turner's discussions of culture and country differences informative and interesting, especially in areas where we had done no other reading. As we read more widely, our notes indicated "too simple," and indeed the book appears to be more a collection of training materials than a thought piece. Its appendix describing the consultancy of the authors, their products, Web site, e-mail, fax and telephone numbers lends credibility to that appearance. Its setting up and demolishing of "straw men" becomes off-putting, but overall we found the book a stimulating read with interesting, if not in-depth, discussions of key issues in managing across cultures.

The first edition of Trompenaars (1993) did not escape the attention of Hofstede (1996), who wrote a biting critique with the title, "Riding the Waves of Commerce." The title reflects Hofstede's view that Trompenaars ". . . tunes his messages to what he thinks the customer likes to hear . . . . The result is a fast food approach to intercultural diversity and communication" (p. 198); and that the seven dimensions are a collection of old anthropological concepts, and the "research" on which the book is based is fundamentally flawed in concept and execution. The exchange of views (see Hampden-Turner & Trompenaars' response, 1997) apparently resulted in the extensive methodology appendix of the second edition. Not willing ourselves to invest our time and effort in judging the validity of Hofstede's critique – on its face, some of it agrees with our own -we leave to the researcher the esoteric methodological issues.

We close this section with a sense of negligence at not having visited some work by H. C. Triandis (see for example, Triandis, 1995). Triandis is without doubt a major figure in the area of cross-cultural research, both in his publications and his training of students to do cross-cultural research. He was across publications one of the most cited authors, but we did not find in our sojourn an oasis of understanding, a particular insight or conclusion that seemed to merit follow-up. Recognizing that on this sojourn we cannot go everywhere (either seeking Triandis or in the other extensive literature), we leave that for our next trip, or the reader's.

We do see in this very broad literature a general terrain – the cross-cultural perspective brings to the forefront the cultural dimensions of leadership, and the issues of communicating, socializing and adapting across cultural boundaries. There is truly a wealth of literature that is (sometimes) fascinating to read and offers descriptions and prescriptions for communicating across cultures. It frustrates, however, not only in its history of "one world idealism" – books like Gudykunst's make clear his views of how one *should* communicate – but more that its focus is on crossing cultures, not conducting business.

From the Expatriate Perspective

Since the advent of nation-states, there must have been expatriates, those adventurers who went "out" to live amidst others. Given the size of the literature in this area, we suspect that ever since that time, the adventurers and those who sent them out have been writing about the experience and the process. Briscoe (1991), in a literature review on developing the global executive, reports ". . . there was more literature on cross cultural adjustment and its relationship to success in an expatriate assignment than in any other area."

The phenomenon of working and living abroad is so widespread among global leaders, so enchanting (see Osland, 1995) and so powerful an experience that we cannot address global leadership without considering the expatriate experience, also. We divide the expatriate literature into two parts: one focused on "managing" expatriates and another on "being" one. Most books have something to say about both – it seems to be difficult to describe "being one" without indicating how they ought to be managed, and vice versa – one can't prescribe management techniques without describing what it is like to be one.

Managing Expatriates
We include here all the processes involved in administering expatriation – selecting, training, rewarding, repatriating et al.

There is a towering figure in this landscape – J. Stewart Black. Amazon.com in June 2000 lists five books authored or co-authored by Black that are specifically related to administering the expatriate process. One of those books, (Black, Gregersen, Mendenhall & Stroh, 1999) cites among its 193 references 27 articles and books by Black, the earliest a 1988 paper on American expatriate managers in Japan. A best practices article by Black and Gregersen (1999), too recent to be included among the 27 mentioned above, summarizes the state of the art into three general areas of best practice: sending the right people (selection) for the right reason (strategy) and providing the right ending (repatriation).

Black may be the most published author that we found prescribing how to manage expatriates, but he has no corner on the best practices library (e.g. Shepard, 1998, for one of many). The importance of selecting for acculturation as well as technical skill, stable family relationships, providing culture training, giving support while on assignment, the expatriate's family support, the difficulty of repatriation and the value of maintaining networks in order to facilitate repatriation – these are well-known best practices. Not only are expatriate management practices widely known, but the practices have been widely known for years (Cagney, 1975). The intriguing thing for a visitor to the area is that as far back as we sampled the literature, few organizations have followed the practices!

At the organizational level, designing and implementing HR systems is a "macro" of managing expatriates that puts best practice into use. Quelch and Bloom (1999), Pucik and Saba (1998), Wilson and Dalton (1998), and Adler and Bartholomew (1992) all fall in one way or another into that subset, as does

Black, Gregersen, Mendenhall and Stroh (1999) and, we suspect, many, many more in the HR literature.

Being an Expatriate

We found two literatures focused on *being* an expatriate – one describing the *experience* of being one and the other offering *how to* advice. The literatures overlap, of course – it is difficult to have a transformational experience without both sharing it and dispensing advice to those about to have such an experience. One author, having been a trailing spouse from country to country to country, decided while in Korea to produce books to help others!

The experience of being. The most interesting for the general reader is the work on the experience of being an expatriate. This literature – on working and/ or living in a country other than one's own – must be huge. Storti (1990) even includes as an appendix a reading list of novels and sojourn descriptions by well-known writers relevant to the experience. Storti's book, written for anyone going abroad who must interact effectively with the local people, takes the view that adjusting to the local culture is "... valuable, desirable, and greatly enhances one's experiences." Its purpose, by sharing the experience, is to help sojourners adjust. His straightforward, down-to-earth anecdotes, descriptions of adaptation and prescriptions are clearly the work of one who has done it. Written by an American with Americans playing the central role in many of the anecdotes, the book has a cosmopolitan flavor that we judge would make it useful for a potential expatriate from most any country. Storti contends that the processes are the same, whatever the country of origin.

Osland (1995), with 14 years of expatriate experience under her belt, attributes her motivation to study (interviews with 35 U.S. repatriates) and write (her dissertation as well as this book) to her own experience. Returning to the U.S., she was frustrated to find that scholarly descriptions of expatriation did not ring true and were of little use to expatriates or their companies in making sense of the experience. Taking as a metaphor Joseph Campbell's hero's journey (1968), she describes the expatriate journey through Campbell's stages, challenges and mechanisms of adjustment. The combination of Osland's experience, her interviews and the hero journey metaphor make for a lively and insightful book. We list a few of those insights that caught our eye: the decision to go is often a visceral call to adventure; there is no way to know what life will be like in another culture until it is experienced; expatriation is transformational because one's normal defense mechanisms don't work the same way; some people see living in another country as an exotic adventure, some see only discomfort and danger; how willing a culture is to accept foreigners may have a greater impact on an expatriate's experience than the similarity of their home culture to the new one; and, heroes have magical friends who protect them, and for believers God is the ultimate magical friend.

Expatriates commonly use words like "adventure" to describe their sojourns, and most seem to believe that the adventure permanently changed them. Storti and Osland give ample examples, but the belief is common in the expatriate literature. A common experience also is the returned expatriates' frustration that nobody back home, neither friends nor employers, seems to care or wants to know what they learned.

How to be an expatriate. "How To" manuals offer advice on how to survive as an expatriate. There are literally hundreds of these books listed in Internet bookstores, providing general advice as well as specialized guidance, (e.g. how to be an expatriate basketball player, how to live cheaply in Thailand). These books are more like travel guides than travelogues – they may be intensely interesting if one is going there, but are filled with irrelevant detail if one is not. We list only a random few references to make the point: Shepard, 1998; Kalb and Welch, 1992; Black and Gregersen, 1998; Rabe, 1997.

After examining literature in both *being* and *how to be* expatriates, we conclude that the expatriate perspective adds an essential element to understanding the global leader – an understanding of the experience and how to manage it. However, it also frustrates by failing to get beyond the adventurer experience to the issues of learning to become a global leader. We save the literature on expatriate competencies for our visit to the competency area.

We began this section with the observation that expatriation is common among global leaders. Is being an expatriate a necessary or only a common experience among global leaders? We return to this question in our conclusions.

From the Competency Perspective

Competencies are the currency of today's HR systems. The strategy view leads us there, but ultimately frustrates because it defines the global leader largely in terms of the tasks, responsibilities and results required to implement global strategies rather than global leader capabilities.

The competency view asks, "What are the knowledges, skills, abilities, motivations and attitudes required to DO those tasks and PRODUCE those results demanded by the strategist?" Competencies are characteristics of the individual leader, rather than the job (see Hollenbeck & McCall, 1999, for a brief review and critique). As we will see, seldom if ever are authors of competency lists able to answer the competency question – What does it take?

While Adler and Bartholomew (1992) began to provide a strategy/competency bridge, as mentioned above, the skills of their "transnationally competent manager" were a mix of "ability to's" (e.g. ability to use cross-cultural skills), experiences (e.g. foreign experience) and personal characteristics (e.g. global perspective).

Briscoe's review in 1991 focused on the U.S. literature, found no global executive competency studies. There were, however, extensive studies of the competencies required for cross-cultural adjustment and success as an *expatriate*. (The reader will recognize that these studies might also have been covered in the expatriate area).

Osland (1995) summarizes in one table extending over two pages (pp. 202–203) the expatriate selection criteria identified ". . . by my study and researchers." The competencies, divided into five areas – motivation, attitude, personal traits, skills and background and family – are all-inclusive, and except for the "superperson" quality of the list, seem as relevant today as then. Osland's reference list, extending from Brein and David (1971) to Black, Gregersen and Mendenhall (1992), illustrates the range of the extensive literature on the competencies of expatriate success. That literature, with studies of naval officers, international students and Peace Corps volunteers (see the review by Church, 1982), as well as corporate executives (Mendenhall & Oddou, 1985), covers a wide range, and includes both U.S. and non-U.S. perspectives (e.g. Torbiorn's study of Swedish expatriates, 1982).

Wilson and Dalton's (1998) more recent review and interview studies of expatriates provide similar findings. They organize their thinking into the Center for Creative Leadership's (CCL) selection/development/support framework, which they hope will ensure expatriate success. Their selection variables include personality (the "Big Five" – emotional stability, extraversion, openness to experience, agreeableness and conscientiousness), and early life experiences (lessons of difference, self-reliance and relationships). As characterizes CCL publications (see also London & Sessa, 1999), this one has an extensive and useful reference list.

Not surprisingly, expatriate success studies emphasize the competencies of adjustment (managing stress, emotional stability) and managing diversity (cultural sensitivity, openness to influence, etc.). Similar to the cross-culture area, they focus on the dynamics and the requirements of living (and working) across cultures, rather than the more inclusive role of leading.

In defining the global leader, competency studies of expatriation fall short because they focus on the ability to adapt to one other culture or country, rather than many (or transnationally), and because cultural adjustment is the focus, NOT executive performance. By the mid-1990s Wills and Barham (1994) described a thriving global leader competency movement: ". . . the creation of comprehensive lists of competencies is a burgeoning industry." Their view reflects Birchall, Hee and Gay's (1996) citation of a number of early 1990s European studies of the competencies of international management.

The Birchall et al. study embodies both the strengths and weaknesses of many of the competency studies. While it is a useful source of non-U.S. references and considerable wisdom about international management, it is based on surveys. Not only is it survey-based, but their study begins with a survey of other surveys of competency studies. Another questionnaire is then used to get ratings of the importance of competencies from 55 valid responses of 102 undescribed respondents. Despite these "technical" flaws, Birchall, Hee and Gay's conclusions - that most jobs have both international and domestic components, require both international business knowledge (strategy, negotiation, marketing) and personal competencies (global awareness and cultural empathy), and that the best development strategy may be to teach people the basics and help them "learn how to learn" – all ring true.

McCall developed a questionnaire, *Prospector*, to measure 11 high potential dimensions for international executive jobs, based on surveys of what it takes to succeed as an international executive (Spreitzer, McCall & Mahoney, 1997). Dividing his dimensions into those of "doing" and those of "being" (following Wills & Barham), the 11 dimensions are:

Doing Competencies:
Seeks opportunities to learn
Seeks and uses feedback
Learns from mistakes
Acts with integrity
Adapts to cultural differences
Brings out the best in people

Being Competencies:
Is open to criticism
Is committed to making a difference
Is insightful
Has the courage to take risks
Has broad-based business knowledge

Dalton (1998) provides another global leader competency framework. Drawing upon de Merode's review (1997), she hypothesize four competencies:

- A high level of cognitive complexity to reason in a complex and constantly changing world;

- excellent interpersonal skills to recognize and work with different customs, values and expectations;
- ability to learn from experiences, a willingness to accept and learn new information; and
- advanced moral reasoning to appreciate the ethical dilemmas of cultural tolerance (p. 386).

We see in the work of McCall, Dalton and Birchall et al. an emphasis on learning competencies and the metacompetency of learning to learn. Hall, Zhu and Yan (2001, *Advances in Global Leadership, Vol. II*) provide further discussion of metacompetencies at some length.

London and Sessa (1999), using a variant of the strategy/task/skill framework, review the literature and endorse the view that the global leader's capabilities are "in addition to" those required in international roles. Recognizing that sensitivity to cultural differences is a key competency for global executives, they suggest a nine-dimensional construct of intercultural sensitivity that captures many of the descriptors used elsewhere for cultural sensitivity (p. 10):

Dimensions of Intercultural Sensitivity

• Comfort with other cultures
• Positively evaluating other cultures
• Understanding cultural differences
• Empathy for people in other cultures
• Valuing cultural differences
• Open-mindedness
• Sharing cultural differences with others
• Degree to which feedback is sought
• Level of adaptability

This list illustrates for us one of the organizing problems of the competency approach – we find competencies at different levels of generality. For example, open-mindedness and adaptability can be thought of as the basis for several of the others on the list. In fact, is not open-mindedness a foundation of adaptability?

London and Sessa also annotate five publications under the heading "Skill Requirements for Successful Executives" (p. 34): Adler's (1997) competencies are a list of tasks preceded by "ability to;" de Merode's (1997) are role demands; Kanter's (1995) describes the cosmopolitan; O'Hara-Devereau and Johansen's (1994) are "three ability to's" and one "area competency;" and Tung's competencies (1997) are another "ability to" list. At the risk of secondhand adaptations from annotations (we worked here from the annotations, although we consulted the originals), we present the competency descriptions for each to illustrate the variety and difficulties in summarizing statements of competencies:

Skill Requirements for Successful Executives

Adler (1997)

- Able to employ cultural sensitivity and diplomacy
- Able to foster relationships that create respect for all parties
- Able to communicate clearly
- Able to solve cultural problems synergistically
- Able to negotiate across cultures

De Merode (1997)

- Motivating cross-cultural teams
- Conducting cross-cultural negotiations
- Recognizing cultural influences on business practices
- Selecting and staffing and evaluating staff indifferent cultural settings
- Managing information across multiple time zones, and organization boundaries
- Building relationships among diverse groups
- Focusing on markets, consistently customizing offering in relation to clients' needs in local markets across many local markets.

Kanter (1995)

- Integrate knowledge
- Move capital, ideas and people where needed
- Develop new communication routes
- Manage dispersed centers of expertise, influence and production
- Learn from and leverage the world marketplace
- Use cultural differences to gain competitive advantage

O'Hara-Devereau and Johansen (1994)

- Ability to understand and communicate across multiple cultures
- Technological competence in a time of rapidly proliferating information
- Ability to create and sustain business teams in a global setting
- Ability to support the complex process of facilitating teamwork

Tung (1997)

- Ability to balance conflicting demands of global integration and local responsiveness
- Ability to work in teams from multiple functions and disciplines, companies and industries
- Ability to manage and/or work with people from diverse racial and ethical backgrounds.

The diversity of content and form in lists of competencies makes integration a difficult task. Undaunted, Pucik and Saba (1998) attempt to bring the various views and approaches to global competencies together. They select five approaches, ranging from Tung's study of expatriate qualities (1981) to Kets de Vries and Mead's (1992) five categories of factors that impact the development of global leaders.

Despite their extensive reference list, Pucik and Saba's effort to summarize (p. 48) misses the range and essence of the studies cited in this chapter, and it did not, for us at least, bring clarity to a clouded field. Their conclusion that "... global managers are defined by their state of mind, in contrast to expatriate/international managers who are identified by location as executives in leadership positions that involve cross-border assignments . . ." seems to add more confusion than clarity. And, although the article presents a summary chart with several lists, they fail to take the next step – the summary list!

Without attempting our own summary, we will note that many of our references cited the importance of the knowing, learning and understanding that fall at least partly in the area of intellectual abilities. Dalton's (1998) inclusion in her competencies of "cognitive complexity" struck us first because she used it as a noun (something one "has") rather than as an adjective descriptive of thinking processes. Pucik and Saba's excellent reference list led us to Wills and Barham's (1994) discussion, the culprits we believe, in using "cognitive complexity" as a state of mind rather than a quality of thinking. Wills and Barham make a strong case for a critical core competence, "cognitive complexity," to function in a role in which ". . . a high degree of complex thinking is required" (p.50). They provide illuminating examples from their interviews of the intellectual demands of the work.

Another competency that is embedded in several of the global lists is the ability to work with global teams. Teamwork, like negotiation, seems to be a part of the global skillset.

We have illustrated the competency perspective with a number of competency lists. Alas, lists alone are no longer enough – today's lists are parts of global leadership models and systems. No doubt, many major global corporations and consulting firms have such models. Brake's (1997) competencies are a part of a larger organization performance system, with competencies grouped into three clusters: business acumen, relationship management and personal effectiveness. Each has five competencies that vary in relevance depending on the organizational level of the person. In addition, Brake includes two appendices of particular interest. One appendix lists Internet information sites for the global leader, a potentially very useful idea that fails in practice. By the time of this writing, only two years after the publication date, six of the 10 Web sites listed could not be found, illustrating perhaps the speed of change in which the global leader operates.

Brake's additional appendix includes "An International Code of Business Ethics," developed in 1994 by the Caux Round Table in Switzerland. A number of authors have emphasized the greater importance in the global arena of an advanced ethics/moral reasoning effectiveness (e.g. Dalton, 1998, Spreitzer et al., 1997) and discussions of cultural sensitivity inevitably raise the issue of relativity of values. Osland (1995) describes the expatriate facing "differences" and learning not to be judgmental. Clearly there is an ethics/moral/social responsibility competence in the global leader profile.

Black, Morrison and Gregersen (1999) present a competency model integrated into a more general performance model. In a kind of "seven habits of the global leader," they describe a core set of four global characteristics (inquisitiveness, perspective, character and savvy) required by every global leader, as well as unique skills and abilities that arise from business-specific "dynamics" of country affiliation, industry, company and functional responsibility. Much of this book is devoted to describing how these characteristics and dynamics interact in the world of global leadership. It is refreshing to find (we see this in Brake also) an emphasis upon the knowledge and understanding of the context (business, industry, environment) in which leadership takes place. It is discouraging, however, to find books so clearly designed with, as Hofstede says, "commerce" in mind. The fact that they include two appendices presenting proprietary cross-cultural instruments available only from their consulting firm undermines the credibility of their otherwise interesting book.

Hay/McBer (undated) describes a system of global leadership with two dimensions: International Adaptability and Universal Competencies. International Adaptability, based on leadership differences among cultures, is represented by three tasks (building business relationships, taking action and exercising authority) that the global leader must be able to handle flexibly, depending on the cultural context. The Universal Competencies are grouped into three areas: sharpening the focus (cognitive or intellectual abilities), building commitment (organization know-how, people judgment, leadership and impact and influence), and driving for success (including self-confidence, need for achievement, social responsibility and initiating action). Their Universal Competencies are foundation competencies (similar to Black et al.) required to "play the game," while International Adaptability determines if one will "win the game." Given the heavy element of "cultural context" in their competency system, we were surprised not to find the emphasis upon openness to influence and cultural sensitivity that most other lists include. Competencies, of course, "do not fall far from the tree," and those familiar with Hay/McBer's basic competency lists will not find any surprises here.

After participating in an extensive competency study (Barham & Oates, 1991), Wills and Barham (1994) stepped back to ask, "Are competencies enough?" Based on a subjective analysis of their interviews with a group of 60 largely non-U.S. executives in international roles, they conclude that competency lists are not the whole story. They describe a "relatively unchanging core" of the person, difficult to see and deeper inside, that must be considered as a whole, especially as it relates to cross-cultural effectiveness. Cognitive complexity, discussed above, is one of those core elements, as are emotional energy and psychological maturity. Fulkerson (1999) takes a similar view that "... faced with emerging globalization, leadership requires broader and more user-friendly concepts and paradigms" (p. 46).

The competency perspective ultimately frustrates for several reasons. Reading over the lists, one can't help but have a sense, like Wills and Barham, that there is more to global leadership than a list of competencies. Also, as our review illustrates, the lists overlap but never quite converge. There may be standard methodologies for determining competencies (each consultancy seems to have its own), but the results are never quite the same and each writer presents a different list. One leaves the area with a sense that everything is there and the conditions are right for the definitive summary piece.

From the Leadership Perspective

The study of leadership has historically been quite separate from the issues of managing across cultures. The theories described in a major reference book (Yukl, 1998) are all U.S.-centric, and the single cross-cultural page of this 508-page volume admits, "Most of the research on leadership during the past half century has been conducted in the United States, Canada and Western Europe. The amount of research conducted in other countries is still limited" (p. 507). On a more promising note, Yukl goes on to point out that, "In the past decade there has been growing interest in cross-cultural research on leadership"

(p. 507), as we see evidenced by the chapters in this volume, specifically Dickson, Hanges and Lord.

A widespread effort to extend the leadership perspective around the world is the nearly 10-year-old Globe Project (House et al., 1999). House describes the worldwide effort to identify dimensions of society and organizations and to develop surveys to measure these and the extent to which these dimensions are universally endorsed characteristics of effective leaders. The promise of the Globe Project piques the interest – there do indeed seem to be leader descriptions that are universally endorsed – and we can expect years of future results. For those seeking the global leader, however, The Globe Project, like the leadership field itself, has the challenge of producing results that are broad enough to impact the operating world of the global leader. Limiting their work, at least so far, to an implicit theory of leadership (how workers see leaders) is only one of the issues likely to be raised about whether the results of the study will apply to broader roles of global leaders.

In our search for the global leader, the leadership field frustrates because of its narrow focus. Its theories and research have had notably little impact on the way leaders lead, whether domestically or globally (Church, 1998). The more practical perspectives (e.g. Kouzes & Posner, 1995 and Kotter, 1988) that have so influenced the practice of leadership in the U.S., if not globally, seem to exist outside the boundaries of the field. And we are yet to find the distinction between management and leadership, a common distinction in U.S. practice, discussed in the literature of global leadership. By limiting itself to some variant of charismatic (leadership) rather than transactional (read *management*), the leadership field has almost guaranteed that it can address only a small (albeit important) part of the responsibilities of executives in global organizations.

Our focus on the academic field of leadership may have set up a "straw person" to criticize. The broader literature of leadership, some of it cited here, has indeed contributed to our defining the global leader and it has incorporated the dimensional approach of Hofstede. Our hope is that as the convergence of leadership and cross-cultural studies described by Dickson, Hanges and Lord (this volume) continues, rigorous theoretical and research-based contributions will enlarge.

From the Adult Learning Perspective

Even a cursory review of the literature on "being" an expatriate (Storti or Osland, e.g.) convinces that people's lives are often transformed by the experience of living in another country. People develop the global mindset, they become cosmopolitan, they extend their perspective and they change their cognitive maps. These changes, as we have observed, may be an essential ingredient of the global executive. How does this happen? How do transformations of personal perspectives take place? After the expatriate descriptions of the experience, where do we go to find the mechanisms for these changes? Although we find training aids designed to assist with the transformation (e.g. Kohls & Knight, 1994; Storti, 1994), what is the process? How do personal transformations take place?

Many areas promise answers to our question – psychotherapy, religion, psychedelic drugs, to name a few, but we won't go there. Instead, we went to the field of adult learning, one that has specifically addressed the issue of personal transformation but has not, as far as we found, addressed the global leader issues. We focus on Mezirow's outstanding *Transformational Dimensions of Adult Learning* (1991).

Mezirow attempts to describe how adults make sense of their experiences, the cognitive structures they use and how these are modified when they no longer fit. It synthesizes viewpoints from education, sociology, philosophy and psychology. In addition, it presents a theory and practice of its own, as well as quite understandable descriptions of ideas of a range of thinkers who have addressed the issue of how people make sense of their experiences.

Mezirow's book is not an easy read. After our second reading we began to see the basic theme: adult learners make meaning of the world through meaning schemes (knowledge, values, beliefs) that make up more general meaning perspectives (frames of reference) that order how we learn and the way in which we learn. Not all adult learning is transformational – *instrumental* learning is about problem solving and rationality, the *search for truth*; *communicative* learning is about understanding what others mean and making ourselves understood, its validity is not based on logic *but on mutual understanding* – language is its tool. *Transformational* learning, using critical reflection to examine our assumptions, involves authenticity or *what should be*.

We see in Mezirow much of the world of Argyris and double loop learning and dialogue (Argyris, 1993), Senge (Senge, Kleiner, Roberts, Ross & Smith, 1994) and the learning organization, Schon and the reflective practitioner (1983), Langer and mindfulness (1989), Fiske and Taylor (1991) and the whole field of social cognitive psychology, as well as numerous others.

The adult learning perspective offers a glimpse of what a global mindset really is and how it develops. In reading in this area, what strikes us as remarkable is how difficult it is to describe a process that most expatriates experience without conscious effort, albeit not without some pain and suffering.

Our sampling in this area is small relative to the amount of writings and, we believe, its potential contribution. The adult learning literature frustrates because its promise is so great, yet even at its best it is inaccessible to the leadership practitioner. The intellectual challenge in covering it (its breadth) and understanding it (its depth), and translating it into global leadership maxims requires a commitment of time and intellectual resources that we have yet to find.

Summary – Defining the Global Executive

We come away from our sojourn in the six areas with the wonderment experienced by, we suspect, most travelers. Our search has taken us many places and far afield, to writings and ideas that we did not know were there, in a far broader sweep than we anticipated when we began, and it has left us feeling that we have only scratched the surface. We turn now to reflection – what have we learned? First we reflect about the journey – what have we learned about the literature? And then we reflect about the global leader.

REFLECTIONS AND CONCLUSIONS

What have we learned from our sojourn? Our descriptions along the way are intended to enable readers to draw their own conclusions about global leadership. Although we resist here the temptation to provide a detailed summary, we have given in to the sojourner's need to tell about the trip. We share here some general reflections from the journey. The literature of cultures has sensitized us to the fact that we inevitably approach experiences with already practiced eyes. Our conclusions and reflections likewise are inevitably both limited and augmented by our previous experiences and what we have seen on this trip.

We present two sets of conclusions, one set about the literature of global leadership, the other about global leadership as a phenomenon.

The Literature of Global Leadership

(1) We began our search seeking a literature of the "global leader." We quickly realized that our search must broaden if we were to have any hope of gaining perspective. Little did we know what that entailed. One reference led to another, and we were soon far afield.

Our first conclusion, then, is that the literature related to global leadership is vast and ever expanding. It is scattered and takes us to places (e.g. the *Singapore Management Review*) that we never intended to go. This review doesn't scratch the surface. With so unlimited a horizon, the searcher eventually quits, rather than concludes, the search. We end our sojourn with the feeling that there is much left that we did not see.

(2) Although vast and scattered, common themes emerge quickly and the reviewer finds a core set of references that serve as touchstones. With themes emerging quickly, one must guard against the temptation to stop the search too quickly.

One common stylistic theme that soon wears thin is an obligatory justification of one's article or study by citing the factors driving the world to globalization – information technology, faster and easier communication and transportation, competitive pressures et al. We vow never again to begin an article with the recitation.

(3) Much of the literature is very engaging, especially the literature of "being" an expatriate. Often written by expatriates or repatriates, who seem to be trying to make sense of their own experiences, one can't read it without wanting to live the excitement oneself. If one has little prospect of ever "going out," one can't help but wonder "What would it have been like for me?"

There are flat places, however. Here we must guard against our own narrow perspective, but for us the strategy work – valuable as we found it – was dull and boring, tough sledding. The literature of adult learning also can be dry and hard, though ultimately rewarding; so can much of the literature of cross-cultural research.

(4) It is easy to get lost in these literatures, to get sidetracked and forget why one came. The articles have interesting and extensive reference lists with entries whose titles promise the secret of the global leader. One trail leads to another. The sojourner must maintain some focus.

(5) The dominant methodology across the literature is surveys, perhaps because of the logistics of gathering other types of data. We found surveys and surveys of surveys to the point that we began to question whether another survey could possibly add anything new and useful. We wondered if surveys could ever encompass the complexity of global leadership. We came away believing that the world does not need another survey of expatriate effectiveness. We question whether Trompenaars or The Globe Project has honestly faced the method issues.

In addition to surveys, or sometimes instead of, we found opinions. Our sample is no doubt biased – one wouldn't write, presumably, if one didn't have something to say – but everyone seems to have an opinion about global leadership. After our sojourn, we, too, plead guilty. Some of those opinions are expressed as given wisdoms (e.g. that all expatriates go through the same stages of adjustment), when more careful analyses indicate that they are not true. And, of course, some opinions are more valuable than others are. We drew the line, occasionally, and simply didn't cite articles (some widely quoted) with opinions too mundane or incomplete.

(6) Although the study of *leadership* has been U.S.-centric to a fault, studies of global leaders are much more centered in western Europe, perhaps reflecting western Europe's more international companies and markets. We found that the expatriate experience has been examined from many directions (from India to Sweden to Japan) with surprisingly common results, although much of the research is inevitably U.S.-based.

(7) When reading the literature, one gets the impression that every newcomer thinks they are the first to visit the global arena. Although there are touchstone references in each area and most works come with extensive reference lists, there is little indication that authors read each other's work. We found it remarkable, for example, that a recent book stated that little is known about the selection of global leaders and international managers. Perhaps the authors were describing their state of mind rather than the state of the art.

(8) The literature is sloppy. We found errors of style and grammar as well as frustrating errors of date, page and title that we are unaccustomed to finding in professional publications. With so many opinions and surveys in publications so widespread, perhaps the standards of publication may simply be lower.

(9) We advise fellow travelers, like the advice given to expatriates, not to be too quick to reject, not to form your opinions too early or on a superficial basis. The literature, despite its flaws, has much to teach. We had the unsettling experience of revisiting articles to find that on second reading we now relished what we had dismissed on our initial visit as irrelevant or simple-minded.

About Global Leadership

(1) We began our search seeking the secret of global leadership. Lest we seem foolish in so quixotic a quest, we point out that many have taken a similarly noble journey. For example, from the introduction to Volume I of this series: "It is the Tower of Babel come to life, and we are all rushing to

figure out the riddle and make it work while moving at the speed of business" (p. xv). Something about the mystery of global leadership invites us to expect a solution.

Our first conclusion is that there is no Holy Grail, no magic bullet, and no rosette stone of global leadership. The riddle has many answers. Global leadership is indeed a multi-sided phenomenon. There are many views with something to offer that when taken alone show only part of the picture. When taken together, despite the inconsistencies and contradictions, a picture of global leadership emerges.

(2) Our second conclusion is that Bartlett and Ghoshal are right – global leadership is about working *across* boundaries. A globalizing world requires an organization (and hence global leaders) that operates across boundaries of country, type of business and function. Crossing boundaries dictates the demands on the leader, the organizational tasks that must be accomplished.

Bartlett and Ghoshal are right, also, that there are many, rather than one, types of global leaders depending on the particular cross-boundary tasks. Typical of the strategy literature, they describe the *tasks* of the transnational organization rather than the *characteristics* of global leaders. We must go to other areas to translate those tasks into the executive qualities or competencies of global leaders. Adler and Bartholomew's classic article began that translation.

(3) Perhaps because they approached global leadership from the strategy side rather than the executive side, Bartlett and Ghoshal missed the boat by failing to recognize the essential difference between crossing boundaries of country (a proxy for culture, imperfect at best) and boundaries of business and function. The essence of global leadership is that it takes place across country/cultural boundaries. The interaction then, of country or culture with the organizational variables of business and function (or whatever) fundamentally changes the task and the characteristics required of effective leaders. The expatriate and cross-cultural literatures are convincing in their descriptions of the drama and the difficulties of crossing cultures.

(4) The organizational variables (the company piece) and the country differences (the culture piece) are very different types of variables in the demands they make on leaders. Increasing the complexity of the company piece – more functions, more businesses, etc. – requires greater cognitive skills, but may not make heavy emotional demands. For example, few of us would find that dealing with the marketing *and* finance of power generators *and* air conditioners threatens our very souls. Although dealing with unfamiliar functions and businesses may increase ambiguity and cause

some anxiety, working within the organizational space is fundamentally different and requires different responses than dealing with unfamiliar cultures, values and languages. Those are the issues that threaten our personal truths.

(5) Seeking the global leader in the literature of global competencies without a common definition and without an appreciation of the company/culture distinction is ultimately a futile effort. There is no shortage of competency lists – there has indeed been a major industry in developing competencies – but none provides a satisfactory answer. When viewed together, as we have done here, we see that the lists don't converge, they are uneven in coverage and level of detail and conceptual clarity, and they are, for the most part, speculative. Admittedly, our search has been selective, but we leave to the reader to judge whether we have selected unfairly simply to support our point. If there is order within the competency lists, we could not find it.

Viewing global leadership through the company/culture interaction lens, however, we see common competencies emerge. As the global leader's role crosses company boundaries, a greater level of the ability to deal with cognitive complexity, to integrate and differentiate, are required. Although the interaction with culture adds to complexity, the thinking process, we argue, is the same.

Another set of competencies emerges for dealing with culture. There is a common set around cultural sensitivity and awareness, openness to experience and curiosity, emotional stability and interpersonal skills, largely coming from the expatriate and cross-cultural literatures.

Global leadership can be dimensionalized in a 2×2 matrix, with dimensions of increasing complexity of the organization on one hand, and of culture on the other. Any particular global leadership task or position (group of tasks) can then be fit into the matrix. Our matrix emphasizes that global leadership resides in the task, is a process. Executives are more or less global leaders depending upon the tasks they are responsible for within the context of country.

There is a paradox that we cannot avoid. Cultural complexity is in the eye of the beholder – one is an expatriate only when one is outside one's own land. Is the expatriate executive a global leader, while the home-country leader in the same job is a domestic manager? There is, of course, no satisfactory answer. As those involved in executive HR work have long known, at the executive level the job and the person cannot be totally separated (Hollenbeck, 1994). Executive jobs differ depending on who does them; where the particular executive comes from (literally and metaphorically) is part of the job. We ask the reader to apply one of those skills required of every expatriate – living with inconsistencies.

(6) "Global mindset" as a term, however lacking in definition, is here to stay. There are descriptors (another is emotional intelligence) that in some peculiar way so aptly fit the phenomenon that they stick. Global mindset is one of those; we found ourselves using it, too. It makes a convenient catchall for gathering the competencies of global leaders, such as cultural sensitivity and ability to deal with cognitive complexity. We offer, however, that global mindset is a characteristic of a person, not of the location of the job as some have suggested. A task may require or benefit from a leader's having a "global mindset," but to define global leaders by mindset and international leaders by their location confuses the process with the competency.

(7) What can we conclude about developing global leaders? If a global mindset is a combination of competencies (knowledges, skills, attitudes and abilities) that enable one to work across both company and cultural boundaries, how does the mindset develop?

We came away from our search convinced that the concepts of adult learning offer a very useful avenue for understanding the development process. The transformation process described there encompasses both the cognitive complexity of crossing organizational boundaries and the emotional complexity of dealing with other cultures.

If our goal were to develop executives capable of dealing simultaneously with the combination of increased organizational and cultural boundaries, the prescribed development would seem to be experiences (assignments, training programs, task forces, coaching, etc.) that embody those tasks. Cross-business experiences (both horizontal and vertical) teach the ability to deal with the complexity of business scope and scale (Bentz, 1987; McCall & Lombardo, 1988). Cross-cultural experiences are well known for developing cultural awareness; expatriate assignments, both living and working in another culture, combine the two.

Is experience as an expatriate necessary to develop the global mindset? The literature presents mixed views. As it turns out, expatriate experiences are more difficult to catalog than they, at first, appear. All are not created equal, they all involve a "from where to where" element. Going "from London to Singapore" is not the same thing as going "from Little Rock to Seoul." And expatriate experiences are not without hazards of their own – our search found a well-established set of best practices for managing expatriation that few companies seem to follow. Bunker and Webb (1992), in describing the impact of stress and coping in learning from experience, do not specifically address the expatriate experience. The dynamics of their descriptions, however, track closely the transformations described both in the adult learning and in the expatriate literatures.

Perhaps the answer to our development question lies in thinking of global leadership as a process of accomplishing tasks – it depends upon some mixture of the task and the executive. In the same way that there is no one global leader, there is no one set of competencies and experiences that prepare an executive for global leadership. Without doubt expatriate experiences can be powerful teachers – whether they are essential for learning the required lessons may depend on the global leadership challenges faced and the person facing them.

If we come away with a single summary conclusion, it is that global leadership remains a fascinating mystery, and the search is not yet finished.

END NOTES

Gessner, Arnold and Mobley close the Introduction to Volume I with the T. S. Eliot's quartet:

> *We shall not cease from exploration*
> *And the end of all our exploring*
> *Will be to arrive where we started*
> *And know the place for the first time.*
>
> (T. S. Eliot, "Little Giddings" from *the Four Quartets*)

Indeed, we arrived at last at home, viewing it differently. In the course of our travels a global executive told us that 50% of what is learned from an international assignment are personal, and 50% business. That was our experience, exactly – our purpose in this review has been to inform, to interest and to raise questions, whether business or personal or both. Back at the place we started with a new perspective, we wonder still:

– Is living in another culture necessary to understanding the culture of others? Can one ever understand the culture of another?
– How important is language? Those who learned it say it is critical, those who don't say it doesn't matter. Both have been successful!
– Which comes first, the business or the culture? Is understanding culture a tool, or is it an end in itself?
– Can good intentions overcome cultural blunders? Or does one have to *know*?
– Are people the same everywhere? Or are they different? Do we learn more by studying the similarities, or the differences?

- Is business business business? Or is it different in different cultures?
- How complex can it get? How many "crosses" can one bear at the same time? What talents are required to deal with so many variables?
- Do diverse experiences in one's home culture contribute to working with others, or is the learning a step function rather than a continuum?
- Is leadership the same everywhere?
- And personally, how would we have done as an expatriate in a very difficult culture? Could we have succeeded?

We end, as should every good sojourn, with more questions than we began.

What are our regrets? Where did we want to get that we didn't quite get? Time and again we found references to the original use of the words, "culture shock" in a 1960 article by Oberg. Having seen, heard and used the phrase so often, for sentimental reasons we wanted to go there. It is not easy to find, however, and we didn't make it . . . this trip.

There is an inevitable, final question that is always asked of travelers. "What was your favorite place?" Most sojourners have difficulty answering this question. To our surprise, as we looked back over our stops, the answer was easy – Storti's little book on crossing cultures. He has the quotes, he has the anecdotes, he has the wisdom (see how he explains in an anecdote, with not a word we can't understand, the process of expanding one's schemas). A foreword describes the book as "enlightening." We thought so, too.

Despite our lengthy sojourn, we end with a final question that we hope the reader shares: "Is there after all an answer to the riddle, a rosette stone of global leadership? Did we somehow miss it?" A new book just crossed our desks with a dust jacket promising ". . . compelling new insights and business tools . . ." with global leadership universals and a global success quotient. Is this the ONE? Well . . . maybe . . . next time.

NOTES

1. We saw several references to Ohmae (1990) discussing similar issues, but no ideas different enough to lead us there.

2. Universalism vs. Particularism; Individualism vs. Communitarianism; Neutral vs. Emotional; Specific vs. Diffuse; Achievement vs. Ascription; Attitudes to Time; Attitudes to the Environment.

ACKNOWLEDGMENTS

Work on this paper was supported in part by the Executive Development Roundtable at the Boston University School of Management, and by the sponsor organizations of the Research Alliance Study of Global Leadership (ABB, Ericsson, Global Research Consortium, Human Resources Futures Association, Johnson & Johnson, Royal Dutch/Shell & Unilever).

REFERENCES

Adler, N. J. (1997). *International dimensions of organizational behavior* (3rd ed.). Cincinnati: South-Western College Publishing.

Adler, N. J., &. Bartholomew, S. (1992). Managing globally competent people. *Academy of Management Executive, 6*(3), 52–65.

Argyris, C. (1993). *Knowledge for action.* San Francisco: Jossey-Bass.

Barham, K., & Oates, D. (1991). *The International Manager.* London: The Economist Books.

Bartlett, C. A., & Ghoshal, S. (1989). *Managing across borders: The transnational solution.* Boston: Harvard Business School Press.

Bartlett, C. A., & Ghoshal, S. (1990). Matrix management: Not a structure, a frame of mind. *Harvard Business Review, 68*(4), 133.

Bartlett, C. A., & Ghoshal, S. (1992). What is a global manager? *Harvard Business Review, 70*(5), 124–132.

Bentz, V. J. (1987). *Explorations of scope and scale: The critical determinant of high-level executive effectiveness* (Technical report 31). Greensboro, NC: Center for Creative Leadership.

Birchall, D., Hee, J. T., & Gay, K. (1996). Competencies for international management. *Singapore Management Review, 18*(1), 1–13.

Black, J. S. (1988). Work role transition: A study of American expatriate managers in Japan. *Journal of International Business Studies, 19,* 277–294.

Black, J. S., & Gregersen, H. B. (1999). The right way to manage expats. *Harvard Business Review, 77*(2), 52–62.

Black, J. S., & Gregersen, H. B. (1998). *So you're going overseas.* San Diego, CA: Global Business.

Black, J. S., Gregersen, H. B., & Mendenhall, M. E. (1992). *Global assignments: Successfully expatriating and repatriating international managers.* San Francisco: Jossey-Bass.

Black, J. S., Gregersen, H. B., Mendenhall, M. E., & Stroh, L. K. (1999). *Globalizing people through international assignments.* Reading, MA: Addison-Wesley.

Black, J. S., Morrison, A. J., & Gregersen, H. B. (1999). *Global explorers: The next generation of leaders.* New York: Routledge.

Brake, T. (1997). *The global leader: Critical factors for creating the world class organization.* Chicago: Irwin Professional Publishing.

Brein, M., & David, K. (1971). Intercultural communication and the adjustment of the sojourner. *Psychological Bulletin, 76*(3), 215–230.

Briscoe, J. P. (1991). *Developing the global executive: report on a literature review.* Boston, MA: Boston University School of Management Executive Development Roundtable.

Bunker, K. A., & Webb, A. D. (1992). *Learning how to learn from experience: Impact of stress and coping.* Greensboro, NC: Center for Creative Leadership.

Cagney, W. F. (1975). Executive reentry: The problem of repatriation. *Personnel Journal, 54*(9), 487–488.

Campbell, D. A. (1984). Preface. In: W. E. Rosenbach & R. L. Taylor (Eds), *Contemporary Issues in Leadership.* Boulder, CO: Westview Press.

Campbell, J. (1968). *The hero with a thousand faces.* Princeton, NJ: Princeton University Press. (Original work published 1949).

Caux Round Table (1996). An international code of business ethics. *Business Ethics: The Magazine of Socially Responsible Business, 10*(1), 36–37.

Church, A. H. (1998). From both sides now: Leadership – so close and yet so far. *The Industrial/ Organizational Psychologist, 35*(3), 57–68.

Church, A. T. (1982). Sojourner adjustment. *Psychological Bulletin, 91*(3), 540–572.

Dalton, M. A. (1998). Developing leaders for global roles. In: C. D. McCauley, R. S. Moxley & E. Van Velsor (Eds), *The Center for Creative Leadership Handbook of Leadership Development* (pp. 379–402). San Francisco: Jossey-Bass.

de Merode, J. (1997). *An annotated review prepared for the Global Leadership Development Research Project.* Greensboro, NC: Center for Creative Leadership.

Dickson, M., Hanges, P., & Lord, R. (2001). Trends, developments, and gaps in cross-cultural research on leadership. In: W. H. Mobley & M. W. McCall (Eds), *Advances in Global Leadership* (Volume 2). Stamford, CT: JAI Press.

Doremus, P., Keller, W., Pauly, L., & Reich, S. (1998). *The myth of the global corporation.* Princeton, NJ: Princeton University Press.

Fiske, S., & Taylor, S. (1991). *Social cognition* (2nd ed.). NY: McGraw-Hill.

Fulkerson, J. R. (1999). Global leadership competencies for the twenty-first century: More of the same or a new paradigm for what leaders really do? In: W. H. Mobley, M. J. Gessner & V. Arnold (Eds), *Advances in Global Leadership* (Vol. 1, pp. 27–48). Stamford, CT: JAI Press.

Fulkerson, J. R., & Tucker, M. F. (1999). Diversity: Lessons from global human resource practices. In: A. I. Kraut & A. K. Korman (Eds), *Evolving Practices in Human Resource Management* (pp. 249–271). San Francisco: Jossey Bass.

Gessner, J., & Arnold, V. (1999). Introduction to conceptual perspectives. In: W. H. Mobley, M. J. Gessner & V. Arnold (Eds), *Advances in Global Leadership* (Vol. 1, pp. 3–8). Stamford, CT: JAI Press.

Gudykunst, W. B. (1998). *Bridging differences: Effective intergroup communication* (3rd ed.). Thousand Oaks, CA: Sage Publications.

Hall, D. T., Zhu, G., & Yan, A. (2001). Developing global leaders: to hold on to them, let them go! In: W. H. Mobley & M. W. McCall (Eds), *Advances in Global Leadership* (Vol. 2, pp. 327–349). Stamford, CT: JAI Press.

Hampden-Turner, C., & Trompenaars, F. (1997). A response to Hofstede. *International Journal of Intercultural Relations, 22*(4), 189–198.

Hay/McBer (undated). *Mastering global leadership: Hay/McBer international CEO leadership study.* Boston: MA: Hay/McBer.

Hofstede, G. (1979). Value systems in forty countries. In: L. Eckensberger, W. Lonner & Y. Poortinga (Eds), *Cross-Cultural Contributions to Psychology.* Lisse, The Netherlands: Swets & Zeitlinger.

Hofstede, G. (1991). *Cultures and organizations: Software of the mind.* London, England: McGraw-Hill.

Hofstede, G. (1996). Riding the waves of commerce. *International Journal of Intercultural Relations, 20*(2), 189–198.

Hollenbeck, G. P. (1994). *CEO selection: A street-smart review.* Greensboro, NC: Center for Creative Leadership.

Hollenbeck, G. P., & McCall, M. W., Jr. (1999). Leadership development: Contemporary practices. In: A. I. Kraut & A. K. Korman (Eds), *Evolving Practices in Human Resource Management* (pp. 172–201). San Francisco: Jossey-Bass.

House, R. J. et al. (1999). Cultural influences on leadership and organizations: Project globe. In: W. H. Mobley, M. J. Gessner & V. Arnold (Eds), *Advances in Global Leadership* (Vol. 1, pp. 171–233). Stamford, CT: JAI Press.

Kalb, R., & Welch, P. (1992). *Moving your family overseas.* Yarmouth, ME: Intercultural Press.

Kanter, R. M. (1995). *World class: Thriving locally in the global economy.* New York: Touchstone.

Kets de Vries, M. F. R., & Mead, C. (1992). The development of the global leader within the multinational corporation. In: V. Pucik, N. Tichy & C. Barnett (Eds), *Globalizing Management: Creating and Leading the Competitive Organization.* New York: John Wiley and Sons.

Kogut, B. (1999). What makes a company global? *Harvard Business Review, 77*(2), pp. 165–170.

Kohls, L. R., & Knight, J. M. (1994). *Developing intercultural awareness: A cross-cultural training handbook* (2nd ed.). Yarmouth, ME: Intercultural Press.

Kotter, J. P. (1988). *The leadership factor.* New York: The Free Press.

Kouzes, J. M., & Posner, B. Z. (1995). *The leadership challenge: How to keep getting extraordinary things done in organizations* (2nd ed.). San Francisco: Jossey-Bass.

Krugman, P. (2000). "Saints and Profits." *The New York Times,* OP-ED, p. 15, July 23, 2000.

Langer, E. J. (1989). *Mindfulness.* Reading, MA: Perseus Books.

Lewis, R. D. (1996). *When cultures collide: Managing successfully across cultures.* London: Nicholas Brealey Publishing, Ltd.

London, M., & Sessa, V. I. (1999). *Selecting international executives: A suggested framework and annotated bibliography.* Greensboro, NC: Center for Creative Leadership.

McCall, M. W., Jr., Lombardo, M. M., & Morrison, A. M. (1988). *The lessons of experience: How successful executives develop on the job.* New York: Lexington Books.

Mendhall, M., & Oddou, G. R. (1985). The dimensions of expatriate acculaturation: A review. *Academy of Management Review, 10,* 39–47.

Mezirow, J. (1991). *Transformative dimensions of adult learning.* San Francisco: Jossey-Bass.

Mobley, W. H., Gessner, M. J., & Arnold, V. (1999). *Advances in global leadership* (Vol. 1). Stamford, CT: JAI Press.

Oberg, K. (1960). Culture shock: Adjustment to new cultural environments. *Practical Anthropology, 7,* 177–182. (original not seen, cited widely).

O'Hara-Devereaux, M., & Johansen, R. (1994). *Globalwork: Bridging distance, culture, and time.* San Francisco: Jossey-Bass.

Ohmae, K. (1990). *The borderless world: power and strategy in the interlinked economy.* London: Collins.

Osland, J. S. (1995). *The adventure of working abroad: Hero tales from the global frontier.* San Francisco: Jossey Bass.

Pucik, V., & Saba, T. (1998). Selecting and developing the global versus the expatriate manager: A review of the state-of-the-art. *Human Resource Planning, 21*(4), 44–54.

Quelch, J. A., & Bloom, H. (1999). Ten steps to a global human resources strategy. *Best Practice* (First Quarter, pp. 18–29); McClean, VA: Booz, Allen, & Hamilton, Inc.

Rabe, M. (1997). *Culture shock! A practical guide.* Portland, OR: Graphic Arts Center Publishing.

Reich, R. B. (1990). Who is us? *Harvard Business Review, 68*(1), 3–14.

Reich, R. B. (1991). Who is them? *Harvard Business Review, 69*(2), 15–26.

Schon, D. A. (1983). *The reflective practitioner: How professionals think in action.* New York: Basic Books.

Senge, P., Kleiner, A., Roberts, C., Ross, R., & Smith, B. (1994). *The fifth discipline fieldbook: Strategies and tools for building a learning organization.* New York: Currency-Doubleday.

Shepard, S. (1998). *Managing cross-cultural transition: A handbook for corporations.* Bayside, NY: Aletheia Publications.

Simmel, G. (1950). The stranger. In: K. Wolff (Ed. & Tran.), *The sociology of Georg Simmel.* New York: Free Press. (Original work published in 1908).

Smith, P. B., & Bond, M. H. (1998). *Social psychology across cultures* (2nd ed.). Needham Heights, MA: Allyn & Bacon. (first published by Prentice Hall Europe).

Spreitzer, G. M., McCall, M.W., & Mahoney, J. (1997). Early identification of international executive potential. *Journal of Applied Psychology, 82*(1), 6–29.

Storti, C. (1990). *The art of crossing cultures.* Yarmouth, ME: Intercultural Press.

Storti, C. (1994). *Cross-cultural dialogues: 74 brief encounters with cultural difference.* Yarmouth, ME: Intercultural Press.

Torbiorn, I. (1982). *Living abroad.* New York: Wiley.

Triandis, H. C. (1995). *Individualism and Collectivism.* Boulder, CO: Westview Press.

Trompenaars, F. (1993). *Riding the waves of culture.* London: Brealey.

Trompenaars, F., & Hampden-Turner, C. (1998). *Riding the waves of culture: Understanding cultural diversity in global business* (2nd ed.). New York: McGraw-Hill.

Tung, R. L. (1981). Selection and training of personnel for overseas assignments. *Columbia Journal of World Business, 16*(1), 68–78.

Tung, R. L. (1997). International and intranational diversity. In: C. S. Granrose & S. Oskamp (Eds), *Cross-Cultural Work Groups* (pp. 163–185). Thousand Oaks, CA: Sage.

Wills, S., & Barham, K. (1994). Being an international manager. *European Management Journal, 12*(1), 49–58.

Wilson, M. S., & Dalton, M. A. (1998). *International success: Selecting, developing and supporting expatriate managers.* Greensboro, NC: The Center for Creative Leadership.

Yukl, G. (1998). *Leadership in organizations* (4th ed.). Upper Saddle River, NJ: Prentice Hall.

TAKE ME TO YOUR LEADER

Howard R. Crabtree

ABSTRACT

Visitors from another planet visit earth to discover the secrets of global company leadership. They learn that, as organizations progress from a traditional to a process-based structure, they require different leadership styles. They discover that the biggest barriers to this style of leadership developing within these organizations are often the beliefs, actions and ego needs of the current leadership.

INTRODUCTION

As the sun begins its daily ascent and casts a hazy dawn light over Mumbai, the streets begin to stir after slumber. Early risers on this day are treated to a sight never before seen on this earth – as far as we know.

Three shimmering green lights appear to be coming straight out of the sun. The lights get bigger and slowly take the shape of flying saucers. Hovering almost silently over the streets these can be seen by everybody to be genuine flying saucers. They are definitely not movie props. There are no Nike flashes in prominent view. Before people can focus on the magnitude of what they are seeing the saucers, with a sound like a soft breeze blowing on a still day, accelerate away towards the industrial part of the city.

It was shift change time at the Acme chemical plant, part of a major multinational company, when the flying saucer landed in the car park. It used the visitors' parking spaces – all of them, and melted some of the tarmac surface. The press had not yet had the time to react to the initial sighting so

Advances in Global Leadership, Volume 2, pages 49–74.
ISBN: 0-7623-0723-4

when, apparently without any doors opening, the occupants of the saucer appeared in the car park, the only people present to greet them were the shift foremen.

The visitors were a little strange looking but other than the fact they were green, not so strange that the foremen felt uncomfortable in their presence. They were, after all, used to American visitors. And when the strangers spoke to them in reasonable English, they relaxed even further. They became totally comfortable when the reason for the unexpected visit was made clear because they knew exactly how to respond.

The travelers, it transpired, were senior managers from the Achme Chemical Company on the planet Triton. Achme, like its earthly near-namesake, was a planet-wide company although it could not be described as global because Triton is, of course, flat. Achme had produced awful financial results for the last two years (about 25 months in Earth time) and the chief executive officer was coming under pressure from the financial community. They believed that the CEO did not have the necessary leadership qualities to direct a planet-wide company. Stung by the criticism, the CEO had decided it was time to take drastic action. He had instructed two of his senior management team to take a couple of company spacecraft and not to return until they had discovered the secrets of planet-wide leadership from this place that he had heard of through the Internet. This place was called "earth" and it had first caught his attention when he had read about stock options in intergalactic compensation surveys. Could the foremen please help them discover the true path to leadership in planet-wide companies?

Of course, the foremen assured the visitors. In fact, they had come at a very good time because they had just received from regional headquarters a video made by the chief executive of the entire Acme Company, which was to be shown to all employees. They would be delighted to show it to the distinguished guests but they would first have to confirm with the regional office – would they terribly mind waiting while they made contact with the appropriate authorities? The plant manager would be in his office in a few hours and he could then place a formal request with the regional office.

It was late that night when the regional vice president got off the telephone with headquarters in New York and gained approval to show the videotape to the Tritonians on condition that they were prepared to sign a secrecy agreement that was being drafted by the intellectual property department.

After spending the night back in their spaceship, at approximately nine the next morning the visitors were introduced to the plant manager and his management team who welcomed them to their plant. It was explained that somebody from the regional headquarters would try to come to Mumbai before they left but it may not happen because it was budget time and, of course, they knew what that meant. New York had asked that they be given a message from the chief executive officer himself. This man's name was known to the Tritonians because he featured prominently in the stock option survey that had caught the interest of their boss. He said that he would have liked to say "hi," at least by telephone, but his schedule would not allow it. At this particular time he was on one of his fleet of company aircraft en route to the Brazilian facility. Maybe he would catch them next time if they could give him a few months notice. He hoped they enjoyed the video and were able to learn from it – if they would leave a forwarding address he would make sure they received a copy of his forthcoming book "Leading the World" as soon as it became available.

The video was a very impressive production taped in the CEO's office in Manhattan – the beautiful Persian rug looked especially magnificent. He explained the mission and vision of the company. They would be the foremost supplier of their particular product in every market they competed in and they would achieve this by exceeding their customers' expectations. They would focus on quality and being the low-cost producer. All employees would play a part in the company's success and managers would be instructed to create mechanisms to solicit their views. He knew the importance of good leadership to the success of the enterprise so he was launching a program that would identify high potential managers from all over the world to be brought to the U.S. to attend a company-developed leadership training program. These would be the people who would ensure the future of the company around the world by leading employees along the true path. He was sorry he would not be able to visit India for another two years because of his busy schedule but he wanted to remind all employees of his "open door" policy. He encouraged them to call him on the telephone if they had comments – he would ensure they got a response to their concerns. Finally, he was proud to announce the creation of a global stock option program covering all employees and allowing them to share in the company's future success. The options would be for one share of company stock for every $250 of earnings – he was sure Indian employees would be excited and motivated by this news.

After viewing the video the Tritonians were given handouts that were to be distributed to employees. They received a little laminated card with the company's vision and mission printed on it, a company baseball hat, a letter from the plant manager telling them to raise any questions they may have about the video with their foremen, and a letter from the benefits department in New York explaining stock options.

The plant manager hoped they had gotten a good understanding of the reasons for the company's global success from the presentation and that they had something worthwhile to take back home with them. The company was very proud of its CEO – he was a very famous man and a great leader. They were very happy that he was now going to pass those secrets on to others in the company. Who knows, one day maybe even an Indian could hope to be a senior leader in this great company.

The Tritonians, sensing that their time was up, thanked them for their hospitality and, wearing their baseball hats (unfortunately a clashing shade of green), returned to their spacecraft and prepared to leave.

At almost exactly the same time as the first spacecraft had put down in the Acme car park, the second was less than a mile away, hovering over Akme Chemical's parking lot looking for a block of non-reserved spaces big enough to put down in. They eventually managed to maneuver the craft into a space by the crowded bicycle shed although they unfortunately melted a couple of reserved parking spaces and a few bicycles on the way.

The shift foremen, who displayed a similar ready acceptance of their strange visitors, also greeted them. It so happened that the regional president of the company was in town and one of the foremen, knowing he was an early riser and that he would want to meet the visitors, telephoned his hotel. The area president was having an early breakfast when the news came through, but he asked for a driver to be sent right away. He did not have to wait because a driver had been stationed at the hotel all night waiting for his call.

He found the Tritonians waiting patiently for him in a conference room when he arrived. He told them how delighted he was to have such obviously important and, dare he say, unusual visitors but, enough about them – they had obviously come to learn about him.

The area president was a German. He had joined the company as a financial analyst in Dusseldorf and had received several quick promotions. He was given an opportunity as finance director in Austria and then was promoted to the country manager position. He then was appointed country manager in Korea, then country manager in Taiwan, before assuming his current position.

Akme was a great company to work for and he was a great example of how leaders were developed in the organization. It was a case of taking high potential people and giving them the opportunity to prove themselves. He had attended formal training programs at the training center in the U.S. but all his real development was on the job. He could talk about the company mission and vision and values and, he hastened to add, he supported them fully. What it was really about, though, was tough business leadership in the trenches and getting employees to perform. Much of the company communication went over the head of the average employee and, frankly, those guys in the headquarters in New York had no idea what they were talking about half the time.

His job was to meet his numbers and that's what would produce bigger bonuses for him and also future promotional opportunities. He tried to telephone his boss fairly regularly but was careful what he told him – he didn't need unnecessary interference from people who didn't understand that his markets were different. Doing business in Asia was not like doing business in the United States, or even in Europe.

He was constantly on the road – he believed it was vital to meet with his people face to face and often. This was the only way he could keep up-to-date and be sure that people weren't "bullshitting" him and were doing what he told them to do. He did not want to give the impression that his people weren't good – this was definitely not the case but it was important to keep the pressure on them.

He developed his people by setting very challenging goals for them – the annual operating plan reviews were always long, difficult negotiations. His people obviously tried to lowball the targets and he probably pushed for more than was reasonable but they always reached a compromise. He believed people grew when they were stretched. His region was going to make all of Akme's other regions look really bad next year because he was going to make sure that Asia beat all numbers by a wide margin. He was particularly proud of the manager of his China business, a young Australian who was destined for great things. He had gotten some very profitable new business that he'd stolen from under the nose of Akme's French subsidiary. He knew that some of the planners in New York had been unhappy with that because the French had been getting great margins but everything is fair in love, war and business and it had really pleased him to know that he'd shown up those cocky Europeans.

His biggest challenge was Japan – he just couldn't get them to be aggressive enough. He'd like to put a European or Australian in there but they did things so differently and stuck together so much that he'd just be setting the expatriate up for failure. Most other countries had expatriate country managers and it worked out well because the locals expected to have foreigners in charge – it gave the country operation a certain status. An expatriate would be a lot easier to communicate with too. These country managers would eventually form the top management echelon of Akme.

The monologue went on for most of the day. Finally the area president decided he had imparted sufficient information. He hoped the Tritonians had gotten a good picture of the keys to Akme's success and would they like to join him for dinner? He hoped they liked ethnic food. They did enjoy their meal even though some of the unfamiliar spices had the interesting effect of changing their skin color from green to purple. When they boarded their spacecraft to return to Triton late that night they were each carrying a small box containing the remains of their meal.

At the Ackme Chemicals plant a security guard guided the spacecraft to an unused plot of land over the road from the parking lot. When the Tritonians emerged they were greeted by one of the plant operators. On hearing the reason for their visit, he invited the guests to the plant control room.

Once inside the control room, they were introduced to the other members of the operating team and were invited to take a seat. One of the operators suggested they were probably hungry after their long journey and they would send out for some breakfast. Plant expenses were in good shape this month so they could afford it.

The team member who had greeted them explained that they had come at a good time to learn how they did things because they had arranged two events for the day. Later that morning they were going to have a couple of visitors. One of their customers had been having some problems using Ackme's product in their formulation and the Ackme team suspected it was being caused by a switch Ackme had made to a different supplier of one of their key raw materials. They had therefore arranged for a representative of the customer and a representative of the supplier of the raw material to visit and discuss the problem with them in hopes of finding a solution. In the early afternoon they had also arranged a video link with the U.K. plant to discuss with their operating team some improvements they had made to their process. They had become aware of improved performance in the U.K. after they had generated a plant efficiency report from the global plant information system. They had also invited a member of the marketing team to the morning meeting and one from the finance team to the second meeting.

While they were waiting for the visitors to arrive, the team members explained that they were essentially self-directed but if they ran into problems they had technical resources they could turn to or they could call the process owner responsible for order fulfillment. Yes, they were aware of the company's mission and vision. The customer who was visiting today was especially important because Ackme was trying to become a major supplier to that industry. Their job in India was to show the customer they could provide real value to him even though he was being asked to pay a high price for Ackme's product. This also put real pressure on the plant to continuously improve their processes so they could keep prices down and still produce high margins for Ackme.

They were aware of this because of education they had received from the process owner and from reading information made available on the company's Intranet. They had also visited customers and understood what they were looking for and how they made decisions concerning their choice of raw materials and suppliers.

They understood that an executive committee developed the overall company strategy in the United States. They believed the CEO's name was Brown or Gray – something like that. There were regional people stationed in Singapore who were available to provide support and assistance to them should they need it. They would participate in reviews with them every six months or so to consider ways the process could be improved and costs could be brought down. All the people involved in the supply chain would be involved in this review. Everybody was aware of what needed to be done to satisfy the customer so there was no real need for them to have a manager on site. The process owner was responsible for removing obstacles from their path – usually created by some zealous bureaucrat in the U.S. who was asking unnecessary questions. Every team member had also received leadership training to help them take charge of situations when no help was immediately at hand.

The rest of the day proved to be an absorbing and enlightening experience as the team had meaningful interactions with customers, suppliers and colleagues. They were able very quickly to broaden the scope of the discussions by accessing the Internet to tap into the global information system for reports and to look at issues on the worldwide Lotus Notes database maintained by the plants. They also included people in other countries into the discussions by e-mail and/or by telephone.

By the time the Tritonians boarded their spacecraft to return home, their heads were spinning. Literally – it happens to Tritonians when they absorb a lot of information. Apparently the centrifugal force allows information transfer to the outer brain cells allowing more information to enter through the central pathway.

Now they were on their way back to Triton and were discussing what to put in their final report. You have probably guessed by now that there were never really three spacecraft or three crews. The Tritonians had cleverly developed some technology, first created by their Bureau of Missing Beings, that allowed them to harness the power of Heisenberg's uncertainty principle. The two crewmembers had visited all three plants at the same time.

"It's interesting" said Ein, "to conjecture how these companies, all of whom are quite successful today, will be doing by the time we get back to Triton."

"I agree," said Zwei. "Acme has a very powerful leader with a planet-wide reach who is famous and the subject of books, but what happens if he gets hit by an asteroid? Akme has developed leaders but they are creating fiefdoms. It's also quaint to see people using air travel to hold discussions with other people on the same planet – and finance people running companies? My goodness, how did that ever happen?"

"There's no doubt that Ackme is the only one that has really grasped what it's all about" said Ein "they're training all their people to become leaders and are putting a lot of effort into ensuring they have the tools to do their job. They're making use of technology and I think they've woken up to the fact that their planet really is one big market. Their fundamental values apply wherever they operate in that market and every employee in every country is aware of them."

"But what are we going to put in our report as a recommendation?" asked Zwei. "You know that we are both in line for top management positions. It's quite clear to me that Ackme is going to be the most successful in the longer term but I'm sure you realize the problem with putting that in our report."

"Yes," said Ein "being the top manager in Acme would be tremendous fun and being one of the top managers in Akme would be great too – all that power, the travel, the fawning, the stock options. I think we need to consider very carefully the impact this report could have on our future lifestyles."

"It was a tragedy," said Zwei, back in his home company boardroom, "Ein just disappeared in the e-toilet – a fatal exception must have occurred and he was just shut down. We had just finished our report describing how the Acme Company had found the true path to planet-wide leadership."

WHAT'S THE POINT?

Why have I used a silly story to make a point about global leadership? I wanted to demonstrate that although the meaning of the words "global" and "leadership" tend to be static, the ideas contained in them are dynamic. The ideas not only change with time, they are also situational. This fact is often not recognized by people working in organizations or by those writing about organizational leadership. They tend to have a fixed view of what the words mean and use this view as a basis for leadership development and succession planning. This view is reinforced by the commonly-held belief that leadership refers only to the leadership of people; that it necessarily requires qualities such as strength of character, decisiveness, charisma, ability to communicate clearly, etc. I shall suggest that, even though these qualities are always desirable in people who lead organizations, they are not sufficient in themselves and often go hand-in hand with character traits that can prevent organizations from developing fully. Am I suggesting that the competency models that have proliferated recently are invalid? Not if the models incorporate a renewal or self-destruct factor that allows top managers to recognize when they need to reconfigure or move on. Unfortunately such a trait is rare, difficult to recognize and is likely to be modified by a taste of power. Corporations tend not to be like the freezer section in the supermarket where products are discounted in price as they approach their sell-by date and are then eventually removed from the shelf. Corporate freezer sections tend to be stocked with product that becomes more expensive and difficult to remove as it approaches and passes its sell-by date. It will eventually be pulled from the shelf but not until it has started visibly to decay and to taint surrounding products. It is for this reason that I believe there has to be a mechanism through which the likely sell-by date is borne in mind during all top leadership selection processes.

To demonstrate, I shall discuss the transition of organizations from the traditional hierarchical model adopted by most companies until very recently to the modern process-based model that is increasingly becoming necessary because of changes in the business environment that have demanded greater speed and flexibility. I shall also look at the very new organization models typified by the "dot coms" of the Internet age. I shall argue that the transition from the traditional to the modern organization requires different leadership styles for each stage of the transition, and I shall also argue that current organizational leadership and basic human nature are significant barriers to this transition of styles occurring.

WHAT IS MEANT BY GLOBAL?

The term "global" has become a regular part of the business vocabulary over the last several years. All self-respecting companies have to describe themselves as "global" even if they have no clear idea of what it means. They can be forgiven for this because it meant something very different only five years ago. It used to be sufficient for a company to have operations in many overseas markets to describe itself as global. True global brands such as Coca-Cola existed but even they were marketed very differently in many markets to allow for local preferences. Many of the differences between markets that organizations encountered just five short years ago do not exist today. A company's competitors in Japan were unlikely to be the same as its competitors in Brazil. A customer's subsidiary in South Africa would have very different needs from the French subsidiary, and the prices charged would certainly be different. Suppliers of raw materials were often locally owned. Pricing was market based because of a lack of transparency across national borders. Employment practices in each country would be different to allow for national idiosyncrasies and local laws and preferences. This led to different management practices in different countries – getting Japanese employees to conform to U.S. methods was not attempted because it was proclaimed by them to be "not the Japanese way."

The fact is that the companies that talked about being global organizations were usually not even close by today's measures. They did not have to be because the differences encountered in selling products in all parts of the world far outnumbered the similarities. Even a simple requirement like single-source manufacturing for the global marketplace was often impossible to achieve because of local laws or requirements designed to boost employment or to protect employment in a country.

Most of the people who run companies today grew up believing the world was a big place, that communications with many countries was very difficult and travelling to them was even more difficult. Five years ago the world of our youth had effectively shrunk to the size of the moon – today it has become a medicine ball and it will soon be a walnut. It stands to reason that even though the fundamental meaning of the word "global" has not changed, the implications for companies are vastly different. The shrinking world has brought tremendous advantages but it has also made life more difficult for the unprepared.

Your Japanese competitor is now doing business in Brazil; your major U.S.-based customer wants to negotiate a worldwide supply agreement and your supplier says that he can, of course, deliver to your door in Malaysia. In fact, you can probably place your order on the Internet and your customer may wonder why he can't do the same. Prices, even for specialty products, are becoming increasingly transparent across national boundaries. These are considerations that were largely unimportant until very recently.

As a result of these fundamental changes, many managers make the mistake of talking about global issues or global products without updating their view of what this really means. They can end up deceiving themselves into believing they have all the bases covered when they really don't. They can also rapidly find themselves out of business. Non-competitive domestic industries are no longer protected by geography or lack of communication and will have to change to survive. Businesses today have to be so much more aware of their environment and to be able to monitor everything in it on a daily basis because it is changing so fast. Their environment is the world so they have to be able to monitor the world on a daily basis. That is truly "being global."

However, this has been made easier by the fact that the world is coming to their door. It would not be outside the bounds of reason to suggest that executives could incorporate the Tritonian Acme into the Ackme organization without having to blow the company profits on inter-planetary travel. Thinking globally used to require conscious attention to the differences that exist between different markets. Now it requires constant attention to the increasing similarities and the opportunities and threats created by them.

WHAT IS LEADERSHIP?

Leadership in a traditional organization is usually viewed as something that resides within a fairly small group of people at the top of the organization. Leadership development is aimed at this elite group or at a pool of people who are regarded as the future members of the top group, the so-called "high potentials." There is nothing wrong with this approach as long as it does not preclude developing leadership throughout the ranks. Unfortunately, in traditional organizations, people are often divided into leaders and led – there is no call for leadership to exist at the lower levels of the organization. Indeed it could even be regarded with suspicion. Leading is something that is the preserve of people whose titles entitle them to consider themselves leaders – "I called this meeting today because I can and because that's what leaders are supposed to do." Leadership comes with the trappings of position such as the salary, car and stock options – it is often an entitlement rather than a job requirement. "Leadership" is also usually viewed as something more than "management" or "supervision." Training and development programs are often aimed specifically at these separate categories. The hierarchical assumption is that supervision, management and leadership are associated with sequential steps on the promotional ladder. I believe that this describes the situation in many, if not most companies today.

In my view no company that considers itself a modern company can afford to think in this manner or to allow its people to think the same. The modern world and the modern business environment are changing so fast that companies can no longer afford to wait for instructions to trickle down a chain of command. They have to promote leadership behavior at all levels in the organization. Obviously, there will be many decisions that can't be made below a certain level in the organization because they require a view of the organization that may only be available at a level where the responsibility is broader. That's a good reason for not making a decision at the shop-floor level – using the fact that a person is not at a high enough level to make a decision is not a good reason per se.

Many companies are realizing that the hierarchical model of organizations is no longer appropriate, and that a flatter, process-driven organization is necessary to cope with the complexities of running a business in a world where speed is critical and where competition, as we saw earlier, is worldwide. The processes in a process-driven organization are different processes from the top-down planned processes of the past. The speed and complexity of the modern environment also means that many processes have to be run in parallel, further adding to the complexity of running the business. Process-driven organizations require people to be educated about the business and its processes as well as being trained to perform specific tasks. Supervision for its own sake is considered to be a non-value-added activity and people at all levels in the organization are required to display leadership behavior in their day-to-day activities. Many modern plants are run using so-called "self-directed work teams" that don't have a manager but do have access to a "staff resource." In such organizations the concept of "boss" has been blurred because a "process owner" may determine what somebody does while their old functional head, which may now be called a "coach," retains responsibility for how well they do it.

These ideas are, of course, not new and are presented more fully in Champy and Hammer's book *"Re-engineering the Corporation"* and Ed Lawler's book *"From the Ground Up."*

In process-driven companies there is clearly a need for leadership *behavior* rather than leaders. This is true at all levels of the organization. Leadership development has to be directed at many people rather than a select few. The set of skills required for leadership behavior, even for the people at the very top of the organization, is also very different than it is in a traditional organization.

MORE ABOUT THE MODERN ORGANIZATION

What is life like inside the modern organization? How are things different?

Command and control management requires that the people running the company have more information than the people do at the bottom. Mid-level managers retain their authority by having access to information that is not available lower down and by being careful about how they share it. Supervisors are used to make sure that people carry out the tasks assigned to them. People are responsible for quite small, narrow pieces of work contained within a functional silo.

In modern organizations where information is entered at the shop floor and where cross-functional teams can view information that cuts across functions and markets, middle managers and supervisors have to find new ways of adding value. People lower down in the organization generally have access to *more* information than those higher up so value has to be created by what is done with the information rather than by the collection and distribution of it. We will see later that companies do not have a choice in this – the Internet will become as important a tool as the telephone in the pursuit of business and those who try to ignore the fact will not survive.

Modern organizations manage processes rather than tasks. The organizational focus is horizontal rather than vertical with everybody looking along their process tunnel to the customer instead of looking up their functional silo to the head of the department. These companies have put in place infrastructures to support the way they run the business. They have often put in place enterprise resource planning systems to enable their move to managing by process. They will have put in place intranets and shared databases to allow rapid exchange of information between people in all parts of the world, and they may have given their suppliers and their customers access to their systems to allow just-in-time supply and sourcing of materials. They will treat all of their customers and suppliers alike even though they may be located in various parts of the world. The way their employees are organized and managed will, increasingly, be standardized around the world. Such companies are committed to a fundamental power shift within their organizations that cannot be reversed. Too much information about the companies' businesses has been distributed to too many people around the world and too much responsibility has been devolved to too many people that interface regularly with the customer to ever go back to how things used to be. These are the truly modern companies.

These companies that have made the transition from traditional to modern are still in the minority but their number is, of necessity, growing every day. Traditionally managed companies, many of whom regard the rapid growth of technology with great suspicion, are increasingly being faced with a barrage of information about e-commerce and the need for them to examine its uses. For the time being, though, there is a great many companies that continue to turn a deaf ear to the voices of change yet that continue to be very successful using the same business model they have been using for many years. Prerequisites for such companies are a customer focus, and customers who, themselves, have not significantly changed the way they do business. Traditional leadership models hold good in these companies and top managers tend to resist as extreme the views of those who suggest that fundamental changes are needed. I will argue that their days are numbered – it may not happen tomorrow, but over the next 10 years such companies will change the way they do business or they will disappear.

The rate at which this change occurs is likely to be slower outside of the United States but I believe the conclusion will be the same. In Europe change will be slowed the most by the need to negotiate everything with the (at least politically) powerful trades unions. In the emerging markets the transition to a process-driven organization will be slowed by a shortage of people with the required educational standard or language skills, or by having available only people who are just too parochial in their outlook. By contrast, the emerging markets have an opportunity like never before to catch up with the rest of the world in technology. Internet connectivity is cheap and affords an opportunity to participate in sophisticated communication. In the early 1990s many companies in the United States and other developed countries started investing heavily in infrastructure that did not make use of the Internet and they now have the worry of how to write off or get a return on these expensive investments.

It is inevitable that as the environment continues to change at an ever-faster rate, the traditional companies will start to feel very uncomfortable. What is going to provide the impetus that will force them to throw out all they now have and fundamentally change the way they do business?

DRIVERS OF CHANGE

I believe there are four fundamental drivers of change. Three of them – the shrinking world, technology and the changing needs of the people that work for them, are forces acting on all companies, however successful they may be. The fourth driver, affecting only some companies but the one that has the most immediate impact is, of course, economic crisis.

Ironically the companies that suffer economic crisis are likely to be the ones that find it easiest to change. They are in the same dilemma as the man who was trapped on a burning oil platform in the middle of the North Sea and who jumped into the burning waters around the platform. When asked how he had come to make the decision to leap into burning waters he explained that he had not made that decision – he had made the decision that he could not stay where he was. Economic crisis will always be the most compelling force for change.

Most traditional companies are probably becoming increasingly nervous about the environment because of the noise they are hearing. They have probably put in place study groups or hired consultants to help them look at the impact of new technology or e-commerce on their businesses. The resultant reports are probably making their way up the hierarchy, and being modified and redrafted at every level.

What will force the change is the surprise discovery one day that their customers are grouping together to buy materials on an Internet-based electronic exchange. They may have been under increasing pressure to provide just-in-time supply because their competitors can do so, or their customers' purchasing agents may have gotten used to customer service agents who can promise material on a specific date without them having to call back. These customers may now have reached a level of frustration that has prompted them to go to the competition. And the competition may be Brazilian.

People will also drive companies to change because of their changing needs. Young people entering the workforce in the United States today are not often interested in, nor do they expect, long-term careers with a single company. The shedding of people that has occurred over the last several years at most large companies and the stock market response to it has convinced most young people that companies are more interested in short-term returns than they are in their people. It is ironic that, as investors in these companies, possibly through mutual fund holdings, they are also indirectly supporting the behavior. Today's employees are therefore looking for something different from work than prior generations did. The concept of a company "family" has been discredited – employees today consider themselves more as long-term contractors with no particular loyalty to any company. In order to retain their services companies are finding that they have to keep them challenged as well as decently paid. They need to make their companies interesting and challenging places to work. This is difficult to do in a traditional company other than for the few at the top. Once again, the change in attitudes is likely to be slower outside of the United States, but it will come. The "new economy" is already up and running in Europe and today's emerging markets produce many of the world's most dynamic entrepreneurs. The way people look upon employment will be difficult to change in some countries – most notably Japan – but the only thing that is likely to abort a steady change is a significant worldwide economic depression.

The recent crop of Internet-based start-up companies was also a factor in forcing the traditional companies to change, and not just because some of them were bought out by the upstarts as a result of their incredibly inflated market valuations. Their influence on modern business was, and will continue to be, huge in relation to their share of total commerce.

In such companies the founders don't worry about what kind of organization they are going to be, it is second nature to build a modern organization because their business objectives, their technology and their people force them into it. These are companies that are all focused on speed and growth. Most of the people who work in these companies are expected to work very long hours, often for low pay but, until recently, with the promise of a massive pay-out from their stock options if the company is successful (and in the recent stock market frenzy it was not always evident what was required to be successful.) Employees are expected to make huge decisions on a daily basis without checking with any higher authority – the kind of decisions that would require several meetings and would need to be elevated several levels up the hierarchy in a traditional company. Life in these companies is very exciting and challenging. Nobody that has worked in this kind of environment is going to fit easily into a traditional company. If the tiny Internet start-up becomes a tech behemoth with a market capitalization greater than the net worth of most blue chips, do you think that employees will accept that their organization now has to be traditionally managed? Despite the pricking of the Nasdaq bubble, this section of the economy will grow and gradually permeate the rest of the economy. Employees from these companies (assuming they are not spending the rest of their lives on a beach somewhere) will gradually infiltrate the rest of industry and the paradigm will shift.

Intuitively it would appear that companies do not have a choice about what kind of organization they want to be. Circumstances will eventually drive them in one direction only and that is towards being a process organization. Even in the absence of an economic crisis, technology and people will be the drivers in even the most traditional organizations. However I shall argue later that there are opposing forces to this movement and they come from a surprising area.

MAKING THE TRANSITION FROM TRADITIONAL TO MODERN

Most of the companies that have begun the transition from traditional to modern have done so in response to a serious business crisis. They knew that something radical had to be done to change their fortunes. Some companies addressed the crisis by slashing non-profitable product lines and by getting rid of huge numbers of people. Investors often looked favorably on these actions and accepted the "restructuring costs" as a necessary expenditure in the journey to improved profitability. Usually if these companies continued to do business in the same old way after their restructuring, they still under-performed. Some companies recognized the need for a much more fundamental change in the way they did business – something that would permeate throughout the organization and give everybody a new way of looking at their work. These were the companies that became process-driven, that saw the need for leadership at all levels and that recognized the increasing global nature of business. The reason these companies saw the need for such change was great leadership. It needed a person at the very top of the organization with the vision to see the need to change the old way of doing things and then to get people at all levels to work in concert with the vision. Senior managers would be given a chance to get on board with the vision but if they could not do so they would be made to leave the company. Jack Welch at GE is probably the best known and most admired example of such a great leader. Ironically, those companies that had the most traditional command and control structure were often easier to change because the structure could be used to enforce change. Seeing the need for change and forcing the organization to change is what I will call phase one of the transition to being a modern organization.

Following the initial expression of the vision it has to be vigorously communicated and championed. In this, the visionary leader is no good alone. There needs to be a constant and consistent message delivered within the organization, backed up by actions supporting the words. Organizations that have just one leader to identify with will run out of steam eventually. Worse, adherence to the vision may exist only in the leader's mind. There has to be a number of disciples preaching a consistent message. Kotter describes this requirement in his article "Leading Change: Why Transformation Efforts Fail." Within a global organization the disciples should be drawn from several different backgrounds and cultures to give legitimacy and credibility to the vision. The message does not have to be identical everywhere in the world – in fact it is probably better if it is interpreted by each of the messengers in his own way and in a way that allows audience identification. Feedback from the people on issues created by the new way of working is also very important before too much frustration is created, which leads to the inevitable "work-arounds" that are anathema to the successful implementation of a process organization. This is stage two.

While this is taking place the systems and business processes of the organization have to be renewed to enable the desired change to take place. This is the area where the leadership mettle is tested as people are asked to do things in very different ways from those they have been used to. Reporting relationships change as process owners are appointed and the role of the old functional head is changed. People have to get the message that things have changed for good – there is no going back. All the systems, practices, and procedures in the organization have to be examined and, if necessary, changed to ensure they are consistent with the required behaviors. This is stage three, which should begin during stage two.

Stage four is the one exhibited by Ackme. Firm leadership and proselytizing become less important and the leadership focus becomes one of enabling – removing barriers from the path of people in the organization whose job it is to satisfy the customer and making sure they have the information and tools necessary to do their jobs effectively.

Stage five is continuous improvement, which may require the company again to adopt a completely different strategy. If it does, the organization should be flexible enough to deal with it so that the process does not need to be kick-started by a charismatic leader again. Organizational change is not a movement from one defined condition to another defined condition; it is a process of preparing the organization to move in whatever direction the market demands. Change in organizations is really preparation for change in the environment.

IMPLICATIONS FOR LEADERSHIP

My premise is that organizational leadership is situational. Charismatic single-minded leaders are required but only in companies that are in need of a stage one transformation. Stage two requires a charismatic single-minded leader who can also delegate authority and who trusts his or her disciples to deliver the message. The demands of stage three are such that the leader must also be somebody who has an understanding of processes and information technology and his role in enabling the future organization.

Stage four leadership requires a coach and facilitator for the organization. The message is established and well known. The stage four leader needs to be able to be observant of what's going on in the organization and help people reflect on their behavior.

At stage five the requirement is for a leader to be totally in tune with the competencies and capabilities of the company, trends in the market and trends in technology such that they know immediately when strategic adjustments have to be made to ensure the future of the company. It is vital for all of this information to cover the whole, global organization.

Now let us consider in a little more detail what the modern organization requires of its people at the helm. Every ship requires somebody at the helm to set the course even if all the passengers are making independent decisions to ensure the required course is maintained. First it requires somebody who is capable of deciding which business the company should be in, and then it needs somebody who can design an organization that allows the people in it to succeed independently in the achievement of the company's overall goals. The organization, and not strong leadership, is the determinant of whether people will be able to successfully perform the organization's processes. In fact, strong leadership of the old fashioned variety may be a real deterrent to the creation of the required organization. Managers within the company must devote more time to managing the environment than managing the people – "managing the white space" as Mike Hammer calls it. Empowerment is an overused word and it is not the correct one to describe the organizational shift that I am referring to, even though the end result may be the same. "Empowerment" suggests moving power from one place in the organization to another when it's really about redefining what we mean by power. The top people in the organization will still determine the direction of the enterprise and approve major capital investments, but it will be because that is the role assigned to them rather than because of their position at the top of a pyramid. People in the middle of the organization will generally be charged with ensuring the people intimately involved in the day-to-day processes have everything they need to do their job at maximum efficiency. It's not about power; it's about everybody fulfilling an assigned role. Where are these leaders, the stage four and stage five leaders, going to come from? How are they being developed? This, I believe, is where the greatest and most insurmountable obstacles to the forces that are driving companies towards transforming themselves into modern organizations are coming from. And the obstacles are arising because of opposition to progress that is coming from a very surprising quarter. This is where human nature plays the key role.

THE OPPOSING FORCES

Let us, for the moment, concentrate on the companies that are in the process of making the transition from traditional to modern organizations. They embarked on the path to change because of a crisis that was, happily for them, followed by the emergence of a great leader. But hold on, there's a problem isn't there? The charismatic leader that forced everybody to change is still in charge. What's he/she doing now? In most cases he's probably still getting mileage out of the old stories about how she saw the need for change and dragged the organization kicking and screaming into the modern era. But, unless this is a unique person we are talking about, they are probably not equipped to lead the organization they have created. People who get to the top by being the super tough decision maker, the charismatic communicators of the one true path to success, struggle in an organization where everyone must lead projects and develop ways to create value all of the time. In most cases, a major personality change would be needed and, although such leaders will still have the respect of people in the organization for what they have done, their war stories are probably producing more groans than genuine applause.

Chris Argyris has an interesting perspective on the problem in his new book, "*Flawed Advice and the Management Trap.*" He believes the conduct and underlying motivations of nearly all managers is ruled by the need to maximize winning and minimize losing and that they see challenges to their authority and policies as signs of weakness. In my own experience I have been amazed at the capacity of senior managers to put a "spin" on facts and to reconstruct reality to ensure that they don't face challenges to their control of a situation. Charismatic leaders have certain characteristics that make them what they are. They possess an absolute certainty about the world and how it should be and they have the ability to communicate this vision compellingly. These are not people who demonstrate great flexibility in their thinking nor do they happily cede control to others. They have a tendency not to listen to information that conflicts with their view of how the world should be.

It's different at the Internet start-ups though, right? No – even the heads of the Internet start-ups tend to be people who have fixed views of how the world should be and who like control. The difference here is that they have no choice about the kind of organization they are going to be in charge of. These companies are generally moving too fast for one person, or even a group of people, to have control over all decisions. Decisions get made and changed constantly – delays can result in market opportunities being lost forever. Even a giant like Microsoft has to operate this way even though Steve Ballmer, like Bill Gates before him, is a control freak. Microsoft cannot afford to wait until all the bugs have been taken out of its software before they ship. They get it to market and capture market share knowing that they can always fix the bugs in future releases. Today's version of Windows 98 is very different from the one I bought in 1998 and has surely been through several releases, each addressing some of the original bugs. People working in Microsoft have much less structure to their daily work than people working at, for example, General Motors, and they have much more ability to make decisions affecting the consumer on a minute-to-minute basis.

Many of the companies that are making the transition to modern organizations, and many traditional organizations that are advised by consultants or where management books are read, are putting in place mechanisms of employee "empowerment." Generally though, these mechanisms are used to confirm that control really resides at the top level – they are used to ward off the threat of real change. Many programs, for example, give employees the ability to make decisions regarding their own work patterns or minor capital investments. The message (spoken or otherwise) to employees is: "Management is prepared to trust you with the following decisions because we believe you will be more motivated through feeling empowered. However, it is still very clear that I am the leader and you are the led." This is very different from saying: "You are responsible for this piece of the operation. If you need help I am here as a resource." Truly modern organizations will have no choice because all the relevant information will reside *only* at the lowest levels. A plant operator of the future will be very much like the air traffic controller of today. The air traffic controller *has* to be empowered. If two 747s are on a collision course there's no time to refer a decision up the line.

My fundamental point here is that many leaders that have overseen the transition from traditional to modern can only take the company to a certain point and are then unsuited to manage the modern organization. Far from recognizing this and stepping aside these leaders will often do whatever is necessary to ensure they retain control, thus stopping the organization from fully making the transition. They believe they are keeping in step with "modern management" but they are still entrenched in the old ways. There are obviously exceptions to this scenario, but my personal observations suggest that they are worryingly few. In the Internet start-ups the internal forces driving the company forward tend to outweigh this factor and produce a modern organization. At the end of the day, a modern organization is no substitute for a good business model so it can't guarantee the success of the organization. After all, 80% or more of Internet start-ups have gone belly up. But, successful or not, the Internet start-ups have contributed to a permanent change to the environment. This change will require companies to have both a good business model and a modern organization in order to be successful, because a modern organization will be a requirement for ensuring the business model continues to be sound.

If the great leader is hindering progress the company's board will see what is happening and ask him/her to step aside, right? Think again. Directors didn't get to be directors by being softies – they are generally leaders of corporations themselves, fond of control and with their own positions to protect. The great leader probably handpicked them for their position on the board and they will no doubt have handed out massive bonuses and stock option grants to make sure he doesn't take his leadership skills somewhere else.

These same people will also have a major influence on leadership development within the company. The great leader may well spend a considerable amount of time on the subject – turning up at leadership development seminars to tell his stories – to ensure there are plenty more just like him in the pipeline. Storytelling by leaders is currently a very popular style of leadership development that overlooks the fact that many, if not most, of the stories in a traditional organization could be irrelevant if not downright harmful. It's also highly likely within an American company that the prospective leaders will have financial or marketing backgrounds. Indeed financial restructuring is seen many times to be as effective in creating value as is business process restructuring. The financial markets have forced this short-term thinking. In the larger companies the future leaders from foreign subs tend to be chosen for their English language and presentation skills, often as a result of attendance at budget meetings which are usually restricted to marketing and finance people. Leaders of modern organizations need to have more process-based skills than those that are usually possessed by people with backgrounds in marketing and finance.

All of the organizational forces are therefore interacting to produce a flow of future leaders that can take control and lead a transition to a modern organization but they are not producing the people to lead the transformed organization.

LEADERSHIP LIFE CYCLES

For the same person to lead a company through each of the stages of organizational transformation would require a very unusual individual because the attributes that make people ideal for one of the stages could be a deterrent for other stages. The educational background may also be a deterrent, particularly if the great leader is an expert in finance. Engineering may be a more suitable discipline for a leader in a modern organization because engineers should have the technical competence to understand how the pieces all fit together. However, engineers also have shortcomings and the truth is that educational background is secondary to other factors.

As the Tritonians showed us, one of the major stumbling blocks to progressing from stage three to stage four is an individual's ego need. There is more glamour that goes along with the stage one and stage two leadership roles. This is part of the reason why the charismatic leaders find it so difficult to let go – the major reason, of course, is that they are convinced they don't have to because they are the best equipped to lead the company at all times. And how dare you suggest that they don't delegate authority and don't listen to their employees' suggestions. You're obviously not watching. And have you noticed how much money employees have made from their stock options?

Should a company, therefore, plan to have a different leader at each stage? Maybe companies need to think about leader life cycles just as they think about product life cycles. But how do you get the CEO to agree with this approach? Not many of the CEOs I know would be likely to suggest that they step aside to make way for somebody with the competencies required to take the company to the next stage. Even if you were able to convince the board of the company of the need for change (and as we saw earlier, this would be very unlikely in the absence of a crisis) it would require great bravery (and probably a lot of money) for them to force the issue.

Of course, this has always been a problem but it is much more severe today because leader life cycles, like product life cycles, are getting shorter and shorter. In the future they will get shorter to the point where the issue of inappropriate leaders will have to be addressed in a very different way from the traditional approach. Many of the people who are leading the traditional organizations today were educated in the 1960s when even engineering students had to stand in line to get some time on the college department's lone computer. Now a computer is an essential office accessory, much more necessary than a secretary is for most executives. The values and tenets by which people of this generation manage have been formed over a 30-year period but early influences tend to be the strongest ones, particularly for the most inflexible leaders. They, incidentally, often are the ones who are the most certain of themselves when it comes to passing on their leadership beliefs. Ten years ago it did not matter much that the person at the top was a bit out of touch because their value set was only a little out of date and the organization could afford to wait for a graceful retirement. Being even five years out of date was not so critical 10 years ago. However, today that same five years can translate to being two leadership generations out of date. Companies cannot wait 30 years for the top man to retire so what can they do? I am convinced that this will be one of the most significant problems boards have to deal with in the future and I predict that many will not face the issue until a crisis occurs and there is a legitimate reason to go back to stage one with a new leader.

I accept that things will inevitably get better eventually because the new business environment is necessarily throwing up a generation of potential leaders that expect their environment to change on a regular basis. These leaders are likely to appear to be flexible compared to yesterday's men. This doesn't get rid of the problem, though; it just reduces the severity.

DEVELOPMENT OF THE GLOBAL DIMENSION

What of the global aspects of the leadership dimension? Many of the issues I have raised in relation to the organization's transition from traditional to modern are merely made more complicated by the existence of global factors. Not many companies have been successful in putting in place enterprise-wide systems on a global basis but it will come. Already communication between employees working in Bethlehem, Pennsylvania and Bethlehem, Israel is simple and real-time. Engineers looking at a potential plant site in Indonesia can take photographs with their digital cameras and transmit them over the Internet so that they can discuss an issue with head office in New York while both parties are looking at the same thing. When information flows this easily it is extremely difficult to control.

I have suggested that "global" will have less and less meaning as markets converge and communications become easier. There will always be cultural differences and, for that reason, it will be good to have a diverse group of leaders drawn from several cultures. I do believe, though, that it will become easier to gain acceptance of business vision, mission and strategies as they apply to satisfying the customer across many cultures than has historically been the case. The "Japanese way" will become the "American way" and vice-versa. I do not see any different life cycle problems arising specifically from the global aspects of leadership.

There is, though, a separate driver for ensuring that future leaders have a global understanding and that leaders from several cultures are deployed that I have not yet mentioned. This arises from a difference in the way businesses are viewed in different markets and how their stakeholders measure their performance. Although there will be a gradual convergence here too, I think it will be slower to occur.

In the United States public companies are under severe pressure to maintain their stock price by meeting short-term financial expectations. Return on investment is a key measure of success and this again tends to be short-term oriented. Employees generally accept that employment is not a right, particularly if the company does not perform well. This over-emphasis on short-term financial performance is one reason why many CEOs come from the finance function.

In Europe the emphasis is much more on measuring future cash flow and the perspective is longer term. A focus on business process comes more naturally to a European businessman than to an American. Product quality tends to be a stronger measure of the fundamental health of a company than the P&L. Employees have an expectation that their employment is going to be of longer duration and, in many cases, there are laws in place that ensure it.

Japanese profit margins drive U.S. managers crazy but their shareholders are used to them and find them to be acceptable. They have traditionally had very rigid employment practices that are now changing, but very slowly.

In today's global marketplace Europeans hold shares in U.S. companies and U.S. citizens hold the stock of Japanese companies. The truly global companies have to satisfy people around the world – either in their role as employees, as stockholders or as members of government. Without a good understanding of the various demands and expectations and the different measurements of success that are being deployed, companies will inevitably fail to meet some of those expectations without even being aware of it. Therefore it is vital to ensure this understanding by the participation at senior levels of people from different backgrounds or people who have the experience of different cultural approaches.

WHAT'S TO BE DONE?

I have raised several issues and asked several questions without providing answers. A key goal of my story about the visitors from Triton was to demonstrate that even where the path to excellence is clear, people will erect walls across the path because of personal needs and wants. This is exactly what Jack Welch saw so clearly when he fired the wall-builders and encouraged the pathfinders. Unfortunately, there are very few Jack Welch's and the great man himself has now announced his retirement. It is a heretical thought but even some people within GE say that he stayed at the helm longer than he should have. Others will say that he exercised very tight control over the organization and that claims of devolution of responsibility have been overstated. Let's assume for the moment that some of that is true. Can you imagine any board telling Welch that his time was up?

Forget the books, forget the fact that you are revered in management circles, forget the company results, Jack – you've stayed too long. Wow! In many cases the problem is compounded by boards continuing to grant massive stock options to the great leaders even when they know they will retire in a year or two. Why do they do this? It's not as a retention tool and it's not because the poor guy (and yes, most are guys) needs the money. It's all about ego. If the board decided to hold back with the rewards the great leader would lose face. Sometimes it's a real pity that the top man's compensation is public knowledge.

It would be nice to be able to believe that there's another way to achieve the same end. When products reach maturity they can still be very successful cash generators so maybe companies can find a way to gain from the experience of leaders who have gone past their sell-by date rather than pushing them out. It would clearly have to be something untainted by the "special projects" stigma, but there has to be a way to make use of all that knowledge and experience. In the end, though, it comes down to ego and will not happen.

Am I saying there's no solution to the problem? Am I saying that companies are going to have to stumble from crisis to crisis to get effective leadership and that the crises will get closer and closer together? That's exactly what I am saying and it will continue until companies and boards redefine what the role of a leader is and take a long, hard look at the arrangements under which the top people are employed. They need to look upon leadership as situational and avoid giving the reins to somebody who may become an inappropriate leader in the future and who may be difficult to dislodge.

In the United States, change would have to be initiated by boards consisting of strong, independent outside directors. Boards need to become more active in soliciting feedback from within their organizations with regard to top management performance and then they must be prepared to act on the knowledge they gain. They should take charge of the leadership development process within the organization to ensure it does not become biased towards producing one kind of leader. This probably requires that boards be staffed with different people than the ones that currently occupy these positions in corporate America because it will require a significant time commitment. It will also require that the task of staffing boards be taken out of the hands of chief executive officers.

Outside of the United States there are some mechanisms, such as supervisory boards, that could be used to oversee the process but these are often used only as talking shops. Their over-weighting with inside directors also usually annuls the effectiveness of company boards. In many countries it will require considerable corporate restructuring before neutral boards can be a reality.

If change is going to occur it seems that it will have to be driven by shareholders willing to vote out boards that don't do their job. It would probably require an even more disastrous drop than the one we have recently seen in the world's stock markets for this to become the generally accepted practice. Please send me an e-mail to let me know if you would like this to happen!

Maybe the Tritonian Achme Chemical Company should change its name to Ach-wire-me!

REFERENCES

Hammer, M., & Champy, J. (1993). *Reengineering the Corporation.* New York: HarperCollins.
Lawler, E. E. (1996). *From the Ground Up.* San Francisco: Jossey-Bass.
Kotter, J. P. (1995). Leading Change: Why Transformation Efforts Fail. *Harvard Business Review,* (March-April), 59–67.
Argyris, C. (1999). *Flawed Advice and the Management Trap: How Managers Can Know When They're Getting Good Advice and When They're Not.* Oxford: Oxford University Press.

TRENDS, DEVELOPMENTS AND GAPS IN CROSS-CULTURAL RESEARCH ON LEADERSHIP

Marcus W. Dickson, Paul J. Hanges and Robert G. Lord

ABSTRACT

Literature on leadership and literature on culture are each rich and deep, but the two were largely unrelated during the first several decades of their development. In more recent years, many researchers have explored relationships between these two literatures. In this chapter, we identify four developments or trends in the last 25 years of cross-cultural leadership literature. First, our understanding of etic or universal findings has advanced and become more complex, but also more realistic. Second, there has been refinement in the definition of "culture" and the identification of the dimensions of culture, with several researchers having identified particular cultural dimensions that seem to be directly relevant to leadership. Third, the social information processing literature has been extended to the leadership and culture literatures. Finally, there is a movement toward larger studies that not only collect data from multiple countries, but also through multiple research methodologies.

INTRODUCTION

Psychologists, management scholars and others interested in organizational functioning have been studying leadership and culture for many years.

Advances in Global Leadership, Volume 2, pages 75–100.
ISBN: 0-7623-0723-4

However, the two topics were largely seen as unrelated for the first several decades of their histories. For example, the cross-cultural psychology chapter in the first edition of *The Handbook of Industrial and Organizational Psychology* (Barrett & Bass, 1976) barely touched on issues of leadership. Similarly, the first edition of Stogdill's *Handbook of Leadership* (1974) had virtually nothing to say about culture and its effect on leadership.

Early literature on cross-cultural leadership tended to be characterized by one of two "themes," which are easily discernible by reading Barrett and Bass' (1976) review. The first theme separates those studies seeking to identify universally accepted leadership qualities from studies seeking to document cultural differences. For example, Mouton and Blake's (1970) attempts to show that the 9,9 management style was universally endorsed, and Sirota's (1968) finding that the managerial style of "consultation" and "joint decision-making" were universally preferred, are examples of studies seeking evidence of universally-endorsed leadership characteristics. In contrast, the work of Foa (1957), Lippitt and White (1958), and Meade and Whittaker (1967) are examples of research that found that preferences for an authoritarian leadership style varied widely across cultures. Second, some studies used a theoretical orientation to guide the research endeavor, whereas other studies simply compared participant responses from two or more countries in an attempt to document the similarities or differences in scale responses across nations. For both of these themes, studies in the second category far outweighed those in the first.

Barrett and Bass (1976) noted that, in the more common atheoretical quest to find cultural differences, the cause of any discovered differences (or similarities) is never clear. Response differences might be due to cultural differences, lack of consistent operationalization and definition of constructs across countries, or even culturally-specific response biases (Dorfman, 1996). In general, Barrett and Bass called for the development of theories explicating why and how culture affects leadership.

Much has changed over the past 25 years. Research and theory focusing on cross-cultural leadership has "taken off," as is evidenced by the broad range of topics covered in a recent two-part special issue of *Leadership Quarterly* (Hunt & Peterson, 1997a), and recent articles and chapters reviewing the literature on leadership in a cross-cultural context (e.g. Dorfman, 1996; House, Wright & Aditya, 1997; House & Aditya, 1997).

In this chapter, we do not purport to present a complete review of the cross-cultural leadership literature, as the aforementioned scholars have ably accomplished this. Rather, we attempt to document the emergence of four trends in cross-cultural research on leadership. First, our understanding of etic or universal findings has advanced and become more complex, but also more realistic. Second, there has been refinement in the definition of "culture" and the identification of the dimensions of culture, with several researchers having identified particular cultural dimensions that seem to be directly relevant to leadership. Third, the social information processing literature has been extended to the leadership and culture literatures. The work being done using this perspective shows promise in explicating the relationship between culture and leadership. Finally, there is a movement toward larger studies that collect data not only from multiple countries but also through multiple research methodologies. While there have been other advances in the cross-cultural literature (e.g. application of multi-level statistical methodology and discussion of cross-cultural response bias), we will focus on these four aforementioned developments in this chapter because these other developments are generally very recent and are more statistically complex than can be adequately addressed in a chapter.[1] We assume as a general starting point the Barrett and Bass (1976) chapter in the first edition of *The Handbook of Industrial/ Organizational Psychology*, because of its influence on the fields of industrial/organizational psychology and organizational behavior.

Development 1: Reconsideration of the Concept of a Universal

Many of the researchers whose work was reviewed by Barrett and Bass (1976) took a view of universal phenomena that, in hindsight, appears to have been overly simplistic. More recently, several different variations of the concept "universal" have been identified (Bass, 1997; Lonner, 1980), including the *simple universal*, which is a phenomenon that is constant throughout the world. In terms of statistical inference, simple universals focus on the mean level of a variable and the extent to which the mean doesn't vary across cultures.

As noted earlier, we believe that much of the leadership-related literature reviewed by Barrett and Bass (1976) were attempts to find what would now be referred to as simple universals. For example, Mouton and Blake's (1970) attempts to document the universal preference for the 9,9 management style is an example of research in which this conceptualization of a universal principle is used. Unfortunately, it appears that the only phenomena that can be accurately classified as simple universals are the most general statements or principles. For example, the facts that humans are aggressive and communicate with each other are examples of simple universals. In the leadership arena, Bass (1997) notes that the statement "whenever a group of people meet, a leader will emerge" is an example of a simple universal.

Although early researchers tended to seek simple universals, our current understanding of the concept of a universal is more complex, and incorporates several different types of universals. The notion of a *variform universal* comes from the cultural relativism tradition, and indicates that there might be subtle modifications of a simple universal when one studies that principle across cultures. In other words, a variform universal refers to cases in which a general statement or principle holds across cultures but the enactment of this principle differs across cultures, whereas in a simple universal both the principle and its enactment are the same across cultures. For example, the simple universal that all people display emotions through facial expressions can be transformed into a variform universal if one asks whether the interpretation of a particular facial expression is the same across cultures (Lonner, 1980). Another example of a variform universal is that even though effective communication skills are seen as essential for effective charismatic leadership throughout the world (den Hartog, House, Hanges, Ruiz-Quintanilla & GLOBE, 1999), the exact behaviors that are considered effective systematically varies. Trompenaars (1993) indicates that while it is considered polite in Anglo countries to wait for a person to finish speaking before saying what is on one's mind, in most Latin cultures, interrupting a speaker conveys interest in what the speaker is saying (den Hartog et al., 1999).

A *functional universal* focuses on the stability of relationships between variables. Functional universals occur when the within group relationship between two variables is the same across cultures. That is, researchers interested in functional universals look for stable patterns and relationships that permit inferences without regard to situational factors. In personnel psychology, the application of validity generalization to identify tests whose inferences are not moderated by situational factors is an example of a search for functional universals. Another example, provided by Bass (1997), is that there is always a negative relationship between laissez-faire leadership and subordinate perceptions of the leader's effectiveness. That is, regardless of culture, the leader who frequently avoids responsibilities and shirks duties is perceived to be ineffective.

A *variform functional universal*, proposed by Bass (1997), also examines relationships between two variables. The twist provided by this type of universal is that even though the relationship between two variables is always found, the relationship's magnitude changes across cultures. In personnel psychology, variform functional universals can be seen in the validity generalization literature in which it is claimed that even though cognitive ability tests predict job performance for all jobs, the magnitude of this relationship is stronger for some jobs (i.e. cognitively complex jobs) than for others. Another example is provided by Bass (1997), who suggests that across all cultures, transformational leader behaviors are seen as more effective than transactional leader behaviors, though the magnitude of this behavior-effectiveness relationship varies by culture.

Systematic behavioral universals are principles or theories that explain if-then outcomes across cultures and organizations (Bass, 1997). Systematic behavioral universals involve theories that claim either (a) a sequence of behavior is invariant over cultures (e.g. Piaget's work on the stages of development), or (b) the structure and organization of a behavior or behavioral cluster is constant over cultures (e.g. the universality of the *g* factor in the intelligence literature) (Lonner, 1980). In other words, this type of universal focuses on causal explanations and the extent to which these causal explanations are useful across cultures. Bass (1997) argues that the transformational-transactional leadership theory is an example of a systematic behavioral universal. Specifically, when leaders exhibit a specific constellation of behaviors identified as "transactional leadership behaviors" (i.e. clarifies work expectations, uses contingent rewards and incentives, monitors employee behavior), then followers are subsequently motivated primarily by self-interest (Bass & Avolio, 1993; Yukl, 1994). If a leader consistently displays behaviors identified as "transformational leadership" (i.e. gets followers to strongly identify with him or her, provides new perspectives on organizational problems, provides developmental opportunities and support, and communicates an enticing vision of the future), then followers are more likely to transcend their own interests and be motivated by the "greater cause" (Bass & Avolio, 1993; Yukl, 1994).

While Lonner (1980) has identified several other types of universals (e.g. diachronic universals, ethologically oriented universals), they are less relevant to the present topic and thus will not be discussed. The utility of this elaboration of the "universal principle" concept is that we now have a taxonomy that should help us make sense of and consolidate empirical findings from multiple studies. For example, at first glance the results of two empirical studies may appear to be contradictory. However, the studies could be reconciled if they were examining different types of universals. Further, this taxonomy should help clarify our thinking about the different leadership theories that may focus on phenomena described by different types of universals.

This is not at all to suggest that we should abandon the search for universals simply because the concept has become more theoretically complex. Similarly, we should not abandon the search for emic phenomena in favor of etic phenomena – both are critical to understanding cross-cultural leadership (or any cross-cultural phenomena, for that matter). Indeed, as Smith (1997) has noted, ". . . what is universally true must by definition be locally true" (p. 628). Peterson and Hunt (1997) argue that the most promising route is to "use analyses of culture-specific scientific concepts as a starting point. We can then allow analyses conducted in several societies and circumstances to drive us toward a more basic construct that we hope will find broad utility"(p. 208). It is promising to note that scholars are beginning to understand the importance of both etic and emic approaches. Hunt and Peterson's (1997b) evaluation of the 10 articles in *Leadership Quarterly*'s special issue (Hunt & Peterson, 1997a) on cross-cultural leadership found all 10 articles to have strong emphases on both etic and emic analyses. We believe that this is as it should be.

Development 2: Defining "Culture" and Integrating the Culture-Leadership Literatures

The construct of culture has been defined in many different ways over the years. For example, Kluckhohn (1951) defined culture as a patterned manner of thinking, feeling and reacting, which is acquired and communicated through symbols and embodied in artifacts. Similarly, Herskovits (1955) defined culture as that part of the environment that is created or modified. In contrast, Triandis (1972) focused on the subjective perception of the man-made part of the environment. Hofstede (1980) defined culture as the set of mental programs that control an individual's responses in a given context.

Erez and Earley (1993) note that the common theme to these various culture definitions is that, in all of the definitions, culture is seen as the shared knowledge and meaning systems used by a particular group of people. It consists of both objective (i.e. tools and artifacts) and subjective (i.e. cognitive categories, beliefs, norms and values components). Erez and Earley make the explicit connection between the subjective component of culture and the concept of scripts and schemas used in the information-processing literature (e.g. Lord & Maher's 1991 work on culture from a cognitive processing perspective).

Additionally, researchers have proposed several dimensions that differentiate one culture from another. Hofstede's (1980) landmark study continues to be one of the most influential and often cited studies of this type. In particular, Hofstede proposed four primary dimensions that differentiate cultures. These dimensions are:

(1) *Power distance*: The degree to which members of a society expect power to be shared equally.

(2) *Uncertainty Avoidance*: The degree to which members of a society feel uncomfortable in unstructured, ambiguous and uncertain situations and create beliefs and institutions intended to minimize the occurrence of such situations.
(3) *Individualism*: The degree to which individuals function independently of each other or are integrated into groups.
(4) *Masculinity*: The degree to which cultures look favorably on assertiveness, aggressiveness and striving for personal success, or instead stress supportive behavior, nurturance and service.

Despite (or perhaps because of) their widespread use, Hofstede's (1980) work has been heavily criticized. For example, his work as a whole has been criticized because of the composition of his scales (e.g. the lack of face validity for the items), and the poor psychometric properties of his scales (e.g. the lack of scale independence and the apparent inappropriate labeling of scales) (e.g. Dorfman & Howell, 1988; Jaeger, 1986; Triandis, 1982). A second criticism of the work as a whole is that cultures may vary by additional dimensions beyond those proposed by Hofstede. For example, the Chinese Culture Connection (1987) reports evidence that a dimension called the Confucian Work Dynamic can meaningfully differentiate cultures. Societies high on Confucian Work Dynamic value persistence, ordering relationships based on status, thrift and possessing a sense of shame, whereas societies low on this dimension value protecting one's face, respect for tradition and personal steadiness and stability. Hofstede and Bond (1988) have found positive relationships between this dimension and the economic growth of Asian countries. A final criticism of Hofstede's work as a whole comes from other researchers who have proposed completely different taxonomies for differentiating cultures, which are argued to more accurately differentiate cultures (e.g. Fiske's 1991 typology of social interactions and Schwartz' 1994 work on values circumplex).

In addition to the criticisms of the work as a whole, specific dimensions proposed by Hofstede (1980) have also been criticized. For example, there is evidence that the individualism-collectivism continuum is not a single continuum, but rather two independent continua (Triandis, 1993). Recent work by Gelfand, Triandis and Chan (1996), for example, has demonstrated that the opposite of individualism is not collectivism, but rather is authoritarianism, with collectivism composing a separate dimension. Another example is Triandis' (1993) argument that Hofstede's uncertainty avoidance dimension is not so much a description of different cultures, but rather a description of the kinds of typical situations that people in that culture confront.

Despite these and other criticisms, Hofstede's dimensions have been very influential in the field, and have received some empirical support by independent researchers (House, Wright & Aditya, 1997). In general, we see Hofstede's dimensions as providing a useful starting point from which to hypothesize about the interaction between culture and leadership.

How do these dimensions of culture relate to leadership? To date there have been several interesting propositions with regard to this question. Hofstede, Bond and Luk (1993), for example, hypothesize that power distance should affect the type of leader seen as effective in a society. The ideal leader in a low power distance culture would consult with his or her subordinates and incorporate their suggestions. House, Wright and Aditya (1997) called this type of leader a "resourceful democrat". On the other hand, a "benevolent autocrat" (House et al., 1997) would be the ideal leader in a high power distance culture. Further, Triandis (1993) conjectured that charismatic leadership might be expected and most effective in high power distance cultures.

Another example of interesting propositions on the connection between these cultures and desired leadership behavior is Triandis' (1993) hypotheses focusing on individualism/collectivism. Specifically, Triandis argues that in highly collectivist cultures, successful leaders will be supportive and paternalistic. That is, they seek to maintain the harmony of the work group, solve workers' personal problems and are generally helpful and considerate. In highly individualist cultures, on the other hand, the ideal leader will allow followers enough freedom to accomplish their own tasks, but will be supportive and provide assistance when needed. The ideal leader in such a culture would value people's distinctiveness and be achievement-oriented and participative.

While these hypotheses are interesting and occasionally counter-intuitive, they are more a product of the cross-cultural literature than of the leadership literature. They seem to be fitting leadership theories into cross-cultural theories rather than applying and testing the existing leadership theories cross-culturally. This lack of integration between literatures is not unique to the study of leadership, but rather extends to other research domains as well (Betancourt & Lopez, 1993). In the next section, we briefly review the cross-cultural generalizability of existing leadership theories.

Generalizability of Existing Leadership Theories. Many leadership theories have been proposed over the years. These theories have ranged from the Ohio State behavioral approach to leadership, to Fiedler's contingency theory of leadership, and even the theory of charismatic and transformational leadership. Some of these leadership theories do not consider either cultural or situational moderators at all (e.g. behavioral leadership approach; the "great man" theory of leadership), while others have specifically dealt with the role of situational moderators (e.g. Fiedler's contingency theory; Path-Goal theory; Vroom-Yetton Normative Decision Model). Though none of these theories have specifically focused on culture, several studies have examined the generalizability and robustness of these theories across cultures. Dorfman (1996) has thoroughly reviewed these studies recently.

As one would expect, there have been mixed results. For example, in the behavioral approach, leadership is believed to be composed of two dimensions: initiating structure and consideration. Dorfman (1996) indicated that there is substantial support for the functional universal status of the relationship between consideration and subordinate satisfaction. However, the studies that he reviewed showed inconsistent results for the effect of initiating structure across cultures.

Misumi's (1984) conceptually similar Performance-Maintenance model of leadership has also received inconsistent support across cultures. Misumi's initial goal was to develop a model of basic functions that are common for all successful leaders (Misumi & Peterson, 1985). The theory's hypotheses that managers should focus on both Performance (planning, guiding, task accomplishment) and Maintenance (preserving the social stability of the group) has received support among Japanese managers (Misumi & Peterson, 1985), Indian managers (Sinha, 1990, as cited in Chemers, 1997) and Iranian managers (Ayman & Chemers, 1983). However, the wide range of studies building on the Ohio State dimensions of Initiating Structure and Consideration have not found unambiguous support for the effectiveness of managers high on both of these dimensions. Blake and Mouton (1964), for example, explicitly argue that the 9,9 leadership style is not always the most appropriate. Thus, these two conceptually similar models have not yielded similar results. Chemers (1997) proposes that this could be due to the different values guiding the expectations and desires of employees in Eastern and Western societies.

Some aspects of Path-Goal theory (House, 1971) appear to be robust. In this theory, the leader's primary function is to motivate followers through directive, supportive, achievement-oriented or participative leadership and to increase followers' payoffs for work goal achievement. Dorfman (1996) discusses a cross-cultural study by Howell, Dorfman, Hibino, Lee and Tate (1994), which obtained some support for the complete universality for supportive leader behavior, some universality for directive leader behaviors and cultural specificity for participative leadership behaviors.

Fiedler's Contingency Theory. Triandis (1993) has recently argued that Fiedler's (1964) contingency theory has a chance to be a variform functional universal if one uses cultural variables (i.e. individualism, collectivism, power distance and uncertainty avoidance) as the parameters of the model. In other words, this theory defines effective leadership differently for different cultures. Triandis argues that Fiedler's "leader-member relations" dimension has a link with the collectivism culture dimension. Good relationships between leaders and their followers should exist if the leader is a member of the followers' in-group and if the leader acts in a nurturant manner. If the leader is a member of the out-group or is not nurturant, then Triandis predicts that the leader will be in Fiedler's Octant 8. Only a very low-LPC leader can be at all effective.

Triandis (1993) connects Fiedler's (1964) "task structure" dimension to the uncertainty avoidance culture dimension. Tasks that are highly structured should be compatible with societies high in uncertainty avoidance since people in these societies like structure and want to avoid uncertainty. In high-uncertainty-avoidance cultures, the contingency model would predict the need for a high LPC leader. Finally, Fiedler's "leader power" dimension has clear connection to the power distance culture factor. Extending contingency theory in this manner increases the likelihood that this theory is a systematic behavioral universal.

Transformational-Transactional Leadership. Bass (1997) has recently presented three propositions arguing that transformational-transactional leadership is a universal concept. First, Bass (1997) claims that there is a consistent hierarchy of relationships between leadership style and various outcome measures (e.g. effectiveness, subordinate effort and subordinate satisfaction). Specifically, even though the magnitude of these relationships varies significantly across cultures, transformational leaders appear to be more effective than (in descending order) leaders who rely on contingent reward, leaders practicing active management by exception, leaders practicing passive management by exception, and leaders who are laissez-faire. In other words, there is evidence for a variform functional relationship between the various types of leadership and effectiveness. Second, Bass (1997) argues that across cultures, transformational leadership measures add to transactional leadership measures in predicting important outcomes, but the reverse does not hold true. Bass notes that this augmentation effect appears to be a variform functional universal, because the magnitude of the relationship varies across cultures. Finally, Bass (1997) argues that across cultures, people's prototypes of leadership and their conceptions of ideal leaders are generally transformational rather than transactional.

Consistent with Bass' proposal, the Global Leadership and Organizational Behavioral Effectiveness (GLOBE) international leadership study being conducted by House and his colleagues has found support for the claim that leadership prototypes are composed of transformational leadership attributes (Hanges & Dickson, in press, a; House, Hanges, Ruiz-Quintanilla, Dorfman,

Javidan, Dickson & GLOBE, 1999; den Hartog et al., 1999). The GLOBE research project, which will be discussed more completely later in this chapter, identified 22 leadership attributes that middle managers from 60 different countries universally endorsed as facilitating effective leadership. Most of these attributes were characteristic of transformational leaders.

While these results may be taken as evidence of the universal nature of transformational-transactional leadership, it should be noted that this evidence is not unambiguous. Research findings in the information processing literature suggest that transformational leadership may not be as universal as Bass and others indicate. We will consider this literature in the next section of this chapter.

In summary, Triandis' (1993) reworking of Fiedler's (1964) contingency theory of leadership is an example of research that exemplifies the recent admonition to "begin with a theory, typically one that ignores culture, and incorporate cultural elements to broaden its theoretical domain" (Betancourt & Lopez, 1993, p. 633). This new contingency theory provides a variform universal conceptualization of leadership. In this theory, culture plays a critical role in determining the type of leadership that is appropriate in a given context. In contrast, Bass (1997) argues that culture is much less important when one is concerned with transformational leadership. He argues that transformational-transactional leadership is a set of explanatory concepts that are useful for all cultures.

Development 3: Culture and Information Processing Views: Leadership Perception

A major development since the Barrett and Bass (1976) review is the application of information processing approaches to leadership. Lord and colleagues (Lord, Foti & DeVader, 1984; Lord & Maher, 1991) conducted a number of studies showing that leadership perceptions are based on both *inferences* from performance and *recognition* based on matching leader characteristics and behavior to leader prototypes. Others have extended this categorization-based approach to cross-cultural issues related to leadership (Erez & Earley, 1993; Hanges, Lord & Dickson, 2000; Shaw, 1990). Shaw notes that many of the difficulties expatriate leaders experience stem from different cultural definitions of effective leadership and culturally based scripts for leadership behavior. Since categories and scripts are learned from experience and are applied automatically, it is difficult for leaders operating in a foreign culture to understand differences in leadership prototypes or to alter their behavior in a culturally appropriate manner. Thus, although the process of prototype matching as a determinant of leadership perception is a simple universal principle, if prototype content varies with culture, prototype matching becomes a variform universal phenomenon.

We are aware of three studies that have used leadership categorization approaches to investigate cultural differences in leadership prototypes (den Hartog et al., 1999; Gerstner & Day, 1994; O'Connell, Lord & O'Connell, 1990). Gerstner and Day compared the leadership prototypes of international students (from France, Germany, Honduras, India, Taiwan, China and Japan) and American students studying in the United States. They found no universal leadership traits, but respondents saw the trait "goal-oriented" as being prototypical in all countries except France and Japan. Other traits were common only among respondents from Western or Eastern cultures. For example, "determined" was prototypical of leaders for respondents from all Western countries (France, Germany, Honduras, India and the United States), while "intelligence" was prototypical of leaders for respondents in every Eastern culture (China, Taiwan and Japan).

Gerstner and Day (1994) also used prototype ratings on 59 traits to generate similarity indices, which were then used to construct a multidimensional representation of country differences in leadership prototypes. The three-dimensional MDS solution was strongly related to the values of each country on Hofstede's dimensions of Power Distance, Uncertainty Avoidance and Individualism. This finding suggests that leadership prototypes reflect the higher level values that characterize a culture.

One limitation of Gerstner and Day's (1994) research is that it used English questionnaires based on studies of leadership using U.S. samples. This approach would not measure dimensions unique to Eastern cultures such as Confucian Work Dynamic (Chinese Culture Connection, 1987) or character-istics specific to a particular country. O'Connell, Lord and O'Connell (1990) used a less restrictive approach to compare U.S. and Japanese prototypes of leaders. They had 120 Japanese students living in Japan generate traits that characterized various types of Japanese leaders (business, finance, education, political and mass media leaders). A native Japanese citizen who had lived in the U.S. and a native American who had lived and worked as an interpreter in Japan then translated these traits into English. Several traits were common among the categories given to Japanese students (fair, flexible, good listener, outgoing and responsible). Comparison of these data to that of American college students (Lord et al., 1984) indicated substantial differences. When traits were ordered in each national sample according to family resemblance values (how widely shared they were among subcategories), rank order correlations for the Japanese and American student was only 0.08. Thus, the overall pattern of traits defining leadership prototypes was quite different for these two samples.

In the most comprehensive cross-cultural comparison of prototypes, den Hartog et al. (1999) examined the extent to which 112 leadership items were seen as "impeding or facilitating unusually effective leadership." They predicted that items indicative of charismatic leadership qualities would be universally endorsed, but they allowed for the possibility that the *expression* of these qualities could vary across cultures. That is, the expression of charisma could be a variform universal. Results based on data obtained from 15,022 middle managers spanning 60 different societies/cultures supported both of these expectations. Three of their six secondary factors (Charismatic/Value based, Team oriented and Participative) were prototypical of outstanding leadership in all cultures. Similarly, many sets of items were universally endorsed. They included integrity (trustworthy, just, honest), charisma (encouraging, positive, motivational, confidence builder, dynamic, foresight), team-oriented (team building, communicating, and coordinating), and an eclectic group (excellence oriented, decisive, intelligent, and win-win problem solver). Universal negative items (undesired behaviors) were ruthless, asocial, irritable, loner, egocentric, non-explicit, non-cooperative, and dictatorial. Many items (35) were also found to vary substantially across cultures, and these included several items associated with charismatic/transformational leadership, such as enthusiastic, compassionate, sensitive, unique and risk taking. This indicates that not all content of leadership prototypes is universal across cultures. Further, qualitative analyses from many countries (Mexico, China, Netherlands, Australia) demonstrated that the expression of charismatic qualities varied across cultures in a manner consistent with variform universals.

Differences in leadership prototypes as illustrated by these cross-cultural comparisons of leadership prototypes highlight the importance of follower-centered views to understanding cultural difference in leadership. Follower-centered views assert that it is the interpretation of *patterns* of leadership qualities, not specific leadership characteristics or behavior per se, that are critical in understanding leadership (Hollander, 1992; Hollander & Julian, 1969). Because schema can differ substantially across cultures, interpretations of the same characteristics or behavior can vary substantially across or within cultures. Thus, perceiver differences can create variform universals of traits or behaviors thought by many to be universal leadership characteristics.

One recent cross-cultural study of implicit theories (Chong & Thomas, 1997) focuses directly on interpretations of leadership, bypassing the measurement of differences in prototypes. The research team focused on two different ethnic groups of New Zealanders – Pakeha and Pacific Islanders. Chong and Thomas argue that these two groups will hold different leadership prototypes, and thus will interpret the same behaviors differently. They also argue that each group will hold different prototypes for Pakeha as compared to Pacific Islander leaders. Thus, they see prototypes as arising from both follower schema and primes from leader characteristics. They provide some empirical support for this proposition, but they did not measure either leadership perceptions or actual prototypes used in forming leadership perceptions.

Network models of cultural constraints. Chong and Thomas' (1997) argument that culturally-based differences in leaders can influence the prototype used by perceivers is consistent with a recent revision of leader prototype theory (Lord, Brown & Harvey, 2000). Lord et al., maintain that rather than being a fixed memory structure that is retrieved from long-term memory, prototypes are actually recreated subject to a variety of situational constraints each time they are used. They suggest that these reconstructions are produced by very fast-acting connectionist architectures that operate automatically to create a perceptual standard appropriate for a specific context. Lord et al., note that national and organizational cultures provide powerful constraints on prototypes. However, important constraints also arise from organizational or group contexts (Emrich, 1999; Pillai, 1996), task type (Hall, Workman & Marchioro, 1998), from the individual perceiver, and as already noted, from leaders themselves.

The implication of the Lord et al. (2000) perspective is that the effects of culture on leadership prototypes would ultimately lie in the nature of cultural constraints on the cognitive networks that produce leadership prototypes. That is, culture serves as an input that partially activates (or inhibits) specific traits associated with leadership, making them more (or less) likely to be used in defining leadership. Moreover, because constraints operate as a whole pattern, rather than in a bivariate manner, the meaning of prototypes is very likely to differ across cultures, again illustrating a variform universal effect. Extending this idea, Hanges, Lord & Dickson (2000) developed an explicit connectionist model of leadership schema, which can be activated by both a sociocultural event and leadership behavior. Importantly, they represent schemas with two levels in this network model – with the higher level being composed of values, attitudes and self-structures, and the lower level involving scripts and specific behaviors. Lord and Brown (1999) emphasize the role of self structures in such networks, arguing that values are organized by and operate through self structures, a perspective that extends Cropanzano, James and Citera's (1993) theorizing on this subject. O'Neill and Hanges (2000) began to empirically investigate such ideas by developing a Pathfinder model of connectionist networks and illustrating that network properties are influenced by cultural values. They demonstrate the critical point at which culture can affect many network properties (e.g. item centrality and schema internal structure) as well as the content of leadership prototypes, providing a more refined explanation of why culture should have variform universal effects.

Self-structures and leadership. Self-structures are also important constraints on leadership prototypes that often operate in conjunction with cultural differences (Hanges, Lord & Dickson, 2000; Lord & Brown, 1999). The dependence of leadership on culture is more evident if one conceptualizes leadership as an ongoing, dynamic, social process rather than merely an aspect of hierarchical organizational structures. For example, Shamir, House and Arthur (1993) maintain that transformational leadership results from leaders engaging the self-structures of followers. Lord, Brown and Freiberg (1999) extend this reasoning even further, arguing that many aspects of leadership derive from the aspect of selves made salient (activated) by leaders. Individuals possess personal, relational or collective self-concepts (Brewer & Gardner, 1996). Lord, Brown & Freiberg (1999) assert that when the personal self is emphasized, leadership stresses transactional qualities; but when the social (relational or collective) selves are stressed, leadership becomes transformational. Experimental work by Jung and Avolio (1999) illustrates this point showing that Asian students, who were presumably socialized to develop a more collective identity, worked best under transformational leadership; whereas, American students, with more individually-oriented identities, did best under transactional leadership. Since cultures vary widely in their emphasis on personal versus social bases for self-definition (Erez & Earley, 1993; Markus & Kitayana, 1991), one might expect the prevalence of transformational and transactional leadership to vary with culture as well.

A closer examination of the role of self-structures in guiding information processing further emphasizes the moderating effects of culture on leadership processes. Because the self is a highly available and richly connected cognitive structure, it is involved in most aspects of information processing (Markus & Wurf, 1987). Yet, only those aspects of the self that are made salient (activated) in any particular situation, i.e. the *working self* (Markus & Wurf, 1987), guide information processing. Leadership processes (Lord et al., 1999), culture (Erez & Earley, 1993) and individual differences (Markus, 1977) are critical determinants of the working self in any particular situation. Hence, we can view these effects as operating by making alternative working selves (e.g. personal versus collective self-views) more accessible.

Markus and Wurf (1987) also argue that the self is a critical self-regulatory structure. It is the source of many self-evaluative motivations as well as standards used for comparison (Catrambone, Beike & Niedenthal, 1996; Smith, Brown, Lord & Engle, 1998). Cropanzano et al. (1993) extend this notion to leadership, arguing that values and self-schema comprise the highest levels in control hierarchies that regulate human behavior. They argue that different types of leadership (transformational leadership, path-goal leadership, reward and punishment based leadership) impact different levels of such hierarchies. Such theorizing provides an ideal basis for understanding the potential impact of culture (Erez & Earley, 1993) because both *values* and *collective versus individual self-orientations* vary substantially across cultures (Triandis, 1989). Further, self-regulatory structures are important *mediational* mechanisms through which we can understand the effects of other factors (Erez & Earley, 1993; Lord & Brown, 1999). Thus, the effects of culture (both national and organizational), leadership and enduring individual differences such as public versus private self-focus (Carver & Scheier, 1981) can be understood through their impact on mediational self-regulatory processes.

In summary, work based on an information processing perspective suggests that two types of schema – followers' leadership prototypes and followers' self-schema – may be particularly important in understanding cross-cultural differences in leadership. Future comparative studies are needed to understand how such schema vary across cultures and how they impact leadership processes. As noted by O'Neill and Hanges (2000), such comparisons should investigate how networks of items vary across cultures, rather than just examining differences in the content of schemas.

Implicit theories and leadership. Perhaps the greatest cultural difference, though, may be the limiting effects of researchers' host cultures on the types of leadership theories they develop. The information processing of leadership theorists, like other individuals, are often constrained by their past experience and implicit theories (Calder, 1977), which are culturally bound. Consistent with an emphasis on individualism, most Western theories of leadership emphasize individual leaders as being critical causal factors. They seek to understand leadership effects in terms of individual qualities, such as traits or behavioral styles of leaders. Collectivist orientations, in contrast, might promote theories that conceptualize leadership as emerging from group, organizational or cultural values or traditions. Such views warrant further exploration. Multi-level theories of leadership (Dansereau, 1995) may reflect some movement away from an individualist perspective, yet we suspect true collectivist views of leadership will not come from researchers immersed in Western cultures.

Another recent trend in cross-cultural research is the documentation of lay theories about the mind and its relation to behavior (Lillard, 1998). Cultures differ widely in terms of the role of rational thought, intentions and individual traits as causes of behavior. European American and Northern European cultures place more emphasis on internal causes and the mind as a mediator of behavior, whereas many Eastern cultures place more emphasis on the situation and external social factors as causes of behavior. Interestingly, young American children also do not see traits as causes of behavior (Lillard, 1998).

Such cultural differences in implicit theories of the mind could be expected to shape the nature and use of implicit leadership theories. For example, Lord and Maher (1991) argue that leadership is recognized by pattern matching or inferred when performance outcomes are attributed to leaders. Both of these processes would, in turn, depend on cultural differences in implicit theories of the mind. Where traits are not central to one's understanding of behavior, leadership prototypes may not exist or may have very different qualities. Indeed, leadership may depend more on situational assessments than attributions of personal qualities (See Emrich, 1999, for an example of how situations can affect leadership perceptions). Similarly, where behavior and events are not typically explained internally, leadership perceptions may not be influenced much by outcome information as Murphy and Jones (1993) have shown. Indeed, where external and extra-mental forces are thought to be extreme, leadership may not be a critical societal construct, which brings into question Bass' (1997) assertion that leadership emergence in groups is a simple universal. All groups, along with other primates, may develop dominance hierarchies, yet in some cultures such differentiation may have little connection with leadership as defined in a European-American tradition.

Development 4: Multinational – Multimethod Studies

Lonner (1980) noted that it is impossible to determine whether a finding is universal or culture-specific by studying one culture, and the ability to unambiguously distinguish between these two extremes does not significantly improve when only two cultures are studied. However, when three or more cultures are explored, similarities and differences can be discerned and one can begin to talk about universal or culture specific findings.

The most often cited of the large multi-national studies of culture is, of course, Hofstede's (1980) research, presented in his book *Culture's Conse-quences*. The dominant dimensions of culture (Power Distance, Individualism, Uncertainty Avoidance and Masculinity) emerged in their best-known form from his work, and have been debated, supported, reviled and revised in the 20 years since the publication of that text. Others have developed different models of cultural dimensions, including Shalom Schwartz (1994) and Alan Fiske (1991), and those too have been the objects of significant research support and critique.

Recent work in the domain of cross-cultural leadership has also started to follow Lonner's suggestions about the assessment of universality. The Chinese Culture Connection (1987), for example, consisted of a group of social scientists that collected data in 22 countries, and identified an additional cultural dimension beyond those identified by Hofstede (1980). Specifically, "Confucian work dynamism" was found to be unrelated to any of Hofstede's dimensions, but it did correlate ($r = 0.70$) with economic growth from 1965 to 1984. More recently, Leslie and Van Velsor's (1998) 12-country study found significant differences (and no universals) between the countries of the European Union and the United States on each of the major SYMLOG dimensions (Dominance-Submissiveness, Friendliness-Unfriendliness, and Acceptance-Nonacceptance of authority).

Currently, Robert J. House and GLOBE research program (den Hartog et al., 1999; Hanges & Dickson, in press, a, b; Hanges et al., 2000; House et al., 1999) have been engaged in an ongoing cross-cultural leadership study that is collecting data from multiple organizations and industries within approximately 60 countries. GLOBE, which was formally started in January 1994, is a multi-phase, multi-method programmatic series of research studies on the relationship between societal and organizational culture and leadership. From its inception, GLOBE has been characterized by the active participation of scholars from multiple cultures. The first phase of the project focused on the development and validation of societal culture, organizational culture and outstanding leader attribute and behavior scales. Phase II consists of data collection and analyses using the scales developed in Phase I. Phase III uses non-questionnaire methodology (e.g. unobtrusive measures, media analysis and focus group interviews) to verify and enrich the information provided in Phase II. Phase IV is in the planning stage and is expected to consist of laboratory studies that will directly test the moderating influence of societal culture on response to, and perceived effectiveness of, identified patterns of leader behaviors and attributes.

Though GLOBE is still a work in progress, several findings and developments have emerged. First, a series of organizational and societal culture scales have been developed and cross validated. These scales draw on and extend the work of Hofstede (1980), Triandis et al. (1986), Kluckhohn and Strodtbeck (1961), and others. The culture scales have desirable psychometric properties (Hanges & Dickson, in press, a) and exhibit construct validity in that they relate to the cultural dimensions of others (e.g. Hofstede, 1980; Schwartz, 1994).

Second, culture was assessed using measures of both the organization or society's values as well as the organization or society's practices. These different orientations to culture assessment draw respectively from anthropological and psychological traditions. Interestingly, the relationships between the values-based and practices-based measures are low, indicating the unique information each perspective provides.

Third, while many different scales of leader attributes and behaviors were empirically derived, a second-order factor analysis revealed that six common factors underlie these scales (Hanges & Dickson, in press, a). These factors are charismatic/value-based leader behavior, team-oriented leader behavior, self-protective leader behavior, participative leader behavior, humane leader behavior and autonomous leader behavior. Interestingly, while these factors largely correspond to well-known dimensions of leadership which were developed primarily from United States samples, the initial factor analysis of these scales was conducted on data which *excluded* the United States.

Finally, the early evidence obtained from GLOBE supports the argument that has already compared the explanatory power of organizational and societal culture on effective leadership perceptions. It was found that for all but one of the second-order leadership factors, both organizational culture and societal culture predict leadership ratings. This leads to the question, which will be addressed by GLOBE, of whether these dimensions of leadership are universal across cultures. Dorfman (1996) indicates that a leadership study of this scope has never been attempted before.

CONCLUSIONS AND FUTURE DIRECTIONS

As mentioned before, substantial progress has been made in our understanding of leadership and culture since Barrett and Bass' (1976) handbook chapter. Indeed, it appears that the field followed some of the Barrett and Bass recommendations. For example, the number of studies involving more than two cultures is increasing. Also, there has been some progress in understanding the dimensions of culture and some attempts to standardize the measurement of constructs across cultures. Despite this substantial progress over the last 20 years, there are many challenges and opportunities remaining in this field.

For example, there is a growing schism between the conceptualization of culture as a construct and the manner by which we measure and assess a group of people possessing that culture. More specifically, researchers realize that, even within a single society, individuals belong to and are influenced by multiple reference groups (e.g. religious, political, occupational, etc). One can speak about the separate cultures of each of these reference groups. The cohort of people that will be clustered together will change depending upon the particular values used to cluster them. Unfortunately, in practice we still label different cultures with the name of the nation in which they are contained. While there may be some justification in making this simplification (House et al., 1997), the increased mobility of the globe's population, the presence of multiple "national" cultures within the boundaries of one nation, and the overlapping of single cultures over national boundaries should combine to make this practice obsolete.

Another area for development is the connection between the organizational culture and leadership literature and the societal culture and leadership literature. Are there any phenomena discovered in the organizational literature that can be transported to the societal level of analysis, the way the concept of culture itself was transported from the societal level of analysis to the organizational? For example, in the organizational literature, Schein (1992) outlines the connection between leadership and organizational culture and how this relationship varies over the life span of the organization. Further, Hambrick and Fukutomi (1991) developed an executive leadership theory that has incorporated this concept of leadership life span. Perhaps this life span concept also applies to societies and the relationship between leadership and societal culture also varies as a function of the society's life stage. An additional question related to cultural life spans is whether organizations in different cultures go through the same life stages in the same order, or whether there is cultural variation in this process.

This relates to another area in which research on cross-cultural leadership needs further refinement. There appears to be a relatively consistent lack of attention given to the question of appropriate levels of analysis. Depending on the question to be tested, appropriate levels of analysis for cross-cultural leadership research could at least include the individual (as in research on individual responses to different types of leadership), the dyad (as in examinations of leader-follower interactions across cultures), the organization (as in examinations of differential organizational effects of leadership styles across cultures), the industry (as in examinations of the relative importance of industry- versus society-level characteristics), or the society (as in examinations of the extent to which societal culture dimensions are predictive of preference for various leadership styles). Hunt and Peterson (1997a) note that only one of the articles in the *Leadership Quarterly* special issue paid more than minimal attention to levels of analysis issues, even though confusion about these issues can be a major cause of analysis errors and misinterpretation of findings.

Bass' (1997) claims of universality for transformational and transactional leadership raise additional questions, especially since these assertions are inconsistent with the information processing literature. Additionally, most of the cross-cultural studies have looked at only a single industry or work group at a time. It is possible that there is a culture by industry interaction in which the preference for transformational leadership varies and the current research paradigms are not sensitive to this interaction. This is especially plausible given Gordon's (1991) argument that organizational culture is primarily influenced by the characteristics of the company's industry.

Finally, we see one particularly promising dimension covered by Barrett and Bass (1976), which has not received sufficient subsequent research. Barrett and Bass identify research showing that level of interpersonal trust or level of faith in people is related to preferred leadership style. For example, Whyte (1963) showed that Peruvians typically had a low level of faith in people. When Williams, Whyte and Green (1966) sorted Peruvian workers by their level of trust in others, those high in interpersonal trust preferred participative and democratic leadership while those low in interpersonal trust preferred more authoritarian leadership styles. The Peruvians with high interpersonal trust closely mirrored workers from the United States in their preferred supervisor-subordinate relationship style. Kluckhohn and Strodt-beck's (1961) "human nature is good" versus "human nature is bad" dimension seems also to draw on this underlying construct. Unfortunately, it appears that this dimension in cross-cultural leadership research has not received nearly the attention that it deserves, given its apparent utility as an explanatory construct, though we do note recent intra-cultural work by Bauer and Green (1996).

In conclusion, much progress has been made in the last 25 years. We have identified and reviewed four of the major developments in this field in the past two decades, along with some caveats and potential areas for additional research. In addition to being a theoretically fascinating field of inquiry, the practical significance of understanding the myriad interactions of culture and leadership cannot be overstated. The continuing trends towards globalization of business, expansion of multinational firms, and multi-nation alliances in business, military, philanthropic, educational, and other settings all create opportunities for cross-cultural leadership misunderstandings, and for greater understanding of these complex phenomena, as well.

NOTE

1. See the recent book edited by Klein and Kozlowski (2000) for a good description of the current state of the field of multi-level research. Additionally, recent work by Hanges and Dickson (in press), Hanges, Dickson and Huang (in press) and Hanges, House, Dickson and GLOBE Associates (2000) provide examples of multi-level research in a cross-cultural leadership context.

ACKNOWLEDGMENTS

An earlier draft of this paper was presented at the 12th annual conference of the Society of Industrial and Organizational Psychology, St. Louis, as part of "Cross-cultural Industrial and Organizational Psychology 1976–1996: Progress, pitfalls, and prospects" (M. J. Gelfand, Chair).

We would like to thank Ashley Culpepper for her extensive work gathering and summarizing much of the literature reviewed.

REFERENCES

Ayman, R., & Chemers, M. M. (1983). The relationship of supervisory behavior ratings to work group effectiveness and subordinate satisfaction among Iranian managers. *Journal of Applied Psychology, 68*, 338–341.

Barrett, G. V., & Bass, B. M. (Eds) (1976). *Cross-Cultural Issues in Industrial and Organizational Psychology.* New York: John Wiley & Sons.

Bass, B. M. (1997). Does the transactional-transformational leadership paradigm transcend organizational and national boundaries? *American Psychologist, 52*, 130–139.

Bass, B. M., & Avolio, B. J. (1993). Transformational leadership: A response to critiques. In: M. M. Chemers & R. Ayman (Eds), *Leadership Theory and Research: Perspectives and Directions* (pp. 49–80). San Diego: Academic Press.

Bauer, T. N., & Green, S. G. (1996). Development of leader-member exchange: A longitudinal test. *Academy of Management Journal, 39*, 1538–1567.

Betancourt, H., & Lopez, S. R. (1993). The study of culture, ethnicity, and race in American psychology. *American Psychologist, 48*, 629–637.

Blake, R. R., & Mouton, J. S. (1964). *The Managerial Grid.* Houston: Gulf Publishing.

Brewer, M. B., & Gardner, W. (1996). Who is this "We"? Levels of collective identity and self representation. *Journal of Personality and Social Psychology, 71*, 83–93.

Calder, B. J. (1977). An attribution theory of leadership. In: B. M. Staw & G. R. Salancik (Eds), *New Directions in Organizational Behavior.* Chicago: St Clair Press.

Carver, C. S., & Scheier, M. F. (1981). *Attention and self-regulation: A control-theory approach to human behavior.* New York: Springer-Verlag.

Catrambone, R., Beike, D., & Niedenthal, P. (1996). Is the self-concept a habitual referent in judgments of similarity? *Psychological Science, 7*, 158–163.

Chemers, M. M. (1997). *An integrative theory of leadership.* Mahwah, NJ: Lawrence Erlbaum.

Chinese Culture Connection. (1987). Chinese values and the search for culture-free dimensions of culture. *Journal of Cross-Cultural Psychology, 18*, 143–164.

Chong, L. M. A., & Thomas, D. C. (1997). Leadership perceptions in cross-cultural context: Pakeha and Pacific Islanders in New Zealand. *Leadership Quarterly, 8,* 275–293.

Cropanzano, R., James, K., & Citera, M. (1993). A goal hierarchy model of personality, motivation, and leadership. In: L. L. Cummings & B. M. Staw (Eds), *Research in Organizational Behavior* (Vol. 15, pp. 267–322). Greenwich, CT: JAI Press.

Dansereau, F. (1995). Leadership: The Multiple-Level Approaches (Parts I & II). Special Issues. *Leadership Quarterly, 6,* 97–450.

den Hartog, D., House, R. J., Hanges, P. J., Ruiz-Quintanilla, S. A., Dorfman, P. W., & GLOBE (1999). Culture-specific and cross-culturally-generalizable implicit leadership theories: Are attributes of charismatic/transformational leadership universally endorsed? *Leadership Quarterly, 10*(2), 219–256.

Dorfman, P. W. (1996). International and cross-cultural leadership. In: J. Punnitt & O. Shanker (Eds), *Handbook for international management research* (pp. 267–349). Cambridge, MA: Blackwell.

Dorfman, P. W., & Howell, J. P. (1988). Dimensions of national cultural and effective leadership patterns. *Advances in International Comparative Management, 3,* 127–150.

Emrich, C. (1999). Context effects in leadership perceptions perceptions. *Personality and Social Psychology Bulletin, 25,* 991–1006.

Erez, M., & Earley, P. C. (1993). *Culture, self-identity, and work.* New York: Oxford University Press.

Fiedler, F. E. (1964). A contingency model of leadership effectiveness. In: L. Berkowitz (Ed.), *Advances in Experimental Social Psychology* (pp. 149–190). New York: McGraw-Hill.

Fiske, A. (1991). *Structures of social life: The four elementary forms of human relations.* New York: Free Press.

Foa, U. G. (1957). Relation of workers' expectations to satisfaction with supervisor. *Personnel Psychology, 10,* 161–168.

Gelfand, M. J., Triandis, H. C., & Chan, K. S. (1996). Individualism versus collectivism or versus authoritarianism? *European Journal of Social Psychology, 26,* 397–410.

Gerstner, C. R., & Day, D. V. (1994). Cross-cultural comparison of leadership prototypes. *Leadership Quarterly, 5,* 121–134.

Gordon, G. G. (1991). Industry determinants of organizational culture. *Academy of Management Review, 16*(2), 396–415.

Hall, R. J., Workman, J. W., & Marchioro, C. A. (1998). Sex, task, and behavioral flexibility effects on leadership perceptions. *Organizational Behavior and Human Decision Processes, 74,* 1–32.

Hambrick, D. C., & Fukutomi, G. D. (1991). The seasons of a CEO's tenure. *Academy of Management Review, 16*(4), 719–742.

Hanges, P. J., & Dickson, M. W. (in press). The development and validation of the GLOBE Culture and Leadership Scales. In: R. J. House, P. J. Hanges, M. Javidan, P. W. Dorfman, V. Gupta & GLOBE Associates. *Cultures, Leadership, and Organizations: GLOBE: A 62 Nation Study* (Vol. 1), Thousand Oaks, CA: Sage.

Hanges, P. J., Dickson, M. W. & Huang, M. (in press). Rationale for GLOBE Statistical Analysis: Scaling of Societies and Testing of Hypotheses. In: R. J. House, P. J. Hanges, M. Javidan, P. W. Dorfman, V. Gupta & GLOBE Associates. *Cultures, Leadership, and Organizations: GLOBE: A 62 Nation Study* (Vol. 1), Thousand Oaks, CA: Sage.

Hanges, P. J., House, R. J., Dickson, M. W., & GLOBE Associates (2000). *Development and validation of scales measuring organizational culture, societal culture, and preferences for leader behaviors and attributes.* Working paper: University of Maryland.

Hanges, P. J., Lord, R. G., & Dickson, M. W. (2000). An information processing perspective on leadership and culture: A case for connectionist architecture. *Applied Psychology: An International Review, 49*, 133–161.

Herskovits, M. J. (1955). *Cultural anthropology.* New York: Knopf.

Hofstede, G. (1980). *Culture's consequences: International differences in work-related values.* Newbury Park: CA: Sage.

Hofstede, G., & Bond, M. H. (1988). The Confucius connection: From cultural roots to economic growth. *Organizational Dynamics, 16*, 4–21.

Hofstede, G., Bond, M. H., & Luk, C. (1993). Individual perceptions of organizational cultures: A methodological treatise on levels of analysis. *Organizational Studies, 14*, 483–503.

Hollander, E. P. (1992). Leadership, followership, self, and others. *Leadership Quarterly, 3*, 43–54.

Hollander, E. P., & Julian, J. W. (1969). Contemporary trends in the analysis of leadership perceptions. *Psychological Bulletin, 71*, 387–397.

House, R. J. (1971). A path-goal theory of leadership effectiveness. *Administrative Science Quarterly, 16*, 321–339.

House, R. J., & Aditya, R. N. (1997). The social scientific study of leadership: Quo vadis? *Journal of Management, 23*, 409–473.

House, R. J., Hanges, P. J., Ruiz-Quintanilla, S. A., Dorfman, P. W., Javidan, M., Dickson, M. W., & GLOBE. (1999). Cultural Influences on Leadership: Project GLOBE. In: W. Mobley, J. Gessner & V. Arnold (Eds), *Advances In Global Leadership* (Vol. 1, pp. 171–233). Stamford, CT: JAI Press.

House, R. J., Wright, N., & Aditya, R. N. (1997). Cross cultural research on organizational leadership: A critical analysis and a proposed theory. In: P. C. Earley & M. Erez (Eds), *Cross Cultural Organizational Behavior and Psychology.* Englewood Cliffs: NJ: Lawrence Erlbaum Associates.

Hunt, J. G., & Peterson, M. F. (Eds) (1997a). International and cross-cultural leadership research. [Special issue]. *Leadership Quarterly, 8*(3–4).

Hunt, J. G., & Peterson, M. F. (1997b). Two scholar's views of some nooks and crannies in cross-cultural leadership. *Leadership Quarterly, 8*(4), 343–354.

Jaeger, A. M. (1986). Organization development and national culture: Where's the fit? *Academy of Management Review, 11*, 178–190.

Jung, D. I., & Avolio, B. J. (1999). Effects of leadership style and followers' cultural orientation on performance in group and individual task conditions. *Academy of Management Journal, 42*, 641–651.

Klein, K. J., & Kozlowski, S. W. J. (Eds) (2000). *Multilevel theory, research, and methods in organizations: Foundations, extensions, and new directions.* San Francisco: Jossey-Bass.

Kluckhohn, C. (1951). The study of culture. In: D. Lerner & H. D. Lasswell (Eds), *The policy sciences.* Stanford, CA: Stanford University Press.

Kluckhohn, F., & Strodtbeck, F. (1961). *Variations in value orientations.* Westport, CT: Greenwood Press.

Leslie, J. B., & Van Velsor, E. (1998). *A cross-national comparison of effective leadership and teamwork: Toward a global workforce.* Greensboro, NC: Center for Creative Leadership.

Lillard, A. (1998). Ethnopsychologies: Cultural variations in theories of mind. *Psychological Bulletin, 123*, 3–32.

Lippitt, R., & White, R. K. (Eds) (1958). *An experimental study of leadership and group life.* New York: Holt, Rinehart, and Winston.

Lonner, W. J. (1980). The search for psychological universals. In: H. C. Triandis & W. W. Lambert (Eds), *Handbook of Cross-Cultural Psychology: Perspectives* (Vol. 1, pp. 143–204.). Boston, MA: Allyn and Bacon, Inc.

Lord, R. G., Brown, D. J., & Freiberg, S. M. (1998). *Understanding the dynamics of leadership: The interaction of self-concepts in the leader/follower relationship.* Manuscript submitted for publication.

Lord, R. G., & Brown D. J. (1999). *Leadership, Values, and Subordinate Self-Concepts.* Manuscript under review.

Lord, R. G., Brown, D. J., & Freiberg, S. J. (1999). Understanding the dynamics of leadership: The role of follower self-concepts in the leader/follower relationship. *Organizational Behavior and Human Decision Processes, 78,* 167–203.

Lord, R. G., Brown, D. J., & Harvey, J. L. (2000). System constraints on leadership perceptions, behavior and influence: An example of connectionist level processes. In: M. A. Hogg & R. S. Tindale (Eds), *Blackwell Handbook of Social Psychology* (Vol. 3: Group processes). Oxford, U.K.: Blackwell.

Lord, R. G., Foti, R., & DeVader, C. (1984). A test of leadership categorization theory: Internal structure, information processing, and leadership perceptions. *Organizational Behavior and Human Performance, 34,* 343–378.

Lord, R. G., & Maher, K. J. (1991). *Leadership and information processing linking perceptions and performance* (Vol. 1). Cambridge: Unwin Hyman Ltd.

Markus, H. (1977). Self-schema and processing information about the self. *Journal of Personality and Social Psychology, 35,* 63–78.

Markus, H., & Kitayana, S. (1991). Culture and the self: Implications for cognitions, emotion, and motivation. *Psychological Review, 98,* 224–253.

Markus, H., & Wurf, E. (1987). *The dynamic self-concept: A social psychological perspective* (Vol. 38). Palo Alto, CA: Annual Reviews.

Meade, R. D., & Whittaker, J. D. (1967). A cross-cultural study of authoritarianism. *Journal of Social Psychology, 72,* 3–7.

Misumi, J. (1984). *The behavioral science of leadership* (2nd ed.). Tokyo: Yuhikaku Publishing.

Misumi, J., & Peterson, M. F. (1985). The Performance-Maintenance (PM) theory of leadership: Review of a Japanese leadership program. *Administrative Science Quarterly, 30,* 198–223.

Mouton, J., & Blake, R. (Eds) (1970). *Issues in transnational organizational development.* Boston: D. C. Heath.

Murphy, M. R., & Jones, A. P. (1993). The influences of performance cues and observational focus on performance rating accuracy. *Journal of Applied Social Psychology, 23,* 1523–1545.

O'Connell, M. S., Lord, R. G., & O'Connell, M. K. (1990). *Differences in Japanese and American leadership prototypes: Initial findings.* Paper presented at the Academy of Management Convention, San Francisco.

O'Niell, O. A., & Hanges, P. J. (2000). *Individual values and the structure of leadership schemas: Verification of a connectionist network.* Paper presented at the 15th Annual Society for Industrial and Organizational Psychology, New Orleans, LA.

Peterson, M. F., & Hunt, J. G. (1997). International perspectives on international leadership. *Leadership Quarterly, 8,* 203–231.

Pillai, R. (1996). Crisis and the emergence of charismatic leadership in groups: An experimental investigation. *Journal of Applied Social Psychology, 26,* 543–562.

Schein, E. H. (1992). *Organizational culture and leadership* (2nd ed.). San Francisco: CA: Jossey Bass.

Schwartz, S. H. (1994). Studying human values. In: A.-M. Bouvy, F. J. R. van de Vijver, P. Boski & P. G. Schmitz (Eds), *Journeys into cross-cultural psychology* (pp. 239–254). Amsterdam, Netherlands: Swets & Zeitlinger.

Shamir, B., House, R. J., & Arthur, M. B. (1993). The motivational effects of charismatic leadership: A self-concept based theory. *Organizational Science, 4,* 577–594.

Shaw, J. B. (1990). A cognitive categorization model for the study of intercultural management. *Academy of Management Review, 15,* 626–645.

Sinha, J. B. P (1990). The nurturant task style of leadership. In: R. Ayman (Chair), *Establishing a global view of leadership: East meets West.* Symposium conducted at the International Congress of Applied Psychology, Kyoto, Japan.

Sirotka, D. (1968). *International survey of job goals and beliefs.* Paper presented at the International Conference of Applied Psychology, Amsterdam, Netherlands.

Smith, P. B. (1997). Cross-cultural leadership: A path to the goal? In: P. C. Earley & M. Erez (Eds), *Cross Cultural Organizational Behavior and Psychology* (pp. 626–639).

Smith, W. G., Brown, D. G., Lord, R. G., & Engle, E. M. (1998). *Leadership self-schema and their effects on leadership perceptions.* Working paper: University of Akron.

Stogdill, R. M. (1974). *Handbook of leadership* (1st ed.). New York: Free Press.

Triandis, H. C. (1972). *The analysis of subjective culture.* New York: Wiley Press.

Triandis, H. C. (1982). Review of culture's consequences: International differences in work-related values. *Human Organization, 41,* 86–90.

Triandis, H. C. (1989). The self and social behavior in differing cultural contexts. *Psychological Bulletin, 96,* 506–520.

Triandis, H. C. (1993). The contingency model in cross-cultural perspective. In: M. M. Chemers & R. Ayman (Eds), *Leadership theory and research.* San Diego: Academic Press.

Triandis, H. C., Bontempo, R., Betancourt, H., Bond, M. et al. (1986). The measurement of the etic aspects of individualism and collectivism across cultures. Special Issue: Contributions to cross-cultural psychology. *Australian Journal of Psychology, 38*(3), 257–267.

Trompenaars, F. (1993). *Riding the Waves of Culture: Understanding Cultural Diversity in Business.* London: Nicholas Brealey.

Whyte, W. F. (1963). Culture, industrial relations, and economic development: The case of Peru. *Industrial and Labor Relations Review, 16,* 583–593.

Williams, L. K., Whyte, W. F., & Green, C. S. (1966). Do cultural differences affect workers' attitudes? *Industrial Relations, 5,* 110–117.

Yukl, G. (1994). *Leadership in organizations* (3rd ed.). Englewood Cliffs, NJ: Prentice Hall.

TRANSFORMATIONAL AND TRANSACTIONAL LEADER BEHAVIORS IN CHINESE ORGANIZATIONS: DIFFERENTIAL EFFECTS IN THE PEOPLE'S REPUBLIC OF CHINA AND TAIWAN

Xiao-Ping Chen and Jiing-Lih Fahr

ABSTRACT

Transformational leader behaviors are defined as those behaviors that make followers more aware of the importance and values of task outcomes, activate their higher-order needs and induce them to transcend self-interests for the sake of the organization (Bass, 1985; Yukl, 1989a, b). These behaviors primarily include six types: articulating a vision, intellectual stimulation, demonstrating high performance expectations, providing an appropriate model, fostering collaboration and providing individualized support. Transactional leader behaviors, on the other hand, are founded on an exchange process in which the leader provides rewards/ punishments in return for the subordinate's effort and performance (Burns, 1978). They often include four types: contingent/non-contingent reward and contingent /non-contingent punishment. We examined the effects of these leader behaviors on subordinates' job satisfaction,

Advances in Global Leadership, Volume 2, pages 101–126.
ISBN: 0-7623-0723-4

organizational commitment and organizational citizenship behavior (OCB) in Chinese organizations. Data from 410 subordinate-supervisor dyads (287 in Taiwan and 123 in the PRC) suggest that while transformational leader behaviors in both samples have a more profound impact than transactional behaviors on employee job satisfaction and organizational commitment, the effects of each specific transformational and transactional behavior are different in the PRC and Taiwan. In particular, among the six types of transformational behaviors, "providing an appropriate model" and "demonstrating high expectation of performance" significantly influenced PRC employees' job attitudes and OCB, whereas "providing individualized support" and "fostering collaboration" had significant influence on Taiwan employees' job attitudes and OCB. Furthermore, among the four types of transactional behaviors, contingent reward and punishment had significant positive impact on PRC employees' job satisfaction and organizational commitment, whereas the job attitudes of the Taiwan employees were not significantly affected by contingent punishment. Instead, it was found that non-contingent reward had significant positive impact while non-contingent punishment had significant negative effect on their job attitudes. In addition, both contingent and non-contingent punishment had significant negative effects on Taiwan employees' OCB, whereas only non-contingent punishment had such negative effects in the PRC. The implications of these findings are discussed in terms of the contingent nature of leadership effectiveness.

INTRODUCTION

Although people in the People's Republic of China (PRC) and Taiwan share many cultural roots (e.g. Confucianism, Taoism, Buddhism), and a set of core values (e.g. group orientation, respect for age and hierarchical position, the importance of face, the importance of relationship, see Lockett, 1988), in the past 50 years these two societies have gone through very different political, economic, and social developments that have created changes in values and beliefs and different preferences for management style and practice. Even though some primary cultural values (e.g. collectivism, relationship-orientation) remain the same, the manifestations of these values and the situations in which they apply may have changed. In this chapter, we shall first explore how the changes in the two societies influence leaders' behavior and people's views of effective leadership. We will then present the results of a large-scale study on the effects of transformational and transactional leader behaviors on a number of employee outcome variables (e.g. job satisfaction, organizational commitment, organizational citizenship behavior (OCB)) in the PRC and Taiwan. Finally we will discuss the theoretical and practical implications of these findings in relation to effectively motivating and leading employees in the PRC and Taiwan.

Numerous books and articles have been published in the past three decades describing the leadership models of Chinese enterprises with most of them focusing on overseas Chinese Family Businesses (CFBs) (Cheng, 1990a, b, c; Redding and colleagues, 1980, 1990, 1991, 1993; Silin, 1976; Westwood and colleagues, 1992, 1997) and few focusing on organizations in the PRC (Ling and colleagues, 1986, 1991; Xu, 1989), despite the fact that PRC has the largest ethnic Chinese population in the world. One reason for such unbalanced research is the rapid economic development in the late 1970s and 1980s in Taiwan, Hong Kong, Singapore and some Southeast Asian countries - where people with Chinese ethnicity control a majority of the financial assets – which caught the world's attention while the PRC was still experiencing political turmoil. Another reason is that it is relatively easier to study the CFBs because they are operated under the capitalist system, whereas PRC enterprises are operated under the socialist system (which is unfamiliar to most researchers who live outside the PRC). The third reason is that traditional Chinese values (especially Confucianism) are relatively well preserved by most of the overseas Chinese; whereas in the PRC, many of these values have been seriously attacked because of the introduction of the Communist ideology and of a series of social and political movements (e.g. the Great Leap movement, the Cultural Revolution, the criticizing Lin and Confucius movement), which made its value system less stable throughout time and thus more difficult to research. In the following, we will discuss the dominant cultural value systems related to leadership in Taiwan and the PRC and how they affect the effectiveness of transformational and transactional leader behaviors in organizations.

Dominant Cultural Value Systems Related to Leadership in Taiwan and the PRC

Personalism and Paternalism in Taiwan
Previous research on the cultural determinants of economic success in East Asia has given rise to the Post-Confucian Hypothesis, which broadly argues that it is the persisting cultural value system rooted in the Confucian ethic, together with certain international economic conditions, that has proven to be fertile ground for successful organizational functioning and entrepreneurial activity in the context of modern economic growth (Kahn, 1979; Hofstede & Bond, 1988; Redding, 1993; Redding & Hsiao, 1990). Taiwan is certainly

included under the rubric. In Taiwan, the sustained core values of Confucianism are *relationship* and *social order*. According to Confucius (Confucius, 1915), a person is defined by his/her relationship with others (*ren zhe, ren ye*) and is embedded in all kinds of relationships. Therefore, one's relationships with others and others' views about oneself are important in one's self-defining process. Furthermore, there are rules and orders in operating these relationships. The so-called "Five Cardinal Relationships" (or *wu lun*), that delineate a hierarchical power structure over key societal relationships (emperor-minister, father-son, husband-wife, older brother-younger brother, friend-friend), serve as guidelines. This Confucian cultural heritage is reflected in the view of leader roles and leadership. Based on extensive leadership research conducted on overseas Chinese, the major forces that dominate the management practice are *personalism* (Redding, 1993) and *paternalism* (Cheng, 1995a, b, c; Redding, 1993; Westwood & Chan, 1992). Personalism refers to the tendency to use personal criteria and relationships as a basis for decision-making and action (Farh, Earley & Lin, 1997). In other words, leaders do not use universal rules in treating employees. Instead they use the quality of relationship as one of the most important bases in their decision-making process. Paternalism refers to a combination of strong discipline and authority with fatherly benevolence and moral integrity (Farh & Cheng, 1999). Paternalistic leaders see themselves as "father figures" of the organization and treat employees strictly, but at the same time show personal care toward employees' well being and demonstrate high moral integrity from themselves.

Empirical studies conducted in Taiwan provide considerable support for these observations. For example, the finding that task-oriented leaders tended to have subordinates exhibiting lower levels of OCB and showing less organizational commitment than people-oriented leaders (Cheng, 1985; Huang, 1986; Huang & Cai, 1998) suggests that employees identify more with leaders who emphasize relationships than those who emphasize task achievement. Moreover, using the case study approach, Cheng (1995a, b, c) found many detailed behavioral examples of the paternalistic leadership of Taiwan CEOs and their corresponding subordinate responses. He concluded that there are three critical components to paternalism. One is "granting favors" (or *shi en*), which refers to leader behaviors that demonstrate personal favors and generosity, go beyond the work domain and are highly personalized. It is obvious that this component of paternalism is closely related to personalism for its focus on developing relationships between leaders and subordinates. Cheng found that in response to the leader's "granting favors," subordinates feel indebted, grateful and obliged to reciprocate. The second component of paternalism, which must be practiced with "favor granting," is to establish a strong authority, or in Cheng's words, "inspire awe or fear" (or *li wei*). The leader's "establishing a strong authority" includes "control and domination, underestimating subordinate ability, building a lofty image for the leader and instructing subordinates in a didactic style" (Farh & Cheng, 1999, p.10). It can be seen that this component of paternalism reflects Confucius' "social order." According to Cheng's research, subordinates respond to the leader's "inspiring awe or fear" with compliance, obedience, fear and a sense of shame. The third component of paternalism is moral leadership (or *shu de*), defined as putting collective interests ahead of personal interests and acting as an exemplar in work and personal conduct. Although this component did not emerge from Cheng's (1995a, b, c) studies, it was found to be an important dimension of effective leadership in Cheng and Zhuang's (1981) earlier study of Taiwanese military personnel.

The above analyses of Taiwan cultural value systems and leadership research findings suggest that in Taiwan leader behaviors that contain elements of personalism (relationship orientation, including the "granting favors" component of paternalism) will be effective in promoting employee job satisfaction, organizational commitment and OCB. Leader behaviors that contain elements of paternalism (excluding "favor granting"), however, will not necessarily be as effective for two reasons. First, "establishing a strong authority" induces compliance, obedience, fear and a sense of shame in the subordinates, which are negative rather than positive feelings. Second, leader's "moral integrity" was not consistently recognized as an important component when subordinates were asked to identify effective leadership, indicating its weaker impact on employees' job attitudes and OCB.

Leader Character and Performance Orientation in the PRC

What people value in leadership in the PRC is different from that in Taiwan because the two core values of Confucianism (relationship and social order) have been strongly distorted and attacked in the PRC during the Cultural Revolution (1960s to 1970s). First of all, the meaning of relationship was given a political interpretation. People were forced to be in two types of relationships with others – comrades or enemies. Everyone had to publicly declare one's relationship with other members of the organization, especially with those who were defined as "enemies" (e.g. landowner, rich peasant, anti-revolutionist, rightist). During that time, drawing a demarcation with the "enemies" was extremely important for one's political survival. The lasting effect of such a practice made "relationship" strategic and instrumental. Furthermore, the "using relationship" mentality remained the same, if not more so, after the PRC inaugurated economic reform and promoted the "getting rich is glorious" (or *zhi fu guang rong*) policy in the 1980s and 1990s. "Relationship" became vital for one's economic survival during this period of time and remains so today. People use "relationships" to get jobs, to get promotions and to get rich. Meanwhile, however, the extreme, pervasive, strategic and instrumental use of "relationship" in the PRC has induced a strong adverse psychology against it. For example, those who get rich fast or get promoted quickly based on their relationships are viewed as less competent in other areas than those who had similar achievements but did not rely on their relationships. Thus personalism is not as appreciated in the PRC as in Taiwan. Leaders who make decisions on the basis of relationships are likely to be viewed as unfair (or *ren ren wei qin*).

Second, the rules and orders of relationships (i.e. *wu lun*) have been strongly criticized and challenged when "rebellion is reasonable" (or *zao fan you li*) was promoted and advocated during the Cultural Revolution. The public humiliation of those who were formerly "authority figures" (e.g. *zou zi pai*) significantly reduced people's respect for authority. Moreover, in many organizations where a majority of the leaders were appointed on the basis of their so-called "political qualifications" (rather than technical and managerial skills), the expert and referent power associated with a leader's position was not assumed in subordinates' minds. Leaders are unlikely to be seen as "father figures" of the big organizational family in the PRC.

While the two core values of Confucianism were distorted and attacked during a series of political and economic movements in the PRC, new thoughts and phenomena emerged. One was the import of Western modern management theories and practices. After the "reform and open door" (or *gai ge kai fang*) policy was proposed in the early 1980s, many foreign enterprises started to form joint ventures in the PRC and brought in modern management thoughts and practices (e.g. performance-based compensation rather than seniority-based or relationship-based compensation). The effectiveness and efficiency of these companies made people realize the rationality behind such practices. Meanwhile, the changes in the system of ownership (e.g. from state-owned to non-state-owned) and changes in the reward system (from fixed pay to organizational performance-related pay) forced organizations and employees to focus more on productivity and profit. Therefore, the implementation of modern management practices has become the common voice of both employers and employees (especially for non-state-owned enterprises).

Another new phenomenon is the strong call for leader character, which is composed of two characteristics. First, effective leaders must do what they say (or *yan xing yi zhi*) and act as a role model (or *yi shen zuo ze*). Due to the requirement of "unifying thoughts" (or *tong yi si xiang*) under the Communist leadership and the severe punishment imposed on dissidents, many people in the PRC have learned to lie to avoid political sanctions. Almost absurdly, many years of positive reinforcement for lying has made it "legitimate" and "reasonable". Many lie to get ahead of others, as how subordinates perceive about some of their leaders. Employees thus do not trust what the leaders say, instead, they pay more attention to what the leaders do. Saying-doing consistency becomes extremely important in order for a leader to be influential. The second characteristic of leader character is that leaders must put public interest ahead of personal interest and not exploit their positions (or *yi quan mo si*). The pervasive corruption in the PRC today (see He, 1998) makes people yearn for honest and upright leaders. Therefore, leaders' moral integrity becomes more important than ever in leading the PRC employees.

From the limited leadership research conducted in the PRC, we found direct and indirect evidence that support our above analyses. For example, using Misumi's (1985) PM leadership scale, (Ling, 1991; Ling, Chen & Wang, 1987) and Xu (1989) found that P (Performance oriented) and M (Maintenance oriented) were viewed as equally important leadership skills by PRC employees. In addition, they found that leader's Character (C) – moral integrity – repeatedly emerged as an important dimension of effective leadership. According to their research, C included two virtues – not acting selfishly and leading by example – and it was found to inspire identification and imitation by subordinates.

In summary, the above analyses of the dominant cultural value systems in Taiwan and the PRC emphasized their different approaches in political, economic and social developments in the past 50 years. It should be noted that these differences are relative in nature and non-exhaustive at best. On the other hand, we claim that on a deeper level many cultural values remain the same in the two societies. For example, communal relationships are more valued than exchange relationships, collective interest should be put ahead of self-interest, and virtuous leaders receive more trust and respect and so on.

Transformational and Transactional Leader Behaviors in Taiwan and the PRC

Transformational Leader Behaviors. Transformational leader behaviors refer to those behaviors that make followers more aware of the importance and values of task outcomes, activate their higher-order needs and induce them to transcend self interest for the sake of the organization (Bass, 1985; Yukl, 1989a, b). These behaviors primarily include six types: articulating a vision, intellectual stimulation, demonstrating high performance expectations, providing an appropriate model, fostering collaboration and providing individualized support (e.g. Podsakoff et al., 1990; Podsakoff et al., 1996). These behaviors are defined as follows:

- Articulating a vision – the extent to which a leader aims at developing, articulating, and inspiring others with his/her vision of the future.
- High expectation of performance – the leader's expectations of followers' excellence, quality, and/or high performance.
- Intellectual stimulation – the extent to which a leader challenges followers to re-examine some of their assumptions about their work and to rethink how it can be performed.
- Fostering collaboration – the extent to which a leader promotes trust and cooperation among employees and gets them to work together toward a common group goal.
- Providing individualized support – the degree to which a leader indicates that he/she is concerned about subordinates' personal feelings and needs.
- Providing an appropriate model – the extent to which a leader sets an example for employees to follow.

It can be seen that among the transformational leader behaviors, "fostering collaboration" emphasizes developing cooperative relationships between team members and "providing individualized support" emphasizes highly personalized care within and beyond the work domain. Thus, these two behaviors contain the elements of personalism and the "favor granting" component of paternalism, and in turn will be effective in promoting employee job attitudes and OCB in Taiwan. In the PRC however, the leader behaviors that are effective will be different. It seems that "providing an appropriate model" captures the essence of the leader character dimension (C), and "high performance expectation" demonstrates the performance orientation of the leader. Therefore, these two behaviors will be effective in promoting employee job attitudes and OCB in the PRC.

> *Hypothesis 1:* Among the transformational leader behaviors, providing individualized support and fostering collaboration will be effective in Taiwan; whereas, providing an appropriate model and high performance expectation will be effective in the PRC in promoting subordinates' job satisfaction, organizational commitment and OCB.

Transactional Leader Behaviors. Transactional leader behaviors, on the other hand, are founded on an exchange process in which the leader provides rewards in return for the subordinate's effort and performance (Burns, 1978). These behaviors often include four types: contingent reward/punishment and non-contingent reward/punishment. The essence of contingent reward/punishment is to reward/punish employees on the basis of their task performance, whereas non-contingent reward/punishment uses criteria that are not related to task performance to reward/punish employees. From the definitions of these behaviors, it can be seen that: (1) the contingent reward/punishment behaviors are more performance-oriented than the two non-contingent reward/punishment behaviors; (2) the non-contingent reward behavior reflects some element of the paternalistic leadership because it shows leader's benevolence and care demonstrated toward employees as human beings, not just as performers; and (3) both the contingent and non-contingent punishment behaviors share some of the "inspiring awe or fear" elements of paternalistic leadership because punishment in general demonstrates leader's "control, domination and didactic style," which were found to induce obedience, fear and a sense of shame in the subordinates in Taiwan. Consequently,

> *Hypothesis 2:* Among the transactional leader behaviors, contingent reward/punishment will have a more significant positive impact in the PRC than in Taiwan, non-contingent reward will have a stronger positive impact in Taiwan than in the PRC, and both contingent and non-contingent punishment will have a more profound negative effect on subordinates' job satisfaction, organizational commitment and OCB in Taiwan than in the PRC.

Relative Effectiveness of Transformational and Transactional Leader Behaviors

Finally, we would like to examine the relative effectiveness of the transactional and transformational leader behaviors. From our earlier analyses, transactional leader behaviors focus more on the exchange process between leaders and subordinates, whereas transformational leader behaviors focus more on developing employees' thought and performance abilities, fostering good relationships and broadening their visions of the company's future. Therefore, the transformational leader behaviors are in general more congruent with the Chinese cultural values, such as communal relationships, collectivism and group orientation, which are shared in both Taiwan and the PRC, than the transactional leader behaviors. Hence,

> *Hypothesis 3:* The effects of transformational leader behaviors will go beyond the effects of transactional behaviors on employees' job satisfaction, organizational commitment and OCB in both Taiwan and the PRC.

METHOD

Participants

The participants in Taiwan included 380 leader-subordinate dyads (the leader/ subordinate ratio was about 1: 3) from a large state-owned telecommunications organization in Taiwan. Participants in the PRC included 205 leader-subordinate dyads from four small-to-middle-sized non-state-owned companies. After obtaining the support of top management in these organizations, we selected leader-subordinate dyads from different levels and different branches of the organizations.

Questionnaires were distributed to supervisors and subordinates in person, and were collected upon completion. Three hundred thirty-nine questionnaires in the Taiwan sample were usable, for a response rate of 87.9%. However, further examination of the responses indicated that only 287 had matched data of the subordinates' response and their direct supervisors' evaluation of their performance. In the PRC sample, 198 questionnaires were usable, but only 123 had matched data of both subordinate and supervisor.

Among the 287 Taiwan employees, approximately 52% of the sample were males, and 80% were married. The average age of the respondents in the sample was approximately 38 years old, and their average tenure in the organization was about 15 years. Six percent of the sample did not complete high school, 30% had a high school degree, 11% had attended some college, and the remaining 53% received a four-year undergraduate or more advanced degree. Among the 123 PRC employees, approximately 65% were male, and 75% married. The average age was about 32, and the average tenure in the organization was approximately 5.5 years. Seven percent of the sample did not complete high school, 35% had a high school degree, 11% attended some college and the remaining 47% received a four-year undergraduate or more advanced degree. Overall, the two samples were comparable in gender, age and education levels.

Measures

Translation. The first stage of this study was the development of a Chinese version of the research questionnaire through a translation-back translation process (Brislin, 1980). To make sure that the translation had the equivalent meaning of the English version, two independent bilingual judges were invited to go through the translation. To make sure that the questions made practical sense to employees, the questionnaire was sent to the personnel officer in the company for suggestions of clarification. The final version was based on the consensus reached among the authors, the judges and the personnel officers in the participating companies. The wording of each item is a little different for the Taiwan sample and the PRC sample because different expressions are used for the same terms in the two societies.

Transactional leader behaviors. Contingent/non-contingent reward and punishment behaviors were measured using a 15-item scale developed by Podsakoff and his colleagues (1984, 1986) with minor modifications to fit the current context. Specifically, Contingent Reward was measured using four items: (1) Gives me special recognition when my work performance is especially good; (2) Rewards me when I do well; (3) Commends me when I do a better than average job; and (4) Personally compliments me when I do outstanding work. The alpha reliability for this scale was .90 for the Taiwan sample and 0.75 for the PRC sample, respectively.

Non-contingent Reward was measured using four items: (1) Often commends me, even when I perform poorly; (2) Is just as likely to praise me when I do poorly as when I do well; (3) Frequently praises me even when I don't deserve it; and (4) Rarely gets upset with me, even when I perform poorly. The alpha reliability for this scale was 0.74 for the Taiwan sample and 0.83 for the PRC sample, respectively.

Contingent Punishment was measured using three items: (1) Would indicate his or her disapproval if I performed at a low level; (2) Shows his or her displeasure when my work is below acceptable standards; and (3) Would reprimand me if any work were below normal. The alpha reliability of this scale was 0.69 for the Taiwan sample and 0.62 for the PRC sample, respectively.

Non-contingent Punishment was measured using four items: (1) Frequently holds me accountable for work I have no control over; (2) Often holds me responsible for things that are not my fault; (3) Is often critical of my work even when I perform well; and (4) Frequently reprimands me without telling me why. The alpha reliability for this scale was 0.78 for the Taiwan sample and .81 for the PRC sample, respectively.

Transformational leader behaviors. The 23-item scale of transformational leader behavior was an adaptation of Podsakoff et al.'s (1990) with minor modifications to fit the current context. In particular, Facilitating Collaboration was measured using four items: (1) Encourages employees to be "team players;" (2) Fosters collaboration among work groups; (3) Gets the group to work together for the same goal; and (4) Develops a team attitude and spirit among his/her employees. The alpha reliability of this scale was 0.92 for the Taiwan sample and 0.85 for the PRC sample, respectively.

Providing Individualized Support was measured using four items: (1) Acts without considering my feelings (reverse coded); (2) Shows respect for my personal feelings; (3) Behaves in a manner that is thoughtful of my personal needs; and (4) Treats me without considering my personal feelings (reverse coded). The alpha reliability for this scale was 0.85 for the Taiwan sample and 0.75 for the PRC sample, respectively.

Providing the Appropriate Model was measured using three items: (1) Leads by "doing" rather than simply by "telling;" (2) Provides a good model for me to follow; and (3) Leads by example. The alpha reliability for this scale was 0.93 for the Taiwan sample and 0.85 for the PRC sample, respectively.

Articulating a Vision was measured using five items: (1) Paints an interesting picture of the future of our department/unit/organization; (2) Has a clear understanding of where we are going; (3) Inspires others with his/her plans for the future; (4) Is able to get others committed to his/her dream of the future; and (5) Is always seeking new opportunities for the organization. The alpha reliability for this scale was 0.88 for the Taiwan sample and 0.70 for the PRC sample, respectively.

Demonstrating High Expectations was measured using three items: (1) Shows us that he/she expects a lot from us; (2) Challenges me to set high goals for myself; and (3) Insists on only the best performance. The alpha reliability for this scale was 0.71 for the Taiwan sample and 0.72 for the PRC sample, respectively.

Intellectual Stimulation was measured using four items: (1) Challenges me to think about old problems in new ways; (2) Asks questions that prompt me to think about the way I do things; (3) Has stimulated me to rethink the way I do some things; and (4) Has ideas that have challenged me to re-examine some of my basic assumptions about my work. The alpha reliability for this scale was 0.85 for the Taiwan sample and 0.70 for the PRC sample, respectively.

Criterion variables. Three criterion variables were included in the current study. Two of these variables (job satisfaction and organizational commitment) were self-reported measures. The OCB was ratings provided by the supervisors for each respondent.

Job Satisfaction was measured using the 20-item short form of the Minnesota Satisfaction Questionnaire (MSQ; Weiss, Dawis, England & Lofquist, 1967). The MSQ has been shown to possess generally good psychometric properties (Gillet & Schwab, 1975) and correlates well with other measures of job satisfaction (Gillet & Schwab, 1975; Wanous, 1974). The alpha reliability for this scale was 0.86 for the Taiwan sample and 0.89 for the PRC sample, respectively.

Organizational Commitment was measured using the 15-item scale developed by Porter, Steers, Mowday and Boulian (1974). This scale was designed to assess an employee's acceptance of the company's goals and values, willingness to exert effort on behalf of the company and maintenance of membership with the company. Previous research (Porter et al., 1974; Mowday, Steers & Porter, 1979) has demonstrated that this scale possesses adequate psychometric properties, and the data pertaining to its reliability and validity are generally positive. The alpha reliability for this scale was 0.91 for the Taiwan sample and 0.87 for the PRC sample, respectively.

Employees' OCB was measured by supervisor ratings. OCB refers to employees' behavior that is discretionary in nature and beyond the level of formal requirements (Organ, 1988). The OCB scale used in the Taiwan sample included five dimensions with 24 items taken from Podsakoff et al. (1990): altruism (5 items), courtesy (5 items), conscientiousness (5 items), civic virtue (4 items) and sportsmanship (5 items). To simplify the matter, a general OCB index was created by assessing average scores on the five scales. The Cronbach alpha for this composite scale was 0.95.

The OCB scale used in the PRC sample, however, was taken from Farh, Early and Lin's (1997) study because this scale was composed of some indigenous Chinese dimensions and we wanted to test its reliability in this study. It included 20 items with five dimensions: altruism (4 items), conscientiousness (5 items), identification with company (4 items), interpersonal harmony (4 items) and protecting company resources (4 items). Again, assessing average scores on the five scales created an overall OCB index. The Cronbach alpha for this scale was 0.87.

Seven-point Likert scales ranging from (1) "strongly disagree" to (7) "strongly agree" were used to assess all of the constructs measured in the present study with one exception in each sample. In the Taiwan sample, the 20-item MSQ scale was assessed with the traditional 5-point scales ranging from (1) "very dissatisfied" to (5) "very satisfied;" whereas, in the PRC sample, the 15-item organizational commitment scale was assessed with a 5-point scale ranging from (1) "strongly disagree" to (5) "strongly agree."

Control variables. Age, sex, educational level, organizational rank and organizational tenure were included in the study as control variables. These variables are relevant because they have been found to relate to employee outcome variables such as job satisfaction and performance (Gordon & Fitzgibbons, 1982; Kacmar & Ferris, 1989; Lee & Wilbur, 1985; McDaniel,

Schmidt & Hunter, 1988). Specifically, age and organizational tenure were measured in years: male was coded as 1 and female as 0. Educational level was categorized into six groups, with 1 for "below high school," 2 for "had high school," 3 for "holding a high school degree," 4 for "had some college," 5 for "holding a college degree," and 6 for "had advanced education." Organizational rank was measured in five categories, with 1 standing for first line supervisor, 2 for administrative officer, 3 for staff manager, 4 for middle level manager, and 5 for high level manager.

RESULTS

Descriptive Statistics

Tables 1 and 2 present the means, standard deviations, reliability coefficients and correlations of all of the variables for the PRC and Taiwan samples, respectively. An examination of the tables indicates that the reliability for all scales was above 0.70 (except the contingent punishment scale). An examination of the zero-order correlations indicates that for the PRC sample: (1) contingent reward and punishment positively relate to subordinates' job satisfaction and organizational commitment (r's range from 0.36 to 0.56, $p < 0.05$); (2) non-contingent reward and punishment are negatively related to subordinates' OCB (r's $= -0.34$ and -0.43, $p < 0.05$); and (3) all six transformational leader behaviors were positively correlated with subordinates' job satisfaction and organizational commitment (r's range from 0.41 to 0.75, $p < 0.05$), whereas fostering collaboration, providing an appropriate model, articulating a vision and high expectation of performance were positively related to OCB (r's range from 0.19 to 0.33, $p < 0.05$).

For the Taiwan sample, however, the zero-order correlation yielded somewhat different results: (1) both contingent and non-contingent reward were positively related to subordinates' job satisfaction and organizational commitment (r's range from 0.17 to 0.48, $p < 0.05$); (2) both contingent and non-contingent punishment were negatively related to OCB (r's $= -0.16$ and -0.25, $p < 0.05$), with non-contingent punishment negatively related to job satisfaction and organizational commitment as well (r's $= -0.30$ and -0.37, $p < 0.05$); and (3) all six types of transformational behaviors were positively related to all three employee outcome variables (r's range from 0.14 to 0.58, $p < 0.05$). In sum, the pattern of zero-order correlations between leader behaviors and employee outcome variables demonstrate different patterns of relationships between the two samples.

Table 1. Means, SD, Reliabilities and Intercorrelations of Leader Behaviors and Employee Outcome Variables (PRC: $N = 123$).

Variables	Means	SD	Alpha	1	2	3	4	5	6	7	8	9	10	11	12	13	14	15	16	17
Control Variables																				
1. Sex	0.66	0.48																		
2. Age	31.90	6.74		0.12																
3. Education	4.00	1.14		0.00	-0.19															
4. Org. Rank	1.76	0.76		-0.24	-0.05	0.35														
5. Org. Tenure	5.60	5.20		0.08	0.57	-0.48	0.15													
Transactional Behaviors																				
6. C-Reward	4.93	1.14	0.75	0.20	0.12	-0.14	0.14	0.13												
7. NC-Reward	3.68	1.48	0.83	0.13	-0.30	-0.06	-0.12	-0.19	0.25											
8. C-Punish	5.03	1.08	0.62	0.09	-0.04	-0.08	0.07	-0.09	0.37	-0.08										
9. NC-Punish	3.78	1.53	0.81	0.1	-0.18	-0.10	-0.06	-0.12	0.05	0.69	0.00									
Transformational Behaviors																				
10. Collaboration	5.05	1.21	0.85	0.15	0.11	-0.13	0.15	0.10	0.63	-0.04	0.47	-0.23								
11. Model	5.02	1.26	0.85	0.25	0.11	-0.05	0.11	0.06	0.63	-0.07	0.47	-0.23	0.78							
12. Support	4.76	1.26	0.75	0.4	-0.00	0.03	0.14	-0.01	0.67	0.23	0.35	-0.06	0.73	0.65						
13. Vision	5.07	1.24	0.70	0.16	0.05	-0.05	0.15	0.06	0.69	0.05	0.47	-0.10	0.77	0.69	0.69					
14. Expectation	4.97	1.36	0.72	0.18	0.03	-0.13	0.11	0.02	0.60	0.07	0.48	-0.11	0.76	0.69	0.71	0.76				
15. Intellectual Stimu.	4.97	1.18	0.70	0.22	-0.01	-0.08	0.23	0.02	0.61	0.12	0.42	-0.02	0.70	0.63	0.69	0.74	0.73			
Criterion Variables																				
16. Satisfaction	5.11	0.83	0.89	0.04	0.13	-0.10	0.13	0.12	0.56	-0.01	0.48	-0.12	0.68	0.69	0.60	0.67	0.75	0.63		
17. Org. commitment	3.80	0.65	0.87	-0.09	0.16	-0.23	0.05	0.20	0.39	-0.10	0.36	-0.11	0.48	0.48	0.41	0.46	0.54	0.41	0.77	
18. OCB	5.14	0.85	0.87	0.03	0.28	-0.33	-0.10	0.30	0.14	-0.34	0.06	-0.43	0.27	0.33	0.08	0.10	0.20	0.08	0.19	0.17

Note: All correlation coefficients are significant at the 0.05 level, except for those below 0.17.

Table 2. Means, SD, Reliabilities and Intercorrelations of Leader Behaviors and Employee Outcome Variables (Taiwan: *N* = 287).

Variables	Means	SD	Alpha	1	2	3	4	5	6	7	8	9	10	11	12	13	14	15	16	17
Control Variables																				
1. Sex	0.52	0.50																		
2. Age	38.10	8.15		0.09																
1. Education	4.00	1.23		0.12	-0.32															
2. Org. Rank	3.39	1.45		0.14	0.41	0.27														
3. Org. Tenure	15.54	9.26		-0.08	0.90	-0.40	0.36													
Transactional Behaviors																				
4. C-Reward	4.67	1.08	0.90	0.05	0.03	-0.10	-0.07	0.05												
5. NC-Reward	3.27	1.05	0.74	0.05	-0.02	-0.07	-0.06	0.03	0.29											
6. C-Punish	4.38	0.82	0.69	0.00	-0.03	0.03	-0.02	-0.03	0.02	-0.35										
7. NC-Punish	2.67	1.05	0.78	0.03	0.06	0.06	0.07	0.05	-0.50	-0.12	0.27									
Transformational Behaviors																				
10. Collaboration	4.99	1.17	0.92	0.10	0.14	-0.09	0.09	0.14	0.63	0.20	-0.06	-0.55								
11. Model	4.91	1.38	0.93	0.10	0.14	-0.04	0.13	0.12	0.67	0.23	-0.09	-0.59	0.78							
12. Support	4.61	1.21	0.85	0.04	0.05	-0.01	0.01	0.04	0.66	0.29	-0.25	-0.74	0.68	0.74						
13. Vision	4.58	1.11	0.88	0.17	0.13	-0.03	0.06	0.12	0.65	0.27	-0.00	-0.45	0.75	0.77	0.63					
14. Expectation	4.82	1.10	0.71	0.10	0.01	-0.04	-0.01	0.02	0.67	0.19	0.14	-0.42	0.64	0.67	0.56	0.75				
15. Intellectual Stimu.	4.57	1.06	0.85	0.16	0.09	0.06	0.14	0.06	0.62	0.26	0.02	-0.45	0.66	0.69	0.60	0.80	0.71			
Criterion Variables																				
16. Satisfaction	3.43	0.51	0.86	0.04	0.25	-0.01	0.22	0.22	0.48	0.22	-0.03	-0.37	0.56	0.58	0.52	0.55	0.51	0.52		
17. Org. commitment	4.80	0.88	0.91	0.08	0.33	-0.09	0.18	0.33	0.33	0.17	-0.04	-0.30	0.50	0.43	0.42	0.46	0.34	0.42	0.72	
18. OCB	5.23	0.90	0.95	0.07	0.12	-0.04	0.16	0.09	0.16	-0.00	-0.16	-0.25	0.21	0.24	0.27	0.16	0.14	0.17	0.22	0.14

Note: All correlation coefficients are significant at the 0.05 level, except for those below 0.11.

Effects of Leader Behaviors on Employee Outcome Variables

To further test our hypotheses, we conducted two sets of hierarchical regression analyses. In the first set of hierarchical regression, we entered all control variables in the first step, and then the six transformational leader behaviors followed by the four types of transactional leader behaviors. The purposes of this test were: (1) to test H1 – that different transformational leader behaviors will have different effects on employee outcome variables in the PRC and Taiwan; and (2) to test H3 – whether the effects of transactional leader behaviors will go beyond that of the transformational leader behaviors or not.

In the second set of the hierarchical regression, we again entered all control variables in the first step, followed by the four types of transactional behaviors and the six transformational leader behaviors. This test had two purposes: (1) to test H2 – that different transactional leader behaviors will have different effects in the PRC and Taiwan; and (2) to further test H3 – whether transformational leader behaviors will have positive effects beyond the effects of transactional behaviors on employee outcome variables in both the PRC and Taiwan. The results of these two sets of regression analyses are presented in Tables 3 and 4, respectively. The amount of variance explained (R^2) and the standardized regression coefficients (β's) reported in these two tables provide an estimate of the unique effect of each leader behavior on the corresponding outcome variables.

Hypotheses Testing

Hypothesis 1 states that among the transformational leader behaviors, providing individualized support and fostering collaboration will be effective in Taiwan, whereas providing an appropriate model and high performance expectation will be effective in the PRC to promote subordinates' job satisfaction, organizational commitment and OCB. Results in Table 3 indicate that among the six transformational leader behaviors: (1) "articulating a vision" and "intellectual stimulation" had no significant effect on any of the employee outcome variables in both the PRC and Taiwan; (2) "high expectation of performance" had a significant positive impact on PRC employees' job satisfaction ($\beta = 0.46$, $p < 0.01$) and organizational commitment ($\beta = 0.37$, $p < 0.01$), whereas its effect was significant only on Taiwan employee's job satisfaction ($\beta = 0.17$, $p < 0.05$); (3) both "fostering collaboration" and "providing individualized support" had no significant effect on any of the outcome variables in the PRC but had significant positive effects on Taiwan employees' job satisfaction ($\beta = 0.15$ and 0.15 respectively, $p < 0.05$), organizational commitment ($\beta = 0.31$ and 0.16, respectively, $p < 0.05$), and OCB ($\beta = 0.25$ for "individualized support", $p < 0.05$); and (4) "providing an appropriate model" had significant positive effects on PRC employees' job satisfaction ($\beta = 0.32$, $p < 0.01$), organizational commitment ($\beta = 0.27$, $p < 0.01$), and OCB ($\beta = 0.38$, $p < 0.01$), whereas its effect was not significant with regard to any of these variables in Taiwan. These results clearly show that the two behaviors (i.e. providing individualized support and fostering

Table 3. Results of Hierarchical Regression Analyses (with Transformational Leader Behaviors entered before Transactional Leader Behaviors) ($N = 410$).

Variables	Job Satisfaction		Org. Commitment		OCB	
	$\beta1$(TW)	$\beta2$(PRC)	$\beta1$(TW)	$\beta2$(PRC)	$\beta1$(TW)	$\beta2$(PRC)
Step 1:						
Control Variables						
Sex	−0.00	0.01	0.08	−0.12	0.04	0.02
Age	0.21	0.06	0.08	0.08	0.10	0.26*
Education	0.02	−0.10	0.01	−0.19	0.03	−0.23
Org. Rank	0.13	0.13	0.04	0.06	0.11	−0.15
Org. Tenure	−0.01	0.02	0.26	0.06	−0.02	0.05
Change R^2	0.08**	0.04	0.12**	0.08	0.03	0.18**
Step 2:						
Transformational Behaviors						
Vision	0.08	0.08	0.12	0.06	−0.11	0.03
Stimulation	0.02	0.12	0.12	0.00	−0.01	−0.16
Expectation	0.17*	0.46**	−0.06	0.37**	−0.00	0.06
Collaboration	0.15*	−0.03	0.31**	−0.08	0.06	0.11
Model	0.13	0.32**	−0.11	0.27*	0.08	0.38**
Support	0.15*	−0.03	0.16*	0.03	0.25*	−0.16
Change R^2	0.37**	0.63**	0.24**	0.33**	0.08**	0.12**
Step 3:						
Transactional Behaviors						
C-Reward	0.08	0.02	−0.03	0.02	0.01	0.01
NC-Reward	0.10	−0.00	0.07	−0.14	−0.11	−0.07
C-Punishment	0.05	0.11	0.05	0.08	−0.13*	−0.09
NC-Punishment	−0.03	0.05	−0.06	0.11	−0.10	−0.33**
Change R^2	0.01	0.01	0.00	0.02	0.02	0.12**
Overall R^2	0.46	0.68	0.36	0.43	0.13	0.42
Overall Model F	15.22**	14.86**	10.34**	5.33**	2.77**	5.12**

Note: * $p < 0.05$, ** $p < 0.01$.

collaboration), that contain a strong flavor of personalism, are effective in Taiwan. In the PRC however, the most effective behaviors are the ones that demonstrate leader character (providing an appropriate model) and performance orientation (high expectation of performance). These results provide considerable support for H1.

Hypothesis 2 states that among the transactional leader behaviors, contingent reward/punishment will have a more significant positive impact in the PRC

Table 4. Results of Hierarchical Regression Analyses (with Transactional Leader Behaviors entered before Transformational Leader Behaviors) $(N = 410)$.

Variables	Job Satisfaction		Org. Commitment		OCB	
	β1(TW)	β2(PRC)	β1(TW)	β2(PRC)	β1(TW)	β2(PRC)
Step 1:						
Control Variables						
Sex	−0.00	0.01	0.09	−0.12	0.04	0.02
Age	0.21	0.06	0.08	0.08	0.10	0.26*
Education	0.02	−0.10	0.01	−0.19	0.03	−0.23*
Org. Rank	0.13	0.13	0.04	0.06	0.12	−0.15
Org. Tenure	−0.01	0.02	0.26	0.06	−0.03	0.05
Change R^2	0.08**	0.04	0.12**	0.08	0.03	0.18**
Step 2:						
Transactional Behaviors						
C-Reward	0.35**	0.43**	0.19**	0.32**	0.12	0.15
NC-Reward	0.14*	0.05	0.11*	−0.08	−0.10	−0.11
C-Punishment	0.08	0.35**	0.06	0.25**	−0.14*	−0.02
NC-Punishment	−0.22**	−0.15	−0.24**	−0.04	−0.18**	−0.38**
Change R^2	0.29**	0.40**	0.16*	0.21**	0.09**	0.20**
Step 3:						
Transformational Behaviors						
Vision	0.08	0.04	0.12	0.03	−0.08	0.09
Stimulation	−0.00	0.11	0.10	0.01	−0.00	−0.10
Expectation	0.15*	0.45**	−0.06	0.36**	0.03	0.04
Collaboration	0.15*	−0.02	0.31**	−0.09	0.04	−0.02
Model	0.11	0.30**	−0.11	0.24*	0.05	0.30*
Support	0.12	−0.03	0.14	0.09	0.14	−0.08
Change R^2	0.08**	0.24**	0.09*	0.13**	0.01	0.04
Overall R^2	0.46	0.68	0.36	0.43	0.13	0.42
Overall Model F	15.22**	14.86**	10.34**	5.33**	2.77**	5.12**

Note: * $p < 0.05$, ** $p < 0.01$.

than in Taiwan, whereas non-contingent reward will have a stronger positive impact in Taiwan than in the PRC. It also states that both contingent and non-contingent punishment will have a more profound negative effect on subordinates' job satisfaction, organizational commitment and OCB in Taiwan than in the PRC. Results in Table 4 indicate that among the four types of transactional leader behaviors: (1) contingent reward demonstrated significant positive effects on job satisfaction ($\beta = 0.43$ and 0.35, respectively, $p < 0.01$) and organizational commitment ($\beta = 0.32$ and 0.19, respectively, $p < 0.01$), but not on OCB, in both the PRC and Taiwan; (2) non-contingent reward had significant effects on Taiwan employees' job satisfaction ($\beta = 0.14$, $p < 0.05$) and organizational commitment ($\beta = 0.11$, $p < 0.05$), but its effect was not significant in the PRC; (3) contingent punishment had significant positive effects on PRC employees' job satisfaction ($\beta = 0.35$, $p < 0.01$) and organizational commitment ($\beta = 0.25$, $p < 0.01$), but had a significant negative effect on Taiwan employees' OCB ($\beta = -0.14$, $p < 0.05$); and (4) non-contingent punishment had significant negative effects on Taiwan employees' job satisfaction ($\beta = -0.22$, $p < 0.01$), organizational commitment ($\beta = -0.24$, $p < 0.01$), and OCB ($\beta = -0.18$, $p < 0.01$), whereas its effect was significantly negative only on PRC employees' OCB ($\beta = -0.38$, $p < 0.01$), but not on their job attitudes. These results suggest that the same reward or punishment behavior can have very different effects on PRC and Taiwan employees' job attitudes and OCB.

Because H2 was about the relative impact of these four types of transactional behaviors on the two samples, we then conducted significance tests of the β values of the two samples on each transactional leader behavior under each outcome variable. The tests revealed: (1) a significant different effect of non-contingent reward on organizational commitment between the two samples ($t_{406} = 2.57$, $p < 0.05$); (2) significantly different effects of contingent punishment on job satisfaction ($t_{406} = -3.86$, $p < 0.01$) and organizational commitment ($t_{406} = -2.57$, $p < 0.05$); and (3) significantly different effects of non-contingent punishment on organizational commitment ($t_{406} = -2.89$, $p < 0.01$), and OCB ($t_{406} = 2.35$, $p < 0.05$). These results suggest that while in Taiwan non-contingent reward had stronger positive effects on employees' organizational commitment than in the PRC, contingent punishment had a much stronger positive effects on employees' job satisfaction and organizational commitment in the PRC than in Taiwan. Moreover, the destructive effect of non-contingent punishment had more impact on employees' organizational commitment in Taiwan than in the PRC; whereas, its negative effect had more impact on employees' OCB in the

PRC than in Taiwan. These results suggest that despite the fact that contingent reward exerted comparable effects in both samples, contingent punishment had stronger positive effects in the PRC, whereas its effect was quite negative in Taiwan. On the other hand, non-contingent reward did not have a significant effect in the PRC but induced significant positive job attitudes in Taiwan. These results provide considerable support for H2.

Hypothesis 3 states that transformational leader behaviors will have a more profound impact on employee outcome variables than transactional behaviors in both the PRC and Taiwan. Results in Table 3 demonstrate that after controlling the effects of the control variables and transformational leader behaviors, the effects of transactional leader behaviors were no longer significant with regard to job satisfaction, organizational commitment and OCB, with the exception that it had an additional significant effect on OCB in the PRC sample (the R^2 change was 0.12, $p < 0.01$). Meanwhile, results in Table 4 demonstrate that beyond the effects of transactional leader behaviors, the effects of transformational leader behaviors were significant with regard to job satisfaction and organizational commitment in both samples (the additional R^2 change attributed to transformational behaviors was 0.08 for the Taiwan sample and 0.24 for the PRC sample, respectively, $p < 0.01$), but were not significant with regard to OCB. Taken together, these results suggest that the effects of transactional leader behaviors on employee job satisfaction and organizational commitment diminish when the transformational leader behaviors are present, indicating that the transformational leader behaviors have a more profound impact on employee job attitudes than the transactional behaviors do. However, their effects do not necessarily go beyond those of transactional behaviors on employees' OCB. These results provide partial support for H3.

DISCUSSION AND CONCLUSIONS

This chapter discussed the differential effects of transformational and transactional leader behaviors in the PRC and Taiwan due to political, social, economic and cultural differences and changes in the past 50 years. A large study conducted in the PRC and Taiwan has shown that leader behaviors that contain the elements of personalism (e.g. non-contingent reward, providing individualized support) are more effective in Taiwan; whereas, in the PRC, leaders who demonstrate modern management practice (e.g. contingent reward and punishment) and leader character (e.g. providing an appropriate model) are more effective in promoting employee job attitudes and OCB.

The differential effects of transformational and transactional leader behaviors found in the PRC and Taiwan speak to the behavioral theories of leadership (e.g. Fiedler, 1978; Hersey & Blanchard, 1977; House, 1971) that emphasize the contingent nature of leader effectiveness. In other words, what determines leader effectiveness is not just the specific behaviors the leader adopts, or the specific styles the leader exhibits; it also depends on the specific situation in which the leader is placed. The situation can be defined by factors such as the organizational structure and culture; employees' values, beliefs, needs, abilities and goals; and the nature of the tasks that need to be accomplished. Leaders will be effective when their behaviors match that required by the situation. To take this point to an extreme, every organization or department has its own culture and characteristics. Leaders then have to choose behaviors and styles that fit the situation to be effective. In our case, it means that leaders who are effective in leading Taiwan employees will need to change their behaviors to lead PRC employees effectively, and vice versa.

The above discussion leads to another important leadership issue. That is, whether leaders are able to change their behaviors and styles to remain effective in different situations. The traditional trait theories of leadership emphasizes the set of traits or characteristics possessed by extraordinary human beings that set them apart from the rest, and states that these traits are stable and effective across different times and situations. According to these theories, leaders are born to be leaders and leadership cannot be taught or learned. We argue, however, that not only different situations require different leader characteristics, as suggested by the behavioral theories of leadership, but also that leaders must change their styles and behaviors to fit the situation's requirements. To take this point further, we believe that leaders are able to make changes to their behaviors in order to remain effective in leading employees (also see Goleman, 2000). How do they do that? We suggest a diagnostic model of decision-making that involves four steps. First, assess the current organizational situation in terms of its structure, culture, employee motivation, ability, values, needs, goals and so on. Second, evaluate a list of leader behaviors that have been demonstrated to be effective in different situations based on previous research and practice. Third, choose a set of behaviors that best fit the requirements of the current situation. And finally, implement these behaviors, evaluate their relative effectiveness and provide feedback for future decision-making situations. These steps should be repeated whenever there are changes made to the organizational system or there are value or behavioral changes in the employees.

We recognize a few limitations of this study that warrant discussion. One limitation is the lack of a quantitative measure of employees' cultural values and preference for management styles in the two societies, which made the connection between the value system and leader behavior effectiveness speculative in nature. The second limitation is that we did not develop an indigenous Chinese measurement of transformational and transactional leader behaviors. Instead, we adopted a modified version of the questionnaires developed in the West. While this limitation does not undermine our main conclusion that the same leader behaviors have differential effects in the PRC and Taiwan, it nevertheless casts doubts on whether these leader behaviors truly reflect PRC and Taiwan employees' view of transformational and transactional leadership. The third limitation of this study is the potential confounds in comparison between one state enterprise as the Taiwan sample and four non-state enterprises as the PRC sample. More comparable samples need to be used in future studies. Finally, due to the survey methodology used in the study, no causal relationship may be inferred. It is equally possible that different leader behaviors induced different subordinates' job attitudes and OCB, or that the differences in subordinates' job attitudes and OCB resulted in the differences in leader behaviors. More systematic and rigorously designed field experiments are needed to determine the causality of leader behaviors and subordinate reactions.

Despite these limitations, the present study has made contributions in understanding the effects of transformational and transactional leader behaviors in Chinese organizations in general and their differential effects in the PRC and Taiwan in specific. Although previous studies of Chinese organizations primarily focused on overseas Chinese Family Businesses, in the present study we investigated a state-owned enterprise in Taiwan and found effects consistent with previous findings. Furthermore, previous leadership research in the PRC was conducted solely in state-owned enterprises; however, our findings from the four non-state-owned organizations in the PRC were again consistent with those found in previous research. These results imply that what employees look for in effective leadership may not change when they work for organizations with different ownership. Rather, it is more related to the deep cultural values employees hold as a member of the society. Phrased differently, effective leader behaviors may travel from one organization to another given the fact that employees of these organizations share similar views of leadership. Therefore, understanding employees' expectations, perceptions and views of effective leadership is the key to understanding the situational requirements (as suggested by the contingent theories of leadership) and to the ultimate success of global leaders.

ACKNOWLEDGMENTS

The authors thank Dr. Xiaolin Zhang for his assistance in data collection in PRC. Part of the study has been presented at the annual meeting of the Academy of Management in Chicago, 1999.

REFERENCES

Bass, B. M. (1985). *Leadership and Performance Beyond Expectations*. New York: Free Press.
Bass, B. M. (1997). Does the transactional-transformational leadership paradigm transcend organizational and national boundaries? *American Psychologist, 52*(3), 130–139.
Brislin, R. W. (1980). Translation and content analysis of oral and written material. In: H. C. Triandis & J. W. Berry (Eds), *Handbook of Cross-cultural Psychology (Vol 2) Methodology* (pp. 349–444). Boston: Allyn & Bacon.
Burns, J. M. (1978). *Leadership*. New York: Harper & Row.
Cheng, B. S. (1985). *Task-oriented leadership behavior and subordinate performance: A supplementary model and its validation*. Unpublished doctoral dissertation, National Taiwan University, Taiwan (in Chinese).
Cheng, B. S. (1995a). *Authoritarian Values and Executive Leadership: The Case of Taiwanese Family Enterprises*. Report prepared for Taiwan's National Science Council. Taiwan: National Taiwan University. (In Chinese).
Cheng, B. S. (1995b). Chaxuegeju and Chinese organizational behavior. *Indigenous Psychological Research in Chinese Societies, 3*, 142–219 (In Chinese).
Cheng, B. S. (1995c). Paternalistic authority and leadership: A case study of a Taiwanese CEO. *Bulletin of the Institute of Ethnology Academic Sinica, 79*, 119–73 (In Chinese).
Cheng, B. S., & Zhuang, S. J. (1981). Factor analysis of effective leader behaviors of rank-and-file military personnel in Taiwan: Relationships among leadership effectiveness, leader roles, and leadership styles. *Journal of Chinese Psychology, 23*, 97–106 (In Chinese).
Confucius (1915). *The Ethics of Confucius*. New York: Putnam.
Fahr, J. L., & Cheng, B.-S. (1999). A cultural analysis of paternalistic leadership in Chinese organizations. In: J. T. Li, A. S. Tsui & E. Weldon (Eds), *Management and Organizations in China: Current Issues and Future Research Directions*. London: MacMillan.
Fahr, J. L., Earley, P. C., & Lin, S. C. (1997). Impetus for action: A cultural analysis of justice and organizational citizenship behavior in Chinese society. *Administrative Science Quarterly, 42*, 421–444.
Fiedler, F. E. (1978). The contingency model and the dynamics of the leadership process. In: L. Berkowitz (Ed.), *Advances in Experimental Social Psychology*. New York: Academic Press.
Gillet, B. J., & Schwab, D. P. (1975). Convergent and discriminant validities of the corresponding Job Description Index and Minnesota Satisfaction Questionnaire scales. *Journal of Applied Psychology, 60*, 313–317.
Goleman, D. (2000). Leadership that gets results. *Harvard Business Review*, (March-April), 21-31.
Gordon, M. E., & Fitzgibbons, W. J. (1982). Empirical test of the validity of seniority as a factor in staffing decisions. *Journal of Applied Psychology, 67*, 311–319.
He, Q. L. (1998). *The Trap of Chinese Modernization*. Hong Kong.

Hersey, P., & Blanchard, K. H. (1977). *The Management of Organizational Behavior* (3rd ed.). Englewood Cliffs, NJ: Prentice-Hall.

Hofstede, G., & Bond, M. H. (1988). The Confucius connection: From cultural roots to economic growth. *Organizational Dynamics, 17*, 4–21.

House, R. J. (1971). A path-goal theory of leader effectiveness. *Administrative Science Quarterly, 16*, 321–339.

Huang, K. L. (1986). Organizational commitment and professional commitment of middle school teachers. *Journal of Taiwan National University, 53*, 55–84 (In Chinese).

Huang, K. L., & Cai, C. T. (1998). The effects of work value and leader behavior on employees' job performance. In: B. S. Cheng, K. L. Huang & C. C. Kuo (Eds), *A Serial Book on Organizational Management in PRC and Taiwan* (Vol. II, 159–204). Taipei: Yuan Liu Publishing Company.

Kacmar, K. M., & Ferris, G. R. (1989). Theoretical and methodological considerations in the age-job satisfaction relationship. *Journal of Applied Psychology, 74*, 201–207.

Kahn, H. (1979). *World Economic Development: 1979 and Beyond.* London: Croom Helm.

Lee, R., & Wilbur, E. R. (1985). Age, education, job tenure, salary, job characteristics, and job satisfaction: A multivariate analysis. *Human Relations*, (August), 781–791.

Ling, W. Q., Chen, L., & Wang, D. (1987). The construction of the CPM scale for leadership behavior assessment. *Acta Psychologica Sinica, 19*, 199–207 (in Chinese).

Lockett, M. (1988). Culture and the problems of Chinese management. *Organization Studies, 9*(4), 475–496.

McDaniel, M. A., Schmidt, F. L., & Hunter, J. E. (1988). Job experience correlates of job performance. *Journal of Applied Psychology, 73*, 327–330.

Misumi, J. (1985). *The Behavioral Science of Leadership.* Ann Arbor, MI: University of Michigan Press.

Mowday, R., Steers, R., & Porter, L. (1979). The measurement of organizational commitment. *Journal of Vocational Behavior, 14*, 79–94.

Organ, D. W. (1988). *Organizational Citizenship Behavior: The Good Soldier Syndrome.* Lexington, MA: Lexington Books.

Podsakoff, P. M., MacKenzie, S. B., & Bommer, W. H. (1996). Transformational leader behaviors and substitutes for leadership as determinants of employee satisfaction, commitment, trust, and organizational citizenship behaviors. *Journal of Management, 22*, 259–298.

Podsakoff, P. M., MacKenzie, S. B., Moorman, R. H., & Fetter, R. (1990). Transformational leader behaviors and their effects on followers' trust in leader, satisfaction, and organizational citizenship behaviors. *Leadership Quarterly, 1*, 107–142.

Porter, L. W., Steers, R. M., Mowday, R. T., & Boulian, P. V. (1974). Organizational commitment, job satisfaction, and turnover among psychiatric technicians. *Journal of Applied Psychology, 5*, 603–609.

Redding, S. G. (1980). Cognition as an aspect of culture and its relation to management process: An exploratory view of the Chinese case. *Journal of Management Studies, 17*(2), 127–148.

Redding, S. G. (1991). Culture and entrepreneurial behavior among the overseas Chinese. In: B. Berger (Ed.), *The Culture of Entrepreneurship* (pp. 137–227). San Francisco: Institute of Contemporary Studies.

Redding, S. G. (1993). *The Spirit of Chinese Capitalism.* New York: de Gruyter.

Redding, S. G., & Hsiao, M. (1990). An empirical study of overseas managerial ideology. *International Journal of Psychology, 25*, 629–641.

Silin, R. H. (1976). *Leadership and Value: The Organization of Large-Scale Taiwan Enterprises.* Cambridge, MA: Harvard University Press.

Weiss, D. J., Dawis, R. V., England, G. W., & Lofquist, L. H. (1967). *Manual for the Minnesota Satisfaction Questionnaire. Minnesota Studies in Vocational Rehabilitation: XXII.* Minneapolis: University of Minnesota, Industrial Relations Center Work Adjustment Project.

Westwood, R. I. (1997). Harmony and patriarchy: The cultural basis for 'paternalistic headship' among the overseas Chinese. *Organization Studies, 18*(3), 445–480.

Westwood, R. I., & Chan, A. (1992). Headship and leadership. In: R. I. Westwood (Ed.), *Organizational Behavior: Southeast Asian Perspectives* (pp. 118–143). Hong Kong: Longman.

Xu, L. C. (1989). Comparative study of leadership between Chinese and Japanese managers based upon PM theory. In: B. J. Fallon, H. P. Pfister & J. Brebner (Eds), *Advances in Organizational Psychology* (pp. 42–49). Amsterdam: Elsevier.

Yukl, G. A. (1989a). *Leadership in Organizations* (2nd ed.). Englewood Cliffs, NJ: Prentice Hall.

Yukl, G. A. (1989b). Managerial leadership: A review of theory and research. *Yearly Review of Management, 15*, 251–289.

LEADERSHIP IN CHINA: RECENT STUDIES ON RELATIONSHIP BUILDING

Dean Tjosvold and Chun Hui

ABSTRACT

There is no hope for creating a better world without a deeper scientific insight in the function of leadership and culture, and of other essentials of group life.

Kurt Lewin, pioneering social psychologist

Supposing is good, but finding out is better.

Mark Twain

If it becomes necessary to oppose a ruler, withstand him to his face, and don't try roundabout methods.

Confucius

Leadership is a special art and a precious contribution to employees, customers, shareholders and managers alike. But the challenge to lead effectively is formidable. Leaders must be credible and consistent, yet flexible and dynamic. They motivate and direct, yet listen carefully and develop a team that wants to do what needs to be done. Today they must often inspire people who are culturally diverse and geographically dispersed.

No wonder then that leadership often disappoints. Over 60% of U.S. employees consistently describe their boss as the biggest source of stress

Advances in Global Leadership, Volume 2, pages 127–151.
ISBN: 0-7623-0723-4

on the job (Hogan, Curphy & Hogan, 1994). Confident, popular leaders too often become frustrated, unwelcomed ones as hopes turn to blame.

Leadership has proved difficult for researchers too. Despite many models and thousands of studies, leadership knowledge is still preliminary and its impact on practice minor (Argyris, 1991; Kouzes & Posner, 1995). Research has shown the limitations of traditional notions that leadership is a simple characteristic of a person, perhaps genetically based, or that it involves a particular kind of action (Dickson, Hanges & Lord, 1999). Research in cross-cultural settings has reinforced the general conclusion that leaders must be flexible. They do not simply follow a script, but must assess the situation and act appropriately. However, specifying this contingency perspective is difficult: Leaders have a great many options in many different circumstances. Leaders must also be credible. How can flexibility and credibility both be attained?

Challenges for leading and for research are particularly daunting in cross-cultural settings, where stereotypes frustrate progress. Although Chinese employees have told us about how they have come to respect and learn a great deal from their Japanese and Western managers, others have complained bitterly about their managers' aloofness and condescension (Wong, Sonoda & Tjosvold, 1999). Western-trained managers in China are often praised for openness, but condemned for insensitivity.

Research on leadership in China has considerable potential for it confronts stereotypes that frustrate leadership practice and research, and can identify underlying elements of effective leading. Our research is a beginning and it shows that researchers can cut through these stereotypes to theorize how one can manage effectively in a culture as discrepant from the American culture as is the Chinese culture. We have found that open-minded, two-way relationships contribute significantly to successful leadership in the East as well as in the West. Leadership is not simply a characteristic of one person but developed by managers and employees together. Our research also demonstrates the value of using the theory of cooperation and competition to identify the nature of these relationships. This elegant theory suggests powerful ways to lead and build leadership capabilities.

The third major contribution of our research is the demonstration of how Chinese values can contribute to successful leadership. Although Chinese cultural values are often thought to impede the development of an empowered workforce, our studies suggest how, when appropriately expressed, they promote effective contemporary leadership.

This chapter has five parts. It begins with a description of the challenges of leading and studying leadership in China. It then outlines the theory of cooperation and competition and describes our field and experimental research findings using this theory. The fourth section discusses how Chinese values and cognitive style can promote productive, open-minded relationships between managers and employees. The final section suggests major procedures to apply research knowledge to strengthen leadership in China.

STUDYING LEADERSHIP IN CHINA

Leadership is a meeting ground for action and science. Leadership must be done as well as understood. Ideas and expectations very much affect the actions of leaders and the reactions of employees. The argument of Kurt Lewin, a father of the scientific study of leadership and groups, that there is nothing as useful as a good theory, applies with great force to leadership.

Our studies have used Deutsch's theory of cooperation and competition to understand leadership in China. The theory helps to move away from inadequate notions of leadership to focus on the relationship between leaders and employees. Considerable research, including between leaders and employees, albeit in the West, has developed this theory. Recent studies in China have begun to explore and expand traditional ideas of Chinese leadership. Indeed, studies using Deutsch's theory suggest how leaders and employees can use power and conflict for the benefit of organizations and themselves.

Confronting Traditional Ideas

Enduring attitudes and expectations shape our understanding and practice of leadership. Chinese leadership has been thought to be autocratic – where followers quickly and automatically follow the wishes and decisions of leaders. China has been found to be a high power distance culture where employees accept hierarchy and unilateral decision making and prefer that their leaders be benevolent autocrats (Bond, Wan, Leung & Giacalone, 1985; Hofstede, 1980; Leung, 1997; Smith, Dugan & Trompenaars, 1996).

However, research has begun to question these traditional notions and suggest their important limitations. Leaders in China are expected to be supportive and nurturing; superior power in China appears not to be so clearly linked to domination and authoritarianism as in the West (Pye, 1985; Spencer-Oatey, 1997).

Building upon Traditional Ideas

Research has consistently supported the Chinese idea that relationships are the basis of organizational work. Authority cannot be assumed. Leaders must earn it by demonstrating a commitment to employees and openness toward them. Studies have shown that employees with high quality relationships with leaders perform their own jobs well and are willing to contribute as good citizens to the organization (Hui, Law & Chen, 1999; Law, Hui & Tjosvold, 1997).

This China-based research is powerful support for emerging research in the West that emphasizes the leader relationship. George Graen and his colleagues have developed an impressive empirical base that the individual relationship between managers and employees has a critical impact on leader effectiveness (Gerstner & Day, 1997; Graen & Uhl-Bien, 1995). Western research on transformational leadership also emphasizes the importance of leaders developing effective relationships with and among employees (Bass, 1997). An important issue is how to build and maintain these relationships in China.

THEORY OF COOPERATION AND COMPETITION

We have used Deutsch's theory of cooperation and competition to analyze the relationships that are critical for leader success. Our aim is not to document that there is one style of leadership that is universally valid. Rather our intent is to explore the extent that the relationships embedded in the theory of cooperation and competition also hold in non-Western cultures, that is, documenting systematic behavioral universals (Dickson et al., 1999). Even if these universals can be documented, how they are applied depends upon the culture and the individual; people have different schematics about cooperation, competition and other key concepts (Dickson et al., 1999).

Morton Deutsch (1949, 1973) argued that how people believe their goals are related has a pervasive impact on underlying expectations and interaction that then affects outcomes. The type of interdependence structured in a situation is proposed to determine how managers and employees interact with each other that, in turn, determines consequences. There are two types of social interdependence: cooperative and competitive. The absence of social interdependence and dependence results in individualistic efforts.

Goal Interdependence

Managers and employees can believe that their goals are cooperatively or competitively related or unrelated (Deutsch, 1949, 1973; Johnson & Johnson, 1989):

(1) In cooperation, individuals' goal achievements are positively correlated; they perceive that they can reach their goals if and only if the others also reach their goals. As they succeed to the extent that others succeed, they encourage and support each other's efforts.
(2) In competition, managers and employees work against each other to achieve a goal that only one or a few can attain. Goal achievements are negatively correlated; each person perceives that when one achieves his or her goal, others fail to achieve their goals. Thus, they are tempted to frustrate and obstruct others from performing well and reaching their goals.
(3) In independence, there is no correlation among goal attainments. Each person perceives that he or she can reach his or her goal regardless of whether other individuals attain their goals. They seek an outcome that is personally beneficial without concern for the outcomes of others.

Of course, most situations are mixes of these pure forms. It is hypothesized that how people believe their goals are predominately related very much affects how they work together.

Interaction Patterns

Between 1898 and 1989, over 575 experimental and 100 correlational studies have been conducted by a wide variety of researchers in different decades with different age participants and tasks, and in different settings. Results of these North American studies, when taken together in meta-analyses, strongly support the generalization that positive interdependence creates promotive interaction (Johnson & Johnson, 1989). Promotive interaction occurs as persons encourage and facilitate each other's efforts to reach their goals. They promote each other's success by giving and receiving help and assistance, exchanging resources and information, giving and receiving feedback, challenging each other's reasoning, advocating increased efforts to achieve, mutually influencing each other's reasoning and behavior, engaging in the interpersonal and small group skills needed for effective coordination, and processing how effectively people are working together and how their effectiveness can be continuously improved.

Competitive interdependence typically results in oppositional interaction in which persons discourage and obstruct each other's efforts to achieve. They focus both on increasing their own success and on preventing anyone else from being more successful than they are. Independent goals discourage interaction as people focus only on increasing their own success and ignore as irrelevant the efforts of others.

Open-Mindedness
.

The dynamics induced by cooperative goals and contributing to effective joint work has been characterized as constructive controversy (Tjosvold, 1998c, 1985b). Controversy occurs when persons discuss their opposing views about how a problem should be solved. It occurs as scientists debate the validity of a theory, but is not restricted to debates over ideas and truth. Negotiating over wage agreements and unfriendly behavior have characteristics of intellectual disagreement as protagonists develop and propose alternative solutions to resolve their conflict.

Research indicates that it is through open-minded, controversial discussion that people combine and integrate their ideas to resolve issues and strengthen their relationships (Tjosvold, 1998c, 1985b). Constructive controversy proposes that open discussion of opposing views is critical for making cooperative situations productive and enhancing. Through controversy, people develop and express their own perspectives on an issue. When confronted with another's opposing views, they feel uncertain about the most effective solution and search for additional information and a more adequate way of understanding the issue. Then they are prepared to integrate other ideas to create new, more elegant conceptualizations of the problem. This exploration of positions and the creation of new solutions during controversy result in high-quality decisions that the protagonists are committed to implementing.

Applying Deutsch's Western Theory

Our studies have used this Western theory to challenge traditional notions of leadership. But many social scientists are skeptical that Western theories can be applied in such collectivist cultures as China, arguing that such a theory has inherent weaknesses in understanding other cultures. An imposed theoretical framework captures the cultural experience of the West, not China. Social scientists should utilize indigenous values and perspectives to understand and appreciate how Chinese people actually experience interdependence and conflict.

Specific objections can be raised to the application of the Deutsch theory. The theory assumes that individuals are self-interested. Their actions and feelings are hypothesized to depend upon whether they believe their self-interests are cooperatively or competitively related. As collectivist rather than individualist, Chinese are thought to pursue the interests of groups rather than their own interests. Is the Deutsch assumption that self-interest motivates social behavior justified in China?

A related objection is that as collectivists, Chinese people are highly oriented toward cooperation, and competition and independence are unfamiliar. Are the Chinese able to interact in competitive and independent ways, or are these experiences infrequent and counter-cultural?

Deutsch argued that conflict is an inevitable aspect of social interdependence and that, even with highly cooperative goals, people conflict. Our research emphasizes the value of constructive controversy for cooperative problem solving. However, the Chinese culture highly values harmony, making conflict anathema. Is conflict an important aspect of Chinese organizations?

A related, though somewhat inconsistent objection, is that conflict, when surfaced, is inevitably competitive, although Deutsch argued that conflict has a cooperative face. The Chinese word for conflict connotes warfare, suggesting that conflict is invariably a win-lose situation. Is a cooperative conflict approach viable in China?

Several central Chinese values are theorized to underline their embracing harmony. Chinese people are thought to avoid conflict because they are particularly sensitive to social face and highly averse to interpersonal hostility and assertive ways of handling frustrations and problems. These values make it difficult to initiate conflict. Simply disagreeing easily and non-verbally communicates an aggressive affront to face. With social face values, can conflict be dealt with directly and open-mindedly?

Chinese society is thought to be a traditional, hierarchical one where employees readily defer to their superiors. Autocratic organizations and leadership are the cultural norm. Open conflict is more consistent with participative management. Is constructive controversy consistent with organizational values in China? Are Chinese organizations using cooperative conflict to serve customers?

Deutsch's theory, like any other, cannot be assumed to apply in another culture, but applying it in China may be particularly questionable. We next review our findings using experimental and field methods.

RESEARCH FINDINGS IN CHINA

A cooperative, bicultural network has tested the Deutsch theory in China. Trained both in the East and West and based in Hong Kong, mainland China, Korea, Japan, Taiwan and other East Asian countries, researchers have debated the theory and developed the methods. Together we have authored the studies upon which this review is based. The network itself has demonstrated the value of cooperative teamwork and constructive controversy! We are most grateful for our colleagues' openness and contributions to the research.

Network members, as well as managers in the region, argued that cooperation and competition were both important phenomena in Asian organizations. Concretely, they translated the major concepts and research questions into Cantonese (the local Hong Kong dialect), Mandarin (the national language of China), Japanese and Korean. This process also simplified and improved the English operations. Interview, questionnaire and experimental methods have all been used to test the theory.

Field Studies on Leadership in Chinese Organizations

Research first was used to determine the extent that the theory of cooperation and competition was useful for understanding leadership in East Asian organizations. Are leaders effective because they have superior power and authority or must they develop strong, cooperative, open-minded relationships with employees? Can authority be assumed or must leaders earn it by demonstrating a commitment to employees and openness to them?

Interviews. We interviewed managers and employees using the critical incident methodology (Flanagan, 1954). Rather than trying to summarize a great number of examples by rating how they generally interact with each other as demanded by most questionnaires, managers and employees described concrete experiences. Interviewers can establish a relationship with the respondents, provide an informal and personal climate, clarify and answer questions and encourage the respondent. Chinese people, with their relation-ship-oriented culture, were thought likely to respond positively to this climate.

The interview had a highly defined structure. Managers and employees described specific interactions with each other by indicating the setting, that which occurred and the consequences. Then they answered specific questions that allow statistical tests of the framework and hypotheses. Interviewees specified their goals and the other's goals, and using 7-point Likert-scale items, indicated how much they perceive that their goals were positively, negatively or independently related and described their reasoning for goal interdependence. They rated the extent to which they expressed their own views fully, considered the other's views open-mindedly, tried to understand the other's concerns, worked together for mutual agreement on this issue, and tried to put together the best of the various ideas expressed. After they rated themselves on these dimensions, the interviewers rated the other on the same items. Managers and employees also described the consequences of the incident for themselves and the organization, and rated the effects of the incident on their work relationship, task productivity and commitment. The examples were also coded and sorted to identify the reasons for cooperative, competitive and independent goals; the interaction behaviors that occurred in them; and the consequences of the interactions.

In an initial study, 89 Hong Kong leaders and employees were interviewed on specific incidents (Tjosvold, Hui & Law, 1998). An open-minded discussion of opposing views between leaders and employees was found to be highly crucial, resulting in productive work, strong work relationships, experiencing the leader as democratic and believing that both the leader and employee are powerful.

In today's global economy, leaders must at times supervise employees working in other countries. Hong Kong senior accounting managers were found to be able to lead employees working in mainland China when they had cooperative goals, but not when their goals were competitive or independent (Tjosvold & Moy, 1998). Then they were able to discuss their views open-mindedly about that which led to stronger relationships and productivity, consequences that in turn induced future internal motivation.

Questionnaires. Surveys complement the interview studies. They allow for the sampling of more people and the use of independent sources for outcome measures. Chinese employees have been willing to respond candidly, but are unfamiliar with questionnaires. The items have been continually reworked to become more concise and clear. Employees are asked to complete the questionnaires when the flow of work allows them sufficient time. We distribute the questionnaire in small groups and explain with examples how they can complete their task accurately. They receive a small gift to reciprocate and show our appreciation.

For example, 170 supervisor-subordinate dyads in a watch case-manufacturing factory in southern China participated in a study on leader relationship and employee citizenship (Law, Hui & Tjosvold, 1997). Employees completed questionnaires involving measures on cooperation, competition, independence and constructive controversy with their supervisor. Their supervisors completed questionnaires on the employee's in-role performance (productivity) and extra-role performance (organizational citizenship).

The overall model tested was that strong cooperative goals, but not competitive or independent ones, promote a high quality relationship between leader and employee, which in turn leads to high levels of job performance and citizenship behavior. Structural equation analysis confirms the underlying causal structure among goal interdependence, leader relationship and job performance and citizenship behavior.

In another study, 106 pairs of supervisors and employees were recruited from 10 state-owned enterprises in Nanjing and Shanghai to participate in a leadership study on goal interdependence, justice and citizenship behavior (Hui, Tjosvold & Ding, 1998). The analysis supported the model that a strong sense of justice promotes cooperative goals, but not competitive or independent ones, which lead to open-minded, constructive controversy. Controversy in turn resulted in job performance and citizenship behavior.

Experiments on Positive Power

Experiments complement interviews and questionnaires in that they directly test causal relationships with high internal validity. They provide an alternative to the heavy reliance on questionnaire survey in management research in China.

Power has traditionally been considered a largely sinister force in organizations. Indeed, power has been assumed to be competitive, where managers use power to overcome resistance and get employees to do what they want to avoid. A critical step is to define power independently of competition, and cooperation as the capacity to affect the benefits and costs of those subject to power (Fiske, 1993; Goodwin, Operario & Fiske, 1998; Thibaut & Kelley, 1959). Equivalently, power is the control over valued abilities that can impact the goals of those subject to power. This definition is similar to traditional measures of power (French & Raven, 1959). Managers and employees have power over each other to the extent that they see each other as having abilities that can impact, either positively or negatively, their success.

Building upon previous experiments in North America (Tjosvold, 1985a, c, 1981), we argue that how power is used depends upon how managers and employees believe their goals are related (Tjosvold & Sun, 1998a). We propose that high power managers who believe their goals are cooperatively, compared to competitively, related to the goals of their employees use their valued resources to assist and support employees.

Eighty participants from a university in Guangzhou were randomly assigned to four conditions: cooperative and competitive goals, high and low power. Participants taking the role of managers and randomly assigned to the cooperative condition read in the instructions that their company has a history in which managers and employees work together. They were also told that the number of chances they would receive in the lottery depended on how well both they and the employees performed their tasks. Managers in the competitive condition read that their company had a history in which managers and employees try to outdo each other. They would receive more chances in the lottery to the extent that they performed their own task more successfully than did the employee.

High-power managers were given the employee problem, three hints that would help the employee solve the problem and its answer. Managers in the low-power condition were given the problem without the hints or answer.

There were three sets of dependent measures using both behavioral and attitudinal operations. To measure actual assistance, the number of written messages sent to the employee with useful hints was coded. Managers also indicated the extent to which they felt they empowered the employees on a questionnaire. The second set of dependent variables involved the level of support given to the employee through sending supportive, encouraging comments. Managers also rated the extent they encouraged the employee. The third set of measures involved attitudes about the other, including the manager's belief that the employee was capable of solving the problem and was appreciative.

Results support the reasoning that high compared to low power provides the capacity to assist employees, but cooperative goals very much contribute to managers' trusting expectations, promotive interaction, encouragement, support and empowerment of employees and provision of concrete assistance. Competitive goals frustrated productive interaction between high power managers and employees. These results suggest limitations of the traditional theorizing of organizational power that assumes a competitive context between the powerful and those subject to power. Cooperative goals appear to be an important basis for developing the positive face of power in organizations.

A follow-up experiment also found that the use of power depended upon goal interdependence. High power managers were more willing to use their resources to support and empower employees with cooperative than competitive or independent goals, especially when the employees demonstrated a high need by being unable to complete the task themselves (Tjosvold & Sun, 1998b).

A third experiment investigated how managers' concepts of power affect their support of employees and use of power (Tjosvold, Coleman & Sun, 1999). Results indicate that the traditional idea that power is limited. So if the leader has more than the employee has, the opposite leads managers to develop a competitive relationship and withhold their resources from employees. In contrast, believing that power is expandable fostered cooperative goals and the provision of useful assistance, especially when employees lacked the ability rather than the motivation to perform well. Even in high distant power societies like China, believing power is expandable and developing cooperative goals contribute importantly to the constructive use of power in organizational life.

A questionnaire study suggests that the relationship between cooperative goals and positive power is not limited to experiments (Tjosvold & Poon,

1999). Traditionally, power has been thought to induce competitive conflicts over scarce resources, which results in powerful units obtaining resources at the expense of less powerful ones. However, power, when defined as control over valued abilities, may encourage managers and employees to manage their conflicts cooperatively by integrating ideas and perspectives. Correlational and structural equation analyses of data provided by 149 managers of budget teams in a public utility in Hong Kong, China indicated that to the extent team members had power, they managed their conflicts cooperatively and productively, which resulted in high quality budgets. Mutual power and cooperative approaches to conflict, even in collectivist China, can help develop quality, mutual solutions to problems, including effective distribution of scarce resources.

Conflict Research

North American research has documented that open discussion of conflicting ideas promotes curiosity, exploration, understanding and integration (Johnson, Johnson & Tjosvold, 2000). When confronted with an opposing view, people have been found to feel uncertain about the most adequate solution, and are curious and seek to understand opposing views. The expression of various views and the defending and articulating of their rationales, and the internal uncertainty and search for more complete information and understanding develop new, useful solutions to the problem that the protagonists accept and implement. Controversy has been found to be highly constructive when protagonists have cooperative goals, for then they are willing to integrate opposing views and reach a high quality agreement. Field research has shown that the dynamics of cooperative controversy can be highly useful for solving a wide array of complex problems for organizations (Tjosvold & Tjosvold, 1991, 1995).

Our studies in China have also indicated that cooperative compared to competitive contexts lead to more openness toward the opposing position and discussant (Tjosvold & Sun, 1998a). In an experiment, Chinese participants placed in the role of managers who were committed to mutual benefit, were interested in learning more about the opposing views, considered these views useful, came to agree with them and tended to integrate them into their own decisions in cooperative compared to competitive situations. They were more attracted to the other protagonist and had greater confidence in working together in the future than were participants in the competitive condition.

More surprisingly, openness itself has been found to be highly valued and useful in conflicts among Chinese. Open discussion, compared to avoiding conflict, strengthened relationships and induced uncertainty about their own position and a curiosity about the opposing view. In particular, they asked questions, explored opposing views, demonstrated knowledge and worked to integrate views (Tjosvold, Hui & Sun, 1998). They characterized protagonists who disagreed directly and openly as strong persons and competent negotiators, whereas "avoiding" protagonists were considered weak and ineffectual. In another experiment, open discussion, compared to avoidance, developed a cooperative relationship and open-minded understanding of the opposing view (Tjosvold & Sun, 1998b).

Field studies also support the value of open-minded discussion in a cooperative context. In a study of 39 groups and their supervisors in Hangzhou, China, work teams in China that used open-minded, constructive discussion with opposing teams promoted product quality and cost reduction, and these discussions were more likely to occur with cooperative than competitive goals (Tjosvold & Wang, 1998). The measures of product quality and cost reduction were taken independently of the measures of goal interdependence and interaction. Earlier studies found that cooperative conflict was useful for Singaporean managers and employees to resolve issues and work productively together (Tjosvold & Chia, 1989; Tjosvold & Tsao, 1989).

A study on conflict values and teams in China involved 106 pairs of employees and their leaders from state-owned enterprises in Shanghai and Nanjing (Tjosvold, Hui, Ding & Hu, 1998). Employees described their conflict attitudes and relationships; immediate supervisors rated team effectiveness and citizenship. Teams that believed conflict was positive were able to work together more effectively and developed stronger relationships. These relationships in turn laid the foundation for team effectiveness and employee citizenship.

Teamwork and Quality Service

Surveys and interview studies have documented the generalization of the theory of cooperation and competition. In particular, the documentation illustrates that cooperative goals and conflict underline productive teamwork and quality service. Cooperative, open-minded discussions of service problems helped restaurant employees work together to serve their customers (Tjosvold, Moy & Sasaki, 1996). When they shared the goal of serving customers well and shared a common task to increase tips for their team, waiters and cooks trusted each other, wanted to share the workload, avoided customer complaints and supported each other. However, showing off one's superior position, demonstrating a distrustful attitude based on the failure to keep word, and background and age differences led to competitive, closed-minded discussions that frustrated quality customer service.

Cooperative conflict, not competitive or avoiding conflict, helped Hong Kong, Korean, Taiwanese and Japanese building contractors work successfully with their subcontractors (Tjosvold, Cho, Park, Liu, Liu & Sasaki, 1998). Manufacturing managers in Hong Kong who handled conflict cooperatively used their frustrations with suppliers in Mainland China to improve product quality (Wong, Tjosvold, Wong & Liu, in press). Managers at the head office in Hong Kong were able to develop new products with colleagues in North America through cooperative goals and open discussion (Tjosvold, 1999). Dealing with customer complaints in Hong Kong were effectively handled through cooperative conflict (Tjosvold, 1998a).

Conflicts over scarce resources have been thought particularly divisive. However, an open-minded discussion helped Hong Kong accountants and managers dig into and resolve budget issues, strengthen their relationships and improve budget quality so that limited financial resources were used wisely (Poon, Tjosvold & Pike, 1998). These discussions were much more likely accomplished with cooperative than competitive goals.

Cooperative goals also promoted the open-minded discussion that helped teams of mass transportation employees obtain the organizational support they needed to reduce costs and improve quality (Tjosvold, 1998b). Cooperative, constructive controversy interactions were also found critical for Chinese staff to work productively and develop relationships with Japanese managers, outcomes that in turn built commitment to their Japanese companies (Tjosvold et al., 1998).

Empowering, open-minded leadership is valued in China. Chinese employees want a relationship with their leaders and, although they may be hesitant to initiate discussions with conflict, expect them to consider their needs and views. Cooperative goals and open-minded discussion appear to be a strong basis for successful leader relationships in China.

CHINESE VALUES FOR OPEN-MINDED RELATIONSHIPS

But how common are cooperative, open-minded relationships in China? Can leaders expect to realize this ideal in practice? It is commonly asserted that underlying Chinese values, while they are relationship oriented, make open, constructive relationships very difficult, especially between managers and employees with power and status differences. While they may induce cooperative goals, the Chinese values of social face and aversion to aggression lead to conflict avoidance. Our studies not only show that Chinese managers and employees can discuss their differences open-mindedly, they also indicate that Chinese values, if constructively expressed, contribute to open, productive conflict.

Social Face

Social face assumes that people attempt to project a desirable image and want assurance that their image is accepted (Tjosvold, 1983). Chinese people have been found to be particularly alert to protecting social face in order to promote relationships (Ho, 1976). Given their sensitivity to the collective and to relationships, they seek harmony and communicate that they view their partners as capable and worthy (Ting-Toomey, 1988). Their collectivism and their understanding of social face lead them to be hesitant about engaging in aggressive interaction that may challenge the face of others. They want to avoid conflict and, once engaged, use compromise and accommodation to deal with conflict (Ding, 1995; Kirkbride, Tang & Westwood, 1991; Leung, 1988; Tse, Francis & Walls, 1994).

However, Chinese values related to face may not make managing conflict more indirect and difficult. Indeed, their sensitivity to protecting face can make the discussions of differences more constructive. When Chinese feel that face is protected or confirmed, they may then openly discuss differences without experiencing social or psychological threat. Consequently, even Chinese who tend to avoid conflict and to be submissive can build cooperation and contribute actively in open-minded discussions.

Chinese negotiators who confirmed social face were able to manage their conflict cooperatively (Tjosvold, Hui & Sun, in press). Participants in an experiment where face was confirmed, in that they received direct feedback that they were seen as effective, emphasized their cooperative goals with the other discussant. They demonstrated uncertainty and curiosity in that they explored the opposing views and were interested in hearing more of the other's arguments. "Confirmed" participants were prepared to pressure the other and dealt with their disagreements collaboratively. They also indicated that they gained knowledge in the discussion, considered the opposing views useful and had come to agree with some of the opposing views. "Confirmed" participants indicated that they made more effort to integrate opposing views than did participants who had lost face. A field study also indicated that confirmation of "face" helped Chinese people to discuss their frustrations cooperatively and productively.

Persuasion and Implicit Communication

Chinese people have been expected to avoid conflict because they assume that conflict requires coercion, and they prefer persuasion. However, conflict can give rise to either persuasion or coercion. Persuasive influence was found to result in feelings of respect, cooperative relationships and openness to the other person and position (Tjosvold & Sun, 1998a). Protagonists who were targets of persuasion, compared to coercion, sought mutual benefit in the discussion, were open to listening to the other person, were interested in learning more about the opposing view and integrated their reasoning. Protagonists in persuasion, compared to coercion, were also more attracted and more confident in their relationships with the opposing negotiators.

Conflict is also thought to be avoided because in the high context Chinese culture, where implicit communication is influential, Chinese people assume that conflict communicates interpersonal hostility (Gudykunst, Ting-Toomey & Chua, 1988; Hall, 1976). However, implicit, nonverbal communication can help develop a cooperative context for conflict discussion. The expression of interpersonal warmth was found to have wide-ranging effects on conflict management (Tjosvold & Sun, 1998b). Participants who discussed with a "warm" rather than a "cold" protagonist developed a cooperative, mutually beneficial relationship. They explored the other's position, incorporated the opposing view and reasoning into their decision and thinking and agreed more with the other person's position than participants in the cold condition. Participants in the warm compared to cold condition expressed greater confidence that they could work with the other in the future.

A field study suggests that even anger can contribute to conflict management in East Asia. Chinese team members who emphasized their cooperative goals were able to discuss their frustrations directly and effectively in order to reduce their anger and solve problems (Tjosvold, 1997b). However, with competitive and independent goals, they refused to consider the other's views, protected their own self-interest and remained frustrated.

Chinese people are thought to be more indirect and discrete in their approaches to conflict (Leung, 1997). Their tendencies to show face, use persuasive influence attempts and communicate indirectly and non-verbally have been assumed to result in conflict avoidance. However, our studies show that these values, when appropriately expressed, can facilitate a controlled, but direct, cooperative and open-minded discussion of opposing views. These values may also promote cooperative conflict in the West (Tjosvold, 1993, 1983).

Cognitive Styles

Research on reasoning styles also suggests that Chinese traditions can strengthen relationship building and improve conflict management. A series of studies found that Chinese people are oriented toward dialectal reasoning, where they strive to reconcile contradictory positions and form syntheses of apparently opposing views (Peng & Nisbett, 1999). This reasoning style would seem to facilitate negotiating in complex social situations, where the best resolution includes elements of opposing positions. Americans, on the other hand, are prone to use formal logic and to seek the truth and the one best solution, which in conflict can lead to finding fault, blaming and rigidity.

However, neither cognitive style is by itself sufficient. Indeed, dialectic reasoning suggests a synthesis. Conflict management requires an integrated use of formal logic and dialectic reasoning. Contradictions and incompatibilities must be debated as well as acknowledged and accepted. The potential utility of various positions should be recognized for, although truth is seldom in the middle, effective decisions typically require a combination of information and insights.

Developing relationships and managing the inevitable conflicts for mutual benefit are highly demanding tasks. When taken together, studies suggest that Chinese or Western values and cognitive styles are not by themselves sufficient to meet these challenges. Managers and employees must work skillfully and diligently, and apply their values and adapt their ways of thinking appropriately if they are to build relationships through cooperative, constructive conflict management.

The Chinese values of social face, persuasion and nonverbal communication need not imply conflict avoidance. When appropriately expressed, these values contribute to open-minded, cooperative conflict management. Organizational values in China support developing effective, two-way relationships among leaders and employees. Chinese leaders are more effective and appreciated when they seek the views of employees and develop cooperative relationships with them.

APPLYING THE THEORY IN CHINA

Our results provide good support for the universalistic aspirations of the theory of cooperation and competition. Chinese managers and employees have clearly distinguished and understood cooperation and competition. They recognize that they can promote their own goals as well as those of team members. It is not necessary to project that Chinese are collectivists who emphasize group interests without concern for their own. They can pursue joint outcomes when they believe their goals are cooperative. They can be both collectivist and individualistic (Earley & Gibson, 1998). Importantly, the theory of cooperation helps us understand and manage Chinese. Instead of simply subscribing to the stereotypes that Chinese like to avoid conflict and open controversial discussions, this theory illustrates ways to induce cooperation with Chinese in conflict situations.

Although research supports the theory in China, results do not imply that actions that develop cooperative goals or communicate an attempt to discuss issues open-mindedly are likely to be different in China than in North America. However, current procedures suggest broad outlines of how Chinese managers and employees may proceed (Deutsch, 1994; Tjosvold, 1991, 1993). The procedures must be modified to take into account the culture, situation and people involved in China. Common sense and sensitivity are needed to modify and apply these steps in the West as well.

Developing Cooperative Goals

Cooperative unity cannot be taken for granted; competition is a viable alternative, one too often realized (Hogan et al., 1944). It is not enough for managers to talk about how they and employees should cooperate, or to blame them for not doing so. People must come to their own conclusion that what is good for one is good for all; success for one is success for all. Moreover, cooperative interdependence needs to be a shared conclusion. One person cannot cooperate alone. Managers and employees alike are committed to working together to reach common goals. Common tasks, joint efforts and shared rewards can convince people they are on the same side.

Common tasks. Managers and employees see that together they are to develop a new product or solve a customer problem. The manager wants them to integrate their ideas and develop one solution. Each person signs off on the final product indicating that he or she has contributed and supports it.

An important common task is to have managers and employees commit to serving customers. To serve customers well requires that they pull together. Learning can also be a motivating common task; all are expected to improve their skills in working with people, selling, operating machinery and to helping each other learn. Common tasks should be challenging. Employees will be motivated to accomplish probable, but difficult tasks, and will recognize that they require everyone's ability and support to do so.

Joint Effort. Managers and employees recognize that they must work together to be successful. They have complementary responsibilities and roles, all of which are needed to succeed. One employee is asked to record ideas, another to encourage full participation, another to be a devil's advocate and to challenge common views and a fourth to observe and provide feedback to help the group reflect on its efforts. They build upon their mutual power: They recognize each other's valued abilities and understand how pooling their resources is required. They have a team identity with their own name and symbol. They discuss the feelings and values they consider important and develop personal relationships.

Shared Rewards. Rewards for task completion should also be distributed. Tangible rewards, as well as praise, are given tó all. Individuals receive a bonus based on the performance of the department and the company's profitability. Managers recognize all members of the department and their accomplishments are written up in the company newsletter. Similarly, everyone is held accountable for unproductive performances. Managers confront a failed common effort and everyone suffers the consequences, rather than singling out one individual.

Managers can help employees realize that their goals are cooperative through a wide range of actions. However, employees themselves must conclude that their primary goals are cooperative so that they feel that they are "on the same side" and are "in this together".

Constructive Controversy

Although a leader can dispense with minor issues efficiently, employees join managers in confronting major important, ongoing issues through constructive controversy. They dig into issues, create alternatives and choose a high quality solution that solves the problems and strengthens the group. They use constructive controversy to explore issues and create alternatives.

Controversy must reaffirm cooperative goals aimed at success. Managers and employees differentiate their views and then integrate them. Teams explore issues thoroughly by protecting and stimulating diverse views. They search opposing ideas and integrate them in order to create workable solutions. Strategies include:

Differentiation. Openness norms encourage everyone to express his or her opinions, doubts, uncertainties and hunches. Ideas are not dismissed because they initially appear unusual, impractical or undeveloped. The rights to dissent and free speech reduce fears of retribution for speaking out. Managers and employees use the golden rule of controversy: Discuss issues with others, as you want them to discuss issues with you. If you want people to listen to you, then listen to them. Articles, books, consultants and experts can provide experiences and ideas that can help the group decide which course of action is superior. Independent people who differ in background, expertise, opinions, outlook and organizational position are likely to disagree.

Managers also assign opposing views. Coalitions are formed and given opposing positions to present and defend. One person is assigned to a critical evaluation role by attacking the group's current preference. Throughout the disagreement, people show personal regard. They criticize ideas rather than attack an individual's motivation and personality. Insults or implications that challenge another's integrity, intelligence and motives are avoided.

Integration. Managers and employees combine ideas. They avoid "either my way or your way" thoughts and try to use as many ideas as possible to create new, useful solutions. They may be able to create a totally new solution.

Controversy discussed in a win-lose, competitive, "I'm right, you're wrong" way, or that questions people's abilities and motives, tears teams apart and creates closed-mindedness and one-sided, ineffective solutions. Skillfully discussed, controversy increases trust and unity between managers and employees.

Organizational leaders and employees must work hard to break out of competitive, conflict-negative ways of working. They can begin by using structured approaches to controversy, such as assigning opposing views to sub-groups and designating someone to be the devil's advocate. They then reflect on their experiences and generate the norms and meanings that will help them discuss their opposing views openly and cooperatively.

Although a theory developed in the West has guided our research, the resulting studies have exposed Western stereotypes of China. Our studies reaffirm the value of relationships, but challenge traditional associations that successful leadership in China entails domination and passivity. Effective leader relationships are characterized by common interests and open-minded, two-way discussion, where leaders support and listen and their employees engage in two-way, constructive controversy.

We realize that cultural differences impact leadership (Tjosvold, 2000; Wall, 1990; Westwood & Chan, 1995). Managers cannot expect that actions taken in an Asian collectivist culture will be understood and responded to as they would in a Western individualistic one (Dikson et al., 1999). Indeed, cultural differences can stimulate the learning needed for one to become an effective, flexible leader (McCall, Lombardo & Morrison, 1988).

However, our research suggests that cooperative relationships and open-minded interaction are valuable in diverse cultural contexts. Leaders can be consistent in working with both Asians and Westerners in their commitment to develop these relationships. But the actions they take to strengthen cooperative goals and open interaction may vary substantially with different employees and organizations. In this way, leaders are both credible and adaptable.

Chinese and Western managers committed to developing participative organizations should welcome our results. Many Chinese employees are prepared and eager to contribute to organizational decision making. Yet developing leader relationships presents a significant challenge. Cooperative, open-minded relationships provide a common ideal and guide for managers and employees to build successful leadership and an empowered workforce. This kind of relationship also guides us through the complexities of cultural phenomena to enhance management across cultural boundaries.

ACKNOWLEDGMENTS

This chapter was supported by the RGC grant project No: LC890/96H and LC 3004/98H to the first author and RGC grant project No: HKU.S.T6197/98H to the second author.

REFERENCES

Bass, B. M. (1997). Does the transactional-transformational leadership paradigm transcend organizational and national boundaries? *American Psychologist, 52*, 130–139.

Bond, M. H., Wan, K. C., Leung K., & Giacalone R. A. (1985). How are responses to verbal insult related to cultural collectivism and power distance? *Journal of Cross-Cultural Psychology, 16*, 111–127.

Deutsch, M. (1994). Constructive conflict resolution: Principles, training, and research. *Journal of Social Issues, 50*, 13–32.

Deutsch, M. (1980). Fifty years of conflict. In: L. Festinger (Ed.), *Retrospections on Social Psychology* (pp. 46–77). New York: Oxford University Press.

Deutsch, M. (1973). *The resolution of conflict*. New Haven, CT: Yale University Press.

Deutsch, M. (1949). A theory of cooperation and competition. *Human Relations, 2*, 129–152.

Dickson, M. W., Hanges, P. J., & Lord, R. G. (1999). Trends, developments, and gaps in cross-cultural research on leadership.

Earley, P. C., & Gibson, C. B. (1998). Taking stock in our progress on individualism-collectivism: 100 years of solidarity and community. *Journal of Management, 24*, 265–304.

Fiske, S. T. (1993). Controlling other people: The impact of power on stereotyping. *American Psychologist, 48*, 709–726.

French, J. R. P. Jr., & Raven, B. (1959). The bases of social power. In: D. Cartwright (Ed.), *Studies in Social Power*. Ann Arbor: University of Michigan Press.

Flanagan, J. C. (1954). The critical incident technique. *Psychological Bulletin, 54*, 327–358.

Gerstner, C. R., & Day, D. V. (1997). Meta-analytic review of leader-member exchange theory: Correlates and construct issues. *Journal of Applied Psychology, 82*, 827–844.

Goodwin, S. A., Operario, D., & Fiske, S. T. (1998). Situational power and interpersonal dominance facilitate bias and inequality. *Journal of Social Issues, 54*, 677–698.

Graen, G. B., & Uhl-Bien, M. (1995). Relationship-based approach to leadership: Development of leader-member exchange (LMX) theory of leadership over 25 years: Applying a multi-level multi-domain perspective. *Leadership Quarterly, 6*, 219–247.

Gudykunst, W. B., Ting-Toomey, S., & Chua, E. (1988). *Culture and interpersonal communication*. Thousands Oaks, CA: Sage.

Hall, E. T. (1976). *Beyond culture*. New York: Doubleday.

Ho, D. Y. (1976). On the concept of face. *American Journal of Sociology, 81*, 867–884.

Hofstede, G. (1993). Cultural constraints in management theories. *The Academy of Management Executive, 7*, 81–94.

Hofstede, G. (1980). *Culture's consequences: International differences in work-related values*. Thousand Oaks, CA: Sage.

Hogan, R., Curphy, G. J., & Hogan, J. (1994). What we know about leadership: Effectiveness and personality. *American Psychologist, 49*, 493–504.

Hui, C. Law, K. S., & Chen, Z. X. (1999). A structural equation model of the effects of negative affectivity, leader-member exchange, and perceived job mobility on in-role and extra-role performance: A Chinese case. *Organizational Behavior and Human Decision Processes, 77*, 3–21.

Hui, C., Law, K. S., & Tjosvold, D. (1997). *The Effects of Cooperation and Competition on Leader-Member-Exchange and Extra-Role Performance In China*. Paper, Hong Kong University of Science and Technology.

Hui, C., Tjosvold, D., & Ding, D. (1998). *Organizational Justice and Citizenship Behavior in China: Goal Interdependence as Mediator*. Paper, submitted for publication. Chinese University of Hong Kong.

Johnson, D. W., Johnson, R. T., & Tjosvold, D. (2000). Constructive controversy: The value of intellectual opposition. In: M. Deutsch & P. T. Coleman (Eds), *Handbook of Conflict Resolution: Theory and Practice* (pp. 65–85). San Francisco: Jossey-Bass.

Kirkbride, P. S., Tang, S. F. Y., & Westwood, R. I. (1991). Chinese conflict preferences and negotiating behaviour: Cultural and psychological influences. *Organization Studies, 12*, 365–386.

Kouzes, J. M., & Posner, B. Z. (1995). *The leadership challenge: How to keep getting extraordinary things done in organizations*. San Francisco: Jossey-Bass.

Law, S. A, Hui, C., & Tjosvold, D. (1998). *Relational Approach to Understanding Conflict Management: Integrating the Theory of Cooperation and Competition, Leader-Member Relationship, and In-Role and Extra-Role Performance*. Paper submitted for publication, Hong Kong University of Science and Technology, Hong Kong.

Leung, K. (1997). Negotiation and reward allocations across cultures. In: P. C. Earley & M. Erez (Eds), *New Perspectives on International Industrial/Organizational Psychology* (pp. 640–675). San Francisco: Jossey-Bass.

Leung, K. (1988). Some determinants of conflict avoidance: A cross-national study. *Journal of Cross-Cultural Psychology, 19*, 125–136.

Leung, K., & Tjosvold, D. (1998). Conflict for doing business in the Pacific Rim. In: K. Leung & D. W. Tjosvold (Eds), *Conflict Management in the Asia Pacific*. Singapore: Wiley.

McCall, M. W., Jr., Lombardo, M. M., & Morrison, A. M. (1988). *The lessons of experience: How successful executives develop on the job*. Lexington, Mass.: Lexington Books.

Peng, K., & Nisbett, R. E. (1999). Culture, dialectics, and reasoning about contradiction. *American Psychologist, 54*, 741–754.

Poon, M., Pike, R. & Tjosvold, D. (in press). Budget participation, good interdependence and controversy: A study of a Chinese public utility. *Management Accounting Research.*

Pye, L. W. (1985). *Asian power and politics: The cultural dimensions of authority.* Cambridge: MA: Harvard University Press.

Smith, P. B., Dugan, S., & Trompenaars, F. (1996). National culture and the values of organizational employees: A 43 nation study. *Journal of Cross-Cultural Psychology, 27*, 231–264.

Spencer-Oatey, H. (1997). Unequal relationships in high and low power distance societies: A comparative study of tutor-student role relations in Britain and China. *Journal of Cross-Cultural Psychology, 28*, 284–302.

Ting-Toomey, S. (1988). A face negotiation theory. In: Y. Y. Kim & W. B. Gudykunst (Eds), *Theory and Intercultural Communication* (pp. 47–92). Thousand Oaks, CA: Sage.

Thibaut, J. W., & Kelley, H. H. (1959). *The social psychology of groups.* New York: Wiley.

Tjosvold, D. (2000). An encounter with a face of Chinese capitalism. *Journal of Management Inquiry, 8*, 87–91.

Tjosvold, D. (1999). Bridging East and West to develop new products and trust: Interdependence and interaction between a Hong Kong parent and North American subsidiary. *International Journal of Innovation Management, 3*, 233–252.

Tjosvold, D. (1998a). *Dealing with Retail Customer Complaints: Managing Conflict for Relational Marketing in Hong Kong.* Paper submitted for publication. Lingnan University, Hong Kong.

Tjosvold, D., & Sun, H. (in press). Social face in conflict among Chinese: Effects of affronts on person and position. *Group Dynamics: Theory, Research, and Practice.*

Tjosvold, D. (1998c). The cooperative and competitive goal approach to conflict: Accomplishments and challenges. *Applied Psychology: An International Review, 47*, 285–313.

Tjosvold, D. (1997a). Conflict within interdependence: Its value for productivity and individuality. In: C. De Dreu & E. van de Vliert (Eds), *Using Conflict in Organizations* (pp. 23–37). Beverly Hills, CA: Sage.

Tjosvold, D. (1997b). *Managing Anger for Teamwork in Hong Kong: Goal Interdependence and Open-Mindedness.* Paper submitted for publication. Lingnan University, Hong Kong.

Tjosvold, D. (1993). *Learning to manage conflict: Getting people to work together productively.* New York: Lexington Books.

Tjosvold, D. (1991). *Conflict-positive organization: Stimulate Diversity and Create Unity.* Reading, Mass: Addison-Wesley.

Tjosvold, D. (1990). Power in cooperative and competitive organizational contexts. *Journal of Social Psychology, 130*, 249–258.

Tjosvold, D. (1989). Interdependence and power between managers and employees: A study of the leader relationship. *Journal of Management, 15*, 49–64.

Tjosvold, D. (1985a). Effects of attribution and social context on superiors' influence and interaction with low performing subordinates. *Personnel Psychology, 38*, 361–376.

Tjosvold, D. (1985b). Implications of controversy research for management. *Journal of Management, 11*, 21–37.

Tjosvold, D. (1985c). Power and social context in superior-subordinate interaction. *Organizational Behavior and Human Decision Processes, 35*, 281–293.

Tjosvold, D. (1983). Social face in conflict: A critique. *International Journal of Group Tensions, 13*, 49–64.

Tjosvold, D. (1981). Unequal power relationships within a cooperative or competitive context. *Journal of Applied Social Psychology, 11*, 137–150.

Tjosvold, D., & Chia, L. C. (1989). Conflict between managers and employees: The role of cooperation and competition. *Journal of Social Psychology, 129*, 235–247.

Tjosvold, D., Cho, Y. H., Park, H. H., Liu, C., Liu, W. C., Sasaki, S. (1998). *Interdependence and Managing Conflict with Sub-Contractors in the Construction Industry in East Asia.* Paper, submitted for publication. Lingnan University, Hong Kong.

Tjosvold, D., Coleman, P. T., & Sun, H. (1999). *Effects of Power Concepts on Using Power to Affect Performance in China.* Paper, submitted for publication, Lingnan University, Hong Kong.

Tjosvold, D., Hui, C., & Law, K. (1998). Empowerment in the leader relationship in Hong Kong: Interdependence and controversy. *Journal of Social Psychology, 138*, 624–637.

Tjosvold, D., Hui, C., & Sun, H. (2000). Social face and open-mindedness: Constructive conflict in Asia. In: C. M. Lau, K. S. Law, D. K. Tse & C. S. Wong (Eds), *Asian Management Matters: Regional Relevance and Global Impact* (pp. 4–16). London: Imperial College Press.

Tjosvold, D., Lee, F., & Wong, C. L. (1992). Managing conflict in a diverse workforce: A Chinese perspective in North America. *Small Group Research, 23*, 302–332.

Tjosvold, D., & Moy, J. (1998). Managing employees in China from Hong Kong: Interaction, relationships, and productivity as antecedents to motivation. *Leadership & Organization Development Journal, 14*, 147–156.

Tjosvold, D., Moy, J., & Sasaki, S. (1996). Managing for customers and employees in Hong Kong: The quality and teamwork challenges. *Journal of Market-Focused Management, 1*, 339–357.

Tjosvold, D., & Poon, M. (1999). *Power, Conflict, and Scarce Resources: Using Conflict to Develop Quality Budgets.* Paper, submitted for publication, Lingnan University, Hong Kong.

Tjosvold, D., Sasaki, S., & Moy, J. (1998). Developing commitment in Japanese organizations in Hong Kong: Interdependence, interaction, relationship and productivity. *Small Group Research, 29*, 560–582.

Tjosvold, D., & Sun, H. (1999). *Using Power to Affect Performance in China: Effects of Employee Achievement and Social Context.* Paper, submitted for publication, Lingnan University, Hong Kong.

Tjosvold, D., & Sun, H. (1998a). *Faces of Power in China: Effects of Social Contexts on Use of Managerial Power.* Paper, submitted for publication, Lingnan University, Hong Kong.

Tjosvold, D., & Sun, H. (1998b). *Openness among Chinese in Conflict: Effects of Direct Discussion and Warmth on Integrated Decision Making.* Paper, submitted for publication. Lingnan University, Hong Kong.

Tjosvold, D., & Sun, H. (1998c). *Persuasive and Coercive Influence: Respect and Cooperative Context for Conflict Management in China.* Paper, submitted for publication. Lingnan University, Hong Kong.

Tjosvold, D., & Tjosvold, M. M. (1995). Cooperation theory, constructive controversy, and effectiveness: Learning from crises. In: R. A. Guzzo & E. Salas (Eds), *Team Effectiveness and Decision Making in Organizations.* San Francisco: Jossey-Bass, 79–112.

Tjosvold, D., & Tjosvold, M. M. (1991). *Leading the Team Organization: How to Create an Enduring Competitive Advantage.* New York: Lexington.

Tjosvold, D., & Tsao, Y. (1989). Productive organizational collaboration: The role of values and cooperative goals. *Journal of Organizational Behavior, 10.* 189–195.

Tjosvold, D., & Wang, Z. M. (1998). *Cooperative goals and constructive controversy in work teams in China: Antecedents for performance*. Paper, Academy of Management Meetings, San Diego, CA, August, 1998.

Tse, D. K., Francis, J., & Walls, J. (1994). Cultural differences in conducting intra- and inter-cultural negotiations: A Sino-Canadian comparison. *Journal of International Business Studies, 24*, 537–555.

Wall, J. A., Jr. (1990). Managers in the People's Republic of China. *Academy of Management Executive, 4*, 19–32.

Westwood, R. I., & Chan, A. (1995). The transferability of leadership training in the East Asian context. *Asia Pacific Business Review, 2*, 68–92.

Wong, A., Tjosvold, D., Wong, W., & Liu, C. K. (1999). Relationships for quality improvement in the Hong Kong-China supply chain: A study in the theory of cooperation and competition. *Journal of Quality & Reliability Management, 16*, 24–41.

Wong, M. L., Sonoda, S., & Tjosvold, D. (2001, June). Organizational learning in a Japanese multinational company in China. Paper. International Conference of Human Resources and Business Strategy, Zhejiang University, Hangzhou, China.

LEADERSHIP AND THE PURSUIT OF STATUS: EFFECTS OF GLOBALIZATION AND ECONOMIC TRANSFORMATION

Jone L. Pearce, Raul R. Ramirez and Imre Branyiczki

ABSTRACT

An analysis of the role of a respected social standing, or status, provides insights into the ways that globalization affects leaders' decisions to undertake organizational change. The review indicates that attaining high status entails advantages, with evidence that many will seek to attain and hold respected positions of social standing. Illustrative observations taken from a larger study of the effects of the transformation of Hungary's political and economic systems after communism suggest that the pursuit of status in differing social circles was a major factor differentiating those leaders who did not seek to make fundamental changes in their organizations from those who did so. These causes are examples of a larger phenomenon: Globalization has the effect of confronting executives from heretofore limited social environments, not only with economic losses to more powerful competitors but also to losses in their status as they come into closer contact with wealthier and more successful others who bestow respect for differing behaviors.

Advances in Global Leadership, Volume 2, pages 153–178.
ISBN: 0-7623-0723-4

INTRODUCTION

Globalization and economic transformation press leaders to make changes to their organizations, and we would expect that the extensive literature on organizational change would provide needed assistance. Yet the change literature tells us surprisingly little about how leaders decide *what* to change in response to indications that change is needed. Despite all the talk of the effects of globalization, the leaders' choices in response to pressures to change their organizations have rarely been addressed. And globalization undoubtedly does create pressures for change. Organizations that may have previously enjoyed little competition due to geographic distance or governmental policies limiting foreign competitors suddenly find that the removal of those barriers through technological or public policy changes force them to confront more effective or wealthier competitors. Many leaders of these organizations scramble to change their organizations, often quite radically, in order to survive, while others do not attempt significant organizational change. We have had an opportunity to observe these wrenching leadership challenges in our study of management and organizational behavior in the societies in transition from communism (see Pearce, 2001, for an overview of these studies).

One of our discoveries was that despite radical changes in the circumstances of organizations after the fall of communism, circumstances that clearly called for radical organizational changes, leaders varied widely in their attempts to change their organizations. In earlier work we analyzed the general slowness of organizational leaders to change their organization as a problem of legitimacy – old behaviors were slow to be discredited and legitimated models of effective behavior were slow to evolve (see Pearce & Branyiczki, 1997). Nevertheless, these leaders did vary a great deal in their attempts to implement organizational change. Some undertook extensive analyses and experimented with organizational changes until they found ones that worked. Others waited passively, or else viewed the challenges as fresh opportunities to gain the old-system advantages they had always sought, advantages that would prove to be meaningless under the new conditions. Yet, our own and others' studies of legitimacy in organizational change speak to the broad direction of change, but tell us little about individual differences. Why these differences in leaders' responses to clear signals that changes needed to be made?

Here we will argue that the pursuit of a respected social standing was one of the key factors in leaders' decisions to try to adapt their organizations to globalization pressures. We observed that with the fall of the Iron Curtain in Europe, organizational leaders in the formerly communist countries found themselves suddenly placed in new social systems, ones where previous behaviors and attributes that had secured places of respect and standing for these leaders were no longer guarantees of current or future respect in the new social circles. That is, many organizational leaders who had occupied their societies' most respected social positions now found that they were deemed to be either harmful or pitiful. We contend that this transformation-induced threat to leaders' respected social standing, as much as any change in incentives, was responsible for the variation we observed in the initiation of change in our studied organizations. While the pursuit of a respected social standing does not account for all of the differences among these leaders' approach to change, it is the one that is comparatively underdeveloped in the study of leadership and change.

These observations led us to wonder why the pursuit of a respected social standing, or what here will be called status, occupies such a minor place in the leadership literature. We hope to fill that lacuna in two ways. First, we introduce relevant scholarship on status taken from the allied disciplines of sociology and psychology. Second, evidence is provided of the importance of these leaders' pursuit of status in undertaking organizational change in response to the political and economic transformations. We hope this will make others' valuable scholarly work on status more accessible to leadership scholars and so encourage greater attention to what we have concluded is a powerful motivating force in organizations.

UNDERSTANDING THE ROLE OF STATUS IN ORGANIZATIONAL BEHAVIOR

A respected social standing, or status, occupies a rather minor place in the leadership, and more broadly organizational behavior, literature. While many of those working in different organizational science traditions, such as Belliveau, O'Reilly and Wade (1996), Benjamin and Podolny (1999), Berdahl (1996), Brint and Karabel (1991), Chung, Singh and Lee (2000), D'Aveni (1996), Dollinger, Golden and Saxton (1997), Eisenhardt and Schoonhoven (1996), Elsbach and Kramer (1996), Gioia and Thomas (1996), Kilduff and Krackhardt (1994), Kirkbride, Tang and Westwood (1991), Kraatz (1998), Long, Bowers, Barnett and White (1998), Sundstrom and Sundstrom (1986) and Tyler (1988), Waldron (1998), Weisband, Schneider and Connelly (1995), have noted status' importance in the organizational settings they have studied, these works are not in-depth theoretical or empirical studies focusing on status itself. The desire to occupy a respected social standing as a driving force has not been completely neglected, but it is a concept that has been used without much theoretical depth. While we cannot know why it has remained so underdeveloped, we can begin to rectify that neglect by introducing our colleagues to what those in allied fields have learned of social status.

The concept of status has been researched by numerous individuals in the fields of psychology and sociology with the intention of better understanding its formation and effects on human perceptions and behavior. However, even here the concept of status is often defined loosely or in different ways and thus is confused with similar concepts.

Defining Status

The study of status is as old as the social sciences themselves (see Scott, 1996, for an historical review). Medieval writers used the term "estate" to describe the existing social hierarchy, which was comprised of three estates: ". . . a religious estate of priests, a military and political estate of knights or lords and the 'common' estate of the ordinary people . . ." (Scott 1996, p. 6). Historically, an individual's status derived from the particular category that person occupied in a social setting. As social divisions became more complex with modernization the term estates gave way as the terms orders, degrees and ranks were added to refer to the multitude of social hierarchies in more fluid societies. Later, political economists introduced the term class, a social ordering based on economic condition (Marx, 1894/1967). Yet Weber's (1914/1978) work is still widely cited in sociology, largely for his description of the complex ways people are differentiated through party, class and status.

Weber's original works were written in German thus presenting a translation issue. Weber uses the German word *Stände,* which was translated directly into the word status and interpreted as status groups with the connotation of a social standing in the community by Roth and Wittich in their widely accepted English translation of Weber's (1914/1978) *Economy and Society.* Weber (1914/1978, p. 932) proposed that status ". . . is a quality of social honor or a lack of it, and is in the main conditioned as well as expressed through a specific style of life." Most individuals accept this translation, but Scott (1996) and Murvar (1985) propose an English translation of *Stände* into the word estate and use the phrase "social estate" to make the direct English translation less specific to the feudal context.

Sociologists have struggled with the distinction between status as a subjective evaluation and status as an objective and structural reality. Wegener (1992) suggests that while the two may have been conflated in earlier times when there was more social stability, modern mobility has had the effect of destroying any consensus on the prestige of different social groupings. The way he handles the problem is to call the subjective evaluation, prestige and the structural condition, status. However, for Weber (1914/1978) like most others, prestige is an aspect of status, it is not synonymous with it. While this Weberian distinction between status and prestige is attractive, unfortunately many in organizational studies equate status with prestige (e.g. Conway, Pizzamiglio & Mount, 1996; Gioia & Thomas, 1996; Kraatz, 1998) thus eliminating the possibility of consistent terminology. The other prominent theorist of social status, Berger (Berger, Conner & Fisek, 1983), defines status as having characteristics that are differentially evaluated in terms of honor, esteem or desirability. Finally, Parsons' (1937) work is widely cited, and to him status is the result of a person's structural position along several dimensions – kinship unit, personal qualities, achievements, possessions, authority and power.

This concern with objectively identifying structural indictors of status is of less interest to the more individualistic social psychologists. For example, Secord and Backman (1974) suggest, ". . . which attributes contribute to status will depend on the persons making the evaluations . . . (p. 274)", making status a wholly individual subjective assessment. However, this hyper-individualism also is unsatisfactory – status is a judgment within a social context and so one would expect evaluations of it to have at least some social consensus. Further, the concept's usefulness as a predictor of individuals' attitudes and behavior becomes limited if it is reduced to an idiosyncratic intra-psychic state.

We address this potential dissensus on the prestige of different status positions by suggesting that the social grouping or referent need always be specified. We propose a formal definition: status refers to position or standing with reference to a particular grouping. To have high social status is to have a respected or honored standing in that grouping. Thus, a person's status is always with reference to a particular grouping and involves others' evaluations that one occupies a respected position there.

Finally, we note that the reference to honor is worth our attention. Status connotes respect and integrity. This helps differentiate status from power. Although some have used status and power interchangeably (e.g. Ibarra, 1993), we suggest the distinction is an important one, particularly in organizations. When people defer to those with high status, they do so because they think deference is the proper thing to do, not because the person wields power over them. Status may be correlated with power in many circumstances, but it is necessary to distinguish deference to those with the power to help or hurt you from deference to those you honor and respect.

Status is not synonymous with power; similarly it is not equivalent to position in an organizational hierarchy of authority. Clearly, those occupying higher hierarchical positions may not be the most honored and respected members of the organization (any professor could tell you that). In the organizational sciences, too many have equated hierarchical position with status. For example, Driskell and Salas (1991) used status interchangeably with organizational rank in their study of stress and decision-making. Nor is status the same as self-esteem (Schlenker & Gutek, 1987) or social capital (Belliveau et al., 1996), although having a high status may contribute to both.

As such a fundamental social fact with important implications for one's own behavior and others' treatment of one's self, it isn't surprising that status has been extensively studied in the fields of sociology and psychology. However, much of this work is not relevant to this discussion of leaders' decisions to undertake organizational change in response to globalization pressures. For example, a major area of inquiry centers on how people of differing statuses behave in interaction with one another (e.g. Blau, 1994; Brewer & Kramer, 1985; D'Aveni, 1996; Greenberg, 1988; Levine & Moreland, 1990; Tyler, 1999; Webster & Hysom, 1998). An important variant of this work is the study of how status differences affect participants' expectations of one another, most prominently Berger et al. (1983) and Berger and Zelditch's (1998) Expectation States Theory. Similarly, normative expectations regarding interaction patterns that support others' claimed status, called "facework" by Goffman (1959), is receiving increased attention with studies of East Asians' cultural preference for interactional support of a respected social standing (e.g. Doucet & Jehn, 1997; Earley, 1997). The sociological and psychological work that is most relevant to this argument is why people value having high status, how others decide whether or not one has high status and how one selects the reference group in which to strive for status.

The Value of High Social Status

If leaders' desires for a respected social standings drive their behavior, it is important to understand why this should be so. Certainly it would appear obvious to readers that having high status leads to desirable advantages and that people will make efforts to obtain those advantages. After all, a major component of the world economy is the production of costly display goods, and many economists have studied "positional goods," those valued not for their intrinsic value but because they compare favorably with others (Hirsch, 1976). Nevertheless, the documentation provided by empirical work in psychology and sociology makes the point vividly (summarized in Table 1).

There is extensive documentation of the advantages that relatively higher social status gives those who have it. For example, status in one domain tends to generalize to other domains. Webster and Hysom (1998) found that higher levels of educational attainment in others led laboratory subjects to assume that

Table 1.   Summary of Empirical Research on Status.*

Factors that Lead to Greater Status	Consequences of Higher Status
Working in a Prestigious Occupation	Higher Status in other Domains
Lineage Prestige	An Assumption that One is Competent in Unrelated Domains
Displaying Status Objects	
Higher Formal Education	Easier Performance Standards
Material Wealth	Disproportionately Higher Rewards
Membership in an Elite Organization	Greater Mobility Opportunities
Superior Task Performance	Greater Deference from Others
Being Articulate and Assertive (without being hostile and dominating)	More Influence Over Others
	Dominant Interpersonal Behavior
Maintaining Eye Contact	Less Expressive Behavior
Occupying a High-status Physical Space (e.g. sitting at the head of the table)	Greater In-group Bias

* See text for citations.

they had greater task competence, even when such competence was unrelated to education. In addition, Szmatka, Skvoretz and Berger (1997) found that those with higher status were held to easier performance standards than were those with lower status. Kilduff and Krackhardt (1994) found that being perceived to have a prominent friend boosted a person's reputation as a good performer. Status also generalizes from organizations to the members who participate in them (e.g. Elsbach & Kramer, 1996).

Furthermore, those with high status receive disproportionately higher rewards, particularly financial ones. Stuart, Hoang and Hybels (1999) showed that having high-status affiliates shorten a firm's time to initial public stock offering, and produced greater valuations compared to firms who lacked high status affiliates. D'Aveni (1996) found that high-status university degrees affected mobility opportunities. This effect seems to be particularly pronounced under ambiguous circumstances – as others seek some evidence of the person's competence. For example, Chung et al. (2000) found that high-status investment banks were more likely to form alliances with others of high status under the more ambiguous circumstances of an initial public offering then in less uncertain underwriting deals. Similarly, Pfeffer (1977) found that occupying a higher social class was a better predictor of organizational advancement in the (pre-deregulated) U.S. banking industry than in manufacturing where there were clearer measures of individual performance.

What is more, those with high status appear to be able to obtain more deference from others, and so to be able to get more of what they want. Berger and Zelditch (1998), Lovaglia, Lucas, Houser, Thye and Markovsky (1998), Szmatka et al. (1997), and Webster and Foschi (1988) all found that those with higher status received more deference from others. Levine and Moreland (1990) concluded from their review of social psychological laboratory research on the subject, that people with higher status have more opportunities to exert social influence, try to influence other group members more often and are indeed more influential than people with lower status. Others have documented differences in behavior patterns consistent with this expected pattern of deference. High-status individuals were characterized as more dominating and less expressive (Carli, LaFleur & Loeber, 1995; Gerber, 1996), and they are more prone to in-group bias than lower status individuals (Ng, 1985).

So occupying comparatively higher status positions provides advantages, such as the assumption of competence in unrelated domains, greater rewards and more deference from others. No doubt this is a partial list. Non-financial advantages are more difficult to track in public records, and these psychologists needed to work only with advantages that may be ethically manipulated in a laboratory setting. Given these status advantages, and the likelihood of others, we should not be surprised that the leaders in our studied transition societies would react with energy and alarm to threats to their respected positions. We would expect the same reactions by leaders, or anyone, whose respected social standing was threatened by changes that undermine their preeminence.

Status Attainment

Sociologists, in particular, have documented how comparatively high status is obtained. Weber (1914/1978) proposed that social worth was based on occupational prestige, lineage prestige, style of life, formal education and, in the long run, material wealth. Having more money seems to be a universal route to higher status. For example, Nee (1996) recorded that as market reforms were introduced in China, the status value of being a cadre (communist party activist) declined in favor of working in private business, because the changes meant cadres controlled an increasingly smaller proportion of financial resources. Similarly, higher levels of education (Bidwell & Friedkin, 1988), working in a high-status occupation (Kanekar, Kolsawalla & Nazareth, 1989; Riley, Foner & Waring, 1988) and memberships in elite organizations (D'Aveni

& Kesner, 1993; Kadushin, 1995) are avenues to higher social status in the larger society.

Task performance in work settings also appears to be a reliable route to higher status (Shackelford, Wood & Worchel, 1996). In this study, individuals enhanced their status by demonstrating superior ability at the task assigned to the group. This suggests that behaviors that are useful to the group or organization may be the basis for a gratitude that generalizes to respect and high social standing.

Yet there appear to be easier routes to high status. Sundstrom and Sundstrom (1986) documented the value of status-object displays. Further, those who spoke more, and were more articulate and assertive without being hostile and dominating (Driskell, Olmstead & Salas, 1993; Skvoretz & Fararo, 1996) received attributions of higher status. Finally, non-verbal behavior such as maintaining eye contact and choosing the head of the table (as opposed to being assigned to sit there) also resulted in others' attributions of higher status (Berger & Zelditch, 1998).

Globalization would certainly affect many of these status characteristics. It is disconcerting when foreigners have never heard of (and so do not appreciate the value of) your alma mater. It is hard to be articulate and talkative in a language you are struggling to master. And since status generalizes from your organization, its relative degradation – because it is becoming impoverished by new demands and because the features that gave it status before are now seen as embarrassments – plunges many participants into new and frighteningly degraded positions. For example, for state-owned firms, having large numbers of employees gives the organization greater political power, and therefore greater claims on state resources. However, globalization shifts the value to efficiency, transforming these "national champions" into over-staffed "dinosaurs."

Status in Which Social Group?

Given the numerous advantages of having high status, it isn't surprising that striving for higher status has been found in many settings. Long ago Barnard (1938/1968) proposed that prestige was an important inducement in organizations, with Maslow (1943) proposing that the esteem of others was one of the fundamental human needs. Troyer and Younts (1997) suggest that one of the primary motivations for individuals' participation in groups is the avoidance of status loss. Waldron (1998) proposes a biological need to strive for status,

> Founded in the principles of natural selection, the central thesis from evolutionary psychology is that particular psychological and physiological mechanisms – in this case for

status – would have been selected for in the history of our species because of the adaptive advantages that . . . status afforded individuals would have been greater access to scarce and sought-after resources (Waldron, 1998, p. 511).

Further, confirmation comes from the study of those who find themselves with conflicting statuses – they tend to emphasize the high ones and downplay the low ones (Elsbach & Kramer, 1996).

Yet in complex societies there are many possible social groupings, making the selection of the group in which individuals will strive for status problematic. To address this question, Frank (1985) reviewed a wide range of research in biology and economics and concluded that the social groups closest to the individual generally will be preferred. Such groups may be closer through physical proximity, perceived similarity or frequency of interaction.

Globalization brings distant groups closer and increases interactions among them. Globalization makes previously unknown or irrelevant groups known and relevant, disrupting existing status relations. To Hungarians under communism, the fact that Western European and North American executives were richer and made more attractive products created no status anxiety – the foreigners were too different and distant to be comparable. But when these foreigners arrived in numbers, set up plants across the street and customers began buying their products, it proved a socially degrading experience for Hungarian leaders. Particularly, when globalization brings groups that are wealthier and have higher performance – two dimensions that are powerful determinants of status – into direct physical proximity and interaction with those who have less of these advantages, it isn't difficult to predict which group's status rankings and values are likely to prevail. For those leaders who had operated in local or national markets, globalization has the same social effect as being forcibly moved from a rural village to the capital city. You find that your respected social standing is gone, and you aren't very good at what is respected in these new social circles. No one likes being seen as an inept rube.

RESPONDING TO PRESSURES FOR CHANGE

To illustrate the applicability of the status research from sociology and psychology to leadership, observations of the desire for respected social standing on leaders' behavior are taken from the first and third authors' longitudinal study of organizational behavior in societies in transition from communism (see Pearce, in press; Pearce, Bigley & Branyiczki, 1998; Pearce & Branyiczki, 1997; Pearce, Branyiczki & Bakacsi, 1994; Pearce, Branyiczki & Bigley, 2000). We were able to closely observe leaders' approaches to changing their organizations in three organizations taken from a larger sample over six years (1989–1995). The pressures for change in Hungary at the time of data collection, and leaders' approaches to change in these three organizations are briefly described here. This is followed by a more detailed analysis of the role of status in those leaders' decisions to make changes.

Economic Transformation in Hungary

During the communist era, Hungary was a pioneer in establishing reforms that provided greater autonomy for enterprise managing directors (the European equivalent of chief executive officers) by implementing different initiatives seeking to mimic marketplace incentives by, for example, mandating monetary incentives for meeting performance targets, generating hard currency (sales outside Soviet-controlled countries), strategic planning requirements, among many others. Also, during this period, political constraints slowly loosened with more foreign travel by managers and professionals and less threat of political retaliation for those who kept low profiles. This is in contrast to other countries, such as Czechoslovakia and Romania, where people and enterprises remained more extensively constrained until the political transformations of late 1989. The Hungarian reform communist government fell to a coalition of conservative parties in contested elections in early 1990. This coalition government struggled with demands for political freedoms and economic transformation in an environment of severe economic collapse. It introduced many new initiatives, but had difficulty seeing all of them through under these extraordinary circumstances. This conservative government was replaced by a left-of-center coalition in 1995.

We have sufficient data regarding leaders' change efforts in three organizations from the Hungarian longitudinal study. All three organizations were state-owned when the study began in 1989, and the two that were not privatized in 1990 struggled with changing privatization mandates, financial regulations and political pressures in what was a highly politicized period for state-owned organizations (for more on this period in Hungary, see Antal-Mokos, 1998; Stark, 1996). The first and third authors collected longitudinal data consisting of structured and unstructured interviews, archival and popular press reports and employee questionnaires from late 1989 through 1996. Only data from the unstructured interviews with the top executives and observations of their actions are used here. The original organizations were sampled to provide as much variance as possible on the dimensions of service/ manufacturing, foreign partner/domestic, and capital city/outlying regions while keeping the sample size small enough for in-depth data collection.

Respected Managing Director Succeeds in Privatizing His Company

The Elevator Company manufactured, installed and serviced elevators for the Hungarian market. In January 1990, the elevator company signed a joint-venture agreement with a Western elevator company in which virtually all of its operating functions were to be transferred to the joint venture by the end of that year. The managing director was successful in taking this company through what was later disparagingly called "spontaneous privatization." This was a highly respected achievement in the early 1990s; countless bureaucratic hurdles in what was still a communist government had to be overcome, and he even had succeeded in generating a bidding war between two Western elevator companies allowing him to negotiate favorable terms for the joint venture (not especially for himself). This consummate performance of skills highly valued prior to the transition had earned him great visibility and respect among the community of executives in Hungary.

The new joint venture moved into a section of the old parent's large industrial plant in late 1990 and began with 75% ownership by the West-European company and 25% by the large state-owned industrial combine. The managing director had been able to select only the most desirable workers from the old parent for what all saw as a more secure employer. This managing director had a great deal of autonomy and was compelled by the new owner to change only the accounting system to conform to the parent's system. There was a local representative of the parent on-site, but his role was strictly advisory, the managing director was free to make any changes he deemed appropriate. In 1991 the managing director worked with his counterparts in Western Europe to change the accounting system, buy new "Western" company cars and office furniture, as well as seeking to purge the company of some of its most egregious old-system practices. For example, the management had long been aware that some of the elevator service technicians would insert "bugs" into the elevators they were responsible for servicing. When the bug disabled the elevator, the technician would offer to provide a better quality service than the company did for a "private fee." One of the managers' first acts when the joint venture was finalized was to crack down on these technicians, stating that the new foreign owners "would not put up with it" (in fact, the new owners knew nothing about this practice). The managers were quite proud of their success in eliminating this irritating problem.

Unfortunately, the Elevator Company's financial performance deteriorated significantly with the recession arising from abrupt economic changes beginning in 1990. Housing was now completely private, and apartment dwellers, who now had to pay for their own services, looked for contracts with more responsive and inexpensive providers. Further, with more freedom to choose their own housing, many people preferred to buy or build houses in the suburbs rather than flats in state-owned apartment complexes, devastating elevator-using new-apartment construction. The managing director rebuffed repeated requests from the parent for a plan that would stop losses under these new economic conditions. The managing director continued to explain that these changes in economic conditions were not his fault, he produced no substantive changes and continued to run deficits. In March 1994 he and a few other executives were fired and two Hungarian-speaking foreigners (descendants of Hungarian émigrés) were retained to undertake the changes necessary to restore the company to profitability.

In analyzing this managing director's reversal in fortunes, he did not appear to work as actively as necessary to respond to the new requirements. One reason was that he did not perceive that the profitability numbers were a serious matter to the new parent, rather than the formalistic exercises they were under reform communism (see Pearce & Branyiczki, 1997; Pearce, 2001, for a more extended discussion of perceptions during the transition).

Nevertheless, at least one reason for his choice not to undertake change seemed to be the very exalted position he occupied among Hungarian executives. He had been a very visible success and so must be competent. His confidence in his own prowess, and focus on the social grouping where he was so respected rather than on his new bosses, blinded him to the seriousness of the latter's concerns. From his perspective they were foreign, "other," and just didn't understand that it was more important to retain the loyalty of skilled technicians than to reduce financial losses.

Recovering Lost Status by Saving a Company
The Porcelain Factory was founded in 1777 by a count on his remote estate near what is now the Slovakian border. It is one of the three prominent Hungarian porcelain manufacturers, valued for its historic line of hand-painted porcelain. In 1990 about 80% of its revenue came from the domestic market, with sales through the state retail distribution network and a few of its own small shops. The managing director began taking newly offered courses in Western management techniques in 1988 and in the spring of 1990 decided he needed to get rid of what he saw as some non-performing middle mangers. However, several of these targeted middle managers were on the company council, an entity with similar rights and responsibilities as boards of directors in market economies. It was one of the reform-era experiments that was intended to provide more local surveillance of companies, but usually was packed with the managing directors' dependent middle managers. In response

to his talk of dismissals, the company council's middle-management member-ship decided this managing director was too dangerous and so fired him in June 1990. This innovative assertion of what previously had been formalistic powers was national news for a while.

The first managing director was followed by one of the deputy directors (equivalent to American vice presidents) who served as acting managing director until a consortium of state-owned banks acquired ownership of the company in bankruptcy proceedings in early 1992. He was demoted back to deputy. During this time, the acting managing director made no changes and he waited. The new board hired a Hungarian-speaking American with some experience in porcelain sales as managing director in late 1992. This third managing director added sales and marketing functions, but ran up large expenses on expensive cars and new office furnishings for himself, while the company continued to be unable to cover its operating expenses (to say nothing of making payments on its large bank debt). Angered by his performance, the board fired him after only one year (October, 1993).

A member of the board then contacted a retired executive from the pharmaceutical industry and persuaded him to move to this remote village to try to save the Porcelain Factory. The executive had had the misfortune to retire before the transition and found that he could not live on a pension decimated by inflation. He accepted the position and immediately began to undertake major organizational changes. In the first week this fourth managing director prepared a brief financial statement for all of the middle managers showing the company's precarious financial situation and repeated the stern warning he had received from the board – either the company can cover its operating costs in one year or it will be shut down. He developed task forces to work on several aspects of their central problem – quality. That first week he also walked the perimeter of the large physical plant late at night with a flashlight looking for the holes in the fences that thieves were using to enter the property and steal porcelain.

This managing director quickly discovered that the company needed a complete restructuring of its work processes but realized there was no money to hire expensive consultants. He reasoned that the Porcelain Factory could get this know-how by becoming a production facility for nearby German porcelain companies capitalizing on the Hungarian company's low labor costs. He had secured a contract as a production facility and began its operations within his first year. The fourth managing director set priorities and developed creative innovations to overcome his considerable constraints. After two years of his leadership, the company was making an operating profit and the German partner was readying plans to form a joint venture to invest in a new facility with the energy-efficient curing ovens this company desperately needed.

Certainly, in this case there were substantial differences in the abilities of the Porcelain Factory's different managing directors – its outlying location had created an isolated environment for the managers who knew only this company and village, and its isolation had made it difficult to recruit talented people. The company did face overwhelming problems: dated products that no one wanted when more stylish Western alternatives became available, quality problems in products (hand-painted porcelain) that would normally be placed up-market as expensive luxury goods, energy-wasting ovens from the 1930s and a distrustful workforce. Nevertheless, none of the earlier managing directors sought status outside their local social circles, circles that did not welcome change. This company was saved because the fourth managing director sought status with reference to shareholders and the broader business community, rather than with reference to the local village. Therefore, he used his extraordinary talents to initiate the changes needed for operational profitability.

The successful fourth managing director had held a position of great respect prior to his retirement. He had worked his way up from chemical engineer to head of the pharmaceutical industry, communist Hungary's successful non-agricultural exporter (with a seat on the ruling Central Committee). He was a man of extraordinary ability who, under more stable circumstances, would have remained a leading figure in the pharmaceutical industry. However, the political changes not only destroyed the respect he had enjoyed (he was a prominent person in the now openly-reviled communist regime), but also decimated his financial standing. The prices of housing and consumer goods quickly moved to Western levels while pensions increased slowly (and pensioners had not had opportunities to save money under communism). Thus, this highly capable, cosmopolitan executive saw his social standing and fortunes collapse. The opportunity to save what many Hungarians considered to be a "national treasure" was an opportunity for him to regain the respected position he had enjoyed (as well as provide the financial support he needed).

An Opportunity to Gain Status
The Specialty Glass Manufacturer made drawn plate glass, laminated security and heat-insulated glass products in a medium-sized city in northern Hungary. Its primary customers were domestic construction and vehicle manufacturers, with about 15% of its sales from exports to the West. The long-serving managing director retired in 1990 after the change in regimes. One of the younger middle managers spoke foreign languages and had been serving as a liaison with a Japanese joint venture that occupied a portion of the

manufacturer's large industrial grounds. This manager's language skills helped him to take advantage of the opportunity to read Western management books and speak with Westerners about their business practices. After a brief service as acting managing director he was appointed managing director in 1991.

The new managing director worked actively to make changes. He reorganized the company, following the form of Western companies in similar lines of business. He completed a large layoff in late 1991, developing an innovative program that actually enhanced employees' trust during this painful process. He established marketing departments, actively pursued promising businesses and worked with the ministries and foreign visitors in the drawn-out privatization process for the Specialty Glass Manufacturer. Nevertheless, despite an operating profit there was little chance of repaying the company's large debts, nor of finding the money to replace the large glass-making furnace that had reached the end of its safe operating life. Three state-owned banks took ownership (in lieu of unpaid debts) in 1992, and when the bank-controlled board blocked the second deal the managing director had negotiated to privatize the company to a foreign firm, he left to lead another local company. The company closed when the glass-making furnace was shut down and the specialty treatment divisions sold to private parties in 1996.

This organizational transformation failed, not because it lacked an energetic and effective leader, but because the state-owned banks that controlled the company were not interested in the formal forgiveness of the unpaid debts on their books involved in a successful privatization. If not for the need to replace the factory's core manufacturing furnace, it probably could have survived until these state-owned banks were privatized or government officials had been able to force the banks' cooperation. The leader had been successful in wrenching large organizational changes in this manufacturing company, all while building the confidence and cooperation of employees through frequent communication via newsletters and meetings. The managing director himself had been quite effective, so much so that he was able to move to a comparable job when he felt he no longer had the board's support.

Again, this managing director was a highly capable individual; however, before the transition his comparative youth would have foreclosed such a responsible position to him. Unlike the managing director of the Elevator Company, he did not come from a position of high status. Rather his status was modest among Hungarian executives. He was viewed as only a valued junior manager. For him, the opportunity to be a respected member of the new rising circle of Western-oriented executives, to be a good manager in the new way, was unleavened by the risk of leaving a respected position in the old. The transition offered him an opportunity to gain status in the new circles, and gain respect in what promised to be the prestige social setting of the future. Thus, he was willing to work hard to master a foreign language and learn all that he could about successful management from foreign sources.

WHY CHANGE?

Most studies of organizational change focus on either the adoption of particular innovations (e.g. Damanpour, 1991; Kanter, 1988) or overcoming what has been called "resistance to a change" (see Burke, 1994; Goodman, 1982; Kotter, 1996). Even those proposing comprehensive models of change (e.g. Nadler & Nadler, 1998) take a decidedly internal focus, giving little attention to how leaders decide what to change. This work has been insightful and useful, but it provides only a limited perspective on organizational change, particularly the kind of massive change required of organizations facing the pressures of globalization and economic transformation. After all, innovation adoption is a rather limited form of change (albeit it may have complex consequences) because what needs to change is assumed. Similarly, those studying resistance to change assume knowledge of what should change, or that what needs to change can be discovered without difficulty. The focus is only on implementation, persuading others to change. The existing change literature has not heretofore addressed the wide variance in leaders' decisions to change and so has not been as useful for understanding the effects of massive economic and political changes on organizations.

The Limitations of Economic Incentives

One reason variation in leaders' decisions to undertake organizational change has received less attention may be that many assume that economic incentives are clear and powerful enough to induce any rational actor to undertake those changes necessary to maximize their outcomes (or those whom they serve as agent). The decision to change is non-problematic, because whether to change or not would be obvious to any sentient being.

Yet, as the Hungarian cases illustrate, not all these leaders responded to the change in economic incentives purported as part of the economic transformations in these countries. Why were economic incentives insufficient? It was assumed by policy advisers that once the profit motive was allowed, organizational leaders would seek to make those transformations enabling them to produce more attractive products more efficiently because the organizations would gain financially. Yet our own observations suggest that as a description of actual leader behavior, this explanation is so stylized as to be meaningless.

Under the old system there were incentives for executives to make their organizations profitable. As the first author has noted elsewhere (Pearce, 1991), in practice under reform communism the financial incentives afforded to executives for reaching financial goals were as attractive as those given to Western-country salaried executives. Rather, the problems with the old system were not incentive problems but capability ones. Executives' actions were constrained and their discretion was limited, fostering bargaining with and lobbying government officials instead of organizational change programs. These constraints undermined the power of the financial incentives in two ways. First, by making actions that would enable managers to achieve financial goals impossible, via numerous bureaucratic constraints. Second, financial in-centives were undermined because in practice financial incentives were attached to targets that all participants realized were impossible, thereby creating a normative expectation that the rewards were an entitlement for effort rather than for results. Measures of results were assumed to be formalistic or symbolic targets. What would actually be rewarded was effort and not being responsible for any bad occurrences. This led to unfortunate misunderstandings with newly arrived Western colleagues, owners and business partners, as we saw happened with the managing director of the Elevator Company. So for most Hungarian executives, the early incentives of the transition did not look sufficiently different from those of reform communism (Pearce & Branyiczki, 1997). This was ambiguity enough to allow leaders to see what they wanted to see.

This blurring of incentives highlights the unexamined assumptions under-pinning theories of directing executives' actions with incentives: that leaders have absolute power and everything else stays constant, making the pay-offs starkly clear. In laboratory studies we can get large changes in individuals' behavior with miniscule differences in financial incentives because the environments are barren of any other signals. Yet executives do not have the same control over organizations that people have over their own bodies, and with changes at the societal level the immediate (and apparently quite long lasting) effect is one of confusion. The changes have so many complex, indirect effects that take so long to work their ways down to individuals that it cannot be said that incentives have changed so much as that incentives have become even more confused. It is not that incentives changes are not noticed, as much as their impact cannot be fathomed. Under this uncertainty it isn't surprising to find so much variability in action. What should be changed in organizations is anybody's guess, and under such circumstances many leaders turn to whatever cues they may gain from their social settings.

Certainly in the long run incentives are shifting, at least in Hungary, which has been quick to mimic the institutional structures of European Union countries. Nevertheless, this work highlights how ambiguous financial signals may appear in practice. The political and economic transition from communism is an extreme case, but it is not unique. All forms of globalization present executives with ambiguous signals. New competitors are different but it may not be possible or desirable to copy them. Perhaps the better course is to change in some other way, or exert political influence to obtain protections as a "national champion?" While leaders may see clear incentives not to fail, deciding what they should change in order to succeed is not always clear.

Yet some leaders did undertake organizational transformations. Why? There were multiple factors involved. One certainly was information or knowledge. Those foreign leaders in our studied organizations arriving from Britain, Canada, France, Germany, Switzerland and the United States brought well-formed conceptions of how organizations should operate. When these foreigners controlled companies, they rapidly sought to impose the standards and procedures used in their home companies. Except for the American managing director of the Porcelain Factory (who had no previous managerial experience), for these foreigners there was no difficulty in deciding what to change; rather for them organizational change was an implementation problem.

However, for the domestic leaders, deciding what to change, or more precisely taking the time and trouble to learn what should be changed, was more problematic. They had an information problem, most knew that, but they varied in their efforts to learn how their organizations should operate under the new conditions. If the foreigners had come by their conceptions of how organizations in their industries should operate by working for decades in their industries, domestic leaders needed to take the trouble to obtain this knowledge. It seemed to us that an important factor in differentiating those leaders who did undertake learning what needed to be changed from those who did not was rooted in each case in their desires to occupy respected positions in their chosen social circles, circles that differed for individual leaders.

Threats to Social Standing

Under the old system there was a widely shared ideal of what a respected manager should do to be a "good leader." As Kostera, Proppé and Szatkowski (1995) have described for Polish managers, the good leader was a good parent – good leaders took care of their employees, found resources for them, tried to protect them and offered ample advice and chastisement when needed. In contrast, bad leaders exploited their employees in order to enhance their own careers, or were weak and foolish and so could not obtain sufficient resources and protection for their dependent subordinates. Under the old system, leaders could obtain status by becoming as close to the ideal as they possibly could.

During the collapse that accompanied the political and economic transformation this ideal came under assault. First, leaders learned that the rich successful Western executives with whom they now came into contact did not share this ideal. What these managers assumed all viewed as respected leader behavior was now openly and directly scorned by prestigious and powerful foreign executives as over-controlling and sloppy. To this new reference group a good leader should focus on performance, be loyal to the organization rather than to their subordinates, and work hard to eliminate cumbersome regulations and practices. In Hungary, a new term was adopted by those holding the new perspective, which distinguished a bad old-system leader, *vezető* (literally, "leader") from the preferred Western model, *menedzser*, (the English, "manager").

These conflicting messages about what one needed to do to be viewed as a respected leader produced a great deal of cognitive dissonance in many leaders, dissonance managed in different ways by different people in the early years of the transition. Some actively embraced the Westerners' ideal of the good leader. Unsurprisingly, most of these were younger people who had been too young to succeed as good leaders under the old system and so had no status to lose by taking the risk. In addition, as we saw for the Elevator Company and early Porcelain Factory managing directors, some leaders were indifferent to the newly imported good-leader model because their status came from local social groupings that hadn't changed what they valued (yet).

The managing director of the Specialty Glass Manufacturer most clearly embraced the new ideal of a respected leader. He self-consciously sought to become a performance-focused manger. The fourth, successful managing director of the Porcelain Factory also held the performance-focused ideal of a good leader, although in his case it had been absorbed decades earlier in his work in the internationally competitive, Western market-seeking pharmaceutical industry under Hungary's reform communism. Interestingly, both of these leaders succeeded by combining elements of both old and new ideals. When the managing director of the Specialty Glass Manufacturer had to cut hundreds of employees, he was careful to do so as paternalistically as possible; for example, not allowing two employees sharing the same household to lose their jobs so no one family would be financially devastated. The managing director of the Porcelain Factory did not shy from personally pressing and hectoring employees who would not change; for example, he went down to the factory floor to argue with porcelain mixers who were reluctant to abandon their informal heuristics for the strict formulas needed to improve quality.

The economic and political transformations in these countries had the effect of placing leaders into closer contact with those who had different systems for conferring respect on organizational leaders. While the Iron Curtain had remained, their richer Western counterparts could be viewed as unambiguous "others" – luckier certainly, but also quite different and utterly incomparable with themselves. The transformation, like globalization more generally, not only upset relatively stable economic systems, it also puts leaders into a different social context, one where important referents view their old practices and standings as less admirable.

Thus, we observed executives struggling with status and standing. While virtually all would be quick to denounce the old system as stupid, many also had built roles for themselves as good leaders that allowed them to maintain respected positions in society. When these images were attacked, unrelentingly attacked, some retreated to the comfort of a familiar circle, while others tried to adapt by adopting at least some of the practices of the Western model of the good leader. This meant taking action to change their organizations (not just care for their people), and demonstrating that they were proactive and performance-focused. Those who more quickly embraced a status based on Western management were quicker to attempt organizational transformations and were more persistent in pushing them through their organizations.

THE POWER OF STATUS

This illustration of the way status can influence organizational behavior suggests insights into the ways that globalization affects leaders' decisions to undertake organizational change. Attaining high status entails many advantages, and substantial evidence from the social sciences was presented indicating that many will seek to attain and hold respected positions of social standing. Observations taken from a larger study of the effects of the transformation of Hungary's political and economic systems after communism were used to suggest that the pursuit of status was a major factor in differentiating those who did not seek to make fundamental changes in their organizations from those who did. Yet, does the field of leadership studies need another concept? Particularly one so closely associated with such well-established ideas as self-esteem and power? As we hope the Hungarian transition cases illustrate, obtaining a respected social status holds great value to many – like money it can be a powerful driver of behavior. Learning more about how status is attained and lost can help us to understand the choices leaders (and others) make. When what needs to be changed is not self-evident – an all too common situation – understanding the drive for status can help predict behavior. It provides the theoretical explanation so often missing in leadership research. For example, it is widely observed that leaders brought in from outside troubled organizations make more changes than those promoted from within (e.g. Wiersema, 1992). An understanding of status suggests an explanation: insiders are more likely to have within-organization reference groups (based on contact over time) and so may be unwilling to make changes that will upset those whose good opinions they value.

The study of status in organizational settings is not without difficulties. For example, we need to determine which reference groups each target individual selects. This can vary widely across individuals and we don't know how easily or quickly individuals may change reference groups over time. We have some guidance in predicting the choice of reference groups (e.g. Frank, 1985), but this doesn't eliminate the need to discover these choices in each setting.

The power of the desire to occupy a respected social status may be most apparent when the accepted routes and attainment characteristics are disrupted, as in political and economic transformation, and in the globalization of previously protected markets. Yet its power in all organizational settings cannot be denied. Professors scheme and pine for titles such as "university professor" that have no material advantage and are understood by only a handful of others. Thousands have undertaken work they despise and sacrificed countless hours of their free time in order to move from a cubicle to an office with real walls. How many people continue to work punishing work schedules because they are afraid of being seen as "less professional" (i.e. having less status)? Our organizations have long given pins, certificates, honorary luncheons and other marks of appreciation intended to bestow status on those they deem worthy. And how many organizations will terminate new managers who are failing at their managerial tasks, rather than demote them back to their old jobs because they assume they could not be effective after such a punishing loss of status? None of us are immune, not withstanding Frank's (1985) observation that so many of us publicly scorn status striving. Something this powerful and pervasive deserves as much attention in our field as economic incentives. Certainly, a more complete understanding of leadership and organizational behavior more generally in the context of globalization calls for closer attention to social status.

ACKNOWLEDGMENTS

Some of these ideas first appeared in the first author's 1998 British Academy of Management Conference address. The Hungarian data collection was supported by Vállalatgazdasági Tudományos Egyesölet (Hungarian Business Economics Society) and an Irvine Faculty Fellowship. The authors wish to thank Alaka Rao for assistance in the literature review, and Chris Zatzick, Lisa Barron, Morgan McCall and Bill Mobley for their helpful comments on earlier drafts.

REFERENCES

Antal-Mokos, Z. (1998). *Privatization, politics, and economic performance in Hungary.* Cambridge: Cambridge University Press.

Barnard, C. I. (1938/1968). *The functions of the executive.* Cambridge: Harvard University Press.

Belliveau, M. A., O'Reilly, C. A., & Wade, J. B. (1996). Social capital at the top: Effects of social similarity and status on CEO compensation. *Academy of Management Journal, 39,* 1568–1593.

Benjamin, B. A., & Podolny, J. M. (1999). Status, quality and social order in the California wine industry. *Administrative Science Quarterly, 44,* 563–589.

Berdahl, J. L. (1996). Gender and leadership in work groups: Six alternative models. *Leadership Quarterly, 7,* 21–40.

Berger, J., Conner, T. L., & Fisek, M. H. (Eds) (1983). *Expectation states theory: A theoretical research program.* Washington, D.C.: University Press of America.

Berger, J., & Zelditch, M., Jr. (Eds) (1998). *Status, power, and legitimacy: Strategies and theories.* New Brunswick, NJ: Transaction.

Bidwell, C. E., & Friedkin, N. E. (1988). The sociology of education. In: N. J. Smelser (Ed.), *Handbook of Sociology* (pp. 449–472). Newbury Park, CA: Sage Publications, Inc.

Blau, P. M. (1994). *Structural contexts of opportunities.* Chicago: University of Chicago Press.

Brewer, M. B., & Kramer, R. M. (1985). The psychology of intergroup attitudes and behavior. *Annual Review of Psychology, 36,* 219–243.

Brint, S., & Karabel J. (1991). Institutional origins and transformations: The case of American community colleges. In: W. W. Powell & P. J. DiMaggio (Eds), *The New Institutionalism in Organizational Analysis* (pp. 337–360). Chicago: The University of Chicago Press.

Burke, W. W. (1994). *Organizational development* (2nd ed.). Reading, MA: Addison-Wesley.

Carli, L. L., LaFleur, S. J., & Loeber, C. C. (1995). Nonverbal behavior, gender, and influence. *Journal of Personality & Social Psychology, 68,* 1030–1041.

Chung, S., Singh, H., & Lee, K. (2000). Complementarity, status similarity and social capital as drivers of alliance formation. *Strategic Management Journal, 21,* 1–22.

Conway, M., Pizzamiglio, M. T., & Mount, L. (1996). Status, communality, and agency: Implications for stereotypes of gender and other groups. *Journal of Personality & Social Psychology, 71,* 25–38.

Damanpour, F. (1991). Organizational innovation: A meta-analysis of effects of determinants and moderators. *Academy of Management Journal, 34,* 555–590.

D'Aveni, R. A. (1996). A multiple-constituency, status-based approach to interorganizational mobility of faculty and input-output competition among top business schools. *Organization Science, 7*, 166–189.

D'Aveni, R. A., & Kesner, I. F. (1993). Top managerial prestige, power and tender offer response: A study of elite social networks and target firm cooperation during takeovers. *Organization Science, 4*, 123–151.

Dollinger, M. J., Golden, P. A., & Saxton, T. (1997). The effect of reputation on the decision to joint venture. *Strategic Management Journal, 18*, 127–140.

Driskell, J. E., Olmstead, B., & Salas, E. (1993). Task cues, dominance cues, and influence in task groups. *Journal of Applied Psychology, 78*, 51–60.

Driskell, J. E., & Salas, E. (1991). Group decision making under stress. *Journal of Applied Psychology, 76*, 473–478.

Doucet, L., & Jehn, K. A. (1997). Analyzing harsh words in a sensitive setting: American expatriates in communist China. *Journal of Organizational Behavior, 18*, 559–582.

Earley, P. C. (1997). *Face, harmony and social structure*. New York: Oxford University Press.

Eisenhardt, K. M., & Schoonhoven, C. B. (1996). Resource-based view of strategic alliance formation: Strategic and social effects in entrepreneurial firms. *Organization Science, 7*, 136–150.

Elsbach, K. D., & Kramer, R. M. (1996). Members' responses to organizational identity threats: Encountering and countering the *Business Week* rankings. *Administrative Science Quarterly, 41*, 442–476.

Frank, R. H. (1985). *Choosing the right pond*. New York: Oxford University Press.

Gerber, G. L. (1996). Status in same-gender and mixed-gender police dyads: Effects on personality attributions. *Social Psychology Quarterly, 59*, 350–363.

Gioia, D. A., & Thomas, J. B. (1996). Identity, image, and issue interpretation: Sensemaking during strategic change in academia. *Administrative Science Quarterly, 41*, 370–403.

Goffman, E. (1959). *The presentation of self in everyday life*. Garden City, NY: Doubleday.

Goodman, P. S. (1982). *Change in organizations*. San Francisco: Jossey-Bass.

Greenberg, J. (1988). Equity and workplace status: A field experiment. *Journal of Applied Psychology, 73*, 606–613.

Hirsch, F. (1976). *The social limits to growth*. Cambridge, MA: Harvard University Press.

Ibarra, H. (1993). Network centrality, power, and innovation involvement: Determinants of technical and administrative roles. *Academy of Management Journal, 36*, 471–501.

Kadushin, C. (1995). Friendship among the French financial elite. *American Sociological Review, 60*, 202–221.

Kanekar, S., Kolsawalla, M. B., & Nazareth, T. (1989). Occupational prestige as a function of occupant's gender. *Journal of Applied Social Psychology, 19*, 681–688.

Kanter, R. M. (1988). When a thousand flowers bloom: Structural, collective and social conditions for innovation. In: B. M. Staw & L. L. Cummings (Eds), *Research in Organizational Behavior, 10*, 169–211.

Kilduff, M., & Krackhardt, D. (1994). Bringing the individual back in: A structural analysis of the internal market for reputation in organizations. *Academy of Management Journal, 37*, 87–108.

Kirkbride, P. S., Tang, S. Y., & Westwood, R. I. (1991). Chinese conflict preferences and negotiating behaviour: Cultural and psychological influences. *Organization Studies, 12*, 365–386.

Kostera, M., Proppé. M., & Szatkowski, M. (1995). Staging the new romantic hero in the old cynical theatre: On managers, roles and change in Poland. *Journal of Organizational Behavior, 16,* 631–646.

Kotter, J. (1996). *Leading change.* Boston, MA: Harvard Business School Press.

Kraatz, M. S. (1998). Learning by association? Interorganizational networks and adaptation to environmental change. *Academy of Management Journal, 41,* 621–643.

Levine, J. M., & Moreland, R. L. (1990). Progress in small group research. *Annual Review of Psychology, 41,* 585–634.

Long, R. G., Bowers, W. P., Barnett, T., & White, M. C. (1998). Research productivity of graduates in management: Effects of academic origin and academic affiliation. *Academy of Management Journal, 41,* 704–714.

Lovaglia, M. J., Lucas, J. W., Houser, J. A., Thye, S. R., & Markovsky, B. (1998). Status processes and mental ability test scores. *American Journal of Sociology, 104,* 195–228.

Marx, K. (1894/1967). *Capital: A critique of political economy* (Vol. 3, edited by F. Engels). New York: International Publishers.

Maslow, A. H. (1943). A theory of human motivation. *Psychological Review, 50,* 370–396.

Murvar, V. (Ed.). (1985). *Theory of liberty, legitimacy, and power: New directions in the intellectual and scientific legacy of Max Weber.* London, Boston: Routledge & Kegan Paul.

Nadler, D., & Nadler, M. (1998). *Champions of change: How CEOs and their companies are mastering the skills of radical change.* San Francisco, CA: Jossey-Bass.

Nee, V. (1996). The emergence of a market society: Changing mechanisms of stratification in China. *American Journal of Sociology, 101,* 908–949.

Ng, S. H. (1985). Biases in reward allocation resulting from personal status group status, and allocation procedure. *Australian Journal of Psychology, 37,* 297–307.

Parsons (1937). *The structure of social action.* New York: McGraw-Hill.

Pearce, J. L. (1991). From socialism to capitalism. *Academy of Management Executive, 5,* 75–88.

Pearce, J. L. (2001). *Organization and management in governments' embrace.* Mahwah, NJ: Erlbaum.

Pearce, J. L., Bigley, G. A., & Branyiczki, I. (1998). Procedural justice as modernism: Placing industrial/organisational psychology in context. *Applied Psychology: An International Review, 47,* 371–396.

Pearce, J. L., & Branyiczki, I. (1997). Legitimacy: An analysis of three Hungarian-West European collaborations. In: P. W. Beamish & J. P. Killing (Eds), *Cooperative Strategies: European Perspectives* (pp. 300–322). San Francisco: The New Lexington Press.

Pearce, J. L., Branyiczki, I., & Bakacsi. G. (1994). Person-based reward systems. *Journal of Organizational Behavior, 15,* 261–282.

Pearce, J. L., Branyiczki, I., & Bigley, G. A. (2000). Insufficient bureaucracy: Trust and commitment in particularistic organizations. *Organization Science, 11,* 148–162.

Pfeffer, J. (1977). Toward an examination of stratification in organizations. *Administrative Science Quarterly, 22,* 553–567.

Riley, M. W., Foner, A., & Waring, J. (1988). Sociology of age. In: N. J. Smelser (Ed.), *Handbook of Sociology* (pp. 243–290). Newbury Park, CA: Sage Publications, Inc.

Schlenker, J. A., & Gutek, B. A. (1987). Effects of role loss on work-related attitudes. *Journal of Applied Psychology, 72,* 287–293.

Scott, J. (1996). *Stratification and power: Structures of class, status and command.* Cambridge, U.K.: Polity Press.

Secord, P. F., & Backman, C. W. (1974). *Social psychology* (2nd ed.). New York: McGraw-Hill.

Shackelford, S., Wood, W., & Worchel, S. (1996). Behavioral styles and the influence of women in mixed-sex groups. *Social Psychology Quarterly, 59*, 284–293.

Skvoretz, J., & Fararo, T. J. (1996). Status and participation in task groups: A dynamic network model. *American Journal of Sociology, 101*, 1366–1414.

Stark, D. (1996). Recombinant property in Eastern European capitalism. *American Journal of Sociology, 101*, 993–1027.

Stuart, T. E., Hoang, H., & Hybels, R. C. (1999). Interorganizational endorsements and the performance of entrepreneurial ventures. *Administrative Science Quarterly, 44*, 315–349.

Sundstrom, E., & Sundstrom M. G. (1986). *Work places: The psychology of the physical environment in offices and factories*. New York: Cambridge University Press.

Szmatka, J., Skvoretz, J., & Berger, J. (Eds) (1997). *Status, network, and structure: Theory development in group processes*. Stanford, CA: Stanford University Press.

Troyer, L., & Younts, C. W. (1997). Whose expectations matter? The relative power of first- and second-order expectations in determining social influence. *American Journal of Sociology, 103*, 692–732.

Tyler, T. R. (1988). The psychology of authority relations: A relational perspective on influence and power in groups. In: R. M. Kramer & M. A. Neale (Eds), *Power and Influence in Organizations* (pp. 251–260). Thousand Oaks, CA: Sage Publications, Inc.

Tyler, T. R. (1999). Why people cooperate with organizations: An identity-based perspective. *Research in Organizational Behavior, 21*, 201–246.

Waldron, D. A. (1998). Status in organizations: Where evolutionary theory ranks. *Managerial & Decision Economics, 19*, 505–520.

Weber, M. (1914/1978). *Economy and society: An outline of interpretive sociology* (Vol. 2, edited by G. Roth & C. Wittich). Berkeley, CA: University of California Press.

Webster, M., Jr., & Foschi, M. (Eds) (1988). *Status generalization: New theory and research*. Stanford, CA: Stanford University Press.

Webster, M., Jr., & Hysom, S. J. (1998). Creating status characteristics. *American Sociological Review, 63*, 351–378.

Wegener, B. (1992). Concepts and measurement of prestige. *Annual Review of Sociology, 18*, 253–280.

Wiersema, M. F. (1992). Strategic consequences of executive succession within diversified firms. *Journal of Management Studies, 1*, 73–94.

Weisband, S. P., Schneider, S. K., & Connolly T. (1995). Computer-mediated communication and social information: Status salience and status differences. *Academy of Management Journal, 38*, 1124–1151.

PART II

LEADING INTERNATIONAL TEAMS AND ALLIANCES

INTRODUCTION: LEADING INTERNATIONAL TEAMS AND ALLIANCES: CONNECTING THE LEOPARD'S SPOTS AT A DISTANCE

William H. Mobley

Globalization and technology bring new opportunities and challenges for leadership. Several chapters in both Volume I and Volume II of *Advances in Global Leadership* have discussed how traditional organizational structures and traditional hierarchical leadership are giving way to new structures, e.g. flatter structures, joint ventures and alliances. Refer to the chapters by Kiely and by Isabella and Spekman in this section and the chapter by Wang (1999) in Volume I. Traditional hierarchical leadership structures also are giving way to distributed, team and virtual leadership processes on a global basis (refer to the Crabtree chapter in Section I and the Kiely and Eyring chapters in this section.) Alliances are growing rapidly. What are the leadership requirements of alliances and how do these requirements generalize to other organizational forms? The Isabella and Spekman chapter in this section speaks to these issues directly. How do we find the global leadership "leopard" and connect the "leopard's spots" in this long distance, distributed, virtual environment?

It is interesting to note that the member firms of the PDI Global Research Consortia (GRC), a group of mature, sophisticated multinational firms from multiple sectors of the economy, are hunting this leopard. GRC members have on their priority research and learning agenda the topic of multinational joint

Advances in Global Leadership, Volume 2, pages 181–184.
ISBN: 0-7623-0723-4

venture leadership and team effectiveness, and virtual/distance leadership and teaming on a global basis.

How can the rapidly expanding communications technology be most effectively used in global teaming and leadership? The chapters by Kiely and by Eyring give us some valuable insights. What is the role of culture in the virtual world? The chapters by Kiely, Eyring, and Gibson, Conger & Cooper look at this issue and suggest that cultural differences are important. Creth (1995) noted the friction caused by "matter" moving at different speeds. She observed that markets, information, currency, goods and people are moving at accelerating rates globally, while cultures, shared values and beliefs, and religions are changing at a much slower rate. We see daily the results of the friction in this differentially moving matter, frictions that cannot be ignored by leaders.

In this section, four informed and informative chapters address issues of structure, connectiveness, teams and leadership. Laree Kiely illustrates how globalization, competition, speed and technology have converged to drive flatter organizations, with team processes and electronic communication at the core. She then leads us through an engaging analysis of international virtual executive teams, and multicultural senior executives in multinational organizations located throughout the world. She articulates the challenges, problems and solutions, payoffs, technology, economic, political and philosophical issues faced by such leadership teams. She differentiates types of virtual teams, then focuses on three areas of difficulty faced in global leadership in a virtual environment – *culture*, *trust* and *collaboration* – and suggests strategic approaches to addressing these difficulties. As did Graen and Hui (1999) and Wang (1999) in Volume I of *Advances in Global Leadership*, she argues for creating a hybrid or blended international corporate or team culture and offers some suggestions for accomplishing this goal.

Isabella and Spekman present a lucid analysis of the nature of strategic alliances and leadership requirements of strategic alliances. They argue that strategic alliances offer the kind of organizational context that encourages development of a new kind of leadership. They see primary roles of alliance managers to include that of visionaries, strategic sponsors, advocates, networkers, facilitators and managers. Further they argue that the attributes of effective alliance leaders and managers are the foundational characteristics of global leaders of the future. Pattern recognition, ability to synthesize and generalize, learning from experience, the cognitive orientation (i.e. how leaders think, see and connect the rapidly changing milieu), openly sharing and caring, a mindset nurtured and invigorated by learning, complexity and ambiguity . . . these are the characteristics they believe global leaders of the future should possess. How many of these factors are included in standard corporate competency models? Finally, Isabella and Spekman provide some valuable guidance on the importance and "how-to" of developing effective alliance managers and leaders.

Gibson, Conger and Cooper join the chorus by noting that much of the research on teams has been country specific, particularly the U.S.; yet international organizations are faced with developing effective team-based systems on a global basis. Drawing on the literatures on small group processes, cultural diversity, cross-cultural leadership, conflict resolution, perception and team effectiveness, they develop a model of *perceptual distance*, the variability in perceptions of a team leader's behavior or the team's behavior in relation to team leadership and team outcomes. They utilize Hofstede's (1984) cultural characteristics of power distance and collectivism to examine the cultural moderating effects on the relationship between perceptual distance and outcomes. They frame some important hypotheses that have implications for leaders and team functioning in different cultures and provide some useful insights on bridging cultural differences.

The Eyring chapter takes a practical look from an Asian perspective of three challenges faced in long-distance leadership: creating an environment of effective communications, particularly in high context cultures; building alignment around business strategy in the cultural context of roles, relation-ships and responsibilities; and fostering individual and group learning in the face of differences in learning styles. Drawing on her experience as an internal and external consultant, Eyring offers some useful suggestions for dealing with these challenges.

Some common themes emerge in these four chapters. Perceptual and cognitive processes appear to be particularly important in cross-cultural, virtual, and alliance leadership and teaming. This is consistent with the emphasis of Dickson et al.'s review of cross-cultural leadership in Section I. Second, the notion that effective leaders, be they global, virtual, alliance or other, must be able to be highly perceptive and must benefit and learn from experience – a notion emphasized by McCall, Lombardo and Morrison (1988) in *Lessons of Experience: How Successful Executives Develop on the Job* – continues to find support. Third, the concept of creating a hybrid, third or blended culture in multinational organizations is receiving increased attention and currency. Fourth, the importance of relationships and the challenges of developing, nurturing and deepening relationships are important in distance leadership and teaming. Electronic communications are not a substitute for face time.

REFERENCES

Creth, S. (1995). Creating a virtual information organization. *Educom Review*, 15–17.

Graen, G. B., & Hui, C. (1999). Transcultural leadership in the 21st century: Challenges and implications for development. In: W. H. Mobley, M. J. Gessner & V. Arnold (Eds), *Advances in Global Leadership* (vol. I). Stamford, CN: JAI Press.

Hofstede, G. (1984). *Cultures consequences: International differences in work-related values*. London: Sage.

McCall, M. W. Jr., Lombardo, M. M., & Morrison, A. M. (1988). *Lessons of experience: How successful executives develop on the job*. New York: Lexington Books.

Mobley, W. H., Gessner, M. J., & Arnold, V. (Eds) (1999). *Advances in global leadership* (Vol. I). Stamford, CN: JAI Press.

Wang, Z. M. (1999). Developing joint venture leadership teams. In: W. H. Mobley, M. J.Gessner & V. Arnold (Eds), *Advances in global leadership* (Vol. I). Stamford, CN: JAI Press.

OVERCOMING TIME AND DISTANCE: INTERNATIONAL VIRTUAL EXECUTIVE TEAMS

Laree S. Kiely

ABSTRACT

Here in the early days of the 21st century, we are hearing those voices around us, which long for the return of the charismatic, individualistic leaders of earlier times. Where are the so-called "leaders of men," the giants of politics and industry who can safely show us the way? We used to be able to recognize them more easily; they stood tall, took little heed of other people's opinions, and spoke authoritatively like him-who-is-to-be-obeyed. But somewhere around New Year's 2000 (or was it earlier?), these titans seem to have become less individualistic. Leadership today seems to be more of a combination of great minds rather than any single intellect. We have come to realize that leaders simply do not and cannot stand alone.

In his book, Organizing Genius, *Warren Bennis (1997) titles the first chapter "The End of the Great Man" and argues that the day of the individualistic, charismatic leader is now past:*

> The myth of the triumphant individual is deeply ingrained in the American psyche . . . .
> In our society leadership is too often seen as an inherently individual phenomenon.
> And yet we all know that cooperation and collaboration grow more important every
> day. A shrinking world in which technological and political complexity increase at an
> accelerating rate offers fewer and fewer arenas in which individual action suffices.
> Recognizing this, we talk more and more about the need for teamwork (p. 1).

Advances in Global Leadership, Volume 2, pages 185–216.
2001 by Elsevier Science Ltd.
ISBN: 0-7623-0723-4

The vastness and complexity of the task in the new century now requires leaders to see far beyond their own individual perspectives, no matter how wise or impressive they may have seemed. To add to Bennis' technology and political complexity, Moran, Harris and Stripp (1993) add culture, rapid change and the shifting nature of work:

> The human family and global business in particular are increasingly intercultural and interdependent. We are in passage from a work culture that conditioned most of us when the Industrial Revolution recast our physical world and reality through mechanization, quantification, and consolidation. We are in transit to a Knowledge Society, dominated by high technology and information processing, a culture marked by mediation (describing and interpreting our world), by simulation and virtual reality (VR), and by circularity (events whipping around us, interacting and shaping experiences). In these circumstances, between epochs, everything we do is cross-cultural and dynamic. (pp. 10–11).

This chapter will focus on what happens to business leadership in an environment like that just described. Clearly the "triumphant individual" is rare, organizational hierarchy is being flattened, team process takes center stage, globalization makes organizations and teams international, and the various electronic communication media become the environment of the new reality. The approach of this chapter will be, first, to examine some of the issues of virtual teams – the challenges, problems and solutions, payoffs, technology, and the array of human, economic, political and even philosophical issues they raise. Secondly, we move to an analysis of three areas of difficulty that face global leadership in the virtual environment: culture, trust and collaboration. As part of this analysis, we suggest strategic approaches for executives to employ in order to solve and preempt some of these problems.

The emergence of "virtual teams" (VT) has become one of the hottest topics in business management literature. And in that literature the subject of leadership comes up often. When it does, however, it is much more likely to discuss middle managers and team members.

What this literature does not talk about much is what goes on with executives *in the new virtual environment of global teams. On one hand, Bennis' "triumphant individual" is passé; on the other hand, executives are still around and functioning as the top leaders of organizations. Although we shall see that most of the research and writing on virtual teams has been done on teams that operate deeper in the organization, it is nevertheless true that senior leaders of international organizations must also collaborate in a virtual environment. The collective knowledge of executive leadership teams plays itself out in a virtual, mediated environment to set the direction and strategy of the entire enterprise. These executive virtual teams may find the challenges of time and space to be even greater, with attendant increases in peril to the organization.*

We want to look carefully and strategically at the needs and challenges facing executive teams who utilize electronic media to run international businesses from widely scattered locations. Our concern is with the international virtual executive team (IVET).

DEFINING INTERNATIONAL VIRTUAL EXECUTIVE TEAMS

For purposes of this chapter, we define international virtual executive teams (IVET's) as groups which are comprised of multi-cultural senior executives (CEO's, presidents, senior vice-presidents, general managers, etc.), are in large, multinational operations or joint ventures, are located in various parts of the globe, have the necessary business acumen, and who make collective, collaborative, and strategic decisions that affect the entire enterprise or a large portion of it. Because business success and the well being of all shareholders and stakeholders depend on the collective and collaborative knowledge and abilities of executive leadership, we must find new and more effective ways to harness that intellectual capital. In other words, to borrow Bennis' metaphor, we must explore new ways of organizing *corporate* genius.

Why Focus on IVETs?

Working as a team with multi-cultural members is difficult enough, but it becomes much more so when the complexities of time, distance, expense, etc., are added to the task of global executives who cannot meet face-to-face. These executive teams then become "virtual" out of necessity, and mediated communication technologies become the means by which they attempt to overcome time and space. The problems that flow from this necessity warrant serious attention. Although business has invested significantly in expensive technology and in understanding and managing virtual teams for project development, problem solving, data gathering and customer service, it has paid much less attention to the virtual environment as it relates to executive and managerial teams.

The New Reality: Virtual Teams

Einstein is reputed to have said that the downfall of this generation would be a perfection of means and a confusion of ends. As technology is perfected, how to best use it remains a mystery. But today both means and ends have become confusing. It's all a blur. Rotating teams of diverse and scattered people conduct business at a dead run on shifting sands. They process vast, morphing databases of fluid information, and aim fast-evolving technologies at moving targets.

A perfect example is the rise of virtual teams (VT) in the late 1990s, the phenomenon of teams whose members are dependent on electronic communication to do their work, "because they are unable to – or prefer not to – meet in person on a consistent basis." (Hagen, 1999). Five years ago the concept of virtual teams was the stuff of brave new worlds poised to become the next wave, waiting on technology to make it possible, wondering what it would be like, in awe of the few companies who had implemented it.

Today the wave has already broken; we're not sure when it broke, but we can tell that it did because we're deep in the reality and the issues of virtual teams. They are happening, succeeding and failing, driving new technologies, promoting and adapting to globalization, wrestling with diversity, pioneering new territory, driving managers crazy, and changing the face of business forever.

The research base on virtual teams is growing, but it has had very little to say about executives and other global leaders. Of course, existing research done on project teams or task forces will have implications for executives as well. The line between leadership manifested by a manager of a project team and "global leadership" is not clearly drawn. As the editors of the first volume in this series observed,

> We struggle with whether the concept of leadership is separate from our concept of management, or whether one is a subset of the other . . . . Thus some authors will describe the challenges of working across multiple cultures simultaneously, as in someone whose job it is to manage a global enterprise . . . . Others will talk more specifically about being an expatriate manager trying to master the intricacies of working in a non-native culture. Both of these perspectives will legitimately be referred to as "global leadership," but the generalizability of the arguments and conclusions from one case to another needs to be carefully considered (Mobley, Gessner & Arnold, 1999, p. xv.).

Thus, we recognize that, like other authors, as we make recommendations to executives, we may be speaking, directly or indirectly, to managers and team members as well. Still, we need to address some significant analysis to top executives themselves.

Necessities and Benefits of Virtual Teams

Ideally, virtual teams are vital to competition in a global market. The VT's immediate access to distant markets and customers and the opportunity for collaboration of geographically divided colleagues is obviously and intuitively advantageous. But company, division and functional boundaries also divide workers. Increased emphasis on customer service means team members need to be available to far-flung clients and customers. Globalization necessitates that cooperative efforts be launched with other related companies or even competitors (Kurland, 1999). In an information-driven age, virtual teams facilitate database enrichment through the centralization of information. Less employee travel and greater centralization of information ideally represents lowered costs and increased effectiveness.

Some firms use VTs to create what one company calls "knowledge centers," calling periodic meetings via a corporate Intranet to build databases and expertise repositories (Hanley, 1999). Solomon (1998) and Lipnack and Stamps (1997) report extended case studies to demonstrate that VTs have intensified customer service and created virtual collaboration with customer teams, producing significant increases in customer satisfaction and loyalty. In addition, studies have shown that virtual teams utilized to promote flexible work conditions are considered desirable by potential employees, making them a recruitment tool for large and small businesses as well (De Lisser, 1999).

Challenges and Problems of Virtual Teams
Early in the game, comparison studies were showing that team face-to-face meetings had systematic advantages over virtual meetings. An early university study comparing face-to-face meetings with electronic bulletin boards (only) concluded, perhaps not surprisingly, that face-to-face is better (Warkentin et al., 1997). However, whether VTs have a "disadvantage" depends on what criteria you apply and the situations you compare. It is widely agreed that face-to-face environments facilitate intense negotiations and problem solving. But with some tasks, such as consulting and data gathering, the VTs may excel. Even when they excel, however, problems and challenges remain. For most team members, there is an initial, sometimes continuing resistance. For some it's technophobia, and technology's promotion of uncomfortable change (Townsend, De Marie & Hendrickson, 1998). For others, it is the inherent limitations of some electronic media: "I don't know about you, but I'm not used to having my rough draft scrutinized by teammates without my being there to explain" (Slack, 1998, p.2).

One very troublesome and systemic disadvantage to VTs is lost creativity and innovation due to reduced informal interaction (Yeung & Langdon, 2000). Some companies, recognizing that the loss of "water-cooler" type interactions represents a liability to creativity and innovation, have assigned VT members to use electronic media for regular social and relational interactions in an effort to get the "water cooler" on-line (Slack, 1999). Hanley (1999) calls this "formalizing informal communities" and reports some success at American Management Systems, Inc. in the creation of a corporate "culture of assistance".

Closely related to the loss of informal communication systems in VTs is the increased difficulty in establishing trust among team members. Duarte and Snyder (1999) devote a chapter to it and virtually every other author on the subject references trust building and trust maintenance as a major challenge. Informal, face-to-face communication that is unavailable to VT members is often a primary channel for trust-building communication. A large study of global VT's by Jarvenpaa et al. (1998) found that trust can be managed and increased in VTs. Teams in various countries were assigned an eight-week collaborative task that included a two-week virtual environment trust-building exercise. The study was interested in whether trust could be increased and also whether perceived integrity (perception that others did what they said they would do), ability and benevolence would contribute to increased trust. The study found that the greatest contributors to increased trust on a VT were, first, integrity, and then ability. Team members' perception that their virtual co-workers were of high integrity seemed to be more vital for trust and team effectiveness than perceptions of co-workers' ability or benevolence.

Lastly, then, consider the last big-ticket problem of global VTs – differences in culture. An extensive review of cultural issues that show up in the work of global VTs is provided in Duarte & Snyder (1999). Preference for working solo among some team members from individualistic cultures will sometimes clash with the need of collectivist members to collaborate and be responsible for the progress of slower team members. Team members from long-term oriented cultures will be more rewarded by opportunities to develop new skills and contribute to future objectives. Team members who are focused on reduced uncertainty will want more structure from managers than members who find uncertainty and ambiguity more acceptable. Members from low power-distance cultures will require less take-charge individualism and more collectivist consultation. These are a few examples of the intercultural complexities that globalization, rotating membership of teams, employee diversity, and techno-logically constrained communication produce.

One of the ways organizations are dealing with individual differences, intercultural problems and the other challenges of VTs is through a combination of assessment and training approaches. Trait-type assessments such as Meyers-Briggs have been commonly employed, and off-site training of many types is common. But as companies see the need for more sophisticated assessments and specific job-related training, they are developing their own assessments related more to skills and preferences, and training team members on the job in more realistic job-specific settings (Baker, 1999).

Types of Mediated Communication and Technologies for Virtual Teams
The conferencing tools these teams employ include real-time or "synchronous" technologies of video conferencing, audio conferencing, desktop and real-time conferencing and electronic meeting systems, plus "asynchronous" or delayed technologies including e-mail, Web pages, database sharing and electronic bulletin boards (Duarte & Snyder, 1997). Actually to say that virtual teams "use" this technology is an over-simplification. Understand that the rise of VTs and the development of the technology making them possible are one intertwined process. It is simultaneously true that technology drives the use of VTs and the use of VTs drives the development of the technology (Hagen, 1999). Solving the problems inherent to the use of VTs will require changes both in team processing and in technology and its use.

Adding up VT's
Most of the authors with whom we have consulted develop some advisory ideas based on their analysis of the problems and challenges of international teams organized for projects or other specific purposes. The advice, however, is generally directed at managers who are responsible for teams with specific organizational assignments. Based on this brief survey, we offer the following observations about the literature on VTs:

- Knowledge about virtual teams is being driven by demands of the market and rapid shifts in the way business is conducted, with the result that formal research is slow to catch up. Most writers' knowledge base is primarily case studies of up-and-running VT enterprises.
- Where executives and upper level managers fit into the VT picture is almost totally missing from the literature. Executive teams appear briefly in their categories list, and a few writers make quick references to executives in passing, but that's about it. The only systematic discussion of leadership at all is in the extensive sections of advice to managers of non-executive teams, and in the occasional treatment of leadership manifested by individual team members.
- Actual communication behavior, that is, what people actually say or write to each other, is recognized by these authors as important, but they put it in as just one of many issues or as an artifact of the more "important" issue of technology. We see this differently. Our perspective, developed below, will be that virtual teams are themselves a process of communication, and that what we're really talking about when we discuss problems of VTs and their

solutions is problems of executive team interaction whose solutions are also grounded in communication choices. The ultimate issue is not a question of having more intercultural training in the virtual environment or being more sensitive to diverse perspectives. Rather, it is the problem of, what we are going to say and how are we going to say it to be effective and efficient.

At least we will attempt to persuade you that these problem areas and the challenges of virtual teams yield to a communication interpretation, and when one does interpret them in this way, the results are significant communication tactics and strategies for effectiveness.

International Virtual Executive Teams (IVETs): The Task

If IVETs existed to simply send instruction and information from headquarters to satellite operations and colonies, the issues would be, perhaps, much simpler. But that is not what teams do; teams are groups of people who have common goals and operate interdependently to achieve goals which could not be achieved by any one individual acting alone. Kenichi Ohmae (1990), who argues that multinational organizations should "decompose the center" or get rid of the headquarters mentality, argues that global companies must make key decisions through the interaction of multiple, international stakeholders.

> No company can operate effectively on a global scale by centralizing all key decisions and then farming them out for implementation. It doesn't work. The conditions in each market are too varied, the nuances of competition too complex and the changes in climate too subtle and too rapid for long-distance management. No matter how good they are, no matter how well supported analytically, the decision-makers at the center are too far removed from individual markets and the needs of local customers (p. 87).

Realistically, however, the stakeholders involved cannot afford the luxury of meeting face-to-face every time an important decision must be made. Thus, we have seen the evolution of International Virtual Executive Teams. IVETs exist in order to make collective decisions, not just to dispense commands or to keep each other informed. Their aim is to make the wisest, most effective and efficient decisions, leading to the most successful implementation in the shortest amount of time. Given that, we should examine those arenas most fraught with challenges and problems in which an IVET must succeed. Keeping in mind that the team must operate collaboratively and in an environment of mediated communication, a "virtual environment," we undertake to examine three critical arenas where the challenges are strong, the problems many and the stakes very high.

1. Navigating through cultural differences

2. Building trust
3. Ensuring collaboration

We have seen in the literature that problems in these three areas create barriers toward the effectiveness and efficiency of IVETs and require the most attention of team members and managers. These arenas or categories of problems are, of course, not discreet; for purposes of analysis, we discuss them separately, and we recommend a series of behaviors, which respond to all three.

Navigating through Cultural Differences

Thinking Clearly about Culture

Ohmae (1990) indicts some lingering assumptions about global organizations by linking them to a distant, outmoded past:

> Colonial administrators – and early global managers – in the old, pyramidal organizations had only crude means to help their people strike an appropriate balance. For the most part, they used brute force: distance and poor communication softened rigidity, and the threat of penalty reinforced shared values. Today brute force is neither necessary nor effective. A new form of organization, organic and amoeba-like, makes that balance easier to achieve (p. 90).

Global business today is dependent upon international cooperation, not the old ethnocentric style of centralized command and control. Effective global leaders must spend a significant amount of time honing their intercultural skills as well as building their business acumen. To quote the Chinese general manager of a multinational pharmaceutical firm: "Doing business here in Beijing is not the same as doing business there in Los Angeles or in London or in Frankfurt. You can't expect to just tell people what to do and have it turn out the way you had hoped". In the 21st century, the reasons for paying attention to cultural differences will increase exponentially.

By their very nature, cultural systems have taught people to think and behave differently from others, and sometimes the differences produce behaviors that are polar opposites from one another. Because of the primitive, tribal need for belonging and the intense desire to manage uncertainty, our cultural systems have also taught us to be suspicious of differences, to think ours is the superior culture. This results both in inclusiveness and exclusiveness. The fact that I know what group I belong to also tells me who does not belong. This would seem almost innate, if there were not the additional issue that many cultures maintain leftover baggage from historical or political events. As Hall, in his seminal work, (1976) has pointed out:

> . . . Anthropologists do agree . . . culture . . . is not innate, but learned; the various facets of culture are interrelated – you touch a culture in one place and everything else is affected; it is shared and in effect defines the boundaries of different groups (pp. 13–14).

In *Managing Cultural Differences*, Harris and Moran (1991) attempt a brief description of how a culture gets to be the way it is. A culture is:

> . . . A way of living developed and transmitted by a group of human beings, consciously or unconsciously, to subsequent generations. More precisely, ideas, habits, attitudes, customs, and traditions become accepted and somewhat standardized in a particular group as an attempt to meet continuing needs. Culture is overt and covert coping ways or mechanisms that make a people unique in their adaptation to their environment and its changing conditions (p. 135).

Chronologically, we could put it this way: cultures evolve as a type of shared history because a group of people goes through a set of common experiences. Those similar experiences cause certain responses. The responses become a set of expected and shared behaviors. Those behaviors become unwritten rules, which become norms that are shared by all people who have that common history or are descendants of that original group.

By the time these commonalties become rules and norms, they have become pre-conscious, or even unconscious; they are a part of us. They become reality – truth, beauty, and justice – and we believe our norms to be the "right" ones and others to be weird, incomprehensible, rude or just wrong.

On a recent trip to China, a colleague of mine tripped over this very issue. We were standing in a crowd of people waiting to visit a temple and the crowd simply "grouped" to go in. My colleague complained to me privately: "Boy these people are rude. They won't line up". So there we were, two people who should know better. How could one of us actually call 1.2 billion people "rude" in their own country!

Rules and Norms
Social scientist Susan Shimanoff (1980) observed that groups of people that share a culture or subculture seem to have sets of unwritten rules – rules that are so imbedded in their culture that they cannot even articulate them, let alone view them objectively. Persons from the outside, when entering or trying to integrate, will often accidentally break the rules. Breaking an unwritten rule offends the insiders and the rule breaker buys a negative reaction.

As a well-known example of unwritten rules, there seems to be a set of expected behaviors in elevators. These rules are not posted on the door, your parents did not sit you down and tell you these rules, they didn't come in a handbook and they are not taught in school. It would be nearly impossible to trace where you first learned this rule of behavior. The rule is, of course, you face the door when you get in. If you turn around and face the other people on the elevator, they become uncomfortable or agitated. They look at their watches, shine their shoes on their pants or look at the ceiling. The theory shows a negative reaction to opposing behavior proves the rule.

Think of times you have gone into a new situation, done something innocently, not even thinking about it, and received a reaction that surprised you – usually a negative reaction. It probably means you have broken an implicit, unwritten rule. For example, many years ago a friend of mine sold his small self-owned software company to IBM. He then took a job in the marketing department of IBM. On his first day of work, people asked why he hadn't done his laundry, or said something ironic about how he would soon be able to buy new clothes. He was shocked; he thought he looked just right – nice jacket, nice tie and a well-pressed BLUE shirt. If you know the history of IBM, at that time people were expected to wear white shirts. It was not in the employee handbook, it was not in the orientation and no one actually tells you because they all just "know", so of course you should know as well.

We should add that many of these rule-like common behaviors come about for a reason. There was a reason why IBMers wore white shirts; their first customers were government and financiers and they were dressing to fit in with their clients – matching their clients' uniforms, as it were. Over the generations, however, the customers changed, but IBM didn't, and to new customer bases, IBM looked stiff, formal and out of touch.

Just as there is usually some reason behind a set of behaviors, as the behaviors continue the reasons may be forgotten, or may even disappear entirely and can no longer be articulated. There's an old story about a woman who, when cooking a ham, always cut off both ends of the meat and threw them away. One day her husband asked why she wasted good meat that way. "It's something about hams", she said, "you just have to do that." Still curious, he asked again. She said, "I don't know, my mother taught me that." So they called the mother. "Why did you teach me to cut off both ends of the ham and throw that meat away to cook it?" Mother replied, "It's just something about hams." Of course when you hear those types of answers -"It's just what you do," "We've always done that," etc – it's a sure sign the reasons are no longer operative and, in fact, are gone. But the mother continued: "Your grandmother taught me that." So they called the grandmother. "Why did you teach us to cut off both ends of the ham and throw that meat away in order to cook the ham?" The grandmother chuckled and said, "I don't know why you do it; I just never had a pan that was big enough."

In highly restricted situations such as IVETs, the differences in our cultural rules and norms can be even more detrimental than elsewhere. To preempt the damage, there are several new "rules" that must become part of our reasoning. The first is that we cannot assume others have exactly the same rules as our own. Second, we must not assume that others are being rude or offensive when their behaviors differ. Third, we must learn to view our norms as objectively as possible. Fourth, we cannot assume that our rules are the right rules; a new set of rules must be negotiated to best fit the circumstances. Nothing will destroy the effectiveness of an IVET more quickly than individuals who have shut down; and nothing shuts down an individual more quickly than negative sanctions.

The very arbitrariness of rules whose origin is forgotten or whose existence is unknown to the people obeying them often makes them difficult to change. For virtual teams to achieve effective teamwork, some of the differences to be negotiated will have to be both inferred through a sensitivity to others and also discovered through a willingness to examine one's self.

A final point, then, about rules, norms, and leadership: Self-awareness is one of the most critical skills for leaders today. The reasons behind our behaviors may have gone away, and we may need to take a look at changing or amending them to allow for more flexibility and adaptation. Complete self-objectivity is impossible, of course, but a willingness to question the assumptions behind our behaviors is vital in an international arena.

Ironically, sometimes our fables surpass cultural differences. I was teaching the "pan" metaphor to a business group in China and one of the participants told me that they had the same fable, only it was played out with a wok! In our international encounters we are often still acting as if our pans aren't big enough, when in the 21st century we may no longer even be cooking in pans. Some of us are still acting like we did when small live meetings of homogeneous team members from the same town were common. As the world changes we have to go back and re-think the way we get things done.

Dimensions of Culture that Threaten the Effectiveness of Mediated Communication

Executive global leaders are not immune to ethnocentrism. While interviewing a Singaporean general manager of a multinational pharmaceutical firm, we were discussing the high percentage and the high cost of expatriates who fail within the first six months of their overseas assignments and are sent home. "I'm not worried about the 40% or so who fail here and are sent home. I am more worried about the 40% who stay here and fail, those who have not learned to love my country and to integrate within it. For example, those who spend all of their free time with other Americans eating only McDonalds and drinking Coke. They do more damage in the long-run." Of course, ethnocentrism and inflexibility are more overt and obvious in overseas assignments, but they still exist in IVETs. Perhaps among some global executives they are more covert, but if so, they are, consequently, all the more insidious. Although at first glance it might seem apparent that language and communication technology would be the biggest hurdles for IVETs, the literature shows, and we are convinced, that the most complex issue, by far, is diversity of cultural background among the executive team members.

How many aspects or dimensions of culture do we have to worry about? It depends on which author you read. Some writers' lists get into double digits as they explore the pitfalls of cultural diversity. Our work as consultants implementing IVETs has shown some of these dimensions have more impact on virtual teams than others, and we suggest the following list as both manageable and IVET-relevant. We shall look at five of these dimensions of culture and the problems they produce, assess their effect on IVETs, then suggest what executive team members can do about them.

Language

Perhaps a culture's most obvious impact on IVETs is in language differences. The problem, however, is not so much that we have different native languages, but rather how we use the one language we share. In general, English is the most commonly shared language in global business today, but that doesn't mean we can really understand each other and certainly does not mean we have access to the same vocabulary or style. For example, the pacing and speed of talk can lead to misunderstanding. Many cultures with a strong politeness norm will not express their confusion. Some suggestions for dealing with these differences in English styles: Pause, wait and read nonverbals if you have access to them through sound or sight. Most importantly, do a process check to ensure understanding. To avoid ambiguity, request feedback to check comprehension.

During a series of interviews of Japanese executives who were members of English-using IVETs, we found that one language-related issue can be overcome by sending written documents ahead of time through e-mail or fax so that ESL team members could be up to speed when the "virtual meeting" occurred. When ESL members had to acquire information verbally and immediately during the decision meeting, they spent so much time trying to understand and trying to translate, they felt unable to participate actively. In fact, decisions were often made without their input because of this translation time problem. This had created resentment, mistrust and crippled collaboration. But an advance look at the written documents gave ESL members the time necessary to get up to speed and collaborate fully.

Articulation difficulties and slang also cause misunderstandings. This problem increases exponentially when trying to converse verbally over mediated tools such as synchronous video or tele-conferencing. Lynn Fan, vice president of marketing at NewTech Infosystems, Inc., gives the example of a Japanese executive who was very confused and offended when a U.S. executive told him he really liked the Japanese executive's proposal and wanted to "step on it." Slang and colloquialisms do not translate well and often cause misinterpretations and conflict. Solutions: (1) Avoid negatives, because a wealth of research says they are difficult to understand. The equivalent idea can be put in the positive, so avoid no's, not's, never's, don'ts, can'ts, and won'ts. Rather than saying, "Don't go into too much detail." say, "Pay attention only to the general trends." (2) Use only observable and literal language; literal language means expressing exactly what you do want. Rather than saying "I'd like to step on it," say, "I would like to do this as soon as possible." Observable language means that which can be seen, heard or actually experienced. Rather than saying, "Don't get too hung up on any one thing," say, "If any one issue raises a concern, please make a note of it and then move on to the next issue." These tools may be difficult to remember in the midst of a meeting, but we have found them to be very effective in solving language issues in IVETs.

One possible exception of the "literal language" rule is the use of stories, metaphors and illustrations. Later in the chapter we show that some cultures are more non-linear and contextual than others are. The people in these cultures are more likely to understand ideas explained through stories than through facts, through pathos (creating a feeling) rather than through logos (facts, statistics, numbers and facts). In addition, collectivist cultures feel more affinity toward you if you share personal stories, especially those from outside of work. The "pan" story is an example of how metaphors can transcend culture differences to create shared meaning.

Finally, consider the possibility that language differences across cultures may actually become *assets*. By calling executive team members' attention to possible misunderstandings, language differences may serve as a reminder to communicate carefully and mindfully. Knowing a colleague's cultural background and language preferences can give us a place at which to begin understanding and collaborating. Taking more care means further enhancing understanding and that leads to better relationships, to trust and cooperation. Perhaps we should be this mindful even when we all speak the same native language.

Tolerance for Ambiguity
Although we now know that an important characteristic for leaders is flexibility and adaptability, especially in the face of rapid change, these perspectives are deep-seated and cannot be changed just by willing them to be so. Some cultures

(and individuals as well) historically have developed a low tolerance for uncertainty. The cultural dimension itself is measured on a continuum from low to high. Tolerance for ambiguity:

> ... Refers to the ability to react to new, different, and at times, unpredictable situations with little visible discomfort or irritation. Excessive discomfort often leads to frustration and hostility and this is not conducive to effective interpersonal relationships with persons of other cultures" (Harris & Moran, 1991, p. 104).

The ability to handle ambiguity and uncertainty is one of many dimensions that differ from culture to culture. In a low tolerance culture, there are more rules and the rules are very specific and inflexible, yet they are often implicit. These cultures often appear more rigid and tend to be more punitive when the rules are broken. Added to this, a high context culture (defined below) that also has a low tolerance for ambiguity is dangerous to a newcomer. Low Tolerance means there are many rules and the High Context means they are more implicit. IVET members can respond to this peril by actively creating and negotiating new rules and making them explicit.

Again, on the surface, differing levels of tolerance for ambiguity look like, and can be, barriers to trust and cooperation. But managed carefully, executive team members with differences in tolerance for ambiguity can be valuable resources for the team. The High Tolerance members will be change agents who take more risks and come up with more creative ideas. The Low Tolerance members will be the ones to create a process with procedures to follow, so that others can be brought on board. In other words, a fully functioning IVET needs both resources.

Power Distance

Some cultures prefer more clearly delineated levels of power and authority. Others resent such clear assignment of authority over others. Part of this is that power is defined differently in different cultures. Depending on the culture, it can be based on one's title, seniority, salary, expertise, age, sphere of influence, etc. Cultures who revere their elders or prefer military-type command and control are called "high power differential". Cultures who believe "all men are created equal," have equal rights amendments and who "empower" their workforce would be considered low power differential.

> The power distance between a boss B and a subordinate S in a hierarchy is the difference between the extent to which B can determine the behavior of S and the extent to which S can determine the behavior of B. "... Power distance, thus defined, which is accepted by both B and S and supported by their social environment is to a considerable extent determined by their national culture" (Hofstede, 1984, p. 72).

More importantly for IVETs is how the power differential issue affects creativity and problem solving. Many Western cultures are low power differential – we resent people who have more power and are disposed to defy them or disagree with them. High Power Differential cultures, however, will not be likely to resist power because of a strong politeness norm or out of fear of sanctions. This means that when the person with the most perceived authority suggests a solution or course of action to a team with High Power Differential members, the suggestion will take on more weight than other ideas. The Perceived Authority's suggestion is most likely going to be chosen, not because it was necessarily right, and certainly not because all options were considered carefully, but because it was the idea of the authority figure in the group. Intentionally or not, the Perceived Authority's idea stifled creativity.

What can we do about this stifling effect of creativity among High Power Differential team members? To enhance creativity and collaboration, the Perceived Authority may need to remain silent or simply ask questions until others have had a chance to voice their opinions. This can be helped by a careful choice of communication technology. Asynchronous tools in virtual environments are excellent for dealing with this cultural dimension. The time delay inherent in these systems enhances members' contributions and ideas without competition from real-time interjections by Perceived Authorities on the team. Later in this chapter we will give you some additional suggestions for virtual environments that allow you to manage power differences in a non-threatening way, and without running afoul of our next culture dimension – the politeness norm.

The Politeness Norm
The politeness norm is one of the ways the High Power Differential plays itself out. It is a form of cultural etiquette or diplomacy closely related to the maintenance of "face." Never underestimate the need of individuals to "save face" and to keep from "losing face." Cultures that have a high power differential and a collectivist perspective have a strong politeness norm as well. It is considered impolite to tell someone in authority bad news or to disagree with him or her. In high power differential cultures, the highest perceived authority is considered responsible for the others. It is a concept that goes back to tribal behavior of hunters and gatherers. If something bad happens, it assumes that the leader is at fault and has failed. The patriarch is in charge and is responsible for the well being of the tribe.

In later human history, telling the king that there was unhappiness or unease within his kingdom was a direct affront; it would make him lose face. If you made the king lose face, his authority with the kingdom would suffer, the well being of his minions would be in jeopardy, etc. This was the beginning of the expression, "shoot the messenger." If you delivered bad news to the king, he was obligated to lop off your head. In this way, a politeness norm can create a group of communication reticents. The problem is, the king may not have liked the bad news, but he needed the information. That was the role of the court jester – the gatekeeper of the kingdom's information. We have already made this point, above: stories, metaphors and examples play a powerful role in communication, not only to illustrate ideas more convincingly, but also to serve as ways to communicate bad news. The jester would sing songs, enact plays and skits, etc. Embedded within this entertainment was the information the king needed to know. But he never had to overtly acknowledge the information.

Consultants and adjutants often serve as the court jesters, not always because of the inability of the internal people to communicate directly and not even because of the risk involved or the lack of courage, but often because of the politeness norm. A corporate client recently told me a story about firing a consultant because he had everyone talking to him and no one talking to each other. "If we can't talk to each other, there is something terribly wrong. We don't treat people badly here. We shouldn't have to hire an outsider for people to have someone to talk to." Well, maybe, but the reticence could have been a result of a culture that was risk-averse and punitive or a culture that had a high power differential, low tolerance for ambiguity, expectations of overt respectful behavior and a strong politeness norm. Maybe the consultant was necessary in this organization.

One way around certain norms or values is to find another norm within that same culture that might be stronger and use it to supplant the dysfunctional norm. If certain executives, because of their cultural heritage, are operating according to the politeness norm of reticence, you may be able to find a value from their culture that supersedes the reticence norm. For example, a cultural collectivist value that is very powerful may come into play. A one-on-one conversation requesting that people discuss issues openly means reminding team members with strong politeness norms that it is in the best interest of the whole organization to assure that information, no matter how troubling, gets out in the open.

Context
In our work with international executive groups we have found context to be the most interesting, complex and confounding of all cultural dimensions. "Context" refers to the need or lack of need of shared background in order to create meaning.

The level of context determines everything about the nature of the communication and is
the foundation on which all subsequent behavior rests (including symbolic behavior) (Hall,
1976, p. 80).

Clarifying how context works, Harris and Moran (1991) observe that:

A high context culture uses high context communications – that is, information is either in
the physical context or internalized in the person. . . . On the other hand, a low context
culture employs low context communications – most information is contained in explicit
codes, such as words." (p. 36).

High context cultures, cultures that require fewer words and depend on the
shared experience of members to generate meaning, are by nature more
homogeneous and have more shared history. For this reason, in a high context
culture such as Japan or Saudi Arabia, there are more implicit rules and
meaning and understanding are shared, implied and assumed. There is more
meaning (and it is more shared meaning) in nonverbal behavior in a high
context culture. The circumstances and shared experiences create the
meaning.

We can all think of little phrases or words that we can utter or nonverbal
signals we can give to our own family members who will know exactly what
we mean without any further explanation. In my family, for example, one
phrase is "Is that you, Sam?" It's a long story, but every member of my nuclear
family knows exactly what it means. That is high context. If you were a
newcomer to my family, it would take about 30 minutes and many verbal
symbols – words – to explain what this phrase means. That's low context. And
even then, I assure you, you still needed to be there to make sense of it.

Low context cultures tend to be more individualistic and heterogeneous, with
multiple histories that are not shared. There is no pre-programmed "memory of
the system," so it takes more information and more words to activate the
system. The problem, of course, is that it decreases information-handling
capacity, thereby increasing the mass and complexity of the system. The rules
must be explicit, verbalized and written down. Shared meaning and
understanding take a lot longer and demand multiple explanations. These
cultures are more verbal and rely more on words and symbols to explain ideas
and concepts. There is more likelihood of misunderstanding here; nonverbal
behavior takes on less meaning or is misinterpreted. There is more
documentation in these cultures and the documents tend to be much longer.

One of our clients is a Japanese-owned company that has colonized
distributors and manufacturers across the globe. When any of the colonized
companies needs to make a decision, it has to go to the Japanese headquarters
first. We were asked to help speed up the decision-making process and to help
them ensure more "yes answers" to their requests from Japan. In addition, the

Japanese sent expats to work in the satellites. These Japanese expats were the only individuals who were allowed to present ideas to the Japanese headquarters. In my interviews with the expats, I asked if they knew which ideas would be given assent and which would be denied before they even took the ideas to the Japanese leadership. They said yes, we know.

Japanese culture is very high context. The members of this society know with less verbal discussion what each other means. They know the context and they know the implicit rules. But implicit rules are just that: implicit, non-articulated, preconscious, non-linguistic. For the outsiders in this case, it was endlessly frustrating. They could not find the patterns in the behavior, yet they were expected to know them. When high and low context cultures work together, we often find that the low context cultures tend to view high context cultures as withholding information and high context cultures tend to view low context cultures as childlike, uncertain, naïve and needing to talk too much.

> A high context communication is one in which little has to be said or written because most of the information is either in the physical environment or within the person, where very little is in the coded, explicit part of the message . . . . A low-context communication is one in which the mass of information is vested in the explicit code, which is typical in individualist cultures. Lots of things, which in collectivist cultures are self-evident, must be said explicitly in individualist cultures. American contracts are much longer than Japanese business contracts. (Hofstede, 1991, p. 60).

High context cultures, however, are often able to articulate what is going on if asked the right questions. With our client, we asked the Japanese expats to articulate any pattern they might have detected in the decision-making process at the Japanese headquarters, and they were able to put it into low-context words for us. Apparently, headquarters most often listened for and agreed to the redeployment of existing resources rather than the request for new resources. Almost any Japanese (high context) person would "just know" this implicitly. The U.S. (low context) counterparts, however, were thrilled to learn this because it changed the nature of their arguments when requesting the "go-ahead" on a new project. They were now able to "profile" their stakeholders and formulate a request that was likely to be approved. As outsiders, they might never have found the pattern that could assure a positive response.

Suggestions for members and managers of IVETs: The more we integrate heterogeneous cultures into teams of people who have to make collective decisions, the more low context we have to be. For IVETs to be most effective they must be low context – at first – and to revert to low context when new members join. But eventually, to be maximally efficient, they must consciously strive to become high context. This means sharing and discussing multiple similar experiences, sharing them in low-context verbal interactions, thus developing shared implicit codes. The more high context a team can become through initially low context shared experiences, the more trust can develop and the more leaders will be able to foster growing collaboration and cooperation. Later in this chapter we will give you actual steps to implement this concept. But let me emphasize this: this kind of trust development, this evolution of a high context culture, cannot begin with mediated communication originally. Use of mediated communication tools will become a context for the shared codes or protocols that can enact the high context, implicit rules. But in order to develop and evolve the high context, low-context, face-to-face interactions are going to be necessary.

A Living-Case Example
The issues of culture play themselves out in very subtle ways among members of international virtual executive teams (IVETs). Perhaps because we expect executives to do great things for our enterprises, we assume they will not be caught up in the subtle problems of culture differences. But real global leaders are made, not born. Part of their development is that they acquire the knowledge and skills necessary to operate outside their own individual culture's assumptions and they learn how to navigate their team's progress through the new international culture of IVETs.

One of our clients, a 42 year-old U.S. CEO, was experiencing many problems with his IVET, largely, we believed, because he did not understand cultural differences, and consequently, did not know how to navigate them. In fact, as he admitted later, culture differences irritated him because he secretly believed his executive team members should act like him. But because they were failing to comply with his wish that they participate more in meetings and act more "empowered," he was about to disband his IVET and start making most decisions on his own, by fiat.

Our client's IVET consisted of the seven international general managers in the overseas manufacturing and distribution operations in China, France, Germany, Holland, Japan, Mexico and Switzerland. He believed, intellectually at least, in the power of teams; the more minds you put on a problem, the better the outcome. But their industry was fast-paced and volatile; success in their market was dependent on how quickly they could think on their feet and make and implement quick, yet effective decisions. All of the team members needed to be located geographically in their own national organizations in order to manage operations, yet the CEO needed their collective deliberations to help him make enterprise-wide, global decisions. To accomplish this, they had regular meetings concerning the many rapid decisions that had to be made. Face-to-face meetings were impossible, so the IVET was created.

The CEO sensed, however, that things were going from bad to worse. In video or audio conferences he was doing all of the talking and, it would seem, all of the thinking. E-mail had taken on a new, formal tone, was received only when he requested information, and seemed more defensive and reactive than informative or helpful. In addition, several other pieces of indirect information were troubling him. First, he had heard from the vice president of human resources (the court jester) that the Japanese were feeling left out and that they were not being heard. (Manifestations of politeness norm, reticence, power differential, high versus low context). In addition, the Chinese vice president of operations said he would get his product out last week. It still wasn't out as far as the CEO could tell and the Chinese general manager did not seem to be aware of this problem (Manifestations of power differential, face saving, politeness norm, tolerance for ambiguity, high versus low context).

On top of this, the German general manager was very angry and very stubborn because the CEO called the German production supervisors and yelled at them to get the product off the line and into the hands of the customers. They were told to do it on budget and on schedule, but it still hadn't happened. (Manifestations of the politeness norm, power differential and high versus low context . . . . The CEO ignored the "chain of command" and caused the German general manager to lose face with his supervisors). The cultural norm of low tolerance for ambiguity, which produces linear, step-wise thinking, led the production supervisors to take the instruction "on budget and on time" as a literal list in order of priorities. Since they could not be on budget they assumed "on time" was a secondary criterion, and the high power differential and high context nature of their workplace kept them from asking, thus creating loss of face.

Last of all, the planned merger between the Dutch and German companies had reached a stalemate. When asked what was the problem, the Dutch general manager simply said, "We'll cooperate when we get our bicycles back". (A manifestation of high context, power differential and also some historical baggage – during WWII, the Germans confiscated the bicycles of the Dutch.) Both the German and Dutch managers were in their late 50s and understood the high context reference to WWII. The U.S. CEO, being in his 40s, had no idea what they were talking about and naively, impatiently said to the whole group "Bicycles, I'll buy you bicycles!" This diminished his credibility with both men and lowered his perceived authority, which was already in question because of his youth.

By the way, this case is not atypical. The CEO is smart and talented, committed to teamwork and his team, knowledgeable about his business and the market, hardworking and rigorous. And he's stymied by what he doesn't realize about the subtleties of culture going on under his nose. In our experience, when executives get in a spot like this, they are typically making some faulty assumptions about the situation, such as: people are basically capable of understanding each other; our issues may be complex, but communicating about them is simple; I'll just tell them to do it; I'll order them or threaten them if I have to; we'll just talk about it, and the right answer will emerge; I'm good at communication so I don't need to understand more; it's the outcome that matters, not the process you use; I've done it a lot, so I must be good at this. Such assumptions in the new realities of international business and IVETs are deadly; we should fear them for their ability to distract executives from the subtleties of cultural problems and challenges. The answer lies in consciously and open-mindedly questioning the assumptions underlying our culture-based beliefs and behaviors. The payoff will be that we can more effectively navigate through cultural differences and use them as guides to help us achieve our goals rather than obstacles that can keep us from getting there.

Building Trust

The idea that cultural differences can be, not just problems, but also criteria for collaboration in a global environment plays out in other areas of concern for international virtual executive teams (IVET). In 1995 Francis Fukuyama combined the concepts of "trust" and "globalization":

> The increasing salience of culture in the social order is such that Samuel Huntington has argued that the world is moving into a period of "civilizational clash," in which the primary identification of people will not be ideological, as during the cold war, but cultural . . . . Where Huntington's argument is less convincing, however, is that cultural differences will necessarily be the source of conflict. On the contrary, the rivalry arising from the interaction of different cultures can frequently lead to creative change, and there are numerous cases of such cultural stimulation (1995, pp. 5–6).

Fukuyama illustrates his point regarding the establishment of trust by discussing various global examples of success due to the synergistic effect of cross-cultural stimulation.

> Every one of the examples used must have started and been constructed through the use of a set of behaviors and interactions that were planned to accomplish greater trust and more effective collaboration. Simply sharing information or doing routine business would not have done the job.
>
> Trust does not reside in integrated circuits or fiber optic cables. Although it involves an exchange of information, trust is not reducible to information. A "virtual" firm can have abundant information coming through network wires about its suppliers and contractors. But if they are all crooks or frauds, dealing with them will remain a costly process involving complex contracts and time-consuming enforcement (Fukuyama, 1995, p. 25).

To put this idea in cultural terms, low trust creates low context groups and forces the responsibility for follow-through into the hands of third parties – usually lawyers – who are not the primary team members. This is neither an efficient or flexible process. In a world where the success of business depends on being nimble:

> The ability of companies to move from large hierarchies to flexible networks of smaller firms will depend, in other words, on the degree of trust and social capital present in the broader society. A high trust society like Japan created networks well before the information revolution got into high gear; a low-trust society may never be able to take advantage of the efficiencies that information technology offers (Fukuyama, 1995, pp. 25–26).

So it is easier for a high-context, collectivist, homogeneous culture to be high-trust. But how can we create a high-trust culture within a heterogeneous group that might add negative historical baggage into the mix? The answer, although it is surprisingly simple, is not easy.

It is this: international executive teams need to "set the stage" for trust and collaboration not just by solving cultural problems that arise ad hoc, but by creating an "Intentional Culture." This is a team-specific culture, negotiated and trained to create the high context team in which trust and intercultural understanding are fostered. This is particularly important in the early stages of mergers, acquisitions and joint ventures. Of course, some kind of corporate culture emerges whenever groups integrate whether we want them to or not. Then the question becomes: Do we want to default to a random or dysfunctional organizational or team culture, or shall we intentionally create one that does what we need it to?

Several years ago, I received a call from a European car manufacturer telling me they were opening a manufacturing plant in one of the southern states. The management was going to be European and the workforce would be hired locally. "Will we have a cultural problem?" "Yes," I assured them, they would. "Well, which way should we go? Should we expect the Europeans to adjust to the Americans or the Americans adjust to the Europeans?" It was a common question, but the wrong one. For generations we have believed that the group with the least formal authority had the "burden of accommodation." But today we know that if we want to effectively deal with and enlist differing cultures, the merging of teams must collectively negotiate a new "intentional" culture.

If executives, members of IVETs, are able to create a new "intentional" culture by negotiating the rules explicitly and through low-context communication tactics at the start, they will become loyal to and develop trust in the process. As the process then becomes understood, the negotiated behaviors become norms, the communicative behavior becomes high context and the people develop trust in each other. To do it, executive team leaders must undertake an intentional enculturation process that every new member must go through. This requires significant development and several face-to-face, low context interaction experiences among team members. It also implies that those responsible for leading the formation of an intentional team culture must be vigilant about possible tensions between national and team cultures.

It sounds like a large task and it is, but it is our experience that the new, emergent culture can be started up in a matter of days and can be sustained through ongoing process checks. We cannot stress this point enough, however, in order for IVETs to be optimally effective and efficient and to use mediated communication most optimally, creating the intentional culture *must start in a face-to-face environment*. Some of the steps in the process may seem very basic, but they need to be undertaken at a high enough level in order to keep members' interest and commitment.

Steps Toward Building Trust
The goal of the collaboration-building process will be to create a new understanding among the team members through a set of shared experiences so that a new collective memory can emerge. The first step of the process involves putting the team members through an intensive workshop in understanding, appreciating and allowing for cultural differences and some socialization experiences. Some programs we have seen suggest simply learning to be more sensitive to cultural differences, but this is not enough. Passive sensitivity and "tolerance" are patronizing and do not allow for using the cultural differences as an asset.

Step 2 is the strategy forming stage where the team members focus on their agreed-upon goals and form their "common ground", the solid foundation upon which they can build the rest of their relationships.

During step 3, the group negotiates what its function will be and how decisions will be made.

In step 4 the group simulates a mediated environment to create protocols for their virtual team behaviors and the most effective use of the mediated tools available to them.

This four-step process is grounded in the social science theories of Walter Mischel (1973) whose revolutionary work in personality demonstrated that deep-seated differences in persons could be changed or adapted to carefully planned situational constraints. In cultural terms, Mischel demonstrated that differences among people could be resolved if context was raised and ambiguity lowered. He called these "strong situations," and provided a set of criteria. Where participants: (1) know the appropriate behaviors; (2) possess the skills for the appropriate behaviors; (3) know the rewards for appropriate behavior; and (4) know the likely outcomes of the appropriate behaviors, the differences they bring to the table tend to be transcended by the strong situation, or, in this case, the intentional, high-context culture.

With IVETs we have learned that creating a strong situation or low-context, intentional culture has outcomes much more valuable than just getting the members in line with the program. When people are allowed to negotiate their own structured environments, they not only go along, they also take individual and collective ownership of the process and will be more likely to sustain it. As they become loyal to the process, the resulting trust in turn strengthens the "intentional" team culture even more.

One footnote – Mischel (1973) also found that failing to create a structured environment results in uncertainty, ambiguity and fear. High uncertainty environments force people to revert back to their original culture, norms, personality and behaviors. In other words, highly ambiguous situations bring differences to the surface; collectively created intentional cultures actually diminish differences and build trust.

Fukuyama wisely argues that "trust" is no longer just an affective emotion or elusive value; it is an economic necessity in the global environment. Historically, trust has been a process that takes time. Western companies forming joint ventures with China have found that it can take five to eight years to develop enough trust to commence an economic relationship. But many ventures today do not have the luxury of time. It is the position of this chapter that a carefully crafted IVET may be able to create the kind of strong situation where team members can develop loyalty to the process fairly quickly, determine some sets of predictable behaviors, build trust towards one another and then accomplish some important and profitable work. Once the intentional culture is established, and trust has evolved, effective and efficient decisions can be made through synergistic collaboration.

Ensuring Ongoing Collaboration

Ensuring ongoing collaboration demands a team that insists on continuous improvement. What is optimal in team process, including executive teams, is understanding problems and opportunities, hearing all possible solutions and ideas, airing disagreements, making effective group decisions and implementing decisions. The previous section outlines the strategic process of forming the trust-fostering IVET intentional culture. This section discusses some of the tactical steps for sustaining and continuously improving the intentional culture. Ensuring ongoing collaboration, however, demands one attribute in the executive leadership team members that can be very elusive in individualist cultures that are more achievement oriented than nurturing. That attribute is an open mind.

For decades (or is it centuries?), business writers and researchers have tried to determine the operational definition of leadership. But in all of our musings, we have rarely listed open-mindedness as a valuable characteristic. In fact, some approaches to leadership have affirmed the opposite – that real leaders should maintain certainty of opinions and require others to follow the leader's wisdom. That is an outmoded view globally, and as we have seen, offends some cultures. Even a few vestiges of the old authoritarian model can cause a team to go in the wrong direction. If the perceived authority speaks up too soon, not allowing for a collective sharing of opinions, it can stifle the exploration of optional points of view, to say nothing of creating resentments and dislikes.

Because some cultures are more hesitant to speak up, more collectivist in attitude, more harmonious in nature, more nurturing in behavior and more polite toward perceived authority, their ideas may not be heard until requested, not heard until later or not heard at all. For leaders who recognize that IVET leadership may require open-mindedness as a primary qualification for eliciting good ideas from all team members, we offer the following tactics for maintaining a collaborative environment on the team.

Tactic 1: Use a Simplified Delphi Technique
For IVETs to achieve collaborative decisions among differing cultures, we suggest a modification of the Delphi technique, developed by Helmer and Dalkey in the 1960s.

The Delphi technique (named after the Delphi Oracle) is a consensus-seeking device wherein anonymous ideas are generated and then run through a filter, but without any group interaction or discussion. (The technique has been referred to as "absentee brainstorming.") Initially developed to elicit individual ideas solely through the mail, it has more recently been adapted to group use. . . for problem solving as well as forecasting. Its key tenet is to seek consensus from experts while avoiding confrontation (Eitington, 1996, p. 217).

The Delphi technique enhances creativity by using individual talents and group synergy. Helmer and Dalkey (1968) write that its purpose is to "systematically combine individual judgments to obtain a reasoned consensus. Its unique feature and potential merit lie in requiring the experts to consider the objections and concepts of other group members in an environment free from bias caused by personalities." (p. 116) We might add here that it frees people from the bias caused by cultural differences. First, questions are constructed and the team members are asked to respond in writing. Second, all answers from all members are then combined and categorized or summarized and distributed to all other members. This is usually done anonymously. The members then rewrite their answers based on the input from the collective summaries and respond to the ideas suggested by other members. Third, the new answers are distributed with the additional comments. The group's leader is responsible for condensing the answers, which must be done carefully so as to keep from biasing the material. Members of the group are asked to resubmit. The final step can be yet one more revision of the answers or a video/ teleconference. There are several variations of this technique, which work exceptionally well in IVETs. In international teams, the Delphi technique is optimal for several reasons. It encourages and enables each team member's contribution, regardless of collectivist or individualist perspective. The individualists will feel like they are being given voice, and the collectivists will believe that the authority figure requested it so it must be done and it is in the best interest of the group at large. It minimizes the politeness norm since the answers are treated as if they are anonymous. It forces input to be low-context, since it has to be put into words. The beauty in this process, as you might see, is how much richer the outcomes are when people are allowed to get their individual information out on the table through writing rather than taking a public, verbal stand. When people take a public stand they have to save face, the reticents do not speak up and the bullies win, whether their information is high quality or not. A further advantage for IVETs is that e-mail and written mediated communication tools lend themselves perfectly to this gathering of data.

Tactic 2: Using the L.A.W.S of Listening:
An executive team that has negotiated the rule of reciprocity will need some specific techniques to realize this ideal of hearing and considering all sides of an issue fairly and completely. We suggest the L.A.W.S of listening approach (Kiely, 1998). This tactic is best used when people are caught in differing opinions; it works in face-to-face situations, but it is especially useful with mediated communication. Mediated communication, by its very nature, is more sequential (turn taking). Although asynchronous is obviously more sequential, the limitations of synchronous media also force more obvious sequential interactions. Many of our high-tech audio tools are still very primitive -more like the old ship-to-shore radio calls where the speaker had to say "over" in order to signal the listener to take his turn. It is true that this type of turn taking is awkward and artificial, but this approach turns it to an advantage. An explanation of the elements of this approach follows.

L. is *like*. This step suggests, when members are disagreeing, that the listener locates and articulates something *likeable* about the dissenting opinion. The rule of reciprocity is served by this step: it requires the listener to consider possible benefits of the opposing point of view prior to refuting or verbally disagreeing with it. This step results in two different and positive outcomes. First, it demonstrates to dissenters that their ideas were given fair hearing. Giving another person's idea fair hearing increases the likelihood that others will reciprocate and give your idea the same fairness and respect. And a second outcome, possibly even more valuable, is that if you open-mindedly consider someone else's point of view, you might actually change your mind.

A. is *"add."* This second step asks the listener to "add" to the dissenter's opinion. This problem-solving model creates "both/and" solutions rather than "either/or" solutions, which are typically more thorough and well thought out. Further, these solutions are more likely to be win-win rather than based on a zero sum game philosophy, which believes only one opinion can survive.

W. is *"worried."* This step invites the listener to tell the idea source what worries him or her about the offered idea. At this point we hear the listener's differing view, but it comes out as a concern rather than an indictment. By this point in the process, our experience is that people are often already building consensus and seeking a working agreement rather than choosing whose suggestions are "right."

S. is *"solution."* The final step suggests that proposed solutions should come last, after the other steps. Here team members propose a solution, as opposed to determining who is "right" or whose idea is "best," criteria that tends to be more competitive and judgmental than collaborative.

We have found that this simple, solution-based model of communicating through differing positions ensures less conflict, higher quality decisions, and full, successful implementation. The Listening L.A.W.S. model can effectively satisfy both collectivist and individualist perspectives, allows for the politeness norm, keeps the power differential in check, and creates a high-context culture in which everyone knows the implicit rules of reciprocity, harmony and creativity.

Tactic 3: A Face-to-Face, Three-day Session
Building a solid IVET is a front-loaded process. To ensure the formation of an intentional culture and a climate of trust and collaboration, we recommend a face-to-face, three-day session to be held in a neutral place (everyone travels, and no local culture dominates the session). The neutral place also cuts down on distractions, since no members are in their usual work area. The three-day

session includes an intensive workshop on using cultural differences to the team's advantage, some socialization experiences, a strategic planning portion and a simulation of the virtual environment.

Tactic 4: Simulation of Virtual Environment Using Mediated Communication Tools

During this three-day session, the team must conduct a simulation of the mediated communication tools to determine protocols and effectiveness, and to provide the skills necessary to run the organization in a virtual environment. This would ideally include a rigorous test of the video conferencing, teleconferencing and on-line tools and behaviors while the members are still in the same facility, but in different rooms – thus, a simulated environment. We suggest the following elements:

- Hook up the remote sites to test.
- Each room is equipped with a telephone with teleconferencing capabilities, a computer with Internet e-mail, two cameras with movable lenses – one to view the group and one to zoom on individuals, multiple monitors or split screens to view multiple sites, a fax machine, a printer, a scanner, a document camera/elmo, a large card with a question mark to signal the need to talk, and a technician.
- Choose a relevant issue for decision. Go through the process via the IVET tools.
- Videotape and play back. Look for snags and determine a better process.

The actual simulation, using the IVET communication tools should involve the following steps:

- Each team member is in a separate room with all equipment and one technician.
- A written report with all factual data relevant to the decision on the table is sent via e-mail and fax.
- The e-mail reply function is used to interject questions for clarification or requests for more information within the text of the document (using different font or shaded areas in the text, as it would show on the screen).
- The CEO compiles all questions and some answers into one document and e-mails back to all without stating who asked what questions.
- Members who have additional answers type the additional text into the document (using different font or shaded areas).

- Data and charts are projected on screens via computer or small document camera.
- A viewing monitor has split-screen capacity in case there are multiple people in one room, so you can see all people or zoom in on one, and so you can view all sites simultaneously.
- Whenever the CEO asks for an opinion, he or she requests an e-mail vote and then polls each person.
- If there are any unanswered questions or unstated concerns, the team is asked to e-mail or call to discuss them individually. If there are changes based on the individual calls the CEO e-mails details to everyone and asks for immediate feedback.
- After the decision is made, the group agrees on a conference call to firm up the details. The CEO writes down a kind of seating chart as if they were in the room with him, and requests input from each individual.
- The final report is amended on the screen as everyone watches. If there is disagreement, the dissenting person speaks up during the conference call.
- The CEO verbally asks all members if they have any problem with going ahead with the decision. Discussion is allowed if there are dissenting votes.
- The team then regroups face-to-face to discuss the process – where it got bogged down, where it worked well, etc. The videotaped process can be played back in clips to see how it worked.
- The team evaluates the process.
- The team completes "what if" scenarios to determine protocols for the future, regarding what types of information should be sent through which types of media/channels and how best to use these tools.

Early detection and elimination of as many problems as possible in the virtual, mediated environment is a must. Many of the problems we saw in the literature and our own consulting experiences could have been detected and preempted if the team had simulated the environment face-to-face, before going "live" at a distance, as in the case of our troubled 45-year-old U.S. CEO of the multinational team. If you're wondering what happened to him, they ended up parceling off the various parts of the business and sold them for minimal profit. Many system problems start as small glitches or misunderstandings, but when we do not have the opportunity to see each other on a regular basis, the small problems can fester and become insurmountable, permanently damaging our relationships and the effectiveness of the team. IVETs who have completed these steps are more able to minimize these "bugs" and to proceed effectively. These teams make better decisions in their virtual, mediated environments with a solid foundation of trust and cooperation.

CONCLUSION

The end of the 20th century may have brought with it the "End of the Great Man," as Bennis argues, because no one person alone can know all there is to know, do all that must be done or create all there might be to create. In the 21st century, we have concluded that decisions must be made by teams of capable people who can harness their collective intellectual capital in such a way as to make nimble, quality decisions. The onset of this century, then, must replace the fading of "The Great Man" with the era of the "Great Team." We are no longer isolated within our own neighborhood, our own culture, our own country or our own worldview. In this *global* environment, this means that International Virtual Executive Teams may well be the future of how business and the global economy are managed. But we have seen that these groups are made up of people who are, necessarily, very different from one another; IVETs can be fragile and are prone to inefficiency and conflict if we fail to understand and develop them carefully.

In this chapter we have discussed the virtual environment, mediated communication and the dynamics of IVETs as executive team members struggle to navigate cultural differences, build trust and ensure collaboration. And we have outlined a model for the creation of an effective and efficient IVET. I hope, if nothing else, that this discussion has convinced you that creating effective international executive teams is a critical issue. Of course, we might get away with muddling along for a while, continuing on as though the game has not changed. But soon, very soon, the need to navigate cultural differences will become urgent. In fact, that boat has already sailed, and we're either on it or we're waving good-bye.

REFERENCES

Angus, J., & Gallagher, S. (1998). Virtual team builders. *Information Week*, 83-83, 86.

Baker, N. C. (1999). Giving teams a winning edge. *Corporate University Review*, 7(1), 29–33.

Bennis, W. (1997). *Organizing genius*. Reading, Massachusetts: Addison-Wesley.

Cleaver, J. (1997). Virtual unreality. *Crain's Chicago Business*, 29(15), 13, 16–17.

De Lisser, E. (1999). Firms with virtual environments appeal to workers. *Wall Street Journal*, b2.

Duarte, D. L., & Snyder, N. T. (1997). *Mastering virtual teams*. San Francisco: Jossey-Bass Publishers.

Eitington, J. E. (1996). *The winning trainer* (3rd ed.). Houston: Gulf Publishing Company.

Fukuyama, F. (1995). *Trust*. New York: The Free Press.

Hagen, M. R. (1999). Teams expand into cyberspace. *Quality Progress*, 32(6), 90–93.

Hall, E. T. (1976). *Beyond culture*. Garden City, New York: Anchor Press/ Doubleday.

Hanley, S. S. (1999). A culture built on sharing. *Information Week*, 16–17.

Harris, P. R., & Moran, R. T. (1991). *Managing cultural differences*. Houston: Gulf Publishing Company.

Henry, J. E., & Hartzler, M. (1998). *Tools for virtual teams*. Milwaukee: Quality Press.

Hofstede, G. (1984). *Culture's consequences; international differences in work-related values*. Beverly Hills: Sage Publications, Inc.

Hofstede, G. (1991). *Cultures and organizations; software of the mind*. New York: McGraw Hill Book Co.

Jarvenpaa, S. L., Knoll, K., & Leidner, D. (1998). Is anybody out there? Antecedents of trust in global virtual teams. *Journal of Management Information Systems, 145*(4), 29–64.

Kiely, L. (1998). *Introduction to business communication: Tools for leadership*. Los Angeles: University Access, Inc.

Kostner, J. (1994). *Virtual leadership*. New York: Warner Books.

Kurland, N. B., & Bailey, D. E. (1999). Telework: the advantages and challenges of working here, there, anywhere, and anytime. *Organizational Dynamics, 29*(2), 53–68.

Lally, R., & Kostner, J. (1997). Learn to be a distance manager. *Getting Results – for the Hands-On Manager, 42*, 6.

Lipnack, J., & Stamps, J. (1997). *Virtual teams. reaching across space, time, and organizations with technology*. New York: John Wiley and sons, Inc.

Lipnack, J., & Stamps, J. (1998). Virtual teamwork: a tale of two approaches. *Training media review, 6*(6), 4–7.

Mischel, W. (1973). Toward a cognitive social learning reconceptualization of personality. *Psychological Review, 80*, 252–283.

Mobley, W. H., Gessner, M. J., & Arnold, V. (Eds) (1999). *Advances in global leadership* (Vol. 1 ed.). Stamford, Connecticut: JAI Press.

Moran, R. T., Harris, P. R., & Stripp, W. G. (1993). *Developing the global organization*. Houston: Gulf Publishing Company.

Ohmae, K. (1982). *The mind of the strategist*. New York: McGraw Hill, Inc.

Ohmae, K. (1990). *The borderless world*. New York: Harper Perennial.

Shimanoff, S. B. (1980). *Communication Rules*. Beverly Hills: Sage Publications.

Slack, K. (1998). Virtual teamwork: tale of two approaches. *Business and Management Practices, 6*(6), 2.

Solomon, C. M. (1998). Sharing information across borders and time zones. *Workforce, 77*, 12–14.

Townsend, A. M., De Marie, S. M., & Hendrickson, A. R. (1998). Virtual teams: technology and the workplace of the future. *Academy of Management Executive, 12*(3), 17–29.

Warkentin, M., Sayeed, L., & Hightower, R. (1997). Virtual teams versus face-to-face teams: an exploratory study of a web-based conference system. *Decision Sciences, 28*(4), 975–996.

Yeung, R., & Langdon, D. (2000). A tangled web. *Accountancy, 125*(1227), 44.

ALLIANCE LEADERSHIP: TEMPLATE FOR THE FUTURE*

Lynn A. Isabella and Robert E. Spekman

ABSTRACT

The premise of this chapter is the following: strategic alliances offer the kind of organizational context that encourages a new kind of leadership and the attributes of effective alliance managers today are the foundational characteristics of global leaders of the future. Drawing on extensive field research as well as work with companies, we examine the alliance context and the challenges it offers to managers. We describe those leadership challenges, and detail both the actions and behaviors required of effective alliance managers and the cognitive characteristics that seem to distinguish them from other line managers. We end with some concrete suggestions about grooming alliance managers, albeit leaders of the future.

INTRODUCTION

The single, vertically integrated company competing as a stand-alone business is quickly becoming an obsolete business model. Bureaucratic enterprises of

---

* Parts of this chapter have been adapted from Spekman, R. & Isabella, L. 2000. Alliance Competence: Maximizing the Value of Your Partnerships. NY: John Wiley.

Advances in Global Leadership, Volume 2, pages 217–244.
Copyright © 2001 by Elsevier Science Ltd.
All rights of reproduction in any form reserved.
ISBN: 0-7623-0723-4

the latter part of 20th century are giving way to the nimble set of almost virtual companies that compete for business on a global basis. Firms now compete as complete value networks against other value networks for share of market in industries as diverse as telecommunications, airlines and pharmaceuticals. In the oil business, firms that drill for oil in the North Sea, the Gulf of Mexico or the Sea of China form partnerships that together represent the trillion-dollar boundary-less global enterprises of tomorrow (Freidman, 1998). An organization is no longer exclusively the people and processes defined as part of the corporate organizational chart. An organization is comprised of its numerous alliances and partnerships that transcend traditional organizational boundaries linking multiple organizations together. To be sure, these global partnerships are growing at unprecedented rates (Harbison & Pekar, 1998).

As more and more organizations become part of global networks, traditional models of management become less meaningful. Hierarchical organizations with a well-established chain of command are not effective. As organizations evolve to meet the challenges of global competition, management practice must also adapt to these new rules and demands. An immediate challenge is for the firm to remain adaptive enough to adjust to the disruptive forces of change and disciplined enough to execute in effective fashion. Brown and Eisenhardt (1998) caution that open boundaries do not mean that managers operate without order. On the contrary, managers learn to adapt to change, actively create their future and redefine the rules of the game.

Recent leadership studies match the evolving organizational reality by describing new leadership skills. Brown and Eisenhardt (1998) illustrate how traditional leadership characteristics (e.g. strategic problem solving) must be replaced by skills in pattern recognition AND ability to generalize. Gregersen, Morrison and Black (1998) talk about global leaders as needing unbridled inquisitiveness, personal character, duality and savvy. McCall (1998) details how experiences (and the lessons learned) combine with talent to create the right leadership stuff. Even those outside corporate leadership, such as Heifetz (1994) or Gardner (1995), offer notions of leadership such as engagement through stories or framing for the audience.

The commonality linking these and other studies is an increasing cognitive orientation toward leading. These most recent studies focus not on behaviors or actions per se. They concentrate on how the individual interprets the world, frames situations, and makes those interpretations accessible to others, such as through stories or lessons. In a world characterized by rapid change, how individuals construe and experience their world is as important, if not more important, than the objective characteristics of that changing milieu (Conger & Benjamin, 1999). Effective leadership derives from how the leader thinks and sees the world and is able to connect to the pluralism and diversity represented in her organizations.

The premise of this chapter is the following: *strategic alliances offer the kind of organizational context that encourages a new kind of leadership and the attributes of effective alliance managers today are the foundational character-istics of global leaders of the future.* Said another way, what it takes to succeed in leadership positions within an alliance is precisely what it will take to guide the global corporations of tomorrow. Being a good alliance manager, we will demonstrate, requires a different way of thinking and seeing the world, and the attributes that enable an alliance manager to be successful are the leadership templates for the future.

This chapter will draw upon our own field research as well as our work with companies. In both instances, we have examined how alliances evolved and the role of alliance managers throughout that process. We will suggest that for these new organizational forms (e.g. alliances and partnerships) to reach their fullest potential, leaders must see and think differently about their roles and how they will maneuver through the organizational landscape. They must be able to synthesize and generalize from conditions of information overload or information scarcity; and share with and care about all types of people and partners simultaneously. The situations they confront will be so new and without precedent (look only at the Internet) that managers will need to approach these situations with the ability to leverage and merge the best of the past with bold and creative initiatives for which there may be no predecessors. They must have a mindset that is nurtured and invigorated by learning, by complexity and by ambiguity.

First, we will look at the alliance landscape to achieve a richer appreciation of why organizations are so drawn to alliances. We will delve into our definition of alliances and the implications of that definition for how we should think about alliances and alliance activity. Finally, we will focus on the characteristics of successful alliance managers and how companies can grow and groom these leaders of the future.

MOVING TOWARD THE FUTURE

Why are Alliances so Popular and Important?

The speed with which companies have adopted alliances and partnerships as a mode of conducting business is unparalleled and staggering. It is estimated that a new alliance is formed every 90 seconds (Harbison & Pekar, 1998). While no single unique reason exists for alliance creation, organizations enter these relationships in an effort to create value that they would have difficulty accomplishing on their own. Some companies use alliances to gain access to an otherwise inaccessible market. Companies who want to do business in China or India must enter into joint ventures with the respective governments. No company has access to oil in Venezuela without an alliance with Petroleus de Venezuela SA, the national oil company. Other companies might want access to technology, which is impossible or too costly to build from scratch. Pharmaceutical companies often partner to gain access to drug technology developed by smaller more focused biotech research labs. Otis Elevator recently partnered with Continental AG because of Conti's technology in lifting belts – an innovative technology Otis hopes will be the first revolutionary development in the elevator business in 150 years.[1] Still other organizations create alliances to reduce costs or share risks. Aerospace companies, such as Boeing or Pratt and Whitney, partner with other companies because the cost of aircraft or jet engine development is so high. When the payback for a jet engine is 20–30 years, having another company sharing costs and risks becomes very attractive.

Finally, organizations partner to learn. Many of the alliances found dealing with the Internet or related to e-commerce are attempts to understand more about this major disruptive change. The amount of dollars at risk in the business-to-business arena alone is in the trillions of dollars. For the traditional brick and mortar retailer or manufacturer there is much to learn from Bicom.com, CheMatch.com, FreeMarkets and a host of infomediaries that have entered this competitive space.

In the spirit of learning, more and more companies are using alliances and partnerships as experimental probes, thereby creating options for the future. In a world where much is possible and little is certain, rather than carefully placing *one* bet on the future, strategists are arguing that having many options, often generated through alliances, is a prudent way to hedge against the future. With several possibilities in place, organizations increase the probability that a few will work and work well, even though most might fail.[2] Learning can happen either way.

Alliances have significant "top line" growth implications and are not just about risk reduction or cost savings. Recent estimates suggest that by 2002, 35% of corporate revenues will result directly from alliance activity – a staggering contribution from the 2% registered in 1980 (Harbison & Pekar, 1998). This potential for value creation makes alliances a force to be reckoned with. It also suggests that how these entities are managed becomes a critical component in the process of value creation. But first we must understand more about what an alliance is.

What An Alliance Is

The Definition of Strategic Alliance

The term alliance or partnership is overused and little understood. The term is in vogue and everyone wants to be your partner or be part of an alliance. An alliance is a close, collaborative relationship between two or more firms with the intent of accomplishing mutually compatible goals that would be difficult for each to accomplish alone (Spekman & Isabella, 2000). Several elements of this definition – collaborate, mutually compatible and difficult to achieve alone – have important underlying connotations:

- *Collaborative* implies that the partners favor cooperation and working together, not of competition and self-interest.
- *Mutually compatible* suggests that the strategic intent of the alliance is based upon a well-matched give and get.
- *Difficult to achieve alone* recognizes that each partner understands the interdependence of the relationship.

These distinctions are critical to make because they focus attention on the underlying logic upon which successful alliances should be built.

Alliances are Managerially Unique

It is safe to say that alliances are not business as usual. Firms must cooperate while simultaneously holding in check the natural inclination to look out for their own self-interest. Managers share decision-making but do not control the actions of their partners. They are compelled to share information but must guard against the expropriation of sensitive knowledge. Alliances lack the permanence of a single hierarchy but have the flexibility to adapt to changing market conditions, new technological disruptions and/or other environmental contingencies. Alliances are fragile organizational forms, yet have the strength to deal with a rapidly changing competitive landscape.

Alliances are governed by a social contract, a spirit that establishes the rules of engagement for partners. This spirit lies at the heart of the alliance and answers the question: "What does it mean to partner?" We envision that partners will share a mutuality of interest, work more in harmony than in a competitive manner and recognize that there is an implied reciprocity in their actions. One partner might concede an issue at one point in time and expect that at a later point the other partner will do the same. In this manner balance happens over time although one partner might appear advantaged at any given moment.

From the dream that first brought the firms together to achieve a certain vision to the point at which the alliance has run its course and the time to end the alliance has come, the role of the alliance manager is essential to guiding the alliance along its life cycle. The alliance manager plays many different roles as the alliance develops and grows. In fact, the same person might not play these different roles, as the skills are different, the demands of the alliance change and the relationship among partners is subject to different tensions and challenges. One person is unlikely to possess all the skills required to see the alliance from cradle to grave.

Exhibit 1 shows the life cycle stages of alliances, the different roles played by the alliance manager, the different decisions that must be made and key business and relationship activities that occur at each stage. This exhibit is intended to illustrate the complex set of issues that affect alliances throughout their life span, demonstrate that alliances are about business *and* relationships, and show that the success of the alliance at any stage is partly a function of the demands facing the alliance as well as a function of the talents and skills of the alliance manager. Alliances may take different forms but each must pass through these different life cycle stages.

While a joint venture is different from a co-development alliance that is different from a buyer-supplier alliance, each must pass from birth to maturity and experience, to varying degrees, similar pressures, tensions and challenges. Exhibit 2 summarizes the common characteristics that span different alliance types. We focus on the similarities since all alliances must share certain characteristics, although they might have different governance structures and goals. For a relationship to be called an alliance, there must exist a certain baseline along these different characteristics.

Alliances are About Business and Relationship
Above all, there must be a compelling business case that creates value that the partners would be hard pressed to create on their own. Time is too short, resources too scarce and expertise is not always available for one firm to act independently. Yet, to assume that alliances are merely a vehicle to execute a business plan faster and less expensively ignores the social aspects of alliance management. Much of the time spent in the successful management of alliances is spent on nurturing the relationship among alliance partners. Successful alliances pay as much attention to the relationship as they do the business. These alliances don't just work at the relationships, but the relationship is an integral part of the dynamics of the partnership. In healthy alliances, the importance of personal contact cannot be overemphasized. The value of establishing a trusting relationship is critical and the open and continuous communications among partners all contribute to the alliance's success (see Exhibit 3).

The Complexity of Alliance Evolution

	Anticipation	Engagement	Valuation	Coordination	Investment	Stabilization
Characteristics	Pre-alliance Competitive needs & motivation emerge	High energy Complementarity Congruence Strategic potential	Financial focus Business cases Analysis Internal selling	Operational focus Task orientation Division of labor Parallel activity	Hard choices Committing Resource Reallocation Broadening scope	High interdependence Maintenance Assessment of relative worth and contribution
Key Business Activity	Search	Identification	Valuation Negotiation	Coordination Integration	Expansion Growth	Adjustment
Key Relationship Activity	Dating	Imaging	Initiating	Interfacing	Committing	Fine-tuning
Role of Alliance Manager	Visionary	Strategic Sponsor	Advocate	Networker	Facilitator	Manager

Exhibit 1.

	Buyer-Supplier Alliance	Co-development/ co-marketing alliance	Joint Venture
Alliance Characteristic	Non-equity, low intensity alliances	Mid-range alliance (might co-mingle assets but not jointly owned)	Equity, high intensity alliances
Trust	Limited to the nature of the alliance; expectation of being honest	Partner is assumed to be more trustworthy than others and is treated in such a manner	Trust has been built over time and is established as a solid foundation; extends throughout the (two) businesses
Commitment	Specific to the terms of the alliance; there is a tendency to test	Commitment takes a longer view and partners are less likely to test	Commitment is focused on joint success and is pervasive; measured over the life of the relationship
Recognized Interdependence	Acknowledgment exists but partners need to be reminded	Partners are sensitive to each other's worry about self-serving behavior and self monitor	The alliance jointly links the fate of the partners such that self-serving behavior is not an option
Symmetry	The extent to which risk and reward are shared is often specified in the terms and conditions of the alliance agreement	Partners' sense of fair dealing extends beyond the boundaries of the alliance	Partners share risk and reward equitably but tend to treat each other as equals.
Open Communications	The tone and content of the exchange of information is specified by the alliance agreement	Communications are more open and cross boundaries at multiple points, often extend beyond the agreement	While certain information might remain proprietary, there is a tendency to speak with one voice and have fewer restrictions on access. Partners might jointly create knowledge

Exhibit 2. An Illustration of Alliance Characteristics Across Alliance Forms.

Joint Planning	Limited in scope and content to the agreement	Less tied to the specifics of the alliance agreement and will spill over to other aspects of the partners' business	Highly linked and essential to the future of the partners' relationship
Coordination of Work	Often coordination needed because of the sequence of workflow and the need to coordinate the movement from A to B. Performance is often monitored separately	Could be high as well but depends on the kind of alliance. Joint work could be done either in parallel or sequence. Performance is measured jointly	Coordination of work is linked to the JV and is monitored by the partners. Both have input into performance outcomes and system changes
Cultural Compatibility	Some level is required to agree on alliance operating principles and norms	Higher level of compatibility would be useful given the degree to which partners co-mingle	Without high levels of compatibility problems are likely to emerge since the partners work very closely. Over time a new, joint culture might emerge

Exhibit 2. Continued.

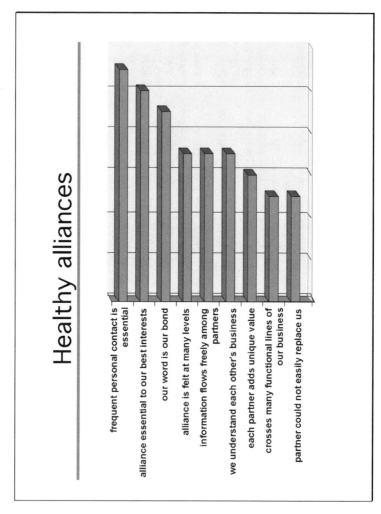

Exhibit 3. Healthy Alliances.

Note: These data present the top reasons managers report their alliances are strong. The length of the bar graph is meant to depict the qualitative difference between the reasons, not a particular value. These data are part of a larger study first described in Spekman, R., Isabella, L., MacAvoy, T., and Forbes, T. (1996). Managing Alliances and Partnerships. Lexington,MA: International Consortium of Executive Development Research.

Business and relationship in a strategic alliance are like strands of DNA. They provide the essential building blocks of the alliance, hold the "code" for the alliance and, because they are intimately intertwined, add both strength and internal support (See Fig. 1). Both are essential to the success of the alliance and to focus on one to the exclusion of the other is to court disaster. The relationship provides the strength for the alliance to weather tough times. It is the safety net that the business can fall on when the market turns bad or the technology is not developing according to schedule. Without this basis of trust or sense of personal commitment, the alliance is likely to languish when all is not going well. Perversely, when the business is good, managers often ignore working on the relationship. Why spend the time? All is right with the world. With no investment in the relationship when business is good, there is nothing with which to grid the alliance when the business is bad. Given the cyclical nature of global markets, managers must be ready for the good times and the bad.

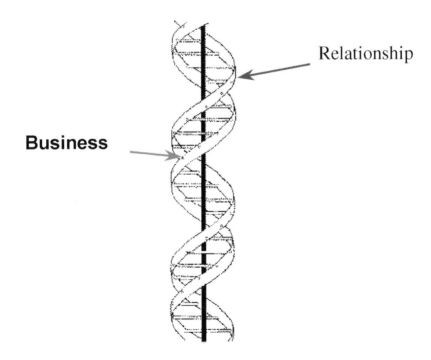

Fig. 1. Business and Relationship are Intertwined.

Alliance Managers Are at the Nexus

At the nexus of this networked organization is a person we call "the alliance manager." The alliance manager is that individual or team of individuals responsible for the strategic alliance. Similar to the classic boundary role person, who sits at the nexus of two or more companies, alliance managers have truly boundary-less tasks. They must attend to a broad range of strategic and operational issues, while operating simultaneously on three levels: across two or more separate parent companies, within the parent companies, and within the alliance and between individuals. Across companies, the alliance manager represents and manages the needs, resources and desires of the partner companies. Within any one particular firm, the alliance manager represents and manages the needs, resources and desires of his or her own company. If a joint venture is involved, the alliance manager maintains close contact with it and with the venture's general manager. On an interpersonal level, the alliance manager creates and maintains relationships with superiors, peers and subordinates in the alliance and their various partner organizations.

Managing across networks by definition creates an awkward set of relationships that require time and talent. Thus, management requires multi-faceted individuals that possess the abilities to be flexible and adaptive to the stage of the network and to the role necessary, and with a set of characteristics that enhances, not detracts, from the network's mission. The talent required to orchestrate joint action at one stage might not be the same as that which is required at another stage. Early stage networks might need an advocate or champion who can build consensus around the key elements of the networks vision and mission. Here one tries to get buy-in – to get others, both in his/her firm and in the partner firms, to develop a similar sense of urgency and to work hard on behalf of the network. As the network matures, different skills are needed and they typically involve ensuring the smooth running of the network and attending to those issues that threaten the network or potentially bog down its workflow. The skills now needed might be ones of a facilitator or mediator. The manager will have to be an honest broker who is respected by the network and viewed as an objective party who is not an advocate for his/her organization, but thinks system-wide (i.e. the entire network).

Because alliances are evolving forms based upon incomplete contracts, the roles of those in leadership positions cannot be constant. Our research[3] shows that the focus of management's attention shifts with the demands of the alliance (See Exhibit 4).

In the beginning, management's role is one of a visionary. As visionaries, management's role hones in on the strategic rationale and vision for the alliance. With that vision, management is best able to scan the alliance landscape for those partners that fit the vision. Once the alliance progresses to engagement, where a partner is chosen, management's role needs to shift to strategic sponsor. As strategic sponsors, management concentrates through strategic dialogue on building the business familiarity necessary to build a solid alliance base. Again, as the alliance moves to valuation, management's role becomes one of advocate, building trust through collaborative give and take. As the alliance begins to move from vision to reality, management's role needs to shift to networker. As networkers, management uses collaboration in teams and partnering skills to create coordination and integration between the partners.

Then, as the alliance develops operationally, management's role becomes more focused on that of a facilitator. As facilitators, alliance management focuses on managing change and building renewed commitment to the alliance. Finally, for an alliance well underway, the role of the alliance manager becomes focused on steering the alliance along its prescribed course.

Working across different levels, with different people with differing perspectives and agendas, requires the ability to be in different places at the same time. Individuals must have an ability to take a broad, strategic perspective, while knowing the details. These managers must appreciate the impact and concerns of many constituents and stakeholders who are part of the alliance network. These managers are indispensable linchpins in the network. Given the recent attention given to the role of alliance managers, their roles and job descriptions are almost newly defined. Thus, the questions become: (1) What skills and competencies are important? and (2) How are critical managers identified and developed?

CHARACTERISTICS OF EFFECTIVE ALLIANCE MANAGERS

The Alliance Manager's Baseline Skills

Our research demonstrated that strong alliance managers possess a set of tangible skills combined with a number of attributes descriptive of their cognitive orientation to learning.

Strong Alliance Managers have Breadth and Depth
Not surprisingly, strong alliance managers, we discovered, know the business, their markets, their products, the core technologies of their company and the corporation itself. Generally through direct experience in both line and staff

Primary Management Roles	ACTIVITIES INHERENT IN THESE ROLES
Visionary	✓ Serves as the driving force behind the alliance's creation
	✓ Paints a picture of the possibilities that forming an alliance creates
	✓ Maintains a broad perspective spanning inside and outside the company
	✓ Understands the computability of strategic intents
Strategic Sponsor	✓ Sells the concept of strategic alliances inside company and beyond
	✓ Has authority to commit resources and key personnel to the alliance
	✓ Is "in" the alliance, not peripheral to it
	✓ Puts in motion alliance opportunities
	✓ Creates an atmosphere that fosters high energy and personal compatibility
	✓ Builds an organization with dedicated resources
	✓ Looks for opportunities across company to benefit the alliance
	✓ Fosters social development for alliance growth
	✓ Provides opportunities to strengthen and evolve the alliance
	✓ Spans many boundaries and layers
Advocate	✓ Sells the value of the relationship to alliance participants
	✓ Sells the value of the specific alliance in question
	✓ Develops support for the alliance
	✓ Constantly pushes the vision forward
	✓ Rallies the right people at the right time
	✓ Makes things happen deep into the company
	✓ Creates mechanisms for support and understanding within the alliance
	✓ Maintains a vigilant focus on the ongoing business of the alliance
	✓ Broadcasts its successes and achievements
	✓ Is internal to the alliance, hands-on and tactical
	✓ Actively owns the day to day alliance
	✓ Allows the alliance to have a large share of mind
	✓ Makes a significant emotional investment

Exhibit 4. Management Roles and Associated Activities.

Networker

✓ Relies on frequent contacts to expedite alliance business
✓ Knows who to ask for help and when to ask
✓ Puts the right people together
✓ Accesses resources quickly and efficiently through others
✓ Creates connections between internal networks of partner companies
✓ Puts in face to face time in order to cultivate trust in key relationships
✓ Engages in and encourages informal activities
✓ See interpersonal activities as key
✓ Bridges communication gaps

Facilitator

✓ Encourages open, honest and straightforward communication among all parties
✓ Facilities effective reviews of "state of the alliance"
✓ Conducts interactions with diplomacy, tact and objectivity
✓ Creates bridges between diverse parties with different interests
✓ Resolves conflicts effectively
✓ Exhibits sensitivity to the needs of all parties

Manager

✓ Shoulders responsibility for sustaining the alliance
✓ Insures that the alliance follows its prescribed path
✓ Maintains relationships critical to alliance success
✓ Maintains alliance momentum
✓ Is daily and constant
✓ Is more tactical than visionary

Exhibit 4. Continued.

positions, they have acquired a strategic overview and broad understanding of critical aspects of the business, as well as solid general management skills. They also have a broad base of knowledge aligned to the organization's business core. Their experiences, both formal and informal, have deepened their expertise in the core while expanding into the surrounding areas.[4]

Strong Alliance Managers Possess Robust and Complicated Networks
Networking and building connections with others are key skills of strong alliance managers. These individuals have integrated network building as an important career activity, seeing almost every contact as a potential opportunity. They reach out to others, get to know other company members outside their functional area, are active in professional societies and never burn bridges during transitions or problem situations. Obviously, the more experiences a potential alliance manager has had, the greater the chances that a broad-based network of contacts has been created. Past successes increase the credibility and respect acquired with the years of building rapport within and through one's professional development and interactions. With a strong network in place, an alliance manager can call on a wide circle of contacts both in his firm and often in the partners' firm.

Interpersonal Savvy is a Must
Because alliances are so heavily dependent on personal relationships, an alliance manager's interpersonal skills have little room for error. Interpersonal skills in an alliance context require the flexibility and adaptability to interact in diverse business and social settings. Knowing how to act appropriately in and with different cultures, and how to interact with business people in non-business as well as business settings are necessary foundations to alliance management. If relationships are a cornerstone of strategic alliances, one's ability to form relationships and make emotional connections often begins with solid one-to-one encounters. In fact, our effective alliance managers echoed observations made by Schein (1981) years ago. Interpersonal savvy involves self-insight, cultural sensitivity, personal flexibility and adaptability in problem solving and repair strategies for mending damaged relationships and patience.

Understanding the finesse needed in "meeting and greeting" is not inconsequential or frivolous in an alliance context. An Asian manager in one of our alliance workshops stated that the social skill most important to his company was a kind of "social stamina." Many business decisions in his company are made over meals and drinks, activities that can stretch long into the evening. Therefore, length of time spent socializing garnered credibility and respect within this company.

Communication Demeanor Makes a Difference

Interpersonal savvy must be manifested not only in actions, but also through communication skills. These communication skills encompass all the fundamental skills of speaking and listening well to others in one-on-one situations, as well as the ability to make another, especially a manager of another culture, feel comfortable and at ease. Strong alliance managers mirror their counterparts as they communicate. Mirroring is simply a term for matching another's gestures, tone, mannerisms and emotional intensity. It is not mimicry; it is behaving with others in ways that create connections, not distance.

The ability to mirror is an under-recognized skill in alliances. With all of the cross-cultural venues in which alliances operate, being able to communicate with very different individuals requires more than knowing how to speak cogently and listen well. It involves knowing how to reflect back on what you are receiving, thus reducing the cultural distance between individuals. Take the Siemens alliance manager who managed the Siecor alliance for over 20 years. Our interview with him gave us a front row seat into the communication skills of a strong alliance executive. His self-presentation changed depending on the alliance partner of which he spoke. When he was talking about the Spanish or Italians or Latin cultures, he was emotional and animated. His eyes brightened, his face echoed his emotion. This was in stark contrast to the demeanor he took on when talking about the Japanese or Chinese with which he engaged. He made less eye contact, was more demure in this speech and appeared quite reserved. This demeanor was again different than when he spoke of his fellow German managers.

Cross-Cultural Tact and Sensitivity are Givens

Another strong root of interpersonal savvy is cross cultural tact and sensitivity. Strong alliance managers understand the power and impact of national culture on business. They understand how to relate to others with different values or perspectives without demeaning themselves or their partners. We know of an alliance manager doing business in Saudi Arabia. Her engineering credentials were exactly what were needed in the alliance at the particular time she became involved. However, given the role of women in the Saudi culture, she alters her work methods. When she travels to Saudi, her husband often accompanies her because she can never travel alone. She is vigilant about her attire and wears the traditional Saudi veil out of respect for her alliance partners. While she may not share the same values, her actions demonstrate respect for the Saudi culture, thereby honoring herself, her company and the alliance partner.

Process Skills Matter

Having the skills required to observe process, act or intervene appropriately is a final component of interpersonal savvy. Process refers not to *what* is done, but to *how* the task is accomplished. Good alliance managers understand process dynamics at a fundamental level. They possess keen observational skills and have the ability to translate what they observe into effective actions or interventions. They know how to read the dynamics in play in real time and act accordingly. When one joint venture manager came into his alliance, first actions involved changing key personnel that the partner had been requesting for months. This was *what* he did. However, *how* he did it communicated volumes to the partner. After listening to the concerns and issues of the partner and alliance executives, he realized that they needed to feel like their voice could be heard. He understood that the process of demonstrating "I'm on your side" was more critical than any objective set of results or any words to the same.

   Process skills are generally underrated in organizations today. They fall into "those soft skills" most commonly and routinely dismissed by MBAs as not the business of business. Effective alliance managers realize that process skills are the business of tomorrow.

The Alliance Manager's Cognitive Attributes

On one hand, all of the skills noted above are skills needed by effective managers in any global business. What distinguishes the best alliance managers is something over and above these baseline skills. These managers, we discovered, tend to possess a set of cognitive attributes that affect how they think and view the world around them. Consider these four alliance managers as they reflect upon their alliance work:

Alliance Manager A: I guess that I don't worry about being the new person in the alliance, or I haven't worried about that. I don't feel any obligation to bend over backwards or to go out of my way to yield or do something different than I would in the normal business transaction just because it is a strategic alliance. I think basically it is a business arrangement.[5]

Alliance Manager B: My objective is very clear. Make as many connections as you can at the main distribution hubs. I am going to lose money on the routes I inherited from them in the short to medium term. I recognize that for the greater benefit of the alliance, we may need to do these things. However, if in three years time, life hasn't gotten any better on those routes . . . .

Alliance Manager C: In 1978 there wasn't much business. It was still very developmental. Company A was putting in some field installations to see what worked and what didn't. Everyone was jockeying for position, so we kept on driving ahead, asking what business do we do next, what markets do we have to win, what challenges do we have to meet. There were lots of meetings and discussions; it was so helpful to sit down and talk for hours.

Alliance Manager D: An alliance manager needs sufficient mental flexibility to adapt to the thinking and the situation of others. That is very important . . . . if you have someone and this happens you may have narrow-minded people who only look at their way of doing things, they will certainly fail in an alliance . . . you have to realize that there are other ways that can lead to success. If you can, you must look at these other ways and consider that they may be even better.

Most executives when queried during our executive seminars quickly dismiss Managers A and B as not being particularly strong. These managers, they argue, are too rigid, not expansive thinkers, and too cause-effect oriented for an atmosphere (alliances) that is much more dynamic, fluid and uncertain.

The strongest debate ends up around managers C and D. Manager C portrays a risk-taking sense of challenge, proactivity and entrepreneurship that is relished. This manager also appears to understand the social noise inherent in an alliance. Manager D, however, is selected consistently by executives in our alliance workshops. Alliance manager D is described as adaptive, flexible and open-minded. This manager seems to understand what Manager A does not – a demonstrable concern for another's point of view.

Our research examined what made individuals like Managers C and D potential alliance exemplars. We discovered that *good alliance managers do, in fact, see and think differently about the world*. We identified six attributes or perspectives associated with strong and effective alliance management. They deal less with skills that individuals have, and more with the cognitive orientation and reference point these managers employ. These are the attributes we assert are the leadership characteristics of tomorrow.

Recognizing and Attending to Multiple Points of View Simultaneously
Strong alliance managers see in multiple dimensions, because they have the ability to consider multiple points of view simultaneously. This is more than simply understanding the perspective of another and understanding that it is different. Good alliance managers actively use this information in explaining what is happening and in forming their solutions in real time. Take the alliance

manager for a joint venture, MonteShell, between an Italian conglomerate, Montedison, and a global energy company, Royal Dutch/Shell, as an example:

> The Shell family view of Monteshell was very negative and to a certain extent, rightly so, because it wasn't up to Shell standards. But, Shell may also have been a bit excessively negative and sort of hypercritical. There was no give and take, just both sides picking on principles. So I made a couple of quite significant concessions on things that had been festering for a while. I've got a long list of unresolved issues and, to break the ice. My object there was to try and break the ice and to show that if we traded off some of our issues, that at least some of the momentum could be won. They were and they weren't big things – but they were personal in a sense because the Italians, you know, the Italian culture very much is focused on honor. If they thought they had been wrongly cheated or undercut, they won't think things in terms of money, they'll think in terms of gestures and the messages that they send. I ended up moving out one guy that the other people thought was no good and that broke things open.

The alliance manager confirmed that he could see the viewpoint of the Italians, see Shells' view, understand the impasse, understand the reasons for that impasse and for each side's interpretations, imagine a different outcome, and offer that path in a way that allows both to come out ahead. His ability to see these multiple perspectives simultaneously created new solutions for the business and repair for the relationship.

Letting the Past Inform, But Not Dictate or Direct

A second attribute is the ability to learn from the past *and* not be constrained by it. Too often managers want immediate answers and solutions to their alliance problems. Their search for answers leads them to inquire *if* others have coped with a similar problem, *if* the problem was solved and precisely what steps were taken in what order. Though rarely articulated, their strategy is to get a success template used by another company with a similar problem, transport it into their alliance, apply it and thereby solve their problem. Unfortunately, this application technique does not always work because alliances are living, breathing entities with unique developmental patterns, pitfalls and possibilities. Each alliance is different.

What happened in the past (or in another company) is just that – something that happened in the past (or in another company). Successful alliance managers use the past to establish generalizable principles to guide their forward assessment of the issue and its resolution. Solutions are not stock answers, but uniquely thought out and creatively applied solutions. One alliance manager we talked with epitomizes this way of thinking: "I act forward by understanding backwards."

Thinking Across Time

Good alliance managers know what is, imagine what is possible and understand all the nuances in between. They think across time, not in time, as one alliance JV manager suggested:

> I read an article about alliances. This article emphasized the fact that one gets all the facts, analyzes them, and puts the picture together and makes the decision based on that. The guys I see that are really doing best are very intuitive in their approach to things. They have done their homework [*the past*], they have a good data bank [*the present*] but they make decisions on the fly and they have to make them with incomplete information because in this day and time, by the time you get complete information, someone else has already done it. [*the future*].[6]

This general manager is demonstrating his ability to think across time and into the future without benefit of having that time.

Seeing Patterns in Chaos and Chaos in Routine

Strong alliance managers have the unique and unusual ability of recognizing patterns in data and disorder in seemingly orderly situations. A simple example brought this home. While waiting to meet with an alliance manager, we found ourselves starring at a painting in her office. One of us commented on the unusual and colorful abstract work. The other commented on the painting of the golfer swinging. During this exchange, the alliance manager entered. Her response was that both of us were right, which is why she loved the painting so much:

> Sometimes I see only colors and lines without a pattern. Others days I immediately see the golfer in the act of taking a stroke. To me it is much like my alliance work. I have to switch back and forth between figure and ground.

Being Clever, Creative and Constantly Curious

Good alliance managers are also clever, creative, ever curious and questioning. These are difficult characteristics to learn; however, they are important ones, because managing an alliance requires a certain type of improvisation. Many global managers, both U.S. and non-U.S., remember the American television show, *McGuyver*. McGuyver was forever finding himself in difficult situations and yet was always able to put together just the right ingredients or use the right mix of items in his surroundings to fashion the perfect bomb, weapon, escape device or aid to ameliorate the situation. So it is with strong alliance managers. They are McGuyver-like in the sense that they are able to fashion innovative solutions in the present because they see something more than what is. They see what is possible. They are able to create order out of whatever materials, insights or tools they have at hand.

Possessing True Wisdom

Good alliance managers are wise. True wisdom is being wise enough not to know particular facts but to know without excessive confidence or excessive cautiousness.[7] Wise people know they don't fully understand what is happening right now. Less wise people assume they know. Unfortunately in alliances, there is a fair amount that is not known completely and fully, making true wisdom a desirable, if not required, characteristic.

THE ALLIANCE MINDSET

Taken all together, strong alliance management requires a different kind of individual mindset, not to mention the spirit of the relationship-embedded enterprise. The term *mindset* refers to the distinctive viewpoints, needs and agendas that determine how an individual views and engages at work (Culbert, 1996). Mindsets help executives make sense of and understand the business world and their daily interactions. The more alliance managers, with whom we have spoken, worked, or gotten to know, the more mindsets appear to create an umbrella encompassing and linking the attributes we've described.

An *alliance mindset* has at its foundation the ability to learn and exercise that learning using a broad repertoire of skills, competencies and perspectives. Managers with an alliance mindset have strongly developed learning orientations,[8] are able to bring order to chaos, thrive on ambiguity and uncertainty and engage artfully with others in community building. Those conditions become a catalyst for learning, not a threat to the status quo.

Our data illustrates that having an alliance mindset, which epitomizes the spirit of learning and challenge of the alliance, is positively related to alliance performance. Recall Alliance Managers A, B, C and D earlier in this chapter. It may not be inconsequential that Managers C and D are associated with a very successful alliance of 25 years, while Managers A and B are from alliances that are either in serious trouble or non-existent. Alliance managers who are strong alliance advocates (i.e. embody the spirit of the alliance) show that they are more likely to be associated with more satisfied alliances (see Exhibit 5).

DEVELOPING GOOD ALLIANCE MANAGERS

Development Takes Time and Effort

Few companies have the bench depth to carefully pick and choose among potential alliance managers. And, most companies do not design management development programs and experiences with an eye toward alliance bench depth. One of the reasons the development of alliance managers is difficult is

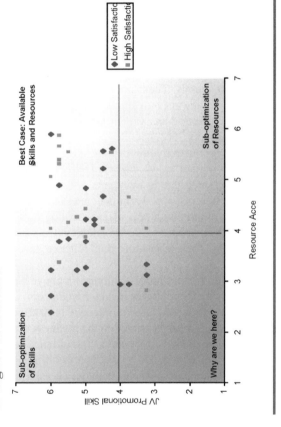

Exhibit 5.

Note: These data are taken from different JV's in the alliance portfolio of a multinational oil company. Each blue and red symbol is a different JV. The axes denote access to resources (the ability to garner the needed capabilities) and alliance competence (as measured by an alliance managers ability to promote the value of the particular both internally and externally).

that there are so many traits that are very difficult to identify, let alone "train" for. Alternatively, if companies merely throw an outstanding line manager into an alliance hoping for alliance development, that company is making a substantial expenditure of people and resources with uncertain results and high costs to both the individual, the company and potentially the alliance. Frankly, most companies should be leery. Firms need to think more strategically about developing not just managers or global managers, but alliance managers, as they will run the companies of the future.

Developing alliance managers takes time and, in some cases, more time than companies are willing to invest or than the individuals are willing to endure. Short-term pressures for results are a disincentive for investing in alliance manager development. In American companies, managerial stars are identified early and promoted quite frequently. These are the individuals who work hard, and desire challenge and rapid upward movement. Companies who provide just that kind of atmosphere for young management talent are rewarded with their unending productivity and results.

Both the talent and their productivity are difficult to lose in today's business environment where speed, market savvy and innovation all increase shareholder returns. Often, these same young managers are at the cutting edge of technology and changing competitive dynamics, making them even more willing and able to push out boldly with new ideas. Creating opportunities that meet these individuals' career needs, while broadening their perspectives in alliance skills, is a challenge. They want more than alliance development may be able to deliver.

At the same time, the issue of continuity of alliance management is critical, particularly when dealing with other cultures in which managers remain in their roles for long periods of time. In Japan, for example, one is an alliance manager for life, whether or not the current job is related to the business of that alliance. This point can best be illustrated by a story about the alliance managers in a joint venture that Corning had with Asahi glass. The two alliance managers, Decker from Corning and Kurata from Asahi, had known each other for over 20 years, as businessmen and friends. The business highs and lows they shared compared equally to the personal times they spent with one another. After Decker died, Kurata was unable to get to the United States for several months. On his first visit stateside, his foremost request after being picked up at the airport was to visit Decker's grave. He spent 20 minutes pacing around the grave, speaking to Decker in Japanese. The Corning executives with him soon learned that he was not merely speaking his condolences, he was literally telling Decker everything that had happened in his absence! Decker was dead, but the relationship and the alliance were still very much alive.

This kind of continuity and resultant dedication to an alliance is far removed from the selection procedures at some companies where alliance managers churn through the partnership. No sooner has one arrived than he or she is summoned elsewhere. We've heard from many Japanese, Korean and Taiwanese managers just how upsetting it is to them to have a manager change every three years. One always ends up re-educating or learning about the new person in the job. And in an alliance context, such re-education is quite costly.

Recognition is crucial. Companies need to acknowledge and appreciate the impact an individual manager can have on alliance development and success. This may seem obvious, but recognizing the need and importance of who is placed into an alliance is a good part of helping an alliance be successful. Alliance manager development is not just a human resources issue; it is a question of developing corporate talent issue that belongs to the entire company.

Companies need to look beyond experiences when identifying alliance talent. Asking the right questions, such as those in Exhibit 6, is as important, if not more necessary, than an objective competence test of global leadership capabilities. These questions seek to identify the depth of the cognitive attributes not necessarily evident in a resume.

These same managers can also learn what it means to partner, for the company and for the alliance. They can learn the importance of the spirit of collaboration within the alliance. In many ways, potential alliance managers benefit from a guided apprenticeship as they move upward in the organization. Companies such as Corning introduce managers into the alliance context sometimes ten years before they assume significant alliance responsibility. Each position is chosen to add increasing depth of perspective and responsibility for that individual manager. The point is not what specific experiences an individual has had; but that thought is given to what experiences that individual needs in that company for a particular alliance context.

Through such a series of professional experiences, and exposure to mentors and role models, new management talent can learn from what the others are doing. These alliance experiences provide an action-learning laboratory, instrumental in leadership development as well as the guided facilitation and reflection necessary to make the learning connection (Conger & Benjamin, 1999).

BEYOND ALLIANCE MANAGER TO FUTURE LEADER

Alliance managers are an integral part of alliance development and success. The skills they need to have or develop represent a unique combination of functional competencies, network competencies, interpersonal competences and a learning orientation and alliance mindset. These managers need concrete expertise and behavioral skills as well as the cognitive capacity and perspectives required to work in a virtual world.

The development of these alliance managers (and future leaders) in part depends upon their company seeing and valuing true alliance activities and the related skills and competencies. Partnering to win competitive position or to dominate the supply chain is not conducive to grooming the kind of skills we advocate for alliance managers. Organizations must first value collaboration,

---

Functional Competencies

• Does this person have the necessary or relevant line management skills for *this* alliance?
• To what extent does this person understand the company, its products and business?
• How might this person's educational background enhance or detract in the position?
• Does this person have a strong understanding of our business and of the alliance's business?

Earned Competencies

• Has this person developed an extensive network within our company?
• Does this person have an extensive business network in the industry of the alliance?
• Has this person developed solid relationships within the partner company?
• Does this individual have credibility in our company?
• Does this individual have credibility and respect outside our company, especially with our partners and in the alliance?

Interpersonal Competencies

• To what degree is this person comfortable in social business situations?
• How does this person demonstrate sensitivity to differences between cultures?
• Is this person considered an effective communicator in diverse settings?
• To what degree does this person easily alter his or her behavior to fit with a new environment or setting?
• Is the person attuned to non-verbal communication?
• Can this person easily sense the mood of a group or individual?

Alliance Mindset

• Does this person have an affinity for complexity?
• Can this person think in terms of patterns, connections and relationships?
• Does this person thrive on challenges?
• Does this person never stop learning from their experiences?
• Is this person described by others as "thinking about and seeing the world differently?"
• Can this person simultaneously consider multiple points of view?

Exhibit 6. Alliance Manager Attributes: Questions for Selection Conversations.

reciprocity, risk taking and experimentation and mutual, system-wide support. Desiring strong alliance managers, but failing to reward allying behaviors or fostering an alliance spirit conducive to cooperation can undermine a company's efforts. Good alliance managers grow up in a culture that supports alliances and allying behavior in a company where the infrastructure and managerial processes reward and encourage cooperation and collaboration with systems that reward the initiative and risk-taking, inquisitiveness and innovation that alliances demand. Placing effort into alliance manager development and the organizational level alliance competence required is equal to developing the leaders of the future.

There are both near and long term benefits to be realized from proactively nurturing the development of one's alliance managers. In the immediate term, one develops the critical mass needed to execute the number of alliances needed. Our observation is that most firms would engage in greater alliance activity but do not have adequate managerial talent. Purposive attention to this gap in management talent will help. In the longer term, one formally makes the alliance experience part of the succession planning process and uses alliance management to supplement other required rotational assignments. One cannot successfully lead a global company if one has not had a set of escalating alliance management experiences. There is too much at stake. The challenges of managing globally can better be addressed if one has had alliance management experience. To lead outside of the traditional trappings of hierarchical authority requires a sense of purpose and vision, a profound respect for one's partner and a delicate hand. Good alliance managers understand that process better than good line managers.

NOTES

1. This breakthrough was described in a newswire press release by Otis Elevator, February 2, 2000.

2. Williamson, Peter, "Strategy as Options on the Future". Sloan Management Review, Spring 1999 (V.40, no. 3), pp. 117–126.

3. The initial research on alliances was conducted through in-depth interviews of alliance managers, followed by an equally extensive survey questionnaire to alliance partners. A more detailed explanation of the methodology can be found in R. Spekman and L. Isabella, Alliance Competence: Maximizing the value of your Partnerships, New York, Wiley, 2000.

4. This has recently been called "T" types by Dorothy Leonard, *Wellsprings of Knowledge* (Cambridge, MA: Harvard Business School Press, 1998).

5. Mention that these quotes are part of our alliance project interview research.

6. Parentheses added for emphasis.

7. A number of the ideas on wisdom have been adapted from Karl Weick, "The collapse of sensemaking in Organizations: The Mann Gulch Disaster," *Wildfire Magazine*, September, 1996, 1–16.

8. These ideas are drawn from some on-going research based up learning orientations. Preliminary themes of this research have appeared in " Learning Mindset: Who has it? Who Doesn't?, " Harvard Business Review, March/April, 1994, p.10.

REFERENCES

Brown, S., & Eisenhardt, K. (1998). *Competing on the Edge: Strategy as Structured Chaos*. Cambridge, MA: Harvard University Press.

Conger, J., & Benjamin, B. (1999). *Building Leaders: How Successful Companies Develop the Next Generation*. San Francisco: Jossey-Bass.

Culbert, S. A. (1996). *Mind-set Management: The Heart of Leadership*. New York, New York: Oxford University Press.

Freidheim, C. (1998). *The Trillion Dollar Enterprise*. Reading, MA: Perseus Books.

Harbison, J., & Pekar, P. (1998). *Smart Alliances: A Practical Guide to Repeatable Success*. NY: Jossey-Bass.

Heifetz, R. (1994). *Leadership without Easy Answers*. Cambridge, MA: Belknap Press.

Gardner, H. (1995). *Leading Minds: An Anatomy of Leadership*. NY: Basic Books.

Gregersen, N., Morrison, A., & Black, J. (1998). Developing leaders for the global frontier. *Sloan Management Review*, (Fall), 21–32.

McCall, M. (1998). *High Flyers: Developing the Next Generation of Leaders*. Cambridge, MA: Harvard Business School Press.

Spekman, R., & Isabella, L. (2000). *Alliance Competence: Maximizing the Value of your Partnerships*. NY: John Wiley.

Schein, E. (1981). Improving Face to Face Relationships. *Sloan Management Review, 22*(2), 43–52.

PERCEPTUAL DISTANCE: THE IMPACT OF DIFFERENCES IN TEAM LEADER AND MEMBER PERCEPTIONS ACROSS CULTURES

Cristina B. Gibson, Jay Conger and Cecily Cooper

ABSTRACT

In this chapter, we propose a theory of perceptual distance and its implications for team leadership and team outcomes. Perceptual distance is defined as the variance in the perceptions of the same social stimulus, which in this case, is either a team leader's behavior or the team's behavior. The general research question that we will address is, "What are the consequences of perceptual distance for team process and outcomes?" Our basic argument is that the relationship between perceptual distance and team processes and outcomes is moderated by two key cultural characteristics: power distance and collectivism. For example, depending upon the dynamics of power distance, large differences in perceptions of a team leader's behavior can negatively impact team productivity. Similarly, depending upon the dynamics of collectivism, significant variations in perceptions of team cohesion can negatively influence conflict resolution.

Advances in Global Leadership, Volume 2, pages 245–276.
ISBN: 0-7623-0723-4

INTRODUCTION

While many research programs have investigated the implementation of work teams and their leadership dynamics in the United States, few have examined the special concerns facing international organizations as they design team-based systems to operate in facilities across the globe. For example, cultural values are likely to vary across operations in different countries, and as such the perceptions, attributions, and interaction styles experienced by teams and their leaders will also vary. From the standpoint of maximizing the benefits of teamwork and leadership, it imperative that we better understand the impact of these cultural processes.

Drawing upon theory and research on team effectiveness, perception and leadership, the goal of this chapter is to better understand one particular dimension of teamwork and leadership in differing cultures. We will explore how the perceptions of team members and their leaders – specifically the degree of differences in these perceptions – impact team processes and outcomes. We refer to this phenomenon as *perceptual distance*. The general research question that we will address is: "What are the consequences of perceptual distance for team processes and outcomes?" We will focus on the critical teamwork process of conflict resolution and the key outcome dimension of productivity. Our basic argument is that the relationship between perceptual distance and team processes/outcomes is moderated by two key cultural characteristics: power distance and collectivism.

We begin our discussion by reviewing the literature on team design, perceptual processes and cross-cultural leadership (see Table 1 for a summary of this literature review). Following this review, we propose specific hypotheses that link these literatures together to develop a model explaining the impact of perceptual distance on team processes and outcomes. We conclude our discussion by describing the implications of our model for explaining variances in team processes and outcomes across cultures.

TEAM DESIGN

A work team is a particular type of work group that has a high degree of interdependent interaction and mutually shared responsibility for achieving specified outcomes (Sundstrom, DeMeuse & Futrell, 1990). While researchers have looked at what contributes to the effectiveness of work groups from a variety of perspectives, most of the criteria for effectiveness can be categorized into three primary dimensions. These include: (1) performance effectiveness in

Table 1. Summary of Literature Reviewed.

Sample of Literature Reviewed	Summary
Team Design	
Cox, Lobel & McLeod (1991)	Groups comprised of collectivists cooperate more than groups of comprised of individualists.
Earley & Mosakowski (2000)	Homogeneous and highly heterogeneous teams outperform moderately heterogeneous teams.
Gibson (1999)	The group efficacy – group effectiveness relationship is tested and moderators are discussed.
Gladstein (1984)	Implicit group effectiveness theories relate to self-report variables but not performance.
Gully, Devine & Whitney (1995)	Level of analysis & task interdependence moderate the cohesion-performance relationship.
Hambrick, Cho & Chen (1996)	Compares the actions of heterogeneous and homogeneous top management teams.
Ibarra (1993)	The organizational context places constraints on the networks of women & racial minorities.
Jehn (1995)	Looks at the relationship between two types of conflict on individual and group-level outcomes.
Jehn, Northcraft & Neale (1999)	Explores the effects of workgroup diversity and task-related moderators on workgroup outcomes.
Kirchmeyer & Cohen (1992)	Examined the effects of constructive conflict on culturally diverse decision-making groups.
Mullen & Associates (1993)	Finds to effects of group cohesiveness on decision-making to be moderated by many factors.
Oetzel (1998)	Measures of individualism-collectivism, self-construal, and group composition are related to conflict in small groups.
Rempel & Fisher (1997)	Higher levels of cohesion can be detrimental to problem solving regardless of perceived threat.
Seers, Petty & Cashman (1995)	Self-managing groups experienced greater cohesiveness and satisfaction than traditional groups.
Watson, Kumar & Michaelson (1993)	Differences between culturally homogeneous and heterogeneous groups disappear over time.
Leadership (particularly relevant to cross-cultural issues)	
Ayman & Chemers (1983)	Factor structures of perceived leader behavior in Iran differed from those of Western samples.
Batt & Appelbaum (1995)	Substantive participation has more possible positive effects than consultative participation.
Bennett (1977)	Explores the generalizability of two leadership scales on Asian managers.
Cohen, Ledford & Spreitzer (1996)	Finds self-managing work team effectiveness is not related to encouraging supervisory behaviors.
Dorfman & Associates (1997)	Finds universality for 3 leader behaviors and specificity for 3 others across countries.

Table 1.   Continued.

Sample of Literature Reviewed	Summary
Leadership (particularly relevant to cross-cultural issues) – Continued	
Gerstner & Day (1994)	Finds significant differences in leadership prototypes between subjects from different countries.
Gibson & Marcoulides (1995)	Found that a 6-factor model of leadership style held across four countries.
Hofstede (1993)	Discusses the shortcomings of U.S. management theories for international managers.
Manz (1992a)	Discusses self-leading work teams as an advancement beyond self-managed teams.
Manz & Simms (1987)	It is important for external leaders of self-managing teams to facilitate team self-management.
Smith, Peterson & Misumi (1994)	Compares the type of guidance used in managing work teams in the U.S., the U.K., and Japan.
Wagner (1994)	Participation is related to both performance & satisfaction though the effects are small.
Perceptual Processes	
Cronshaw & Lord (1987)	Finds empirical support for the social information processing theory of leadership perceptions.
Hanges, Lord & Dickson (2000)	Proposes an information-processing model relating culture and leadership.
Lord (1985)	Uses an information-processing explanation of leadership to discuss measurement issues.
Lord, DeVader & Alliger (1986)	Leadership perceptions are related to certain personality traits.
Lord, Phillips & Rush (1980)	Perceiver characteristics are significantly related to leadership perceptions.
Rush, Thomas & Lord (1977)	Implicit leadership theories pose a threat to the validity of leadership behavioral questionnaires.
Weiss & Adler (1981)	Found that implicit leadership theories are not affected by differences in cognitive complexity.

terms of outputs, (2) group processes, and (3) member attitudes (Cohen & Bailey, 1997).

The dimension of performance effectiveness typically includes output measures of productivity, quality and customer satisfaction. Group processes manifest themselves in conflict resolution, decision making and problem solving. Attitudinal outcomes include measures of employee satisfaction and trust. In the model we are proposing, we focus specifically on the performance output measure of productivity and on the group process variable of conflict resolution, because research suggests that both of these outcomes are most critical across multinational facilities and that they are also the most challenging to manage given potential cross-cultural differences in team dynamics (Erez & Earley, 1993; Earley & Moszakowski, 2000; Gibson, 1999).

The importance of conflict resolution within teams has been illustrated by Gladstein (1984) who found that group ratings of the openness of communication and the supportiveness associated with conflict resolution were positively associated with group ratings of satisfaction and possibly performance. She interprets her findings thus: "Open communication, supportiveness, fair weighting of individual inputs, and discussion about how to do the work help group members feel good about their jobs and their team. This satisfaction and self-reported effectiveness may be related to revenue attainment in the long-run . . . . Thus, though these variables may not predict performance, they are associated with other important outcomes" (1984: 512).

More recently, Seers, Petty and Cashman (1995) found that the group process variable of team-member exchange, which assesses the level of reciprocal collaborative and cooperative efforts within a team, was the variable most highly related to group production efficiency. In a similar vein, Jehn (1995) examined 79 work groups and 26 management teams from a large freight transportation company and found that conflict impacted group outcomes, dependent on the type of conflict and the type of task. She identified two types of conflict – task and relationship. Relationship conflict had a negative effect on attitudinal outcomes such as satisfaction and intent to turnover, but had no relationship with performance, regardless of the type of task. On the other hand, task conflict was significantly related to effectiveness but was moderated by the type of task. For routine tasks, task conflict was detrimental to group processes, whereas for non-routine tasks task conflict was not detrimental and was sometimes beneficial for group process.

In addition, three key facets of team design impact productivity and conflict resolution: team composition, group culture and group cohesion. These facets are particularly pertinent in multinational organizations that utilize team-based systems across different cultures. The differing national cultures featured on teams represent highly different contexts that impact the mechanisms, which influence processes and outcomes. We address each of these features in turn in the following sections.

Team Composition

Two basic literatures speak to the issue of team composition: cultural diversity research and small groups research. The cultural diversity literature (e.g. Cox,

1993; Cox, Lobel & McLeod, 1991; Jackson and associates, 1995; Watson, Kumar & Michaelson, 1993) studies team members' demographic backgrounds and highlights demographic variables presupposed to relate directly to cultural attributes, values, and perceptions. The benefits of cultural diversity are often attributed to the variety of perspectives, values, skills, and attributes that diverse team members contribute (Maznevski, 1994).

The small groups research literature addresses team composition effects (e.g. Hackman, 1986, 1987; McGrath, 1984; Turner, 1987), and shows that the relationship of heterogeneity to performance is mixed and subject to a number of constraints imposed by the work setting (McGrath, 1984; Nemeth, 1986). Much of this research finds that team similarity is positively associated with team effectiveness and interpersonal attraction (Hambrick & Mason, 1984; Tsui et al., 1992). Homogeneous team members generally report stronger affinity for their team than do heterogeneous team members (Ibarra, 1992). Attitude similarity and demographic homogeneity have generally been shown to be positively related to group cohesiveness (Jackson et al., 1992). Demographically similar groups tend to exhibit higher satisfaction, and lower absenteeism and turnover (e.g. Jackson, Brett, Sessa, Cooper, Julin & Peyronninet, 1991). These findings are consistent with the well-established principle that people are attracted to similar others (Byrne, 1971), and the proposition that heterogeneous groups experience more conflict (Jehn, Northcraft & Neale, 1999). Beginning with Steiner (1972), a stream of research has treated the composition of groups primarily in terms of the resulting process losses that prevent a group from reaching its performance potential. These process losses potentially result from the differing perceptions, attributions and communication patters that result from heterogeneity (Adler, 1991).

Team Culture

Emerging from team interaction are shared understandings among members, which have been called alternately a "hybrid culture" (Earley & Mosakowski, 2000), "third culture" (Casmir, 1992; Graen & Hui, 1999), team-based mental models (Klimoski & Mohammed, 1994), or synergy (Adler, 1991). A hybrid team culture refers to an emergent and simplified set of rules and actions, work capability expectations and member perceptions that individuals within a team develop, share and enact after mutual interactions. To the extent these rules, expectations and roles are shared (Rohner, 1987; Shweder & LeVine, 1984), a strong culture exists. These characteristics need not be completely shared among team members – just as cultural values are not uniformly shared among societal members (Rohner, 1987) – but there needs to be significant overlap among team members.

Several perspectives posit the importance of shared group culture for team functioning. For example, effective groups often display a shared conception of their expectations and rules (Bettenhausen, 1991; Hackman, 1987). When team members perceive shared understandings with other members, the positive effect and propensity to trust generated by such a discovery fuels performance improvement (Klimoski & Mohammed, 1994) and bolsters group efficacy (Bandura, 1997).

Using a series of three studies, Earley and Mosakowski (2000) showed that effective teams are those with a strong team culture because shared member expectations facilitate individual and team performance and communication. A strong team culture may derive from overlapping and pre-existing character-istics of team members or newly developed patterns of team member interaction. Their investigation demonstrated that during the initial interaction phase, national heterogeneity had a detrimental impact on team functioning. This disadvantage was not a monotonically decreasing function; rather the impact was consistent (both split and heterogeneous teams were inferior) in contrast to a homogeneous team. Over time, however, the impact of heterogeneity on team performance and other team outcome variables was related in a curvilinear fashion. After forming ways to interact and communicate, highly heterogeneous teams appeared to create a common identity.

It may be that leaders play an important role in creating and managing hybrid cultures. Graen and Hui (1999: 23–24) suggest that, particularly in multi-national organizations, managers create hybrid cultures by bridging the home office and overseas office cultures, which can facilitate the proper handling of seemingly incongruent values and priorities. Furthermore, they argue that the ability to develop hybrid cultures can be enhanced through developmental experiences in multinational settings.

Team Cohesion

Teams vary in the extent to which team members feel attached to the team, often referred to as *cohesion* (Gully, Devine & Whitney, 1995). In their meta-analysis of the impact of team cohesion, Gully et al. (1995) found a positive relationship between cohesion and performance, but the effect was larger for studies using a group level of analysis. The relationship between cohesion and performance was also dependent upon the type of task involved. When tasks were highly interdependent and required coordination and communication, the cohesion-performance relationship was stronger, implying that interdependent tasks groups are better able to capitalize on the benefits of cohesiveness.

In the second meta-analysis, Mullen et al. (1993) looked at the effects of group cohesiveness on decision-making quality. Supporting Janis' (1972) proposition that cohesiveness was a necessary but not sufficient condition for groupthink, their results showed that there was not a simple effect of cohesiveness on quality of decision making. They found that antecedent conditions had to be present in order for the two constructs to be related. Once antecedent conditions were accounted for, Mullen et al. (1993) found that different components of cohesiveness had varying effects. The more a measure of group cohesion reflected interpersonal attraction, the greater was the propensity for cohesion to impair the quality of group decisions. The opposite was true if the cohesion measure reflected commitment to the task.

These findings suggest that cohesion is generally related to performance outcomes, but under certain conditions may be detrimental to group decision-making ability if the cohesion stems from interpersonal attraction. Rempel and Fisher (1997) supported these findings in their investigation of the effects of perceived threat and cohesion on the decision-making ability of groups. They found that groups reporting high or increasing levels of cohesion experienced decreased problem-solving ability regardless of perceived threat. However, groups with lower levels of cohesion experienced decreased problem solving with an increase in perceived threat.

When taken together, these findings illustrate the relevance of studying cohesiveness in work teams. As highly interdependent types of groups, work teams should be able to reap more of the potential benefits, which can stem from cohesion. Moreover, assuming that their primary task does not require considerable amounts of decision-making, these groups will not be subject to the risk of groupthink, a potential detrimental effect associated with cohesion.

CROSS-CULTURAL LEADERSHIP

A key technique for grappling with the aforementioned features of teams is through team leadership. One of the most significant areas of influence for leaders of teams is decision-making. This leadership dimension was first identified by Lewin and his associates (Lewin, Lippitt & White, 1939; Lippitt & White, 1947) who studied autocratic versus participative leadership roles in teams and their impact on group decision making and decision implementation. In providing direction for a work team, the leader has a basic choice between implementing decisions using the resources of the group members or by using the leader's own resources. In other words, the leader could choose to engage in either participative or autocratic behavior. To the extent the leader uses participative behavior, a team gains autonomy and eventually may become self-managed. It has been further suggested that a system of self-direction will have a positive impact on the team members' feelings of competence and self-control (Deci, 1975a, b). And finally, theorists have suggested that self-direction instills a sense of purpose that extends beyond the immediate performance of the task (Manz, 1992a, b; Manz & Simms, 1987).

Effects of Participation

While quantitative research on leadership decision-making styles over the last several decades has not produced firm conclusions on the performance effects of a participative decision style, descriptive case study research has generally found positive relationships with group performance (Yukl, 1998). Wagner (1994) found that participation had a small but positive relationship to team effectiveness. However, participation effects can differ depending upon whether the type of participation is substantive or consultative (Wagner, 1994). For substantive participation, research has shown a consistent positive relationship with performance outcomes. However, the effects of consultative participation were not as positive as the effects for substantive participation. Most of the positive outcomes that researchers have found in relation to consultative participation were behavioral in nature. Few, if any, effects of consultative participation on performance outcomes have been found. One exception is a study by Batt and Appelbaum (1995). They directly compared the effects of substantive and consultative participation across two different industries: telecommunications and apparel. Substantive participation was positively related to satisfaction, organizational commitment and perceptions of output quality for both samples. Although consultative participation was not related to any of these outcomes for the telecommunications employees, there was a significant effect on organizational commitment for sewing operators.

In some settings, certain participatory leader behaviors may have a negative impact. Cohen et al. (1996), for example, found that supervisors using encouraging behaviors with self-managed teams had a negative impact on team performance. In support of a more direction-oriented approach, Brewer, Wilson and Beck (1994) found that police sergeants who spent more time monitoring team performance typically had higher performing units. The underlying rationale for this approach is that teams without a clear sense of direction spend a great deal of their time wallowing around and frustrated because they receive confusing instructions about their purpose (Hackman, 1986). Research suggests this may be true – an engaging statement of purpose orients and empowers teams (Walton, 1985; Mohrman, Cohen & Mohrman, 1995).

Cross-Cultural Differences in Reactions to Participative Leadership

The vast majority of these studies have been conducted in U.S. settings. Unfortunately, cross-cultural research on leadership has been quite limited. As Yukl (1998) points out, however, most of the leadership research of the latter half of the last century has been conducted in the United States, Canada and Western Europe. As a result, it strongly reflects the cultural biases of Western society such as those identified by Hofstede (1993, p.81): "In a global perspective, U.S. management theories contain a number of idiosyncrasies not necessarily shared by management elsewhere. Three such idiosyncrasies are mentioned: A stress on market processes, a stress on the individual, and a focus on managers rather than workers."

In recent years, there have been studies to rectify this problem though the total number remains small (e.g. Den Hartog et al., 1999; Dorfman et al., 1997; Gerstner & Day, 1994; House et al., 1999; Smith, Peterson & Misumi, 1994). From the standpoint of leadership decision styles and power distance, there is an even smaller body of research. While there are various forms of universal qualities as identified by Dickson, Hanges, and Lord in their chapter in this volume, it is generally believed that numerous attributes viewed as character-istic of leaders are likely to vary strongly by culture (Lord & Maher, 1991). In addition, conceptions of the most important characteristics of effective leadership appear to vary by culture, such that the meaning and evaluation of numerous leader behaviors depends on the cultural context (Den Hartog et al., 1999; Gibson & Marcoulides, 1994; House et al., 1999).

In some cultures, an effective leadership style might be characterized by paternalism, while in other cultures a more participative and peer-based style may be more positively associated with the attribution of leadership. Research conducted by Ayman and Chemers (1983; 1986), for example, demonstrated that sensitivity to group norms was a more critical component of leader behavior in Iran and Mexico than in the United States. These differences are likely to result in different leadership prototypes or profiles around the globe (Bass, 1990: Hofstede, 1993). One of the more widely cited studies examining leadership prototypes across different cultures by Gerstner and Day (1994) did indeed find reliable differences in leadership perceptions by culture. Work by Redding (1990) and Chen (1995) identified a leadership prototype called paternalism, which is a style combining clear and strong authority with concern and consideration. The leader's authority is not easily shared or delegated, and all initiatives are believed to flow outward from the formal leader (Silin, 1976). Preferences for this style appear to vary by culture (Dorfman et al., 1997; Dorfman, 1994; Hofstede, 1993).

Cultural Values as Key Mechanisms Influencing Leadership and Teamwork

The intercultural differences obtained in the studies described in the previous section can be partially explained by differences in cultural values. Although variations within countries do exist, people within a given country often share common values and these values can be utilized to distinguish one country's culture from another (Hofstede, 1980; Shweder & LeVine, 1984; Triandis, 1989). As Dickson, Hanges, and Lord similarly point out in their chapter in this volume, two cultural values that appear to be especially critical in leading work organizations are power distance and collectivism (Hofstede, 1980; House et al., 1999). Power distance represents the degree to which members of a culture accept and expect that power in society is distributed unequally (Hofstede, 1980; House et al., 1999). Cultures low in power distance will try to minimize inequalities, favor less autocratic leadership and favor less centralization of authority. Research suggests that the U.S., Australia, Canada, Denmark, Austria and France are low in power distance (Hofstede, 1980). On the other hand, cultures high in power distance will be characterized by greater acceptance of inequalities, more autocratic leadership, and greater centralization of authority. Research suggests that Malaysia, the Philippines, Panama, Guatemala and Puerto Rico are high in power distance (Hofstede, 1980). In these high power distance cultures, leaders are often viewed as effective even if they are highly directive (Kanungo, 1980, 1982).

A second key cultural value pertinent to the management of teams is the level of collectivism that characterizes a facility. Collectivism describes the strength of ties between individuals in a society, the degree to which members are integrated into groups and the extent to which members of a society value their membership in groups (Hofstede, 1980). Countries such as Peru, Chile, Puerto Rico, Taiwan, Singapore and Malaysia are highly collectivistic. Countries such as the U.S., Australia, New Zealand, Italy, and France are low on collectivism. Preliminary evidence suggests that in collectivistic cultures, leader directive behavior is more important than when collectivism is low (Bennett, 1977; Hofstede, 1980).

Cultural values, in turn, shape perceptions, cognitions, and preferences in teams (Gibson, 2000; Gibson and Zellmer-Bruhn, 2000). There is some empirical evidence to support this. Hofstede (1991) found that in high power distance cultures, managers were more often satisfied with a directive leadership style from their supervisors, whereas managers in low power distance cultures preferred a participative supervisor. Smith, Peterson and Misumi (1994) have shown that managers in high power distance countries employ a greater use of rules and procedures than managers in low power distance cultures. Finally, although House et al. (1999) found that several aspects of leadership were universally endorsed (i.e. charismatic and value-based leadership behaviors), they also obtained preliminary evidence that collective value orientations are positively related to team-oriented leadership endorsement, and that power distance is negatively related to participative leadership endorsement. The authors concluded that "societal cultural variables have non-trivial influences on culturally endorsed leadership theories and explain, in part, why there is variance across cultures with respect to what is expected of leaders" (1999: 218).

In perhaps the most comprehensive investigation of a cultural contingency model of team effectiveness, Gibson and Zellmer-Bruhn (2000) explored a sample of 52 teams across four countries that varied based on power distance and collectivism. Using rich qualitative analyses of team members' language about teamwork, referred to as teamwork metaphors, they demonstrated that power distance and collectivism impact the meaning members ascribe to teamwork and to their expectations of team leadership. In the high power distance cultures, team members tended to utilize teamwork metaphors containing information about hierarchy such as the family and military metaphors. In the low power distance cultures, team members used teamwork metaphors such as sports metaphors that contained very little information about status and hierarchy. Stated another way, the meaning team members ascribed to teamwork in high power distance cultures included prescriptions for status relationships and in turn shaped members' expectations regarding hierarchical relationships in teams. Based on their interview results, the authors argue that teams in a high power distance culture, which have military or family metaphors, will be more effective when managed in such a way that recognizes status relationships and incorporates these into the team structure. Teams that utilize sport metaphors in a low power distance culture will be more effective when status relations are equal within teams.

Findings such as these point to the importance of cognitive and perceptual processes in teams, particularly with regard to team leadership. We explore these processes from the point of view of perceptual theory in our next section.

PERCEPTUAL PROCESSES

According to social perceptual theory (Allport, 1955; Tagirui & Petrullo, 1958), human beings experience other individuals phenomenologically. This is due to the great complexity of social stimuli, limitations in our information-processing capabilities and individual differences. As a result, we construct proximal representations of what we see and experience about others. As Bruner (1957) suggests, perception therefore serves essentially as an act of categorization. Perceivers have learned that certain stimulus elements are commonly associated with one another, and these in turn become meaningful categories. Given that these categories provide guidelines for classifying information, we can think of perception as a form of problem-solving technique. The technique allows perceivers to ascertain whether the stimulus individual possesses characteristics that would place them in any one of several categories (Shaver, 1975).

Perceptions of Leadership

Among many organizationally relevant perceptions, individuals develop classification schemes for the behaviors of leaders (Hanges, Lord & Dickson, 2000). The process becomes even more fine-grained in that different behaviors may be perceived to represent different leadership styles. For example, on the dimension of decision-making, the demonstration of certain types of behaviors can result in leaders being categorized as either "participative" or "autocratic" leaders.

Brewer (1988) contrasts two general perceptual modes - person-based or categorical. In the person-based mode, which tends to occur when the perceiver has low cognitive demands, perceptions are based primarily on the features and behaviors of the person being perceived, and information is integrated to form a unified impression of the person. Such a stimulus-based processing represents a leader-oriented view of leader perceptions. In contrast, the categorical mode of social perceptions predominates under higher cognitive load conditions, which would be expected when a team member interacts with multiple others or observes an entire group interacting. Under this mode, the purpose and processing goals of the perceiver determine the relevance of perceptual categories, and these knowledge structures guide information processing. This mode corresponds to a perceiver-oriented model of leader perceptions and is the view that we adopt in this chapter.

This view emphasizes the importance of perceiver constructs (Lord & Maher, 1991) in explaining leadership perceptions and their impact. Extensive work in this area (Eden & Leviatan, 1975; Hall & Lord, 1995; Hanges et al., 2000; Maurer & Lord, 1991; Rush, Thomas & Lord, 1977; Weiss & Adler, 1981) has demonstrated that prior beliefs about leader behaviors affect the perceptions of leaders and the encoding, recall and rating of leadership behaviors. It is the events, behaviors and traits *as perceived by others* – not as they occur in any objective sense – that are crucial in explaining leadership perceptions (Hollander & Julian, 1969; Lord et al., 1986). For example, Lord et al. (1980) partitioned variance in ratings of leaders into three components: subjects' group context, the leader being rated, and the group member actually doing the perceiving and rating. Group context explained between 10 and 27% of the variance in ratings on measures of leadership. Leader effects were also important, explaining between 19 and 52% of the variance. But consistent with the perceptual view of leadership, perceiver effects were nearly just as important, explaining between 17 and 44% of the variance in ratings.

To understand the role of leadership perceptions in determining team processes and outcomes, it is critical to distinguish between the perceptual processes associated with leaders' self-perceptions, and those associated with team members' (followers') perceptions of the team leader.

Leaders' Self-Perceptions

The self is a person's mental representation of his/her own personality, social identity and social roles (Kihlstrom & Cantor, 1984). The mechanisms by which self-relevant information is processed, stored and organized into a certain structure have mainly been conceptualized by models of social cognition. According to this approach, a person's self-perception is formed through experience and thought, and encoded in memory alongside mental representations of other objects in the physical and social environment (Kihlstrom et al., 1988). On the structural level, the self-perception can be viewed as a collection of schemas, prototypes, goals or images (Sherman, Judd & Bernadette, 1983). Each schema contains information, traits, roles and behavior, as well as knowledge of rules and procedures for making inferences and evaluating one's own functioning and development. Not all information about the self is accessible at any particular moment. The part active at any moment is called the "working self" (Markus & Kunda, 1986; Markus & Wurf, 1987). Compared to deeper levels of the self-concept, the working self is more accessible, malleable and tied to prevailing circumstances. The configuration of the immediate social environment determines the facet of the self that is most accessible (Erez & Earley, 1993).

Self-perception is to a large extent an agent of its own creation (Gecas, 1982). Much of our own personal self-regulation operates in the service of developing and maintaining an acceptable self-perception. Stated another way, we act in ways that maintain our sense of self. Three motives in the service of the self can be identified (Erez & Earley, 1993): (1) the need for self-enhancement, as reflected in maintaining a positive cognitive and emotional state about the self; (2) the self-efficacy motive, which is the desire to perceive oneself as competent and efficacious; and (3) the need for self-consistency, which is the desire to sense and experience coherence and continuity.

A leader's own behavior is often derived from his or her self-perception. Leader behavior, in turn, will be directed by a desire to maintain the self (Erez & Earley, 1993). A leader will tend to search for, critically examine and demonstrate particular behaviors that are consistent with his or her sense of self. For example, a leader's self-perception might include beliefs associated with follower participation in decision making, such as: (1) it helps employees develop self-confidence, (2) it is just and necessary, (3) it reaffirms the leader's membership in society, and (4) it promotes a positive self-image for the leader by advocating values respected by a given society. The first two beliefs are related to the self-efficacy motive, the third belief is related to the self-enhancement motive and the fourth to a self-consistency motive.

Team Members' Perceptions of Leaders

There is only a small body of research that has explored the implications of subordinates' perceptions and leadership. This literature, however, has not examined the *impact* of individual differences in perceptions of a leader's behavior, but rather it has focused on ascertaining what characteristics lead to the attributions of leadership. For example, Lord (1985) and Lord and Maher (1993) found that perceptions of leadership ability could arise via two different processes. First, leadership could be inferred based upon the perceiver's knowledge of the focus individual's past performance: "Because leadership is commonly viewed as a determinant of good performance, leadership is an inference made about people associated with good performance" (Lord, 1985: 102). So the entrepreneurial founder of a new venture that becomes a successful business enterprise is often attributed the quality of "leadership." Secondly, a person could form their perception of leadership by being exposed to his or her behaviors or traits through day-to-day interactions with that person in an organizational setting.

According to this theory, categorizations are made based on the match of stimulus properties (actual leader behavior) to abstractions or prototypes derived from characteristics common to a category. Perceivers use degree of match to this ready-made structure to form leadership perceptions (Lord & Maher, 1991). Several laboratory studies have shown that the fit of individuals' behavior to observers' prototypes of leadership affects leadership ratings (Cronshaw & Lord, 1987; Fraser & Lord, 1988; Lord et al., 1984). Results are consistent with a model in which at first a person is classified in terms of leadership based on his or her behaviors, and then further inferences about the person are based on the perceivers' implicit leadership theories and general knowledge associated with leadership categories, rather than the person's actual behavior. In Brewer's (1988) terms, most processing is category-based rather than person-based.

Differences in Perceptions

From the perspective of the model presented in this chapter, it is important to note that perceptions often differ. Given variations in experience, personality dispositions, empathic ability, interpersonal skills and cognitive complexity, individuals will necessarily have different perceptions of the same social stimulus (Kelley, 1963; Shaver, 1975). In addition, there may be transient motivational factors that can influence perceptions related to the immediate context (Shaver, 1975). As a result, a leader may have different perceptions of his or her own behavior than does the team he or she leads. This is because, when asked to describe his or her own behavior, a leader will often do so in terms of his or her self-perception (Lord & Maher, 1991). However, there are many other factors that may impact whether actual leader behavior demonstrated is consistent with these self-perceptions. In addition, whether followers perceive this behavior as consistent with the leader's intentions is also subject to many constraints and impacts.

Members of the same work group may have varying perceptions of the team's collective behavior. Perceptual differences among team members can be explained by the fact that certain group members have more or less contact with the team and that important background factors differ among members. In addition, the history of their interpersonal relations may lead team members to interpret the team's behavior in differing ways.

We use the term *perceptual distance* to describe the degree to which there are significant variations among the perceptions of individuals of the same social stimulus – in this case, either perceptions of the leader's decision-making behavior or of their team's cohesiveness. Under our terminology, *high* perceptual distance would imply large differences or variations in perceptions of the same stimulus whereas *low* perceptual distance would imply only small or no differences between individual perceptions.

The concept of perceptual distance has certain parallels to the construct of "social distance" proposed in the charismatic and transformational leadership literature (Shamir, 1995), but it essentially describes a different dimension of social perception. In the leadership literature, for example, the term "social distance" refers to the effects of leaders on subordinates or followers at varying degrees of *organizational distance*. For example, it has been hypothesized that there will be fundamental differences in the perceptions of a leader's behavior between the subordinates who comprise the leader's most immediate circle of relationships and subordinates who do not have direct contact with the leader (Shamir, 1995). These varying perceptions are due largely to fundamental differences in the influence processes employed by the leader with "close up" versus at "a distance" relationships. In close situations, the leader will rely more upon personal example and observable behavior to influence, whereas distant relationships demand that the leader employ rhetorical skills and the articulation of a guiding vision. These differences in influence approaches will result in different categorizations of what constitutes "leadership" given a follower's proximity (or distance) from the leader. While still a phenomenon based on perception, social distance, in this case, refers to the *hierarchical* and *work relationship* distance between subordinates and their leader that in turn creates differences in the perceptions of what constitute their leader's behaviors.

Our conceptualization of "perceptual distance" differs. It is not dependent on organizational or hierarchical distance but rather is a product of person-specific differences shaped by an individual's past experiences, personality dispositions, empathic ability, interpersonal skills, and cognitive complexity as well as the ongoing dynamics of the relationship with the social stimulus. These differences may cause a leader and the team or individuals within a team to have varying perceptions of the same social stimulus. In contrast to "social distance," variations in these perceptions can therefore occur among individual members of a team who are at the *same* relational or organizational distance from the leader and from one another.

INTEGRATING TEAM DESIGN, LEADERSHIP AND PERCEPTUAL THEORY: PROPOSED RELATIONSHIPS

We propose that the potential consequences of perceptual distance, both in terms of team processes and outcomes, will also depend on the cultural context in which teams are embedded. In other words, significant perceptual differences in a low power distance culture are likely to have different implications for team performance outcomes than in a high power distance culture. Similarly, perceptual differences among team members in low versus high collectivism cultures may lead to important differences in how team conflict is resolved and in the quality of intra-team communication. Specifically, integrating team design, leadership and perceptual theory, we propose several relationships (see Figs 1 and Table 2) concerning perceptual distance vis-a-vis team performance outcomes and team process outcomes. We will start with the former.

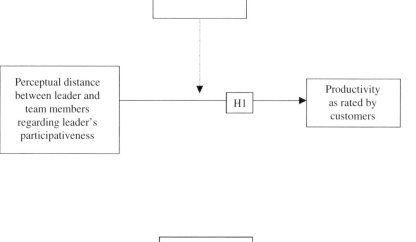

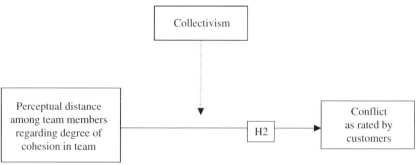

Fig. 1. Proposed Relationships.

Perceptual Distance Between the Team and a Leader

We view perceptual distance between a leader and team members as most critical when the stimulus is the degree to which the leader is participative. Stated another way, when a team leader and team members differ in their perceptions regarding the leader's behavior, this may have detrimental effects on performance outcomes such as productivity. Whether or not this is the case is likely to depend on the level of power distance prevalent in the cultural context.

In a high power distance culture, we argue that perceptual distance between the leader and team members regarding their leader's participativeness will have little or no impact on the team performance outcomes. We argue that this

Table 2.   Specific Predictions.

	Low Power Distance	Hi Power Distance
High Perceptual Distance (large differences between leader and team members' aggregated perceptions of leader's behavior)	H1a: low productivity	H1b: high productivity
Low Perceptual Distance (small differences between leader and team members' aggregated perceptions of leader's behavior)	H1a: high productivity	H1b: high productivity
	Low Collectivism	Hi Collectivism
High Perceptual Distance (within team – large differences among team members' perceptions regarding level of cohesion)	H2a: high conflict resolution effectiveness	H2b: low conflict resolution effectiveness
Low Perceptual Distance (within team – small differences among team members' perceptions regarding level of cohesion)	H2a: high conflict resolution effectiveness	H2b: high conflict resolution effectiveness

occurs for four particular reasons. The team members' deferential attitude towards the formal power of their leader (Chen, 1995; Hofstede, 1991; Redding, 1990) allows group members to tolerate wide variations in perceptions of leader behavior without sacrificing performance outcomes. This tolerance will also allow group members to accept differences in leader-member relations without feelings of resentment arising to the point that they negatively impact group performance.

Secondly, the prototypes of leadership behavior in high power distance cultures will generally not place a premium on participative decisions, and therefore varying perceptions of the leader's behavior along this decision-making dimension will be far less meaningful than in a low power distance culture. Expectations are that the leader may demonstrate an inconsistency of behavior in decision-making styles and that this is permissible behavior. Differences are therefore not seen as dysfunctional.

Third, in a high power distance culture, it is important to maintain smooth interpersonal relations and to try to be agreeable under difficult circumstances. This includes being sensitive to what others are feeling and then adjusting one's behavior. Moreover, as Tjosvold and Hui point out in their chapter in this volume, conflict in high power distance cultures such as China is often avoided because it is assumed to communicate interpersonal hostility rather than simply disagreement. Because of these concerns and values, team members in a high power distance setting may be reluctant to indicate a lack of understanding or to point out or challenge a leader's inconsistencies and mistakes to save the leader's face (Earley & Randel, 1997). Face refers to the evaluation of a person based on internal and external social judgments (Earley, 1999). Particularly in high power distance cultures, a person's behavior in organizations reflects, in part, his or her attempt to establish and maintain face across a range of social settings (Earley & Randel, 1997).

Finally, as Chen and Farh note in their chapter, "personalism" is a dominant feature of management practice in high power distance cultures such as Taiwan and China. Personalism (Redding, 1993; Fahr, Early & Lin, 1997) is the tendency for leaders not to use universal rules in their treatment of subordinates. Instead the quality of the relationship with a particular subordinate becomes an important basis in the leader's decisions to involve that individual in decision making. Therefore a leader may involve one subordinate extensively in a decision while excluding others or minimizing their involvement. Subordinates accept these variations as normal behavior. There are few expectations of universal treatment as one would find among team members in a lower power distance culture, and therefore greater acceptance of differences in leader-member relations.

On the other hand, in a low power distance culture, the opposite of the aforementioned outlined points is likely to be true. As previously reviewed, in a low power distance culture, team members are likely to have a less deferential attitude toward leadership. And they are also likely to have higher expectations of consistency between ideal and realized leader behavior. Thus, team members will be far less accepting of perceptual distance between the leader and team members. In these cultures, this type of perceptual distance will be interpreted as inconsistency in stated and actual leader behavior, and this inconsistency in behavior is likely to be interpreted as a sign of weak leadership. In a low power distance culture, this type of perceptual distance is more likely to generate confusion among team members and possibly resentment toward the leader. As a result, the leader's ability to influence the group toward achieving team performance outcomes will be far more limited. This is likely to impede the overall effectiveness of the team's task efforts as certain individuals resist the leader's directives. Given the above discussion, we propose the following:

Hypothesis 1: Power distance will moderate the relationship between leader-member perceptual distance (regarding the leader's participativeness) and productivity such that:

H1a: When power distance is low, the relationship between perceptual distance and productivity will be strong and negative.
H1b: When power distance is high, there will be no relationship between perceptual distance and productivity.

Perceptual Distance Within Teams

A second type of perceptual distance captures differences among team members in their perceptions of the same stimulus. Here we focus on the level of cohesion as the critical stimulus. Team members may vary in the extent to which they perceive the team to be cohesive. This is because team members' personal characteristics shape their expectations of group characteristics, appropriate interaction rules, group efficacy beliefs and group identity (Earley & Mosakowski, 2000; Lickel, Hamilton, Wieczorkowska, Lewis, Sherman & Uhles, 1998; Markus & Kitayama, 1991).

In teams with differences in perceptions, subgroups or factions may exist (Earley & Mosakowski, 2000; Lau & Murnighan, 1998; Ravlin et al., 2000). These subgroups may create "faultlines" (Lau & Murnighan, 1998). Faultlines are the ". . . hypothetical dividing lines that may split a group into subgroups based on one or more attributes" (p. 328). Analogous to the geological faultlines under tectonic plates, faultlines arise from a combination of team member attributes. Faultlines may underlie how team diversity affects functioning (Jackson et al., 1995; Lau & Murnighan, 1998; Zenger & Lawrence, 1989).

When faultlines exist, members retreat toward preexisting subgroup identities for ego protection in the face of challenges or threats. Instead of forming a unitary identity, this creates a potential for relational conflict (Earley & Mosakowski, 2000; Jehn et al., 1999; Lau & Murnighan, 1998). For example, Fielder (1966) conducted a study of heterogeneous groups with Dutch and Belgian members who reported a less pleasant atmosphere and experienced more communication problems than homogeneous groups. Subgroup identities provided for easy retreat that subgroup members hesitate to abandon. The persistence of multiple subgroups is more likely within a team that has heterogeneous perceptions (Davison, 1994; Hambrick et al., 1996).

We argue that heterogeneous perceptions within a team regarding the level of cohesion will be particularly detrimental in a highly collectivistic culture. In a collectivistic society, members call for greater emotional dependence on one another than individuals from individualistic societies, and tend to define themselves in relation to the groups in which they are members. If these groups are goal-oriented, as are work teams, collectivists subordinate personal goals and prioritize the goals of the group. In other words, collectivists generally give priority to the collective interest (Triandis, 1995).

Because they identify with groups to a greater extent, collectivists draw a distinction between the groups in which they are members (in-groups) and others (out-groups) (Chen et al., 1998). In highly collective cultures, there is a strong sense of who is "in-group" and who is "out-group" (Earley & Gibson, 1998; Triandis, 1995). As such, we can assume that collectivists would expect other members of their group to associate with the group to the same extent that they do themselves. If social identities are valued by collectivists, then variances in perception of cohesion should be threatening to social identity, because it signifies that differences exist in the bonds that individuals feel toward the group. This condition should be detrimental to the process of a group in a collectivistic culture by decreasing cooperation and affect-based trust between group members (Chen et al., 1998). We expect that this will have a degenerative effect on conflict resolution in the team.

In support of this notion, Kirchmeyer and Cohen (1992) examined the effects of constructive conflict on decision-making groups that were culturally diverse. In a laboratory exercise, 45 four-person groups recorded their recommendations regarding a business problem, and afterwards members individually completed a questionnaire on the experience. Ethnic minorities contributed considerably less to decisions than non-minorities did. However, with increasing use of constructive conflict, groups made more valid and important assumptions, and the performance and reactions of ethnic minorities improved at rates either the same as or greater than those of non-minorities. Thus, for managers facing growing ethnic diversity in the workplace, the practices of constructive conflict offer a promising approach to group decision making.

Similarly, Oetzel (1998) found that the degree of collectivism was a significant predictor for turn-taking and initiating conflicts in heterogeneous groups, and for competitive conflict tactics across all groups. More specifically, in interactions between Japanese and European Americans in a decision-making activity, he found that collectivism had direct and indirect effects. Collectivism had a direct effect for initiating conflicts, with European Americans initiating more conflicts than Japanese. The relationships between collectivism and turn taking, and between collectivism and conflict tactics were mediated by self-construal.

Based on this initial evidence, and the theoretical frameworks presented earlier, we propose the following:

Hypothesis 2: Collectivism will moderate the relationship between team member perceptual distance (regarding the level of cohesion in team) and effective team conflict resolution, such that:

H2a: When collectivism is low, there will be no relationship between perceptual distance and effective team conflict resolution.
H2b: When collectivism is high, the relationship between perceptual distance and effective team conflict resolution will be strong and negative.

IMPLICATIONS FOR TEAMS AND THEIR LEADERS

Our model has practical implications for both teams and their leadership. First, low power distance cultural settings may be more sensitive to differing perceptions of a leader's behavior. Therefore team leaders in these settings must be especially alert to the differences between self-perceptions of their leadership behavior and those held by the teams they lead. Wide perceptual distance between a leader and his or her team can potentially undermine the effectiveness of a team leader. Given this dynamic, it becomes essential that team leaders in low power distance settings understand and identify those leadership behaviors that require great consistency in their demonstration to team members. While we focused on the dimension of participative decision making in this chapter, we suspect this principle applies to other leadership behaviors as well. While decision making is among the most obvious, other areas such as conflict resolution, praise and recognition, communication of goals, and influencing tactics directly shape team outcomes and therefore should be considered as equally important leadership behaviors.

Once leaders have identified those leadership behaviors requiring greatest consistency of demonstration on their part, they need to establish various vehicles or means to assess how team members actually perceive their behavior on an ongoing basis. Among the more common assessment tools today would be formal 360 degree feedback processes. For example, we are aware of one firm that uses 360 feedback with team leaders at various transition points in the progress of the team's task. At the same time, it is would also be useful to hold one-on-one feedback sessions with individual team members and possibly structure group feedback to the leader at different stages of a task. Feedback built around dialogues rather than simply survey instruments can provide a greater richness of data to the leader and may offer more profound insights into why perceptual differences exist in the first place. Finally, we recommend that team leaders negotiate norms and expectations about their behavior at the very beginning of a team's formation and then hold periodic assessment reviews to see whether expectations and norms have shifted due to events or other factors.

As our proposed model for teams suggests, leaders should identify their critical behaviors influencing team outcomes and obtain feedback on them, and, in addition, in collectivistic contexts, it is critical that team members share perceptions of team characteristics to arrive at a better understanding of what each perceives, expects and is comfortable with. Lane, DiStefano and Maznevski (1997) suggest a three-step process that involves (1) understanding differences in perceptions, (2) bridging the differences, and (3) integration.

To help in understanding perceptual differences, we suggest that cross-cultural teams hold an initial session at the beginning of each project to discuss expectations about specific team behaviors, which are felt to be critical to the team's success. Each member might be asked to describe their preferred approach, identifying where problems might arise across members. From this, potential problem areas could be identified along with possible solutions. This of course assumes that team members are able to articulate cultural norms, which in reality may not necessarily be the case. Given this dilemma, it would be useful to have an internal company consultant who could advise teams at the onset what they might expect in terms of cultural differences, and how these might manifest themselves in dysfunctional ways.

We would also recommend that formal feedback sessions are established at certain specified junctures in the project team's life, in which individual members share their perceptions about the team processes and perceptual differences are identified. Such a process assumes a level of comfort with open discussions, which again may not always prove to be the case given cultural differences. One way to address this dilemma would be for team members to identify a team member who could serve in an ombudsman's role. Team members bring their concerns to this individual in a confidential capacity. The ombudsman, in turn, alerts the team to potential problems. In addition, the team ombudsman canvasses the membership from time to time to determine whether strong perceptual distance has arisen among members along specific team process dimensions.

In addition, it is important to keep in mind the notion of bridging identified by Lane, DiStefano and Maznevski (1997). Bridging requires finding commonalties among members and *de-centering*. The latter term refers to the process of sending and receiving communication with the other person's perspective in mind. The fundamental idea of de-centering is empathy - feeling and understanding as another person does. This may require some initial training for the team in active listening and interpersonal behavioral skills. At the very least, the team leader should in part be selected on the basis of his or her emphatic ability given the influence of the position.

The final step of integration requires blame-free explanations and problem-solving – again something the team's leader might model and reward in his or her own actions. In their research, Maznevski and her colleagues (Maznevski, 1994; Maznevski & Chuboda, 2000; Maznevski & Peterson, 1997; Lane et al., 1997) found that the single best predictor of effective group integration is team members' willingness to suspend blame for problems and to explain problems by trying to understand how members' different perspectives could have led the group as a whole to experience difficulties. This leads the team onward toward exploring alternatives and building a shared reality, developing trust and common rules, and building confidence in the team's ability to use different perceptions productively.

In conclusion, teams and their leaders need to be more aware of the role of individual perceptions and their influence on team processes and performance. Unfortunately, in the quest to accomplish their tasks, teams often become focused largely on task accomplishment itself and fail to reflect and learn from the impact of psychological forces that may ultimately hinder what they are seeking – a successful project outcome. To overlook such forces, however, can mean that a team may pay a significant price when it comes to realizing its full potential as a working group.

ACKNOWLEDGMENTS

This research was made possible with funding provided by the Carnegie Bosch Institute for Applied International Management Research, the University of Wisconsin Initiative for World Affairs and the Global Economy, and the National Science Foundation Grant No. SBR 96–31748. The researchers would like to acknowledge the time and effort extended by all of the respondents in this research together with their associated staff. Special thanks to Rauol Zapata in Puerto Rico, Joylie Agustin and Ricardo Lim at the Asian Institute for Management in the Philippines, and Michael Segalla at the Hautes Etudes Commercials in France. We would like to express our appreciation for the administrative support, translations, and transcriptions provided by Paula Bassoff, Ryan Billingham, Peter Bruhn, Florence Brunell, Joan Donovan, Steve Gibson, Kerry Jung, Francisco Lloveras, Rachel Ritterbausch, David Robinson, Carol Troyer-Shank, and Richard Zapata at the University of Wisconsin.

REFERENCES

Adler, N. J. (1991). *International dimensions of organizational behavior.* Boston: PWS-Kent.
Allport, F. H. (1955). *Theories of perception and the concept of structure.* New York: Wiley.
Ayman, R., & Chemers, M. M. (1983). Relationship of supervisory behavior ratings to work group effectiveness and subordinate satisfaction among Iranian managers. *Journal of Applied Psychology, 68*, 338–341.
Ayman, R., & Chemers, M. M. (1986). The emic/etic approach to leadership orientation and job satisfaction of Mexican managers. Paper presented at the meetings of the International Association of Applied Psychology, Jerusalem, Israel.
Bandura, A. (1997). *Self-efficacy: The exercise of control.* New York: W. H. Freeman.
Bass, B. M. (1990). *Bass and Stogdill's Handbook of Leadership* (3rd ed.). New York: Free Press.
Batt, R., & Appelbaum, E. (1995). Worker participation in diverse settings: Does the form affect the outcome, and if so, who benefits? *British Journal of Industrial Relations, 33*(3), 353–378.
Bennett, M. (1977). Testing management theories cross-culturally. *Journal of Applied Psychology, 62*, 578–581.
Bettenhausen, K. L. (1991). Five years of groups research: What we have learned and what needs to be addressed. *Journal of Management, 17*(2), 345–381.
Brewer, M. (1988). A dual process model of impression formation. In: T. K. Srull and R. S. Wyer, Jr. (Eds), *Advanced in Social Cognition* (Vol. 1, pp. 1–36). Hillsdale, NJ: Erlbaum.
Brewer, N., Wilson, C., & Beck, K. (1994). Supervisory behavior and team performance amongst police patrol sergeants. *Journal of Occupational and Organizational Psychology, 67*(1), 69–79.
Bruner, J. S. (1957). *Contemporary approaches to cognition: A symposium held at the University of Colorado.* Cambridge: Harvard University Press.
Byrne, D. (1971). *The attraction paradigm.* New York: Academic Press.

Campion, M. A., Medsker, G. J., & Higgs, A. C. (1993). Relations between work group characteristics and effectiveness: Implications for designing effective work groups. *Personnel Psychology, 46*, 823–850.

Casmir, R. (1992). Third-culture building: A paradigm shift for international and intercultural communication. *Communication Yearbook, 16*, 407–428.

Chen, C. C., Chen, X., & Meindl, J. R. (1988). How can cooperation be fostered? The cultural effects of individualism-collectivism. *Academy of Management Review, 23*(2), 285–304.

Chen, B. S. (1995). Chaxuegegu and Chinese organizational behavior. *Indigenous Psychological Research in Chinese societies, 3*, 142–219.

Cohen, S. G., & Bailey D. E. (1997). What makes teams work: Group effectiveness research from the shop floor to the executive suite. *Journal of Management, 23*(3), 239–290.

Cohen, S. G., Ledford, G. E., & Spreitzer, G. M. (1996). A predictive model of self-managing work team effectiveness. *Human Relations, 49*(5), 643–676.

Cox, T. H. (1993). *Cultural diversity in organizations*. San Francisco, CA: Berett-Koehler Publishers, Inc.

Cox, T. H., Lobel, S. A., & McLeod, P. L. (1991). Effects of ethnic group cultural differences on cooperative and competitive behavior on a group task. *Academy of Management Journal, 34*(4), 827–847.

Cronshaw, S. F., & Lord, R. G. (1987). Effects of categorization, attribution, and encoding processes on leadership perceptions. *Journal of Applied Psychology, 72*, 97–106.

Davison, S. C. (1994). Creating a high performance international team. *Journal of Management Development, 13*, 81–90.

Deci, E. L. (1975a). *Intrinsic motivation*. New York: Plenum.

Deci, E. L. (1975b). Notes on the theory and meta theory of intrinsic motivation. *Organizational Behavior and Human Performance, 15*, 130–145.

Den Hartog, D., House, R. J., Hanges, P. J., Ruiz-Quintanilla, A., & GLOBE (1999). Some emics and etics of culturally endorsed implicit leadership theories: Are attributes of charismatic/transformational leadership universally endorsed? *Leadership Quarterly, 10*, 219–256.

Dorfman, P. (1994). *Cross-cultural leadership research: Issues and assumptions*. Paper presented at the SIOP Conference Symposium, Nashville, TN.

Dorfman, P. W., Howell, J. P., Hibino, S., Lee, J. K., Tate, U., & Bautista, A. (1997). Leadership in Western and Asian Countries: Commonalities and Differences in Effective Leadership Processes across Cultures. *Leadership Quarterly, 8*(3), 233–274.

Eagley, A. H. & Johnson, B. T. (1990). Gender and leadership style: A meta-analysis. *Psychological Bulletin, 108*, 233–256.

Earley, P. C. (1999). *Face, harmony, and social structure: An analysis of organizational behavior across cultures*. New York: Oxford University Press.

Earley, P. C., & Erez, M. (1987). Comparative analysis of goal-setting strategies across cultures. *Journal of Applied Psychology, 72*, 658–665.

Earley, P. C., & Gibson, C. B. (1998). Taking Stock in Our Progress: 100 Years of Solidarity and Community. *Journal of Management, 24*, 265–304.

Earley, P. C., & Mosakowski, E. (2000). Creating hybrid team cultures: An empirical test of transnational team functioning. *Academy of Management Journal, 43*(1), 26–49.

Earley, P. C., & Randel, A. E. (1997). Self and other: Face and work group dynamics. In: C. S. Granrose, & K. Oskamp (Eds), *Cross-Cultural Workgroups*. Thousand Oaks, CA: Sage Publications.

Eden, D., & Leviatan, U. (1975). Implicit leadership theory as a determinant of the factor structure underlying supervisory behavior scales. *Journal of Applied Psychology, 60*, 736–741.

Erez, M., & Earley, P. C. (1993). *Culture, self-identity, and work*. New York: Oxford University Press.

Fahr, J. L., Earley, P. C., & Lin, S. C. (1997). Impetus for action: A cultural analysis of justice and organizational citizenship behavior in Chinese society. *Administrative Science Quarterly, 42*, 421–444.

Fiedler, F. E. (1966). The effect of leadership and cultural heterogeneity on group performance: A test of the contingency model. *Journal of Experimental Social Psychology, 2*, 237–264.

Fraser, S. L., & Lord, R. G. (1988). Stimulus prototypicality and general leadership impressions: Their role in leadership and behavioral ratings. *Journal of Psychology, 122*, 291–303.

Gecas, V. (1982). The self concept. *Annual Review of Psychology, 8*, 1–33.

Gerstner, C. R., & Day, D. V. (1994). Cross-cultural comparison of leadership prototypes. *Leadership Quarterly, 5*, 121–134.

Gibson, C. B. (1999). Do They Do What They Believe They Can? Group-Efficacy and Group Effectiveness Across Tasks and Cultures. *Academy of Management Journal, 42*(2), 138–152.

Gibson, C. B. (2000). From knowledge accumulation to transformation: Phases and cycles of collective cognition in workgroups. Working paper, University of Southern California.

Gibson, C. B., & Marcoulides, G. A. (1995). The cultural contingency approach to leadership: Examining the invariance of a leadership model across four countries. *Journal of Managerial Issues, 7*(2), 176–193.

Gibson, C. B., & Zellmer-Bruhn, M. (2000). Intercultural Analysis of the Meaning of Teamwork: Evidence From Six Multinational Corporations. Working paper, University of Southern California.

Gibson, C. B., Zellmer-Bruhn, M., & Schwab, D. S. (2000). Team Assessment in Multinational Organizations: Development and Evaluation Across Cultures. Working paper, University of Southern California.

Gladstein, D. L. (1984). Groups in context: A model of task group effectiveness. *Administrative Science Quarterly, 29*, 499–517.

Graen, G. B., & Hui, C. (1999). Transcultural and global leadership in the twenty-first century: Challenges and implications for development. In: W. H. Mobley, M. J. Gessner & V. Arnold (Eds), *Advances in Global Leadership* (Vol. 1, pp. 9–26). Stamford, CT: JAI Press, Inc.

Gully, S. M., Devine, D. S., & Whitney, D. J. (1995). A meta-analysis of cohesion and performance: Effects of level of analysis and task interdependence. *Small Group Research, 26*(4), 497–520.

Hackman, J. R. (1986). Leading groups in organizations. In: P. S. Goodman (Ed.), *Designing Effective Workgroups*. San Francisco, CA: Jossey-Bass Publishers.

Hackman, J. R. (1987). The design of work teams. In: Lorsch (Ed.), *Handbook of Organizational Behavior* (pp. 315–342).

Hall, R. J., & Lord, R. G. (1995). Multi-level information-processing explanations of followers leadership perceptions. *Leadership Quarterly, 6*, 265–287.

Hambrick, D. C., Cho, T. S., & Chen, M. (1996). The influence of top management team heterogeneity on firms' competitive moves. *Administrative Science Quarterly, 41*, 659–684.

Hambrick, D. C., & Mason, P. (1984). Upper echelons: The organization as a reflection of its top managers. *Academy of Management Review, 9*, 195–206.

Hanges, P. J., Lord, R. G., & Dickson, M. W. (2000). An information processing perspective on leadership and culture: A case for connectionist architecture. *Applied Psychology – An International Review, 49*, 133–161.

Hartog, D. D., House, R. J., Hanges, P. J., Ruiz-Quintanilla, S. A., & Dorfman, P. W. (1999). Culturally Endorsed Implicit Leadership Theories. *Leadership Quarterly, 10*(2), 219–256.

Hofstede, G. (1980). *Culture's consequences: International differences in work-related values.* Beverly Hills: Sage.

Hofstede, G. (1991). *Cultures and organizations: Software of the mind.* London: MacGraw-Hill.

Hofstede, G. (1993). Cultural constraints in management theories. *Academy of Management Executive, 7*(1), 81–94.

Hofstede, G., Neuijen, B., Ohayv, D. D., & Sanders, G. (1990). Measuring organizational cultures: A quantitative study across twenty cases. *Administrative Science Quarterly, 35,* 286–316.

Hollander, E. P., & Julian, W. (1969). Contemporary trends in the analysis of leadership perceptions. *Psychological Bulletin, 71,* 387–397.

Howell, J. M., & Frost, P. J. (1989). A laboratory study of charismatic leadership. *Organizational Behavior and Human Decision Processes, 43,* 243–269.

House, R. J., Hanges, P. J., Ruiz-Quintanilla, S. A., Dorfman, P. W., Javidan, M., Dickson, M., & Gupta, V. (1999). Cultural influences on leadership in organizations: Project Globe. In: W. H. Mobley, M. J. Gessner & V. Arnold (Eds), *Advances in Global Leadership* (Vol. 1, pp. 171–234). Stamford, CT: JAI Press, Inc.

Ibarra, H. (1993). Personal networks of women and minorities in management: A conceptual framework. *Academy of Management Review, 18,* 56–87.

Jackson, S. E., Brett, J. F., Sessa, V. I., Cooper, D. M., Julin, J. A., & Peyronnin, K. (1991). Some differences make a difference: Individual dissimilarity and group heterogeneity as correlates of recruitment, promotions, and turnover. *Journal of Applied Psychology, 76*(5), 675–689.

Jackson, S. E., May, K. E., & Whitney, K. (1995). Understanding the dynamics of diversity in decision-making teams. In: R. A. Guzzo, E. Salas & Associates (Eds), *Team Effectiveness and Decision-Making in Organizations* (pp. 204–261). San Francisco: Jossey-Bass.

Jackson, S. E., Stone, V. K., & Alvarez, E. B. (1992). Socialization amidst diversity: The impact of demographics on work team oldtimers and newcomers. *Research in Organizational Behavior, 15,* 45–109.

Janis, I. L. (1972). *Victims of groupthink.* Boston: Houghton-Mifflin.

Jehn, K. (1995). A multimethod examination of the benefits and detriments of intragroup conflict. *Administrative Science Quarterly, 40*(2), 245–282.

Jehn, K. A., Northcraft, G. B., & Neale, M. A. (1999). Why differences make a difference: A field study of diversity, conflict, and performance in workgroups. *Administrative Science Quarterly, 44,* 741–763.

Kanungo, R. M. (1980). *Biculturalism and management.* Toronto: Butterworths.

Kanungo, R. N. (1982). Work alienation and the quality of work life: A cross-cultural perspective. *Indian Psychologist, 1,* 61–69.

Kelly, G. (1963). *A theory of personality: The psychology of personal constructs.* New York: Norton.

Kihlstrom, J. F., & Cantor, N. (1984). Mental representations of the self. In: L. Berkowitz (Ed.), *Advances in Experimental Social Psychology* (Vol. 17, pp. 2–48). New York: Academic Press.

Kihlstrom, J. F., Cantor, N., Albright, J. S., Chew, B. R., Klein, S. B., & Niedenthal, P. M. (1988). Information processing and the study of the self. *Advances in Experimental Social Psychology* (Vol. 21, pp. 145–78). San Diego, CA: Academic Press.

Kirchmeyer, C., & Cohen, A. (1992). Multicultural groups: Their performance and reactions with constructive conflict. *Group & Organization Management, 17*(2), 153–170.

Klimoski, R., & Mohammed, S. (1994). Team mental model: Construct or metaphor? *Journal of Management*, *20*, 403–437.

Lane, H. W., Di Stefano, J. J., & Maznevski, M. L. (1997). *International management behavior*. Malden, MA: Blackwell Publishers.

Lau, D. C., & Murnighan, J. K. (1998). Demographic diversity and faultlines: The compositional dynamics of organizational groups. *Academy of Management Review*, *23*(2), 325–340.

Lewin, K, Lippitt, R., & White, R. K. (1939). Patterns of aggressive behavior in experimentally controlled social climates. *Journal of Social Psychology*, *10*, 271–301.

Lewis, A. W., & Fagenson-Eland, E. A. (1998). The influence of gender and organizational level on perceptions of leadership behavior: A self and supervisor comparison. *Sex Roles*, *39*(5/6), 479–502.

Lickel, B., Hamilton, D. S., Wieczorkowska, G., Lewis, A., Sherman, S. J., & Uhles, A. N. (1998). Varieties of groups and the perception of group entitativity. Unpublished paper.

Lippitt, R., & White, R. K. (1947). An experimental study of leadership and group life. In: E. E. Maccoby, T. M. Newcomb & E. C. Hartley (Eds), *Readings in Social Psychology* (pp. 495–511). New York: Holt Rinehart, & Winston.

Lord, R. G. (1985). An information processing approach to social perceptions, leadership and behavioral measurement in organizations. *Research in Organizational Behavior*, *7*, 87–128.

Lord, R. G., & Maher, K. J. (1991). *Leadership and information processing: Linking perceptions and performance*. Boston: Unwin Hyman.

Lord, R. G., De Vader, C., & Alliger, G. (1986). A meta-analysis of the relation between personality traits and leadership perceptions: An application of validity generalization procedures. *Journal of Applied Psychology*, *71*, 402–410.

Lord, R. G., Foti, R., & De Vader, C. (1984). A test of leadership categorization theory: Internal structure, information processing, and leadership perceptions. *Organizational Behavior and Human Performance*, *34*, 343–378.

Lord, R. G., Phillips, J. S., & Rush, M. C. (1980). Effects of sex and personality on perceptions of emergent leadership, influence, and social power. *Journal of Applied Psychology*, *65*, 176–182.

Magjuka, R. J., & Baldwin, T. T. (1991). Team-based employee involvement programs: Effects of design and administration. *Personnel Psychology*, *44*, 793–812.

Manz, C. C. (1992a). Self-leading work teams: Moving beyond self-management myths. *Human Relations*, *45*(11), 1119–1140.

Manz, C. C. (1992b). *Mastering self-leadership: Empowering yourself for personal excellence*. Englewood Cliffs, NJ: Prentice-Hall.

Manz, C. C., & Simms, H. P. (1987). Leading workers to lead themselves: The external leadership of self-managing work teams. *Administrative Science Quarterly*, *32*, 106–128.

Markus, H., & Kitiyama, S. (1991). Culture and the self: Implications for cognition, emotion, and motivation. *Psychological Review*, *98*, 224–253.

Markus, H., & Kunda, Z. (1986). Stability and malleability of the self-concept. *Journal of Personality and Social Psychology*, *51*, 858–866.

Markus, H., & Wurf, E. (1987). The dynamic self-concept: A social psychological perspective. *Annual Review of Psychology*, *38*, 299–337.

Maurer, T. J., & Lord, R. G. (1991). An exploration of cognitive demands in group interaction as a moderator of information-processing variables in perceptions of leadership. *Journal of Applied Social Psychology*, *21*, 821–839.

Maznevski, M. L. (1994). Understanding our differences: Performance in decision-making groups with diverse members, *Human Relations*, 47(5), 531–552.

Maznevski, M. L., & Chuboda, K. M. (2000). Virtual transnational teams: An adaptive structuration approach to understanding their performance. In press, *Organization Science*.

Maznevski, M. L., & Peterson, M. F. (1997). Societal values, social interpretations, and multinational teams. In: C. S. Granrose & K. Oskamp (Eds), *Cross-Cultural Workgroups*. Thousand Oaks, CA: Sage Publications.

McGrath, J. E. (1984). *Groups, interaction, and performance.* Englewood Cliffs, NJ: Prentice Hall.

Mohrman, S. A., Cohen, S. G., & Mohrman, A. M. (1995). *Designing team-based organizations.* San Francisco, CA: Jossey-Bass.

Mullen, B., Anthony, T., Salas, E., & Driskell, J. E. (1993). Group cohesiveness and quality of decision making: An integration of tests of the groupthink hypothesis. *Small Group Research*, 25(2), 189–204.

Nemeth, C. J. (1985). Dissent, group process, and creativity. *Advances in Group Processes*, 2, 57–75.

Neuberg, S. L. (1989). The goal of forming accurate impressions during social interactions: Attenuating the impact of negative expectancies. *Journal of Personality and Social Psychology*, 56, 374–386.

Neuberg, S. L., & Fiske, S. T. (1987). Motivational influences on impression formation: Outcome dependency, accuracy-driven attention, and individuating processes. *Journal of Personality and Social Psychology*, 53, 431–444.

Oetzel, J. G. (1998). Explaining individual communication processes in homogeneous and heterogeneous groups through individualism-collectivism and self-construal. *Human Communication Research*, 25(2), 202–224.

Ravlin, E. C., Thomas, D. C., & Ilsev, A. (2000). Beliefs about values, status, and legitimacy in multicultural groups: Influences on intra-group conflict. In: P. C. Earley & H. Singh (Eds), *Work Behavior Across Cultures*.

Redding, S. G. (1990). *The Spirit of Chinese Capitalism.* New York: Walter de Gruyter.

Rempel, M. W., & Fisher, R. J. (1997). Perceived threat, cohesion, and group problem solving in intergroup conflict. *International Journal of Conflict Management*, 8(3), 216–234.

Rohner, R. (1987). Culture theory. *Journal of Cross-cultural Psychology*, 18, 8–51.

Rush, M. C., Thomas, J. C., & Lord, R. G. (1977). Implicit leadership theory: A potential threat to the internal validity of leader behavior questionnaires. *Organizational Behavior and Human Performance*, 20, 93–110.

Schweder, R. A., & LeVine, R. A. (1984). *Culture Theory: Essays on mind, self and emotion.* New York: Cambridge University Press.

Seers, A., Petty, M. M., & Cashman, J. F. (1995). Team-member exchange under team and traditional management. *Group & Organization Management*, 20(1), 18–38.

Shamir, B. (1995). Social distance and charisma: Theoretical notes and an exploratory study. *Leadership Quarterly*, 6(1), 19–47.

Shaver, K. G. (1975). *An introduction to attribution processes.* Cambridge, MA: Winthrop Publishers.

Sherman, S. J., Judd, C. M., & Bernadette, P. (1989). Social cognition. *Annual Review of Psychology*, 40, 281–326.

Shweder, R. A., & LeVine, R. A. (1984). *Culture theory: Essays on mind, self, and emotion.* New York: Cambridge University Press.

Silin, R. H. (1976). *Leadership and Value: The Organization of Large-Scale Taiwan Enterprises.* Cambridge, MA: Harvard University Press.

Smith, P. B., Peterson, M. F., & Misumi, J. (1994). Event management and work team effectiveness in Japan, Britain, and the USA. *Journal of Occupational and Organizational Psychology, 67*, 33–43.

Steiner, I. D. (1972). *Group process and productivity.* New York: Academic Press.

Sundstrom, E., DeMeuse, K. P., & Futrell, D. (1990). Work teams: Applications and effectiveness. *American Psychologist, 45*(2), 120–133.

Tajfel, H. (1982). *Social identity and intergroup relations.* Cambridge: Cambridge University Press.

Taguiri, R., & Petrullo, L. (1958). *Person perception and interpersonal behavior.* Stanford, CA: Stanford University Press.

Triandis, H. C. (1989). The self and social behavior in differing cultural contexts. *Psychological Review, 96*, 506–520.

Triandis, H. C. (1995). *Individualism and Collectivism.* Boulder, CO, Westview Press.

Turner, J. (1987). *Rediscovering the social group: A self-categorization theory.* Oxford: Basil Blackwell.

Tsui, A. S., Egan, T. S., & O'Reilly, C. A. III (1992). Being different: Relational demography and organizational attachment. *Administrative Science Quarterly, 37*, 549–579.

Wageman, R. (1995). Interdependence and group effectiveness. *Administrative Science Quarterly, 40*, 145–180.

Wagner, J. A. (1994). Participation's effects on performance and satisfaction: A reconsideration of research evidence. *Academy of Management Review, 19*, 312–330.

Walton, R. E. (1985). From control to commitment: Transforming workforce management in the United States. In: R. H. Hayes & K. B. Clark (Eds), *The Uneasy Alliance: Managing the Productivity-technology Dilemma.* Boston: Harvard Business School Press.

Watson, E. W., Kumar, K., & Michaelson, L. K. (1993). Cultural diversity impact on interaction process and performance: Comparing homogeneous and diverse task groups. *Academy of Management Journal, 36*, 590–606.

Weick, K. E., & Roberts, K. H. (1993). Collective mind in organizations: Heedful interrelating on flight decks. *Administrative Science Quarterly, 38*, 357–381.

Weiss, H. M., & Adler, S. (1981). Cognitive complexity and the structure of implicit leadership theories. *Journal of Applied Psychology, 66*, 69–78.

Yukl, G. A. (1998). *Leadership in organizations.* New Jersey: Prentice Hall.

Zenger, T. R., & Lawrence, B. S. (1989). Organizational demography: The differential effects of age and tenure distribution on technical communication. *Academy of Management Journal, 32*, 353–376.

THE CHALLENGES OF LONG-DISTANCE LEADERSHIP: A VIEW FROM ASIA

Alison R. Eyring

ABSTRACT

This chapter takes a practical look at three challenges faced by long-distance leaders: creating an environment of effective communication, building alignment around business strategy and fostering individual and group learning. While these are clearly challenges that span all continents, the chapter focuses on how they are played out across Asia. Cultural issues associated with these challenges and the use of electronic communication and collaboration tools to help overcome these challenges are discussed. While the perspective taken in this chapter is from that of Asia, it is hoped that the lessons learned are relevant around the globe.

OVERVIEW

In this chapter, the term, "long-distance leadership" is used to refer to a range of individual and organization capabilities and processes needed to lead a distributed organization. In distributed organizations, employees may be separated from one another by geography, time or culture. They may work from home, participate in global teleconferences, or manage staffs that live on the other side of the world. The evolution of distributed organizations has created a whole new vocabulary with terms like *virtual organization, distributed teams,*

Advances in Global Leadership, Volume 2, pages 277–300.
2001 by Elsevier Science Ltd.
ISBN: 0-7623-0723-4

and *technology-enabled communication and collaboration tools*. This new lexicon allows us to describe how people and organizations function when physically apart.

There are many reasons why companies are more likely to become physically distributed. The need to reduce costs is perhaps the most common reason on a global level. In the U.S., employees' needs for more flexible work arrangements and desire for improved quality of life have been key drivers of telecommuting. This in turn has created a large number of distributed organizations. For example, the number of telecommuters in the U.S. rose from 4 million in 1990 to over 11 million in 1997 (von Hoffman, 1998). In contrast, telecommuting is seldom practiced in Asian companies.

A key enabler of distributed organizations has been the rapid expansion of Web technology, accessibility of phone lines and increased bandwidth. Managers can now interview candidates online, conduct meetings with participants calling from around the world, and conduct strategy development sessions over the Web. Teams can coordinate work schedules, conduct meetings and exchange documents and ideas without ever seeing one another. These scenarios, while increasingly common, vary greatly due to differences in organization and group norms as well as the availability and accessibility of enabling technologies. For example, broadband or hi-speed lines are easy to access and relatively inexpensive in places like the U.S. and Singapore, while quite expensive and even inaccessible in Thailand or parts of India.

This chapter focuses on three challenges faced by long-distance leaders in Asia:

1. Creating an environment of effective communication
2. Aligning people with strategy and customers' requirements
3. Fostering individual and group learning

For the purpose of this chapter, a "leader" is defined as someone who helps set objectives, motivates others to achieve these objectives and is responsible for their attainment. This individual may or may not be in the role of a manager with traditional reporting lines. When the role of a long-distance leader is specific to a manager, the term "manager" will be used. Long-distance leaders in Asia face the same difficulties as any leader; but, they often find that physical and cultural distance add significant complexity to their job.

While the perspective of this chapter is from that of a practitioner, some observations about the relevant literature may be useful as background. This is not intended to be a comprehensive review of the literature, but to help create an appreciation for the diversity of the related research and practitioner writing.

Perhaps the most significant body of knowledge contributing to our understanding of long-distance leadership comes from the study of telecommuting and the areas of remote management and virtual teams which evolved, in large part, from this literature. Jackson and van der Wilan (1998) describe the shifting focus of telecommuting research and practice over the past 30 years. In the U.S., and to a lesser degree in Europe, telecommuting has evolved from a solution to energy consumption and commuting requirements in the 1970s, to an approach to balancing work and family demands and addressing skill shortages in the 1980s, to a contributor to more productive and effective workplace design in the 1990s. The emphasis in the telecommuting literature today seems to be on how to make these working arrangements work through improved management and by better leveraging technology to improve communications, collaboration, learning and performance (von Hoffman, 1998; Maruca, 1998; Haywood, 1998; Lipnick & Stamps, 1997; Jackson & van der Wielen, 1998).

Within the discipline of Information and Decision Sciences, the study of remote management and virtual teams also has examined how to leverage technology to work and make decisions more effectively (Townsend, DeMare & Hendrickson, 1996) and the relative impact of and preference for alternative forms of electronic communication (Dimmick, Kline & Stafford, 2000). In the disciplines of psychology and management science, researchers have examined the behavioral challenges of managing remote teams and the challenges of working as a member of a physically distributed team (Jarvenpaa, Knoll & Leidner, 1998). Over the past few years, these disciplines seem to be converging. Behaviorally oriented researchers have begun to learn more about the importance of enabling technologies; while at the same time, the technology focused researchers have begun focusing more on the critical human dynamics, such as trust, in remote collaboration. Increasingly, the practitioner literature is focused on helping managers of virtual teams improve performance through skill development, improved work practices and structure, as well as improved use of technology (Duarte & Snyder, 1999; Kostner, 1994). The research in the area also seems to be converging with studies of long-distance learning, virtual teams and teleworking in general (see Igbaria & Tan (Eds), 1998). The vast majority of writing in this area focuses on a given country and does not examine relevant cross-cultural variables.

The second body of knowledge that is critical to understanding the challenges of long-distance leadership is that of cross-cultural management. The research in this area is broad and complex. Hofstede (1980) and Trompenaars (Trompenaars & Hampden-Turner, 1998) provide what are perhaps the two most commonly known conceptual frameworks for describing cultures along a number of different variables. "Power-distance" and "collectivism vs. individualism" are two cultural dimensions that are particularly relevant for long-distance leaders in Asia. Elashmawi and Harris (1993) also describe the impact of cultural differences such as perceptions of time and communication patterns on management and human resources practices.

Cross-cultural research focusing on team behavior also provides useful context for long-distance leadership in Asia. This is because long-distance leaders in the region typically manage culturally diverse teams. Cross-cultural team research has focused on how culture impacts team performance (Salk & Brannen, 2000) and their ability to make decisions (Oetzel, 1995). Recently, Earley and Mosakowski, (2000) examined the impact of cultural diversity on team performance. One of the challenges of long-distance leadership in Asia is the large number of cultural factors that impact performance. This makes it difficult to isolate cultural influences in large organizations across the region where long-distance leaders may manage teams with more than five different national cultures, languages and even time zones.

What is an "Asian" Perspective?

To call any perspective "Asian" is simplistic. Over half of the earth's population falls into this category, and the language and cultural differences across the region are striking. Within most countries found under the "Asian" umbrella, one finds multiple cultural groups, multiple languages and great diversity across age cohorts, gender and socio-economic status. For example, Singapore is home to Chinese, Malays, Indians, Armenians and Eurasians among others, while Indonesia has over 350 known ethnic groups. The People's Republic of China (PRC) too may be better understood in the context of the differences found within the European continent than as a uniform whole. Even the concept of "Asian" has different meaning to different people in the region. For example, if you ask an Indian or Pakistani if they are "Asian" they are most likely to say "no," whereas a Chinese person is more likely to say "yes." Few managers in Asia would include the individualistic Australians and New Zealanders under the Asian umbrella, although regional organizational structures typically group them together.

Having said this, there are many market, organizational and cultural features across this diverse region that differentiate it from the "West." Until fairly recently, government controls limited competition in many industries. While many controls remain, the norm today is to deregulate and to privatize government-owned businesses. This has led to increased competition, over-supply, margin pressures and now an ever-increasing rate of organizational change. Increased competition and margin pressure is driving a number of Asian companies to venture outside their local markets and to expand their operations regionally and globally. This is no different from what has happened in the West, but it is a fairly recent phenomenon in the region and one that shows no signs of slowing down. In fact, as the region rapidly recovers from the recent financial crisis, we can expect even greater change. All this change is accompanied by a fairly painful human toll and, not surprisingly, some resentment over perceived loss of traditional values.

From a technology perspective, significant changes also are impacting the experience of long-distance leaders in Asia. Currently, the existing tele-communications infrastructure, with a few exceptions, is less developed than in the West. Access to phone lines and the Internet is still limited in many countries. In addition, telephone lines and bandwidth can be very expensive. This has slowed the use of teleconference facilities and establishment of company intranets. However, across the region today, the telecommunications industry is being deregulated and the increase in competition is driving down prices and increasing access. We can expect this to continue to change radically over the next few years.

During the past century, multinational companies (MNCs) with a regional presence in Asia typically ran their businesses as a number of separate legal and operational entities, each headed by a country manager. In these local companies, employees reported to local managers who in turn reported to a country manager. Thus, only at fairly senior levels did managers report out of country. This meant that the need for a good command of English, which is considered the international language of business of Asia, was needed by only a small number of executives. Most employees had no need to work with colleagues in other countries. With a country manager who funneled information into and out of the company, it was clear who was the boss. In addition, interdepartmental conflict or conflicting priorities could be resolved fairly quickly by the country management.

Given the changing competitive landscape, companies in Asia have begun implementing new organizational structures thought to provide certain performance advantages. A growing number of MNCs, and some of the larger regional Asian companies, have shifted away from purely geographic structures to a mixture of functional, product, customer and matrixed configurations. A growing number of companies also have shared service or central processing centers in one country and centers of expertise distributed across the region or worldwide. To make things more complex, many also have matrix structures with some local managers reporting to both a local executive and a regional or sometimes global manager.

It is difficult to separate the fact that long-distance leaders exist in greater numbers today in Asia from the fact that they exist because growing numbers of MNCs have implemented matrix functional structures and begun centralizing some functions across the world or region. One result of these new organizational structures is that a growing number of managers in Asia are reporting to managers in other countries. Also, a number of MNCs now run global business units from Asia with those in the West reporting to a global business unit head in places like Singapore, Hong Kong or Sydney. These structures also require a growing number of more junior employees to work on projects, which have leaders who are physically remote. Thus, a growing number of employees across the region must work with colleagues of other cultures, religions and language groups. Also, a growing number of manager and project leaders now find themselves managing across time, distance and culture.

The Challenge of Communication

Effective communication is defined as a match between the intended and interpreted meaning of a message. Even among people of the same background and at the same location this may not occur. Not surprisingly, what may start out as a simple communication to an individual or small work team can become a difficult and painful experience for long-distance leaders in Asia.

A key challenge for the long-distance manager in Asia is learning how to regularly communicate across multiple cultures and language groups. Unlike long-distance leaders in large countries like the U.S., these leaders engage in a large number of cross-cultural interactions repeatedly throughout the day. Learning cross-cultural techniques, such as recognition of cultural biases when sending and receiving messages, and different styles of communications, such as direct and indirect speech patterns, is essential. The long-distance leader must be multi-skilled and appreciative of the differences in different cultures.

Interpersonal communications across Asia, with a few exceptions, are described as "high-context" communications. This means that most of the message's meaning is conveyed through the context of the message or in non-verbal clues rather than explicit words. Asians may say "yes" with their mouths, but "no" with their facial expressions, body language or actions.

While Asians as a whole tend to be less direct than their U.S. counterparts, there is significant diversity across the region. For example, the Batak of Indonesia are a small tribe of people known for their directness, while their

Javanese neighbors are so indirect they may be likened to the shadow puppets popularly used in traditional entertainment in Southeast Asia. For business purposes, Australia is often grouped into an Asian zone or region. However, it is not uncommon for managers with regional responsibility to spend much of their time resolving conflicts caused by communication failures between Australian employees and their Asian counterparts.

In addition to cultural diversity, physical distance combined with availability of telecommunications technology creates special challenges. Long-distance leaders must be able to communicate and collaborate using a range of delivery mechanisms. More importantly, they must understand physical limitations and local acceptability. For example, one long-distance manager in an MNC began using a Web-enabled Notes database for group collaboration in the region. The IT specialist in Thailand reported that intranet connections were sufficient to allow all group members to use this tool. After several months however, the manager found that team members in Thailand were not using the Notes discussion database. During a personal visit, she asked one of the team members to show her the discussion database and found that it took seven minutes for the first page to load on the browser. After a bit more investigation, she learned that the IT manager in Thailand that conducted the earlier tests had access to a very costly, high bandwidth line, while the team members had a regular phone line. Although none of the team members pushed to fix the problem – an action that reflects a cultural dynamic – the lack of adequate Internet access prohibited basic access to the database.

Since communication across Asia is mostly high-context communication, and it is relatively less direct than in the West, face-to-face communication is the preferred mode. Unfortunately, this is often not feasible when team members are in different locations. Thus, long-distance managers must frequently use a range of alternate methods, including written memos, voicemail, e-mails, teleconferencing and video conferencing. It's ironic that, although most communication across the region is "high-context," virtually all long-distance leaders in Asia must rely on electronic communication and collaboration tools that force people to be more explicit in their messages. In other words, they must communicate in a low-context way with high-context people. Not surprisingly, employees in Asia often complain about e-mail and company intranets, as they perceive a loss of "human touch" in the workplace.

Organizational changes across the region place a growing demand on employees to speak English. This means that a large number of employees have to interact and work together in a second or even third language. This can be both tiring and frustrating. A practical challenge of long-distance leaders in Asia is English language diversity. While English is definitely the language of business, the levels of English fluency vary widely across the region. In countries like Singapore and Malaysia, English understanding among employees tends to be high, while in Korea, Japan and Thailand, English fluency drops significantly at levels below the most senior management. The English spoken in each country is influenced by the grammar, syntax and pronunciation of the mother tongue, slang from Western films and TV programs, home and working environments and even the age of the speaker. This sometimes results in dialects unrecognizable to the native English speaker. For example, in Singapore, the government recently launched the "Speak Good English Movement" to address the use of "Singlish," which has developed into a unique blend of English, Cantonese and other local dialects.

Mandarin, which is considered the second language of business in the region, is equally diverse. For example, the PRC and Singapore use simplified Chinese characters, while Hong Kong and Taiwan use traditional characters. While people in the PRC and Singapore both speak Mandarin, their accents and use of idiomatic expressions are more diverse than those of English speakers in the U.S. and England. Furthermore, while the written characters for Mandarin and Cantonese are the same, the verbal languages are completely distinct. This makes written communications in Chinese characters quite difficult to comprehend across countries where Mandarin or Cantonese is spoken.

Companies in Asia, whose structures require cross-national managers, typically use English-speaking ability as one of the selection criteria. However, people reporting to this person may not speak English. This places a great burden on the bilingual managers to translate documents between levels. It also makes it more difficult for the long-distance manager who may not speak the local language to gauge what is happening in the organization without the filter incorporated by his or her direct report.

The use of electronic communication and collaboration tools poses advantages and disadvantages in Asia. On the positive side, because English is a second or even third language for many Asian employees, these tools allow non-native English speakers time to reflect on and compose a message. This is particularly helpful to people who are not fluent or completely comfortable conversing in English. Needless to say, another advantage is the speed by which messages can be distributed to large groups of employees.

The downside of these tools is that because emotion and non-verbal messages are stripped from the written explicit message, the recipient may trust the information less. This lack of trust makes the message less likely to be accepted and acted upon. These low-context messages are also more difficult to accurately interpret. This may cause conflict that escalates when e-mails are copied to larger audiences, or worse when copied to ranking managers.

Inappropriate use of e-mail often causes conflict that is difficult to resolve. This is due in part to the inability to talk face-to-face about the problem. In Asia, it also invokes issues of face and loss of confidence in the sender. One story that illustrates this problem occurred in an MNC where one group developed the practice of labeling e-mails with emotions that they felt at the time of writing the messages. One manager in the Middle East sent an e-mail (which was labeled "flame") to his work group sharing his frustration with the rate at which certain HR programs were being implemented in his region. One of his managers used the "reply to all" feature and copied the HR executive responsible for the program worldwide. Needless to say, the HR executive felt frustrated that he had not been spoken to directly about this issue, but it was several months before the two managers were able to discuss this issue face-to-face. While this dynamic is universal, it seems that recovering from such conflict is sometimes more challenging in Asian countries. For example, American expressions like, "it's water under the bridge" or "forgive and forget" have no counterpart in countries like China or Indonesia.

While long-distance leaders in the region don't have the luxury of frequent face-to-face meetings, it is common to schedule something around the business planning or budget review processes. These face-to-face meetings are important for establishing relationships among geographically and culturally diverse employee groups, and serve as the basis for building the trust that is so critical to working together. Companies like Hewlett Packard, Motorola and Shell regularly bring together managers and professionals from across the region to review business performance, plan for improvements and build relationships.

Because long-distance leaders may only bring their people together once a year, quarter or month, they often find that their agendas are filled with information sharing. This information overload prevents more time spent reflecting, making decisions or generating new ideas. While this is not unique to long-distance leaders, it is a costly issue in Asia, as regional travel tends to be relatively expensive. It also highlights the need to learn how to use electronic communication and collaboration tools for information exchange so that meeting time can be freed for more important objectives.

Overcoming the Challenges of "Long-Distance" Communication

Much has been written about how to communicate effectively across cultures (see Gudykunst, 1991). In her book, *Managing Virtual Teams*, Haywood (1998) provides an excellent summary of ways to overcoming communication problems in distributed teams. The following suggestions focus on how long distance leaders in Asia can become more effective communicators (beyond the general cross-cultural communications guidelines).

First, consider the appropriateness of different electronic communication tools for sending different types of messages. In Asia, face-to-face communications will almost always be the preferred mode of message delivery. Teleconferences are less favored and written communication via e-mail is least preferred for employees in remote locations. Videoconferencing seems subordinate to teleconferencing because it is less flexible in terms of location. This is important when meeting participants are separated by multiple time zones and one or more are joining the meeting early in their morning or late at night in their specific time zone. Also, time delays in videoconferencing are still common in Asia due to limited bandwidth, and the separation between what people see and what they hear can be disconcerting. Find out what the technical limitations exist in different countries before using more advanced electronic communications or group collaboration tools. In general, lower-tech methods (e.g. teleconferencing or e-mail) may be easier to use across a number of countries in the region than higher tech methods (e.g. NetMeeting, Web-enabled Lotus Notes databases). Finally, long-distance leaders need to help define when it is appropriate to use e-mail and when they should be copied on team correspondence. Experience shows that they also should teach employees to consider each e-mail a candidate for public review and to consider the impact it might have if read by someone other than its intended recipient.

When team meetings are held via teleconference or videoconference, allow people time to prepare adequately beforehand. Provide participants with an agenda and some discussion points prior to the meeting so they can be prepared to participate. This is particularly important if the teleconference participants are a mixture of Western and Asian employees.

Finally, use third parties to obtain feedback on how effective the different modes of communication are for different stakeholders. It is likely this feedback will be difficult to obtain directly from subordinates or team members in remote countries, especially if the relationship is newly established.

The Challenge of Alignment

The concept of organization alignment is fairly broad and can encompass many things. In their book, "The Power of Alignment", Labovitz and Rosansky (1997) provide a useful framework for organizational alignment that encompasses dimensions of horizontal and vertical alignment. For the purpose of this discussion, the focus will be on what they call "vertical alignment" which refers to the synchronization of individual performance with business strategy. While this is challenging for any leader, it is particularly difficult for leaders who must do work on a long-distance basis. This section outlines challenges long-distance leaders face when trying to align performance objectives with behavior. These challenges include clarifying roles, relationships and responsibilities; creating a common direction; and gaining "alignment" across cultures and countries. Suggestions on how to enhance alignment are also provided. While a key element, the issue of compensation and rewards is not addressed due to the complexity of this issue.

In the U.S., a discussion of linking individual performance with business strategy and objectives often centers on measurement and compensation. In companies in Asia, a discussion of such alignment often focuses on the need to clarify roles and responsibilities as they relate to achieving certain organizational objectives. The story told by a Chinese manager helps to understand why this is important:

> Unlike the U.S., with its 3 Rs of reading, 'riting and 'rithmetic, China's 3 Rs are roles, relationships and responsibilities. Roles are defined by one's birth order within the family. Birth order dictates the relationship among family members. These relationships then define the responsibility one family member has for another.

If you watch a Chinese movie or listen to members of a Chinese family in the PRC speaking today, they will refer to siblings as "eldest sister" or "second brother." Even aunts and uncles have their place in the order.

Understanding how one fits into the social order is important in most Asian countries. In functional or matrix organizational structures, long-distance leaders face a great deal of role ambiguity. Employees may feel uncomfortable not knowing how their own manager or project leader fits into the overall organizational hierarchy. Before long-distance leaders can begin to align individual and organizational objectives, they must first meet employees' needs in terms of clarifying roles and responsibilities.

Once a reasonable understanding of roles, responsibilities and relationships in a distributed work group has been established, the long-distance leader is better able to unite her team around a common vision, business strategies and business priorities. The most common impediment to alignment is the difficulty in bringing people together to debate, share ideas and co-create a common vision, idea or plan.

When "vision" or "strategic intent" statements are simply cascaded from the top of the organization, they are often derailed at the layer of management reporting outside their own country. One reason for this is that such statements often take on different, and at times unacceptable, meanings in different countries. For example, the senior management of one regional marketing company developed an objective to "delight the customer." The term "delight" was not easily translated into Thai and a number of influential Thai employees felt the word itself had negative connotations. Time pressure and lack of foresight had precluded the mostly Western expat executive team members from consulting their employees in different countries before agreeing on this objective. While the objective was effectively cascaded and translated into local measures in most countries, much time and energy was wasted in Thailand. While a fairly mundane example, this is played out repeatedly by MNCs across the region.

A common approach for overcoming a problem such as this is to bring a group together to identify a common direction. However, it's is often quite difficult for long-distance leaders in Asia to bring their people together for face-to-face meetings. Barriers include distance between countries across the region, airfare costs and time required to obtain visas. For example, one executive in Singapore brought his direct reports together for a two-day meeting on a small island in Indonesia that was accessible by ferry from Singapore. The meeting was almost cancelled because one of the team members carried a South African passport and the Indonesian government did not wish to issue him a visa. Another long-distance leader had team members in New Zealand, Malaysia and India. This meant that any time they met face-to-face at least one person would be required to travel over eight hours for what could be a one-day meeting.

Even when leaders bring their groups together, they may need to work with cultural dynamics that can make it difficult to build a common mindset. In general, people in Asia tend to be more inclined to respect the authority of people higher up in the organizational hierarchy, regardless of whether they are a direct or indirect supervisor. This means they are less likely to "push back" when they don't understand or disagree with higher-ranking individuals. This impacts the ability of all leaders in Asia to create a common mindset and to cascade strategy and objectives effectively in a two ways. First, cascaded strategies and objectives may not be understood – but the person to whom they are cascaded is less likely to ask questions or say they don't understand. Second, even if they are understood, the receiving individual or group may not disagree or confront the higher-level objective even when it doesn't make sense. Add the variable of distance to the equation and these problems are magnified. Potential causes include lack of an adequate relationship due to insufficient face-to-face time and cultural differences. Lack of adequate English skills becomes a real issue in countries such as Thailand and Korea if the people to whom the objectives are cascaded are lower-level employees.

Even when a common direction is agreed upon by members of a distributed work group, long-distance leaders in functional or matrix organizations face the challenge of pacing their alignment process with other leaders in the organization so as to not create confusion among employees in one country. In geographic-based organizations, a country manager receives a set of business targets or strategies either directly from his manager or through a board of directors for the legal business entity, and can then drive an integrated alignment process within the country. In functional or matrix organizations, strategies and objectives are cascaded from a number of business or functional heads in one country to multiple business or functional heads in a receiving country. Because markets differ so widely across Asia, cascading objectives into an organization is more difficult and varied for different parts of the organization. Thus, the cascading process typically occurs at different paces due to leadership differences or practical issues, such as size of the business or group. Within a country, employees reporting to different managers and business lines are understandably confused and the need for role clarity often creates perceived stress. This is a particularly great challenge to companies in Asia that have implemented functional or matrix structures.

When implementing an alignment process, long-distance leaders also face the challenge of resistance within countries. Within all countries, people differ in terms of how open they are to influences from other countries, however in countries with recent deregulation and nationalism (e.g. the telecommunications industry in Singapore and Philippines), companies are more likely to face this issue. The resistance to change is sometimes expressed as "that won't work here" or "you just don't understand this country." While both statements may be correct, they often have the unintended consequence of the long-distance leader pushing harder, and the local employees resisting more. Sometimes this resistance is not communicated openly, but the process is sabotaged subtly and is invisible to the long-distance leader. Within Asia, long-distance leaders must be sensitive to this issue when business strategies and objectives are cascaded to them. They need to take time to explain and educate, and get early buy-in and even involvement in the creation of the strategy from those who will be affected. The emotional commitment of employees can make all the difference to successful implementation. Of course, this is a dilemma for leaders who are pushed to act quickly across multiple countries.

Long-distance managers attempting to build alignment face a dilemma. On one hand, they must develop relationships and trust not only with people for whom they are responsible in other countries, but with other employees in the country who interact with their people. On the other hand, they are faced with increasing workloads and time and cost pressures. As they travel more, they have less time to spend with each person and it becomes more difficult to manage performance problems, resolve conflicts and set direction. In response, they begin using various forms of electronic communication to save time. However, the more they rely on remote communication and collaboration tools, the harder it is for them to create effective relationships. Clearly, the use of electronic communication and collaboration tools is one solution for exhausted people with increasing workloads and great complexity in their work caused by distance and cultural diversity. To be successful, however, they need to balance this with face-to-face time. Some of the face-to-face time must be spent establishing group norms for how to work remotely.

Overcoming the Challenge of Alignment
Building alignment is an area where the saying, *"go slow to go fast"* is particularly relevant. Long-distance managers in Asia must take time to first build alignment around clarity of roles, responsibilities and relationships among distributed work groups. Consider the use of training programs to help develop this and use discussion to clarify roles and responsibilities. This discussion should include defining the roles team members play in their own countries, and how they should relate to others. Ensure that the group discusses the use of any remote communication and collaboration tools they will use if this has not already been done. Once this is established, team members can begin the iterative process of agreeing and cascading business strategy and objectives to people at lower levels of the organization.

Over the past 20 years, Western companies have made significant advances in the use of measures to drive strategy execution and to track performance. Measurement has become a valuable tool for building alignment. (Kaplan & Norton, 1996; Rucci, Kirn & Quinn, 1998). While the use of good measures is one way to help build alignment around common strategies, the concept of business measurement systems and performance measurement is a relatively new phenomenon in Asia. Most companies are still in the early stages of the learning process. One suggestion for long-distance leaders is to begin the process of educating their team members about the use of measurement as a tool for creating alignment long before the time comes to begin using the measures. Keep in mind that the use of explicit measurement is likely to create discomfort and concerns about failure.

The Challenge of Fostering Learning

Deregulation, increasing competition and oversupply has accelerated the rate of organizational change across the region. This has led to an increased emphasis placed on attracting, retaining and developing employees with different skills and mindsets. While this is true around the globe, what began in the U.S. in the 1970s and evolved over 30 years has really just begun in the past five years in Asia. These changes can be expected to accelerate. To cope with changing organizational requirements, long-distance leaders in Asia must effectively foster individual learning and development. They also must create mechanisms to promote creation and sharing of knowledge among members of their work teams or organizations. The following section explores special challenges long-distance leaders face in promoting individual and group learning in Asia. Suggestions for doing this more effectively are also provided.

As background, it is helpful to describe how children are taught across Asia. Cultural norms for education are important because they influence how people learn as adults and how people expect to learn. From a very young age, children in countries such as Singapore, Hong Kong and Japan are taught to respect the authority of the teacher. This is demonstrated by not questioning the teacher's accuracy and by following instructions. Emphasis is placed on instilling discipline and accuracy, and less attention is paid to encouragement or building the self-esteem of the learner. In class, students spend significant amounts of time, even at very early ages, focusing on acquiring a great deal of content knowledge. Feedback from the teacher is very explicit and it is common for a teacher to say "incorrect!" Children are not encouraged to ask why, but to master new concepts and to memorize content. The pressure to succeed academically is great for students and their families.

The result of this teaching style has been phenomenal achievement in mathematics and the hard sciences. What was regarded as less important in the past, and hence was not developed, were creativity, self-management, self-confidence and a questioning attitude. This "Asian" style of education has helped develop adults who, in general, expect standards for performance to be fairly explicit, are often capable of memorizing a great deal of information and are motivated to be "right." Having said this, it is important to recognize that educated young adults in Asia today are much more Westernized than their parents in terms of global or cross-cultural awareness, English-speaking ability and exposure to Western values and culture.

This educational system influences expectations for learning in the work environment in Asia. It is commonly believed that learning happens in a classroom, and that a teacher or expert has the answers and does the "teaching." The expectation of both managers and their subordinates – that most learning happens through structured classroom experiences – exceeds an understanding that most learning happens on the job. Thus, the move towards experiential learning and on-the-job coaching is fairly recent, although New Zealand and Australia prove to be exceptions in the region.

For the long-distance manager, finding experiential developmental opportunities for their subordinates can be difficult, as it often requires travel to other countries. They may face both individual resistance and governmental restrictions. For example, it can be extremely difficult to get a visa for a Pakistani to work on a developmental project in India. Another example occurred in one Western MNC, where a manager based in Singapore tried to send one of his Sri Lankan employees, who was on a developmental assignment in North America, to Pakistan for a short-term developmental assignment. The employee turned it down because his family was concerned about fighting in Pakistan. Furthermore, the employee enjoyed his lifestyle in the U.S. and was hesitant to leave it to work in what he considered to be an unpleasant working environment. Managing this process was time-consuming and frustrating for both the employee and manager.

Ensuring adequate developmental feedback is a challenge for all managers. In Asia, providing direct feedback on performance is not a norm, and when it does occur, it comes from one's manager. For a long-distance leader, it become difficult to provide developmental feedback to subordinates or team members from peers located in the same location or who are physically distributed. Limited opportunities to observe the employee's performance also makes it very difficult to provide useful developmental feedback. Currently, structured, multi-rater feedback tools are being utilized to a greater extent, but still are uncommon.

Across Asia, the availability and quality of local training resources varies widely. For the long-distance leader, this means that it may be impossible to have her direct reports or organization participate in a common training program without incurring significant costs in terms of international travel.

Depending on the type of training delivered, a lack of adequate English skills can make it difficult to implement a common training program within a business unit that spans the region. For example, in one MNC, which is organized into global functional business units, one business unit planned to roll out a common training program worldwide. The U.S.-based manager responsible for implementing this program pushed to roll it out quickly across several countries. Because a functional business unit leader drove this, the option of implementing the program by geography was not considered. Fortunately, regional experts were able to convince their U.S. counterpart to slow down the implementation process so that the program could be rolled out across business units within each country. Thus, the process was slower, but total costs were significantly lower because each business unit within the country was then able to use the same translated program and to share costs for training delivery

A final challenge long-distance leaders face in helping to develop their subordinates or team members occurs when e-mail becomes the primary means of contact within a project team or work group. When this happens, a long-distance leader has difficulty assessing individual development needs. In the absence of good performance information, managers may focus too much on single events or small problems without understanding the context in which they occur. This may lead to inaccurate judgments about understanding or capability. Also, when employees are forced to communicate in a second or third language, they may find it difficult to express issues or concerns. This may be misinterpreted as a lack of capability or motivation.

So far this section has focused on issues long-distance leaders face in promoting individual learning and development in Asia. Equally important is how they can foster the creation of or sharing of knowledge among members of their team or work group. Research shows that lack of a relationship between the source and recipient of knowledge is a key barrier to knowledge sharing and implementation of best practices. (O'Dell & Grayson, 1998). Two concepts are helpful when exploring how long-distance leaders can build relationships among distributed team or work groups: (1) the notion of "care" as described by Von Korgh (1998); and (2) the cultural construct of "face".

Von Krogh describes "care" in organizational relationships as a key enabler for knowledge creation. He quotes philosopher Milton Mayeroff when saying that, "to care for another person, in the most significant sense, is to help him grow and actualize himself" (p. 137). Care, he says, gives rise to trust, active empathy, real help, non-judgmentalism and courage to allow others to experiment. While many leaders implementing knowledge-sharing programs or processes have learned that knowledge sharing will not occur without trust, this concept of "caring" helps one to better understand what brings about trust, and thus the ability to create and share knowledge.

Another concept that is useful to long-distance leaders promoting group learning or knowledge sharing is the concept of "face." We can describe "face" as the image of one's self that he would wish for others to see. Argyris (1997) notes "all of us design our behavior in order to remain in unilateral control, to maximize winning and minimize losing, to suppress vulnerability, risk and embarrassment, and the appearance of incompetence." The concept he describes parallels that of "face" in Asia. While the concept of "face" seems fairly universal, Westerners and people across Asia differ in how they "save face." In the U.S. and Australia, for example, people protect or "save face" by speaking out and demonstrating their knowledge, and possibly by challenging ideas of others. They are not very likely to worry about saving another's face when working with a group. They are likely to believe that challenging others ideas is a good mechanism to arrive at the "best" solution. In Asia, people are more likely to save their own face by not calling attention to oneself or by risking making a mistake. Other members of the group will help them save their face by not calling attention to their mistakes or by putting them in the awkward position of having to speak out. Challenging others' ideas is done in Asia, but tends to be subtler. It seldom happens in unfamiliar or new teams.

In team or work group gatherings, "face" drives different behaviors. In a global teleconference, for example, team members who are from the U.S. or Europe are more likely to speak out spontaneously and to direct questions to one another without considering the impact of their statement on others in the teleconference. In this way, they protect their "face" and feel good about their contribution to the group process. Team members who are from China or Southeast Asia may be less likely to speak out and will typically direct their comments or questions to the leader. In this way, they also protect their "face" and feel good about the group process. Unfortunately, this behavior sometimes leads Westerners to assume that Asians are not creative or able think independently; while Westerners' behavior may lead Asians to perceive them as rude and undisciplined in their thinking processes. Ironically, both actions may, in fact, be barriers to learning when they are used as defensive routines created to keep the person's self image intact.

Because it takes money and time to bring distributed team members together, a leader may be tempted to be the only one who travels, or to use e-mail or electronic collaboration tools to foster group sharing. These actions may prevent or stall the process of trust building. One long-distance IT project leader helped to overcome this problem by creating a photo album of team members. He took this album on each trip and reviewed the pictures with remote team members, and even their customers. Reactions to this were quite positive, as the distributed team members had not had the chance to see one another, although they had been working together for several months. At Shell in Singapore, for example, dispersed project teams are encouraged to attend a team-building session before they kick off a project. In the workshop, team members agree on how they will make decisions, resolve conflict and leverage the electronic tools available. This helps them to clarify roles, relationships and responsibilities even when face-to-face encounters are limited. It also helps to prevent the inappropriate use of e-mail, which can contribute to group conflict.

As group decision support systems and groupware programs have become widespread, they have made possible electronic meetings and decision-making in a variety of situations. For example, in electronic brainstorming, team members enter ideas whenever they want and the computer software compiles and disseminates the ideas. The benefits are anonymity, quantity of ideas generated, filing of ideas for later consideration and wide distribution. This technology helps overcome one of the problems of communicating at a distance, but does not overcome the problem of people who do not know each other being unwilling to share ideas and information. Because electronic communication or problem solving focuses on facts and not feelings, it also may be less effective in gaining employee commitment to agreed actions.

Finally, long-distance leaders in Asia often may face the challenge of getting their people to think differently, and in many instances, to generate new ideas or approaches to work even when they do come together for face-to face meetings or workshops. The use of facilitated group techniques and time to interact in smaller groups is becoming more common as leaders discover ways to create an environment of open communication among people who seldom interact.

Overcoming the Challenges of Fostering Learning

As companies across Asia integrate and enhance learning systems, the job of fostering individual development will become easier for the long-distance manager. The development of long-distance learning technology also will help; however, implementation needs to be carefully managed, as it will go against firmly entrenched beliefs about how one learns. Rather than bringing remote team members together for training, long distance leaders in Asia might gain more benefit by spending time with them creating greater awareness about how people learn, and discussing learning and development tactics. Once this framework is understood and shared by team members, it will become easier to develop specific development plans and to discuss these with individuals and the group in general.

To better understand development needs, long-distance leaders need to take time during visits to observe their team or work group members interacting with peers or customers. By taking time to develop relationships with people working with and around their subordinates or team members, the leaders also may be able to obtain indirect developmental feedback.

As mentioned earlier, the use of multi-rater performance input is fairly new across Asia, although its use is growing rapidly. Long-distance leaders can leverage these tools to gain better insights, but must be cautious against moving too quickly to quantitative rating scales as their use differs across cultures. For example, a "5" in Singapore may be equivalent to a "3" in Hong Kong.

One of the top priorities for a long-distance manager who wishes to foster group sharing or learning is to dedicate time to building relationships among members of the project team or work group. This is best accomplished face to face. If the group does not already have a history together, use group processes that enable people to discuss issues and concepts in small teams without having to voice these directly to the leader. Use this time to define when it is appropriate to use which electronic communication tool, and to establish a shared understanding of roles, responsibilities and relationships. Finally, develop skills in the use of basic communications techniques espoused by proponents of learning organizations (e.g. use of inquiry/advocacy, left-hand column, ladder of inference) among team or work group members. These are especially useful when team members return to their own work place and must rely heavily on teleconferences for group discussions.

Opportunities for Future Research

Most organizational problems worth solving require some coordination across multiple departments. Similarly, overcoming the challenges of long-distance leadership requires integration of learning from across the disciplines of psychology, management and the information and decision sciences. In Asia, this is difficult because almost all of the research is conducted by Westerners in Western countries and so may or may not be appropriate. Urban congestion and work/family balance are starting to become bigger social issues in Asia. We can assume they will drive greater demands for organization flexibility over the coming decade in the region. Like the West about 20 years ago, organizations in the region will increasingly be required to manage employees who are physically distributed. Thus, the need for cross-disciplinary research in the region is more important now than ever.

This chapter has highlighted practical challenges faced by long-distance leaders in Asia. The discussion has highlighted the intermingling of physical and cultural distance, and the interplay between culture and the effectiveness of electronic communication and group collaboration tools. Hopefully, it has raised more questions that it has answers. In the future, long-distance leaders in Asia will benefit from research that answers questions such as:

(1) What forms of electronic communication and remote collaboration enable, and which detract from, organizational effectiveness in Asia?
(2) How can organizations in Asia best introduce and manage tele-commuting?

Table 1. Key Challenges for Long-Distance Leaders in Asia (and some possible solutions).

Challenge	Solutions
Creating an environment of effective communication	• Use lower-tech (and higher context) methods – especially early in group formation • Teach employees to consider each e-mail a candidate for public review and when to avoid its use • Allow people to prepare beforehand when conducting a teleconference or videoconference • Provide a structured agenda and discussion points before the teleconferences or videoconferences • Use third parties to obtain feedback on the effectiveness of the different modes of communication • Ensure group members are aware of communication differences across cultures, and skilled in cross-culture communication techniques
Aligning people with strategy and customers' requirements	• Invest time in physically bringing the group together to define and/or understand direction • Go slow initially to ensure real understanding and don't assume silence indicates agreement or understanding • Involve those who will be affected early in strategy development to ensure national cultural differences can be handled when these are implemented • Leverage structured learning events to discuss to clarify the staff roles, responsibilities & relationships • Discuss the use of remote communication and collaboration tools • Spend more time educating team members about using measurement as a tool
Fostering individual and group learning	• Spend time with employees to create greater awareness about learning and explore mental models • Take time during visits to observe team or work group members interacting with peers or customers • Leverage multi-rater performance tools, but move to this slowly • Dedicate time to build relationship among members of project team or work group so that feedback can be shared among team members • Develop skills in basic communication techniques

(3) What factors contribute to high performance in highly diverse, distributed teams in Asia?
(4) How can long-distance leaders bridge the contextual gap created by low-context communication and collaboration tools?

CONCLUSIONS

Any leader faces a number of challenges when physically apart from his or her team or organization. This chapter has focused on three of these challenges and has tried to provide insights into the nature of the challenge as played out across Asia. Hopefully, the examples and possible means of overcoming these challenges will serve useful to managers and project leaders working in the region.

Following are a few conclusions we can draw from this chapter:

First, long-distance leaders in Asia need to balance the need to act quickly and decisively with the need to engage remote employees and team members and to build trust. As the rate of change in Asia accelerates, this will become harder to do. Whereas long-distance leaders in the U.S. and much of Europe can achieve results with strong task focus, they will fail to achieve long-term results in Asia with this orientation.

Second, long-distance managers in Asia must be cautious when introducing or relying on electronic communication and remote collaboration tools. Clearly, these tools can be effective and enhance group performance. However, they may impede group development or cause interpersonal conflict that can be quite difficult to overcome in Asia. Long-distance leaders are wise to use these resources to supplement face-to-face interactions rather than to substitute for them. Long-distance leaders must balance the need to be fast and efficient with the need to communicate with and interact with people in a way that makes sense in their cultures. Over time, e-mails and intranets will become more common across the region. The challenge for the long-distance leader is to seek every opportunity to effectively use face-to-face time and to leverage electronic interactions as an enabler to group and organization effectiveness.

Finally, long-distance leaders in Asia must understand how education in the region shapes expectations for learning. When leveraging long-distance learning tools, they must find ways to replace the "context" gap in teaching just as they must fill the "context" gap in other forms of communications. Lastly, they must appreciate the difficulties of developing people separated from them by distance and culture and learn how to shape new team norms for peer coaching and feedback that are generally unfamiliar across Asia.

REFERENCES

Argyris, C. (1993). *Knowledge for action: A guide to overcoming barriers to organizational change*. San Fransisco: Jossey-Bass Publishers.

Dimmick, J., Kline, S., & Stafford. (2000). The gratification niches of personal e-mail and the telephone: Competition, displacement and complementarity. *Communication Research, 27*(2), 227–248.

Duarte, D. L., & Snyder, N. T. (1999). *Mastering virtual teams: Strategies, tools and techniques that succeed*. San Fransisco, CA: Jossey-Bass Publishers.

Early, P. C., & Mosakowski, E. (2000). Creating hybrid team cultures: An empirical test of transnational team functioning. *Academy of Management Journal, 43*(1), 26–49.

Elashmawi, F., & Harris, P. R. (1993). *Multicultural management: New skills for global success*. Tokyo: Gulf Publishing Company.

Gudykunst, W. B. (1991). *Bridging Differences – Effective Intergroup Communications*. Newbury Park, CA: Sage.

Handy, C. (1995). Trust and the Virtual Organization. *Harvard Business Review* (Reprint), May-June.

Haywood, M. (1998). *Managing virtual teams: Practical techniques for high-technology project managers*. London: Artech House.

Hofstede, G. (1984). *Culture's Consequences*. Beverly Hills: Sage Publications.

Igbaria, M., & Tan, M. (Eds) (1998). *The Virtual Workplace*. London: Idea Group Publishing.

Jackson, P. J., & van der Wielen, J. M. (1998). Introduction: Actors, approaches and agendas. In: Jackson, P. J. & J. M. van der Wielen (Eds), *Teleworking: International perspectives: From telecommuting to the virtual organization*. London: MPG Books Ltd.

Jarvenpaa, S. L., Knoll, K., & Leidner, D. E. (1998). Is anybody out there? Antecedents of trust in global virtual teams. *Journal of Management Information Systems*, (Spring).

Kaplan, R. S., & Norton, D. P. (1996). *Translating strategy into action: The balanced scorecard*. Boston: Harvard Business School Press.

Kostner, J. (1994). *Virtual leadership: secrets from the round table for the multi-site manager*. New York: Warner Books Inc.

Labovitz, G., & Rosansky, V. (1997).*The Power of Alignment: How great companies stay centered and accomplish extraordinary things*. New York: John Wiley & Sons, Inc.

Lipnack, J., & Stamps, J. (1999). Virtual teams: The new way to work. *Strategy & Leadership, 27*(1), 14–19.

Maruca, R. F. (1998). How do you manage an off-site team? *Harvard Business Review*. (Reprint). July-August.

O'Dell, C., & Grayson, C. J. (1998). If only we knew what we know. *California Management Review, 40*(3), 154–174.

O'Hara-Devereaux, M., & Johansen, R. (1994). *Globalwork – Bridging Distance, Culture and Time*. Jossey-Bass.

Salk, J. E., & Brannen, M. Y. (2000). National culture, networks and individual influence in a multinational management team. Academy of Management Journal, Vol. 43.

Straus, S. G., Weisband, S. P., & Wilson, J. M. (1998). *Human resource practices in the networked organization: Impacts of electronic communication systems. Journal of Organizational Behavior, 5* Supplemental, 127–154.

Townsend, A. M., DeMarie, S. M., & Hendrickson, A. R. (1996). Are you ready for virtual teams? *HR Magazine, 41*(9), 122–127.

Trompenaars, F., & Hampden-Turner, C. (1998). *Riding the Waves of Culture* (2nd ed.). New York: McGraw-Hill.

von Hoffman, C. (1998). Managing telecommuters. *Harvard Business Review- Management Update* (Reprint U9803D). March.

von Krogh, G. (1998). Care in Knowledge Creation. *California Management Review, 40*(3), 133–153.

PART III

DEVELOPING GLOBAL LEADERS

INTRODUCTION: GROWING THE LEOPARD'S SPOTS: DEVELOPING GLOBAL LEADERSHIP

Morgan W. McCall, Jr.

What would people look like if they were "born" global leaders? Would they have learned five or six languages as a child? Would they have parents from different cultural backgrounds? Would they have moved around a lot? Been educated in countries other than where they were born? Have parents who were global business leaders too? Or do we mean "a born leader" literally, as in genetically gifted such that they came into this world with essential global competencies like empathy, cultural sensitivity, being a good listener, adaptability and flexibility? Perhaps there are genetic markers for such things, but as several authors suggested in the first section of this book, we aren't even in agreement about what the global competencies are, much less where they come from.

In Section I, we turned to ABB's Percy Barnevik for a practitioner's perspective on what a global manager was, so now we turn to him for an opinion on where they come from. His experience has taught him that "global managers are made, not born. This is not a natural process . . . . Obviously you rotate people around the world. There is no substitute for line experience in three or four countries to create global perspective. You also encourage people to work in mixed-nationality teams. You *force* [his emphasis] them to create personal alliances across borders, which means that sometimes you interfere in hiring decisions" (Taylor, 1991, 95).

Advances in Global Leadership, Volume 2, pages 303–307.
2001 by Elsevier Science Ltd.
ISBN: 0-7623-0723-4

So much for born that way. Not only are global leaders not born, he is saying, but developing global perspective is a decidedly unnatural act. You have to be forced. The natural process, if you will, has to be upset to develop a global leader. It's a good thing he doesn't think he needs very many of them.

The authors in this section tackle the challenges of development head on. First comes Charles Corace of Johnson & Johnson who lays out, pipe by pipe and valve by valve, a systemic approach to developing leaders (Chapter 11: "Building a Leadership Pipeline"). Drawing on his considerable experience in developing global leaders, he outlines a strategic approach to the challenge. He argues that the only way to have global leaders at the end of the day is to work hard at it, and that means integrating the various and numerous human resource subsystems around a common purpose, and linking the whole thing to the business strategy. He uses the metaphor of a pipeline to indicate that you start by considering the input, and then follow the process as it goes through a number of transitions along the way. If Barnevik is right about the need to intervene to foster development, by force if necessary, then it takes such a process – one that identifies the critical points of intervention, creates procedures for making interventions and follows through over time.

In the next chapter Hall, Zhu, & Yan (Chapter 12: "Developing Global Leaders: To Hold on to Them, Let them Go!") focus us on three critical aspects of the pipeline. First, they struggle with the same issues raised in Section I – how can you develop global leaders if you don't know what they are? After reviewing various competency models, they develop the idea of meta-competencies – those skills and abilities that make it possible for future global leaders to acquire the new competencies they need in order to adapt to the changing world. From there the authors go on to suggest that developing a global mindset involves a fundamental transformation, and that the only way to achieve it is through an extended assignment requiring real work in another country. That, they hypothesize, offers the lessons of global leadership if the recipient has the metacompetencies to learn them. But, they observe, it is not as simple as that. There is a tension between what an organization needs in terms of performance in these jobs and what is required to actually develop in these jobs. They point out that this tension really flares at repatriation, a notoriously difficult time when so many former expatriates feel unappreciated, underutilized and undervalued by the company that sent them abroad. These authors look at this process in detail, suggesting some ways to approach this intractable problem.

To this point in the section, global leadership development had been discussed as a generic process. However, one might ask if it really is the same for everyone, regardless of nationality or gender. Is the same process appropriate, for example, for a Filipino executive working for a European corporation as it would be for a European working for that company? Or, given the obvious disparity in the number of women in the senior ranks of international corporations, is a process that works for men somehow insufficient to develop global women leaders?

It is this latter issue that interests Adler, Brody, and Osland (Chapter 13: "Advances in Global Leadership: The Women's Global Leadership Forum"). To shed some light on the special case of women they use a detailed case study of a U.S.-based corporation that made a concerted effort to maximize the leadership development of its talented women around the world. They provide some fascinating data collected in this organization about the differences in perceptions and attitudes between male and female managers, and among women of different nationalities. In both cases there are substantial differences! In describing in detail the program developed by this company exclusively for its best-regarded women, Adler et al. raise some challenging questions for developing women leaders. Above all it surfaces the issue of whether or not women aspiring to global leadership positions should receive special treatment and special programs. On the one hand, consistent with the Hall chapter, it is clear that women need access to global experience if they are to acquire global perspective. Consistent with the chapter by Corace, access for women comes about when a system or process is in place to assure it. But on the other hand, and in contradiction with the Hall et al. premise about international assignments, the special circumstances faced by women (especially family obligations), leads these authors to recommend greater flexibility in the nature and duration of the international assignments they are given.

Taken as a whole, the chapters on developing global leaders agree on many issues but leave others unanswered. There is consensus, for example, that you need to know what qualities you are looking for in global leaders, but less consensus when it comes to what those qualities are. In fact, it's not even clear what a global company is – is it measured by the percentage of revenue generated outside of the home country? By the number of employees outside of the home country? Or does the definition of global lie more in the mindsets of executives or even the metacompetencies that are prerequisites to developing global perspectives and skills? Harkening back to the discussion in Section I of this volume, there is progress toward understanding what global leadership is all about, but consensus remains elusive.

While there is still considerable debate about what exactly a global leader is and how many different types there may be, there is general agreement that there is a shortage of them. In the absence of a definitive answer to what a global manager is, the need to develop a *philosophy* about what global means and what types of leadership it requires becomes paramount. Only then can a systematic approach be created to develop the talent needed to achieve that business philosophy. A shortage of talent defines the business case for paying special attention to neglected and underutilized talent pools of women and people from emerging nations. Disagreements – or at least reasonable questions – remain about whether these "special cases" should receive special treatment, and if so, what form that treatment would take.

There is also considerable agreement across authors that global learning comes from global experience, and that there is no substitute for going outside of one's home country and working with people and business models from different countries. Adler et al, for example, in addressing what they see as the special needs of women managers, still conclude that it is critical that they hold higher visibility international assignments and serve on global task forces. Hall et al. make the strongest statement, arguing compellingly that development of international perspective comes through lengthy international assignments with real work. It is this extreme position that surfaces disagreements among the experts. Crabtree, for example, in Section I of this volume, suggested that for senior executives global homogenization might make expatriate assignments less crucial. Adler et al. argued that recognition of women's special circumstances suggests more flexibility in international assignments, including shorter terms.

International organizations have long been concerned about repatriation of their expats, struggling with how to best use what they have learned, finding home-country assignments with as much responsibility and challenge, and preventing turnover of experienced international executives. These chapters add a new wrinkle to the traditional concerns by linking repatriation directly to development. Corace's pipeline argues implicitly for processes and mechanisms to take advantage of repatriation as a learning opportunity, and Hall et al. are direct (and again controversial) in asserting that "to keep them, you have to be willing to let them go."

Finally, there seems to be a consensus that developing global leaders is about learning. Hollenbeck (Chapter 1) set the stage for this in his review of the literature by highlighting how an adult learning perspective clarifies the processes involved in the development of global executives. In this section all the chapters pick up on that theme by emphasizing learning and growth. Corace talks about creating an environment to support learning, including timing interventions to correspond to critical points in the learning cycle. The Hall et al. chapter identifies the metacompetencies of identity and adaptability as crucial to developing global leadership skills from international assignments – another way of saying that it takes good learners to make the most of the developmental potential in assignments. Adler et al. focus on learning interventions particularly suited to women.

So, can global leaders be developed, or should we focus our efforts on identifying and selecting (and stealing) exceptional people who somehow – through genetics or experience – have already acquired whatever it takes? Perhaps the message in these chapters is that effective global leadership can be developed, but not without considerable thought and intensive effort. In other words, it isn't easy, and it isn't an exact science. But the rest of the message hinges on one's assessment of the availability of talent. If already-effective international managers are abundant and available, then why invest in building a development pipeline? Instead, the time and effort should go into processes of acquisition and retention. But if such talented people are rare, as Barnevik asserts, and if talented people who are talented in the ways a specific business strategy calls for are rarer yet, then development is a necessity, not an option. There is some comfort in knowing that we are making progress in understanding what that entails.

REFERENCES

Taylor, W. (1991). The Logic of Global Business: An Interview with ABB's Percy Barnevik. *Harvard Business Review, 69* (Mar-Apr.), 91–105.

BUILDING A LEADERSHIP PIPELINE

Charles J. Corace

ABSTRACT

At the outset, I would like establish that there are no simple answers or magical solutions to quickly address the complex challenges of developing an effective supply of leadership talent. The concepts and insights provided here reflect the collective wisdom of a talented team of professionals within Johnson & Johnson who are responsible for the executive development of its senior leadership team. Over the past three years our department team has been effectively delivering senior-level leadership experiences, while at the same time conducting extensive internal and external research and developing approaches to strengthen the Johnson & Johnson leadership pool.

Our lessons learned over this period of time can be boiled down into these four factors:

• *Simplicity is the keystone to adoption.*

When plans or strategies get so complex that they can not be effectively described to your key stakeholders within five minutes, you are headed down the road of organizational "mumbo jumbo," which then only the content experts will understand and value.

• *Alignment, with the business imperatives, sustains engagement.*

If success is dependent on the commitment of line leadership, then the investment of their resources must directly contribute to the achievement of the their business goals.

Advances in Global Leadership, Volume 2, pages 309–325.

• *Synergy is achieved through integration.*

While there are multiple processes involved in the development of leadership talent, it must function as a synchronous operation in order to produce the greatest impact.

• *Execution is critical to learning; learning is critical to success.*

Success is achieved through refinement of imperfect strategies and applications.

In the Lewis Carroll novel, "Alice's Adventures in Wonderland" the King of Hearts is asked, "Where shall I begin?" To which he gravely replies, "Begin at the beginning and go on till you come to the end: then stop."

The King of Hearts' directions may be fine for the White Rabbit. But for organizations seeking a supply of leaders for the future, things are considerably more complicated. While there are places to start, there is no "beginning" because the effort is already underway, and becoming more strenuous all the time. There is no "end" because the need is ongoing and increasing. And to "stop" would trigger the organizational spiral equivalent to Alice's plunge down the Rabbit Hole.

There is a Chinese proverb, which says, "If we don't change our direction we're likely to end up where we're headed." With that in mind, let's look at where the leadership supply situation is taking us.

In 1998 McKinsey and Company published the results of "The War for Talent," a study assessing the "talent problems faced by 77 large U.S. organizations." After gathering data from corporate officers, vice presidents of human resources and 200 high potentials in each organization, the study concluded that "companies are about to be engaged in a war for senior executive talent that will remain a defining characteristic of their competitive landscape for decades to come." The senior leaders of these organizations identified a current shortage of talent. Combine this shortage with the lack of human capital investment over the past 10 years and the decline in the executive population over the next 15 years, and the result is a potential organizational "Achilles heel." If where we are headed is an exposed Achilles heel and victimization in the war for talent, then what can we do to change our direction?

There is no lack of initiative launched by organizations scrambling to close the leadership gap. But what is too often missing is a sustained strategy for aligning resources and focusing efforts to achieve dominance in the highly competitive talent market. *In the war for talent, the critical weapon is commitment.*

The marketplace battlefields of history are littered with those who enter the fray with a fierce competitor without the resolve to win. Those who fall are often the victims of short-term expectations and short attention spans. Resources are allocated, then suddenly reallocated. Abrupt refocus and reorientation follow periods of frantic concern and activity regarding the latest issue.

This yo-yoing of organizational energy resembles the accounting principal of LIFO – Last In/First Out. But while LIFO may be effective in accounting for raw materials and supplies, when it comes to resolving complex, long-term organizational problems, the result is fragmented, diluted resources. Because people are unclear about what is truly valued by the organization, it also creates a situation where they are reluctant to commit themselves to a common direction.

To address the complexity of the leadership supply issue, organizations need to align key stakeholders and processes in a way that achieves focus and maximizes impact. Three elements must be in place to make this work:

(1) **A description** of the kind of leader the organization wants
(2) **A commitment** to approaching leadership supply as an integrated process, rather than a series of organizational activities or initiatives
(3) **A clearly defined set of critical success factors** for guiding the actions to be taken and assessing results

Over the past several years organizations have funneled considerable effort into defining the characteristics and behaviors of effective leaders, typically creating overall competency frameworks with function-specific iterations for finance, information management, sales and operations and so forth. While customizing a basic model to encompass specific technical attributes is desirable, the true value lies in how they are used and applied. Having open applications of the leadership profile sustains and reinforces its importance. Where there are highly visible applications, such as sourcing and selecting talent, performance and development planning and assessment and succession planning, the competency framework operates as a set of guiding principles. But without integrating the competencies into the critical human resource processes, the result will be another addition to the list of failed organizational initiatives.

There are a number of ways to develop a leadership profile. One option is to go with one of the standardized leadership frameworks developed by various consulting firms. Based on exhaustive analyses of 360 feedback systems, these profiles draw on a huge database, which shows that a high percentage of critical leadership success factors are common to many organizations. This provides a solid foundation for a leadership competency framework, such as the example from Teams Inc. of Phoenix, Arizona in Fig. 1.

While it is fast and efficient, the drawback to a generic framework is just that – it's generic and may be seen as a one-size-fits-all solution that doesn't really suit an organization's unique needs. Overcoming this perception barrier and creating buy-in with those responsible for applying the profile is a key factor in using these standardized instruments successfully.

For organizations that decide to build their own leadership competency frameworks, success is directly related to how active the people who will apply it are in its development. To pull together an effective team for creating a

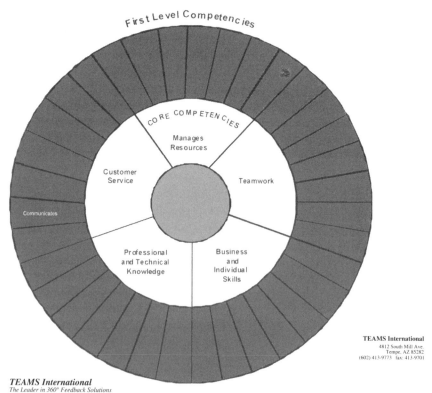

Fig. 1.

leadership framework, human resource organizations should support the process, and line leaders should provide the bulk of the input. Involving your line leaders early and actively helps create the operating-level buy-in necessary to sustain the framework as a supporting process, as opposed to just one more initiative *du jour.*

Once there is a clear description of what your organization values and desires in its leaders, the next step is to assure that you have an integrated process linking the steps for developing an effective supply of leadership talent.

When the supply of talent significantly exceeded the demand, organizations were in a position to cast a net into the talent pool, then pick and choose among the catch. Today, as shown in McKinley's study, "The War for Talent," the demand for leadership talent exceeds the supply of leaders with the experience or the potential to create and sustain growth. Let's view this situation in terms of a production process. When raw materials are abundant and cheap, there is less concern with effective sourcing. Loss through spillage or inefficiency during production does not pose a problem, because the cost is not high and there is a sufficient supply of material on hand. There will be sufficient end product without hurting the bottom line.

On the other hand, if the product were investment-grade diamonds and the raw material a 100-carat hunk of carbon, the situation would be approached very differently. First of all, finding a rough diamond of that dimension is not an everyday occurrence. Following its discovery, the specimen would be placed in the hands of an expert diamond cutter, responsible for extracting the precious essence from the raw material. The cutter studies the diamond in the rough for a long time, since there is only one chance to capture the core component. This accomplished, the gem proceeds to the polishing table where each facet is shaped and formed to capture light and exude brilliance. Mishandled by the cutter or polisher, the raw material will never reach its full market potential.

Similarly, in today's leadership marketplace we can't afford to squander resources. The supply of raw material is restricted, demand is burgeoning and the cost of loss is steep. To compete in this volatile environment and realize a representative market share of leaders, we need to align all organizational resources and leverage the skills of every participating unit in the process.

The quality improvement processes of the 1970s and 1980s were born out of a need for survival. Many of our industries were being challenged to the point of extinction by competitors producing higher quality, more reliable products. In order to survive, companies were forced to examine not only the types of products they offered, but also more importantly, the quality of these products. As a result, to this day there is a strong emphasis on improving processes to assure quality.

Taking a lesson from history, the victors in the war for talent will be those who view leadership supply as a challenge demanding a holistic response, with speed, reliability and process excellence as cornerstones. In this interdependent process, strength comes from the deep functional expertise of individual units, leveraged through lateral linkages. The most obvious lateral linkage is the sharing of a common vision and focus in achieving the desired outcome – a robust supply of leadership talent.

Figure 2 illustrates one approach for creating an effective supply of leadership talent, highlighting critical process elements.

Value Proposition

• The key features of your organization, which attract potential candidates

Acquiring Talent

• Processes focused on sourcing, selecting and obtaining candidate commitment

Assessing Talent

• Determining current and future capability of the talent pool

Developing Talent

• Building functional and leadership capabilities of the talent pool

Transitioning Talent

• Providing support to those selected for greater organizational responsibilities, improving their opportunity for success

VALUE PROPOSITION

Gone are the days of a seller's market. In the past, an organization with a strong presence in the marketplace simply relied on its reputation to attract talent. In today's consumer-oriented markets, however, buyers have ready access to information regarding every aspect of an organization's performance – not only business results and industry ranking, but social responsibility and employee satisfaction as well. When potential candidates choose to explore employment opportunities, deep-seated personal needs and values guide them. The organization that does a good job of communicating its features and benefits to prospective candidates creates a vital bond and captures a larger share of the talent market.

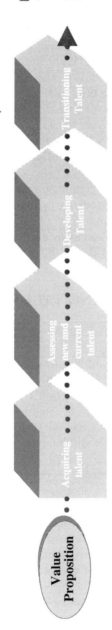

Fig. 2.

In this highly competitive talent marketplace, you must be crystal clear about the benefits and opportunities your organization provides prospective candidates. Key attractors for today's talent pool include the chance for business impact, an innovative climate and commitment to defined values and performance-based reward systems. With the advent of the "dot-com" organizations, there is an additional profile developing. Dot-com's have reversed the financial indicator "the time value of money" to "the money value of time." Knowing that speed is of the essence, they have to pay richly for the talent who will produce the next cyber breakthrough in the shortest period of time. In this "Who Wants to be a Millionaire" marketplace, the supply of breakthrough talent is limited and clarity of who you are and what you are about is everything.

After having communicated what your organization is capable of bringing to the talent marketplace, the guiding philosophy must be "What you see is what you get." Truth in advertising is everything. Organizations that promise X but deliver Y can't hide from the fallout. In today's wired environment, information about a company is shared worldwide and its performance as an employer is common knowledge.

ACQUIRING TALENT

After developing a core value proposition, the next step is to create a marketing strategy that delivers your message to targeted candidate groups. While a product may have a broad range of features and benefits, having a single approach for marketing the product to a diverse array of customers is a strategy doomed to failure. Likewise, an organization's value proposition has to be carefully positioned for different groups of candidates. While college graduates and current jobholders may be looking for many of the same things in a prospective employer, they do have different priorities, and your marketing messages should be tailored to focus on what matters most to each.

With the establishment of a clear value proposition and targeted communications strategy, the next phase is to assure there are processes and support for promoting, evaluating and closing the deal. Talent acquisition is no longer a one-way street where you pick and choose among the large number of respondents to an advertisement or college visit. If you have been effective in drawing candidates to your doorstep, then the real challenge begins – promoting the features and benefits of your value proposition while choosing the candidates who bring the most to the current position and have the greatest promise of growth. Once there is a meeting of the minds between candidates seeking opportunities and your organization's need for talent, it's imperative to move quickly and close the deal. If your decision process is a prolonged series of reviews and approvals, then you're likely to lose candidates to other organizations. Just as organizations choose from a range of candidates, in today's market candidates choose from a range of offers and go with companies whose actions match their words.

ASSESSING NEW AND CURRENT TALENT

Building a robust leadership supply begins with a pool of talent that enables you to observe not only what people accomplish, but, and most important in terms of future potential, how they go about it. While there are many approaches to assessing the leadership potential of the talent pool, the most important is to use identified leadership competencies as the base. Assessing talent accurately requires multiple inputs for describing current capability and future potential. Good sources include performance management, succession planning, assessment centers, special task forces or project teams and action-learning experiences. In addition to supporting the formal assessment process, using leadership competencies brings form to the informal gut-level assessment that is in continual operation.

In many organizations, the objective of the assessment phase is to identify the winners. But from a human capital investment mindset, a much broader perspective would be to use the process to identify those with leadership potential, as well as determine the developmental investment required to enhance the entire talent pool. With the scarcity of talent in today's marketplace, organizations can ill afford to let the pool stagnate. After all, not everyone develops at the same pace. Some require time to learn through experience and realize their full potential.

Traditionally assessment focuses on *performance* – the results attained, and *potential* – the ability to meet greater organizational challenge. But as we face a future of continuing change, there will be an increasing value placed on ability to learn and grow. *Learning potential may become the new criteria for the millennium.* For organizations today, "survival of the fittest" no longer fits developmental needs.

DEVELOPING TALENT

Rarely does talent, once seeded into an organization, flourish on its own to become everything the organization needs and wants. Even if you go outside for a "ready now" leader to fill a void, there is a strong probability that your high-profile hire will plateau at the current level if there is not an effective development process in place.

An effective development process is one where the individual, the individual's manager and the organization share the responsibility. The primary responsibility rests in the hands of the individual, as in "You can lead a horse to water." An organization may provide world-class support and managers may take a proactive role in the development of their staff, but unless individuals commit to the process, there will be no growth and the status quo will dominate. It's up to the individual to seek feedback, develop a plan and engage in actions that enhance personal effectiveness.

The primary role for mangers is to lead by example, demonstrating an active and visible commitment to their own development. In addition to the position of role model, they should strongly support the development of those who work with them, thus providing ongoing communication and feedback.

With individuals committed to personal development, and managers actively supporting the growth of their employees, the key responsibility of the organization is to provide a culture that nourishes learning and growth. Because nothing reinforces the desired culture more than actions, it's critical for organizations to provide the resources and tools that enable their people to realize their development plans. To become part of the cultural fabric of an organization, development must shift from a discretionary to a critical strategic business process, measured and evaluated according to the value it creates.

While development is tailored to specific needs of individuals, there is a common framework that can be applied, such as the integrated process illustrated in Fig. 3. Keep in mind that this is an ongoing process, requiring assessment and reassessment to support continuous growth

Integrated Development Process:

- **Define Personal Goals**: What would you like to do, and what type of organization best fits your style?
- **Define Professional Goals**: What is required for you to get where you'd like to be in terms of formal education, industry experience and organizational expectations?
- **Identify Developmental Gaps**: Seek formal and informal feedback. Sources could include 360 feedback, personal assessment, coach/mentor.
- **Define Developmental Goals**: Establish specific targets which, when achieved, will provide the skills, abilities or behavior sets for success.
- **Determine Developmental Resources**: What approach will be most effective in reaching these goals? On the job, special assignment, formal education, coaching/mentoring?

Fig. 3.

- **Implement the Plan**: Growth comes from experience. While observing the experiences of others may be beneficial, it seldom results in permanent personal change.
- **Follow up and Learn**: Seek feedback on your progress in attaining your goals. The additional insights enable you to make course corrections that greatly increase your achievement level.
- **Reassess:** Development is a dynamic process, demanding continual engagement in this framework.

TRANSITIONING TALENT

While the previous stages of the process focus on getting and developing leadership talent, the objective of transitioning is to improve new leaders' success rates as they move into positions of greater responsibility. Organizations can no longer take a wait-and-see position when it comes to the success potential of their leaders. In Morgan McCall's "High Flyers," in contrast to development, he refers to this assessment mentality as "The Right Stuff" profile. The cost of this Darwinian approach is a needless loss of leaders who could have performed successfully given appropriate support.

The 3 S's characterize assessment environments:

Surprise: Prior to appointment to a leadership position, there is little or no discussion with individuals regarding promotion potential, let alone potential future positions. The new leader receives the news generally one week before the organization.

Sink or Swim: The new leader is thrown into deep water with no lifeline. Management assumes, based on past performance, that these high performers know how to swim and will be able to deal with the new challenges, sharks included.

Support (not): In conjunction with the sink or swim mentality, there is little or no proactive support. Once the kingmakers anoint the new leader, they move on to the running of the kingdom and leave the anointees to figure it out and fend for themselves.

As one would assume with this process, there will be survivors and casualties. The casualties generally fall into two categories: "lost in battle" and the "walking wounded." Those lost in battle are easy to identify – they end up being relieved of the assignment or leaving the organization. Often, these individuals successfully resurrect their careers in other organizations and regain their champion status. The walking wounded are harder to spot. While they survived the baptism by fire, these people have been so damaged in the process that they seldom reach their full potential. The walking wounded learn to survive by providing what the king wants, as opposed to what may be best for the kingdom. In this scenario the individual fails to grow and the organization loses.

In the war for talent, no organization can sustain the casualties derived from throwing leaders onto the battlefield without proper support.

In their work, "Right from the Start," Michael Watkins and Dan Ciampa of Harvard point out that what new leaders do during their first six months largely determines their success or failure over the next three years. The key for organizations, then, is to assure that new leaders are prepared for their experience and supported during this critical initial phase.

New leader preparation should be an integrated process addressing three phases: prior to assignment, at assignment and during the first 180 days. Prior to being assigned to a leadership position, candidates should have a clear understanding of the personal and professional requirements – the critical success factors. Many succession-planning processes focus on the candidate's readiness, primarily in terms of the functional demands of the position. Certainly if there are functional gaps, the time to acquire those skills or experiences is before being assigned the position, not on the job. But there is another aspect of readiness that is often more critical and seldom addressed – the personal component. This can be defined as the person's willingness to take on the increased demands of the new position. While candidates may be ready in terms of their background and experiences, it's often their willingness that determines success or failure. Some factors affecting willingness include the type of challenge offered by the new position and the value it brings to one's career, as well as demands on self and family. A willing candidate's personal goals and values are aligned with the organizational opportunity at hand.

When assigned to a position of greater responsibility, there needs to be a clear set of expectations about the outcomes to be achieved over the first 60, 90 and 180 days. When expectations are not spelled out, the new leader and senior management naturally form their own assumptions. Since these assumptions are seldom in alignment, a derailment process begins, resulting in losses on two levels. The first and most obvious loss is current business opportunities as well as potential future growth. The second and perhaps more significant loss is the high potential individual. When a new leader derails, your organization not only loses its investment for developing this individual, but, with a limited number of developmental opportunities available in any organization, you have precluded the growth of another potential leader.

Through purposeful planning, this critical transition period can become a launching pad for personal and organizational success, and not a talent- and resource-devouring gauntlet for the survival of the fittest.

CRITICAL SUCCESS FACTORS

The essential concepts in this process for building a pipeline of leadership talent are quite basic. While these components are common to many organizations, the real challenge is to integrate the overall process seamlessly. Organizations typically attempt to achieve integration through structure. But while having key processes report up through an organization can support integration, this does not assure success. In fact, despite the best structural efforts, organizational silos often prevail. What is required for seamless integration is a shared set of success factors operating within each component, and across the entire leadership pipeline process, as shown in Fig. 4.

Fig. 4.

This integrated process achieves two main outcomes:

- Development and retention of leadership talent
- Development of a supportive organizational culture

This model reflects the true complexity of building an effective leadership talent pipeline. First, the primary activities (horizontal) need to be integrated and aligned. Then, within each of these areas, the critical success factors (vertical) must be defined and applied, thus supporting alignment across the entire process.

Key Components
- **Strategy** – The commitment and the plan that defines how it will be achieved. The objective is to have a simple statement of the desired outcome, with shared understanding and commitment across all segments and levels of the organization.
- **Catalyst for Change** – Reinforcements to the strategy. What are the organizational rewards and incentives for performance? Without significant upside or downside reinforcements, people attach zero value to the new direction and the status quo prevails.
- **Roles** – Who does what to drive the process at the individual, managerial and organizational levels? While the concept of "we are all in this together" helps solidify shared ownership and responsibility, the organizational "we" lacks the specificity for performing real tasks and accomplishing critical objectives.
- **Resources** – Assets (financial, human, time) committed to realizing the strategy. More often than not, additional headcount and budgets are not forthcoming, so financial and human resources need to be reallocated. In addition, current commitments have to prioritized in order to free up time.
- **Systems** – Processes and tools aligned to accomplish the strategy. There are two questions here: One, do you have the technological systems, infrastructure and supporting operating platforms you need to produce the defined outcomes? The second issue deals with alignment. Like a sports team with great individual contributors, are these systems and processes aligned and operating together to create added value, or do they compete as independent centers of excellence?

THE THIRD DIMENSION

As if the framework just described isn't already complex enough, consider the implications of developing a supply of leaders capable of superior performance in the global marketplace. While the content of the leadership framework presented here is global in its basic makeup, what is valued and how they are applied – the context – can have significant regional variability. To assume otherwise would imply that people around the world fundamentally see and value things the same way.

MOVING FORWARD

If you think of building the leadership supply pipeline as a journey, which organizations need to embrace, then what has been outlined here is a map highlighting critical paths. In determining the most effective path to take, there exist all kinds of maps, each with its own purpose. For instance, there are maps that represent the regions of the world as well as country and city maps. If we wanted to get to 322 Main Street in "Anywhere," USA, a map of the United States would fail to do the job. While it could establish a general direction and get us close to our destination, it would lack the specific detailed information required to drive up to the doorstep. On the other hand, a city map in all its detail would be useless if we didn't know where we were in the larger landscape. In other words, both perspectives play a role in getting us where we need to be.

The leadership supply process we've described is like a regional map, intended to give you an overview of the critical features in the landscape, assess your current location and set a course for reaching your desired destination. As with any map, there are a number of different routes you can follow. So before you take to the road you need a realistic assessment of where you are and a course that suits your organizational capabilities. In the desire for quick results, the direct route may seem like the obvious choice. But if it takes you over rough terrain, and your organizational vehicle isn't equipped to deal with hazards and obstacles, then perhaps allowing time for a less direct route would be more prudent.

Perhaps the King of Heart's advice to "Begin at the beginning and go till you come to the end" isn't so absurd after all. For in the complexity of building a pipeline of effective leadership talent, wherever you are now is the beginning, and taking action is an end as well as a means.

The work of creating a leadership supply can be frustrating as well as challenging. But once you realize that the process is never complete, its rewards begin to evolve. The greatest satisfaction may be in the growth of individual leaders, who, through their leadership, make a real difference for the people they work with and the organizations they build. If at times you feel you must be crazy to take on such a daunting challenge, consider the comments of the Cheshire Cat to Alice.

"But I don't want to go among mad people," Alice remarked.

"Oh you can't help that," said the Cat, "we're all mad here. I'm mad. You're mad."

"How do you know I'm mad?" asked Alice.

"You must be," said the Cat, "or you wouldn't have come here."

Because there is no single correct route to take, you will need to travel minus step-by-step directions. And you'll never arrive at the point where you can stop. But if you take to the road as an organization, genuinely committed to moving forward, keeping a steady focus on where you want to be and staying in it for the long haul, you will navigate the talent supply landscape with increasing effectiveness. And the rewards of the journey will be great.

REFERENCES

Carroll, L. (1987). *Alice's Adventures in Wonderland*. St. Martin's Press, Inc.

Ciampa, D., & Watkins, M. (1999). *Right From The Start: Taking Charge in a New Leadership Role*. Boston: Harvard Business School Press.

McCall, M. W. (1997). *High Flyers*. Boston: Harvard Business School Press.

McKinsey War for Talent Team (1998). *Winning the War for Talent*. McKinsey & Company, Inc.

DEVELOPING GLOBAL LEADERS: TO HOLD ON TO THEM, LET THEM GO![1]

Douglas T. Hall, Guorong Zhu and Aimin Yan

ABSTRACT

"It has become impossible for me – or for any one individual – to know everything that needs to be known about all the changes in market conditions, products, manufacturing, and distribution for each country or region. So, in the final analysis, you have to find the right people for the right problems – and then trust them to take the right actions."
– Interview quote from Hay/McBer International CEO Leadership study (McBer & Company, 1995).

It has become almost a cliché that the environment of the current global economy demands new leadership qualities. Change has always been rampant, but the world has never been more frantic than it is now. Development of information technologies and globalization of industries have expanded business horizons and shifted the competition landscape in fast speed, and multinational companies are facing significant uncertainty, ambiguity and increasing strategic discontinuity (Hitt, Keats & DeMarie, 1998). More than ever, management executives are looked upon to "weather the storm," to consistently engender performance at levels well above competitors (Darling & Box, 1999). It is a common understanding that "in the end, leadership is the primary factor in the performance of a company," as C. R. "Dick" Shoemate, chairman and CEO of Bestfoods, commented in *Fortune*'s cover story on the most admired companies (October 11, 1999).

Advances in Global Leadership, Volume 2, pages 327–349.
2001 by Elsevier Science Ltd.
ISBN: 0-7623-0723-4

Questions remain, however, regarding what makes the needed global leadership, and how to find or develop the "right people" before we can "trust them to take the right actions." Some writers have claimed that the process of identifying and developing global leaders is nothing but a fad (Bonnstetter, 2000). If you agree with this assessment, then there is no need to read further. But, if not, join us in thinking about how we are going to develop the global leadership required for future business growth. In this chapter we will examine how international assignments can be an effective way to development global leadership. We will also present a new way of viewing the relationship (or "psychological contract") between the individual and the organization. And, finally, we will make an argument for a counterintuitive approach to managing the expatriate and repatriate assignment processes.

THE PROMISE AND THE PROBLEMS OF INTERNATIONAL ASSIGNMENTS

In some ways, using international assignments for leadership development is not new. For example, in the late 1980s, academicians, consultants and executives themselves predicted that chief executives in the year 2000 would be experienced abroad (*Wall Street Journal*, Feb. 28, 1989). Also, executive development has always been identified as one of the top strategic objectives for international assignments (Global Relocation Survey, 1999). Successful companies have proven the value of such assignments, as the most admired *FORTUNE* companies are twice as likely as other companies to structure carefully planned career assignments across countries. Bestfoods uses "cross-border assignments" so that individuals learn to lead in different cultures, and American Express takes a similar approach, incorporating international assignments to ensure that people have the required capacities to lead the company to future success (Fortune, 1999).

It is no longer a question of whether you need to use international assignments for leadership development – it is a question of how to make the best of them. Of those companies who see international assignments as essential in their succession planning, how many have actually seen their high potentials stay and advance in their careers? The reality of international assignments is often far less rosy than what we see in the development plan (Black, Gregersen & Mendenhall, 1992).

When we examine international assignments, as Black et al. point out, there is a contradiction between what firms say about the importance of the international experience and how they actually manage it. That is, they say it is tremendously important to the firm, yet it is often managed in a laissez faire manner that belies its stated importance. Our assessment is that companies really do mean it when they state that these international stints are strategically important. The problem lies in how to make the management of these tours more effective.

Thus, we would propose that at least two steps be taken to make the international assignment process more effective. First, it needs to be made *clear on what is meant by success* in an international assignment. Second, organizations need to open themselves up to the risk of letting their international managers go and to put development before retention. And, strange as this may seem, we will argue that, in a Zen-like way, *this developmental, "let-them-go" attitude will actually enhance retention!* These two issues – defining success and valuing freedom and development – are intertwined with a learning perspective in global leadership context. We will explain in more detail in the following sections.

GLOBAL LEADERSHIP IN THE NEW ECONOMY

In the current business environment, it's the survival of the smartest. Qualities such as adaptability, multiple-perspective-taking, comfort with uncertainty, cognitive complexity and broad vision have become part of the basic "competency tool kit" of successful leaders. It is dangerous, however, to assume that common factors exist among leaders of multinational firms that transcend the boundaries of nations. People can't take for granted that leadership skills learned in one country apply to other places in the world. Many firms have had too many experiences where the lessons of successful experience at home simply did not work when they were applied in an international context.

Let's consider an example: UPS (Harvard Business School, 1987). The company started to implement its mission to "unite the world with service" in Germany in 1976, as part of its global development initiative. The first step was simple enough: to start a ground package delivery system like the one the company has in the United States, but on a smaller scale. To staff the operation, the company started with 20 UPS managers from the United States. They were chosen based on their competency as managers, their ability to communicate and their adaptability. Some instruction in German was seen as a plus. The group of managers landed Germany hoping to extend their record of successful leadership.

The results of the German operation: After four years, with a $50 million loss in 1979, it was an embarrassing failure. What happened? The managers, who had been so successful in the United States, applied what they had learned to the German business. But when they began interviewing prospective drivers, it became clear that they had no buildings, no trucks and no information in German about the company, and thus the interviewees had no real evidence that the company even existed! Without any fluency in the German language and any understanding of the culture, their interviews were unsuccessful. Also, the managers had no profile of the ideal "German UPSer." They could not learn anything about the applicants, and the applicants gained no information about the German UPS organization.

And there were other personnel problems. The wage rate that they could pay (seven marks per hour in 1976) was far below the local market value for the sort of motivated, committed workers that were found in the U.S. organization. Absenteeism and theft were high, far higher than in the United States. Also, half of the new company's work force was made up of "guest workers" (semiskilled migrant workers). Although a similar hiring practice had been successful in the United States, this gave UPS a negative reputation in Germany and resulted in UPS being viewed as an undesirable place to work.

There was a myriad of other ways that the managers were tripped up by the differences between the U.S. context in which they had experienced such success and the German environment. And compounding the problem was an arrogant attitude that they had little to learn about managing. As John Christensen, one of the original 20 and the regional personnel manager from 1978 to 1984, stated:

> Most of the early American managers we brought over did not understand or recognize the immense cultural differences. It was like fighting World War II all over again. Americans adopted a "holier and better than thou" attitude, while the Germans secretly sabotaged the American manager. Even some of the best managers in America were like fish out of water in Germany (HBS Case No. 9–488–017, p. 2).

A lesson from this case: Leadership skills acquired in one country will not necessarily be adequate for success in a global environment. And openness to learning is essential.

NEEDED QUALITIES FOR GLOBAL LEADERS

What, then, are the qualities that would help a leader avoid some of these UPS-like pitfalls when dealing with the challenges of the international business context? Although different studies have identified different sets of so-called global leadership competencies, we have determined three key points in our review of the literature. First, global leadership entails more fundamental personal qualities than technical skills. Second, learning ability is the building block supporting the development of fundamental skills. And, third, global leaders focus on future adaptability rather than temporary success. Let us examine some of the studies that are particularly relevant here.

A recent benchmarking study by Hay/McBer on the "Mastering Global Leadership" identified two dimensions of competencies. First of all, global leaders are skillful in international adaptability. They are in a much stronger position to respond proactively to international challenges when they align business strategies, policies and behaviors with cultural requirements. At the same time, these successful global leaders share universal competencies that transcend national boundaries: broad scanning, analytical thinking, conceptual thinking, acting for longer term success, clarifying complex situations, and understanding organizational and industry dynamics.

As Daniel Goleman, author of *Emotional Intelligence*, pointed out, neither technical expertise nor intellectual ability distinguished stars from average global leaders. He cites studies of executives in Latin America, Europe and Japan, which showed that executives who failed were almost always high in expertise and IQ. The critical deficit was in emotional intelligence. In Japan, over half of the failed executives showed a major deficit in emotional intelligence, as did three-quarters of the failed executives in Germany (Goleman, 1998). And in Latin America, because of the "huge rate of change in recent years," virtually all of the leaders who failed were lacking in emotional intelligence. Goleman quotes Kevin Murray, director of communications for British Airways, who said, "Organizations going through the greatest change are those who need emotional intelligence the most." (Goleman, 1998, p. 42).

In Goleman's view, there are five basic emotional and social competencies that make up emotional intelligence: self-awareness, self-regulation, motivation, empathy and social skills. Global leadership qualities involve a composite of these fundamental social and emotional qualities that are difficult to change, although they can be developed. In a similar vein, Hart and Quinn (1993) found, in a study of 916 firms and their leaders, that CEOs having higher behavioral complexity produced the best overall firm performance.

Gender and Global Leadership Skills

Although it is clear that these qualities are critical for all leaders in the global environment, there is mounting evidence that women, as a group, may score higher in these emotional and relational competencies than men, according to Joyce Fletcher (1999). A review of several comprehensive management studies conducted by various research-oriented consulting firms (such as Personnel

Decisions International) concurs with Fletcher's assessment, giving higher marks to women in the following performance areas:

- Motivating others
- Fostering communication
- Producing high-quality work
- Listening to others

The two areas where the results were mixed (i.e. men scored higher on half of the studies and women scored higher on the other studies) were strategic planning and analyzing issues. Both of these are in the more analytic, rational areas. In the emotional and social competencies, the women leaders scored consistently higher (*Business Week*, 2000). These findings might suggest that women might be more capable of showing the adaptability required in an international move, although work-family issues may complicate the picture. But our bet would be that, when more gender research is done on expatriation and repatriation, women may have an advantage.

More Basic Qualities: Metacompetencies

Hall (1986b, 1996) has proposed that beneath the key global competencies, which can change with the environment from time to time, there are even more fundamental *metacompetencies*, which enable the person to learn new competencies independently. And, as McCall (1998) has shown, learning how to learn is a critical ingredient in the development of leadership talent. (An example of a general metacompetency, not necessarily a leadership competency, would be reading. Once a person can read, he or she can acquire other learning independently from all kinds of sources of the written word.) Two metacompetencies that Hall has proposed are *identity* and *adaptability*.

If a person has adaptability, he or she is able to identify for him- or herself those qualities that are critical for future performance, and is also able to make personal changes necessary to meet these needs. But adaptability alone is not enough. The person also has to change his or her awareness of self, so that he or she internalizes and values that change. Thus, the second metacompetency is identity: the ability to gather self-related feedback, to form accurate self-perceptions and to change one's self-concept as appropriate. Adaptability without identity can be a mindless reaction to the environment, with no self-direction. Identity changes without adaptability would be simply "navel-gazing" – very self-aware inaction. With adaptability and identity change, the person has learned how to learn.

Both fundamental competencies and metacompetencies are needed to make a strategic global leader. Strategic leadership reflects a leader's ability to anticipate, envision, maintain flexibility, think strategically and work with others to initiate changes, which creates a strong vision and sustainable competitive advantage for a company (Ireland & Hitt, 1999). No wonder that a recent survey of 1,450 executives from 12 global corporations found that the ability to "articulate a tangible vision, values, and strategy" for their firm was the most important of 21 competencies considered to be crucial skills for global leaders to possess in the future (Davids, 1995).

The common thread of learning ability ties our three key points about global leadership together. To develop skills that involve metacompetencies and that are future oriented, leaders must have an opportunity to develop qualities in learning ability.

DEVELOP GLOBAL LEADERSHIP THROUGH INTERNATIONAL ASSIGNMENTS

You Can't Grow Global Skills Without Global Experience

To develop these qualities in leaders, the traditional methods of development will no longer work. These methods have typically involved domestic activities, such as formal training courses, job rotations (within the home country) and perhaps some form of a mentoring process. What's needed now is all of these – and more!

What more is needed? International assignments. Increasingly, we are seeing leading companies (e.g. 3M, Motorola) requiring international experience as part of their succession planning process (Seibert, Hall & Kram, 1995). An international assignment is often a kind of emotional upending experience, where the person's fundamental assumptions about his or her identity and about work, relationships and business are deeply challenged. And because many of the person's routine "programs" for accomplishing results no longer work in a foreign environment, the person is forced to become adaptable – or to fail. Thus, the two basic metacompetencies – self-awareness and adaptability – receive a "kick start" in the international context.

In terms of more specific skills, international assignments have been regarded as an important way to develop future global leaders who can navigate their firms effectively through the complex waters of international competition (Adler, 1991; Black, Gregersen & Mendenhall, 1992). As a part of pursuing a global business strategy, many firms are requiring high potential managers to have served in at least one important international assignment. Companies believe that the best way to develop global strategic thinking is to put people in different international assignments. It is claimed that there is really no substitute for on-the-ground experience (Allard, 1996).

Defining "International Assignment"

And what do we mean by an international assignment? We observe that many companies engage in a wide range of practices that they label "international assignments." In some cases a person might be assigned to an action learning project involving opening a new office in Budapest or to a global task force charged with creating a new work-life policy. While such assignments might involve frequent international travel and close interaction with people who speak different languages and come from different cultures, we would argue that such work does not represent a great deal of international and cross-cultural immersion.

We would argue that for an assignment to produce true global learning it should be one that is a "real" job, with a long time frame, with accountability for results and interaction with other people (who one sees as different from oneself) with whom one is interdependent. Although we recognize that shorter-term assignments, such as service on project teams or task forces, can have important developmental qualities, we would argue that nothing could compete with the learning power of a real job where the results matter in the manager's future career. Working as a member of a project team in a new country simply does not put the person's identity on the line the same way that having personal responsibility for the success of a business (or some other operation) in that country does. Thus, we would say that for an international assignment to have the most meaningful development potential, it should meet these criteria:

- The person is physically relocated to another country, where he or she lives full-time,
- the duration of the assignment is at least two years, and
- the person works closely with local people and is interdependent with them for achieving performance results.

Why International Assignments are Such Powerful Growth Engines

International assignments as a means of leadership development are more challenging than domestic executive development. An international assignment exposes managers to novel situations and great uncertainty. What had worked in the past for the manager does not necessarily work in this new environment (as in the UPS case), forcing the person to adapt. And it is this process of experiencing surprises, where one's standard "routines" no longer work, that stimulates a cycle of exploration, experimentation with new behaviors and reflection on these new skills. In this way, the person develops not only new skills, but also a new understanding of oneself – a *transformed identity*.

Let's look at it another way – an international tour contains many of the elements of an assignment that we know are developmental, based on the work of McCall, Lombardo and Morrison (1988). Often the international assignment involves a start-up or a turn-around process, which provides wonderful stretching experiences for development. Starting something from scratch produces learning situations, such as identifying what's important, building a team, surviving adversity and realizing the power of leadership. Succeeding in a fix-it assignment helps the person learn to be tough and persuasive and to be tough and instrumental.

And then, in some cases, the international assignment entails a huge jump in scope, going from running a relatively small domestic operation to being head of, say, the company's business in Europe. With a sudden move to a larger operation, the person has no choice but to learn how to depend on other people (she can no longer do it all herself) and to think like an executive.

Routine-Busting and Identity Growth

Also, being suddenly immersed in a foreign context – where just getting through the mundane activities of everyday life (having a telephone installed, hiring a new employee, getting directions while driving) – is a struggle, a powerful personal and professional role transition, requiring communication across language and culture boundaries. There are constant surprises, where the person comes up short and is told that his or usual programs for behavior no longer apply. These daily challenges and "routine-busting" upending experiences provide compelling personal feedback and force a person to become aware of new choices, to explore situations and his or her own identity in a new way and to try out new behaviors (Hall, 1986a). These new choices can create a cycle of growth, in which the person experiences increased adaptability and a heightened sense of self as an agent, which in turn can lead to more awareness of choice – and the cycle repeats itself.

Of course, the person does not always deal with these tasks successfully. There can be many setbacks and failures. And learning how to deal with these hardship experiences is also another building block for development (McCall et al., 1988). This sort of surprise and sense making is part of any transition into any new role (Louis, 1980), but the situations are stronger when the boundaries crossed are international. And the more powerful the role transition, the more profound the identity changes will be.

Out of this deep change, the individual develops a *new perspective or mindset*. This is not just a new view of oneself (identity) but a new view of one's organizational and professional role. This change goes far beyond a change in the skill set – it is a change in the *person*. We know that these deep changes in personal identity occur as a result of being confronted with a higher level of complexity in the environment (Kegan, 1980, 1995), and this is precisely what happens in an international assignment. But wait – it is even more complex than that. Not only does the person develop new perspectives, but he or she also *develops skills in the taking of new perspectives, and developing and holding multiple perspectives*. This ability to acquire and hold multiple, perhaps competing, perspectives (i.e. the ability to see a situation through another person's eyes) is a quality of a more "evolved" identity, in Kegan's (1980) terms.

Learning From Experience

According to Kolb's (1984) learning theory, international assignments allow managers to complete a learning cycle: from Active Experimentation to Concrete Experience to Reflective Observation to Abstract Conceptualization, on a consistent, firsthand basis. Traditional practices of doing and managing international businesses while staying at the corporate headquarters are limited from a learning point of view. While short international visits by managers are helpful for problem solving and decision making, this practice of "remote control" is insufficient for the individual to accumulate a complete experience – from effective perception and sense-making to problem definition, and from data collection to decision making. Only when the person is engaged full-time in the international location, working and living there, is she or he generating the concrete, everyday experiences and having to make the real everyday choices that trigger this learning cycle.

Thus, it seems clear that the international assignment is a powerful natural intervention in a person's life. It is an incredible source of both task learning and personal learning (Hall, 1986). It causes people to become more adaptable and to extend their identities. It helps them learn how to learn. No school, no matter how richly endowed, could produce more learning. No training program can do so either. One executive described this learning process while looking back on his assignment drilling for oil in a rain forest: "That was the purest time of my life. No offices, no memos. Conditions were horrible, but oh, it was exciting. I can't describe the exhilaration of that time." (McCall, Lombardo & Morrison, 1988, p. 63.)

REDEFINING SUCCESS IN INTERNATIONAL ASSIGNMENTS

If the international assignment is such a key component of the leader's career development, the next question that arises is: What makes for a successful outcome in this experience? Actually, how we define the term "success" for an overseas assignment to some degree determines how successfully we develop global leaders.

Just as companies often expect too little in their definition of an international assignment, we would argue that they also often set the bar too low on what outcomes they expect from the assignment. In many cases, "success" to the company means simply that the person has completed the assignment. There may be little concern with how the person applies and shares the information learned from the overseas work. As one interviewee in our research on repatriation stated, "I learned so much from my international assignment. I don't think my company has been able to take the advantage they could take from my learning."

In addition, we can look at outcomes during the expatriate phase itself. Not all expats experience the same high degree of learning, as did our above respondent. Many studies have shown that expatriated managers often isolate themselves from local people and fail to learn much about the business, the culture or themselves (Tung, 1988). And, of course, in many cases the company loses the expat to competitors, and the assignment is not completed (Halcrow, 1999).

Generally speaking, then, the outcomes of an international assignment can be assessed from the perspectives of the individual and that of the firm. Thus far in the research literature, most studies have implicitly taken the perspective of the company. In addition, most of the research to date has focused on short-term outcomes. Therefore, we suggest the need to expand our knowledge of international assignments to include explicit attention to longer-term outcomes and to the inclusion of what constitutes a successful outcome for the individual.

Perhaps the most widely used measure for the immediate outcome of an assignment has been full-term completion of the assignment (vs. premature return). For the firm, therefore, a successful assignment entails the timely and effective completion of organizational tasks. In contrast, an assignment would be recorded as a failure if the key organizational objectives attached to it were not achieved. For the individual, on the other hand, a successful assignment might mean strong performance, learning and personal growth and job satisfaction.

And we can also think in terms of time frame – both the immediate and the longer-term effects of the assignment. A key component to the success of the assignment is the follow-up process that occurs when the person is repatriated back to the home country. From the individual's perspective, success in completing an international assignment can also be reflected in his longer-term career growth and continued development opportunities, such as future challenging job assignments, promotions or enlargement of responsibilities. (These opportunities could be either within the present firm or in other organizations.)

In a similar vein, there are also longer-term measures of success for the organization. From a human capital perspective, as the firm has invested large sums in developing the employee through the international assignment, effective future utilization of the new expertise may be critically important. Therefore, a longer-term success measure would be whether this new expertise is institutionalized and utilized through retaining the repatriated manager, applying his learning in future assignments or transferring his new expertise to other employees.

These success criteria are illustrated in a two-dimensional diagram in Fig. 1, showing the benefits to the individual and the organization, as well as the

BENEFITS

	Individual	Organizational
Expatriation (Short-term)	- Task performance - Skill building, learning, & growth - Job satisfaction	- Accomplishment of organizational tasks - Achievement of objectives
Repatriation (Long-term)	- Continued development - Attractive future assignments - Promotion - Enlargement of responsibility	- Retention of repatriated employee - Utilization of new expertise - Transfer of expertise

Fig. 1. Possible Success Criteria for International Assignments.

Source: Yan, Zhu, and Hall (2000).

shorter- and longer-term effects. The criteria from both rows in the table, then, integrate the assessment of success from the two stages of the international assignment, the expatriate stage (top row) and the repatriation stage (lower row).

Since most companies are results- and goal-driven, how we define the term "success" for an overseas assignment determines to some extent how successfully we develop global leaders. As discussed earlier, development in international assignments entails changes in both competencies and met-acompetencies that cannot be measured by instant skill acquisition or capability improvement. It is important for companies to foster employees' learning when they are overseas. It is even more important for employers to recognize, value and utilize their learning after they come back. For example, the firm could build an institutional architecture that would transfer country-specific learning to organizational memory. Unfortunately, however, many companies are not taking advantage of their expatriates' knowledge.

On the other hand, if people returning from international assignments find themselves and their learning unappreciated, which more often than not is the case, they may decide to leave the company. This is not only a waste of human capital investment – it squanders leadership resources. To develop global leadership through international assignments, organizations need to appreciate learning that unfolds over a longer period of time. Expatriate managers are a source of long-term competitive advantage because of the knowledge (often tacit) that was gained from exposure to international markets. To leverage this knowledge, multinational corporations must build infrastructures that facilitate the assimilation and institutionalization of expatriate learning.

A "CAREER FIT" MODEL FOR UNDERSTANDING THE FIRM-EXPAT RELATIONSHIP

Matches and Mismatches in Expectations

After we sort through the success criteria, we find that there is a paradox in terms of how both parties perceive the role of international assignments in their employment relationship. While the in-depth knowledge and skills developed and utilized in a specific organization over a long period of time are still valued, the world is moving toward an environment in which cross organizational adaptability and learning skills are more important. The skills and competencies effective in the first scenario tend to be static and technical. Competencies and abilities gained in the second scenario tend to be dynamic, learning-oriented and strategic. Between the scenarios there is a paradigm shift in leadership development. If the norm is that one should work in the same firm over a lifetime, anyone pursuing a protean career would be perceived as an opportunist. However, if the norm stresses that cross-firm experience and adaptability developed as a result of cross-firm career experiences are the most valuable, staying within the same company for a long time is neither a recommended career path for an individual nor a preferred practice of a focal company.

Yan, Zhu, and Hall (2000) have proposed a theoretical model for understanding how each of the two parties, the organization and the individual may frame a particular overseas assignment. The model integrates psychological contract theory (MacNeill, 1985; Rousseau, 1995) and agency theory (Smith, 1937). One dimension describes whether the assignment reflects a psychological contract that is *relational* (long-term, continuing) or *transactional* (with no commitments beyond the current assignment). The other dimension describes whether the perceiver is the individual or the organization.

Considering the full array of possible combinations, the yield is four scenarios in a 2-by-2 matrix, as shown in Fig. 2. In *mutual loyalty* (Cell I), both parties view the contract as relational and are committed to a long-term relationship. In a *protean contract* (Cell IV), both parties understand the relationship as transactional, with no future commitments. Using the language of agency theory, a*gent opportunism* (Cell II) is a case in which the organization (principal) considers the international assignment as part of a long-term relationship, but the employee (agent) sees it as transactional. Finally, *principal opportunism* (Cell III) represents a mismatch in which the organization treats an international assignment as a short-term transaction, and the individual perceives it as relational.

What Can Go Wrong?

International assignments are marriages made in heaven that often end up in hell. Let us use our model of psychological contract fit to explain how this can happen.

First of all, the assignment usually starts with impossibly high expectations. The organization "courts" the employee with sweet promises of a glowing future career: "We have extremely high hopes for you. You are one of the chosen few, and this will be a key stepping stone in your future path. We are happy to make this huge investment in your development." This sort of selling is often required, as the move may entail great sacrifices for the spouse or partner and the family, and it may take the person out of a more predictable

		INDIVIDUAL	
		Relational	***Transactional***
ORGANIZATION	***Relational***	Cell I **Mutual Loyalty**	Cell II **Agent Opportunism**
	Transactional	Cell III **Principal Opportunism**	Cell IV **Protean Contracts**

Fig. 2. The Two Sides of the International Assignment Contract.

Source: Yan, Zhu, and Hall (2000).

domestic career path and away from contact with a mentor and a peer network. In short, the company sells the assignment as mutual loyalty: This is a long-term "deal" on both sides (Cell 1). Then several things can happen during the expatriate assignment. On one hand, things can change on the company side. Mergers, divestitures, emerging lines of business, and other unforeseen changes can occur. Or, the corporate office might lose contact with the person ("out of sight, out of mind"). One result of all of these developments might be that the person no longer appears valuable to the firm, so that the international assignment comes to be seen as just another assignment, a transaction in the organization's view (Cell III, principal opportunism). Or, perhaps the employee might develop great visibility in the foreign assignment, in a hot job market, and receive some tempting calls from recruiters. She might jump ship (Cell II, agent opportunism).

Now, what if she completes the overseas assignment (short-term success) and is repatriated back home? In many cases, at the appointed time for the foreign assignment to end there may not be a good follow-up job for the person. Or the subsequent jobs that are available may not fit with the person's geographical or work-life preferences. As a result, the person might find herself in a "special assignment" or in a job that is below her capabilities, feeling frustrated and stuck. After having successfully completed this highly challenging, very exciting, visible and high-stakes overseas assignment, and after being personally transformed, coming home with a new identity as the "returning heroine," she experiences an "ego crash."[2] Suddenly, what had been portrayed as a very promising, long-term career, full of glowing potential, now looks like a dead end. Whereas before the overseas assignment, the company was talking "loyalty" all around, now it is saying, "Hey, it's a new career contract now. You have to use your network and find your own next job." Again, we've moved to Cell III (principal opportunism, with the company shifting from viewing her career as a long-term relationship to viewing it as a transaction). Now it is also possible that there might be a more positive set of outcomes in which both parties come to see a new world of change and opportunity, so that both shift to a more transactional view (Cell IV, protean career). The employee might see her new skills and identity developed overseas as qualities that she wants to take in new directions, perhaps even outside the firm at some point in the future. And the company might see that this talented person is in great demand externally and will have to be continuously "recruited." Thus, there could be a realization on both sides that it is, in Jack Welch's words, a "one day contract."

Thus, by looking at the expectations for the future of the employment relationship from both parties' perspectives, we can see how one or both might come to change the psychological contract. And because, as we said at the outset of this section, the expectations at the start of the expat assignment were so impossibly high, it would be almost impossible to meet them. The odds that both parties would have these dreams realized would be quite low. And when the expectations reach those heights, the fall is hard. For whichever party feels treated opportunistically, the sense of betrayal is strong.

ABOUT THAT FREEDOM PARADOX: WHAT SHOULD THE ORGANIZATION DO?

So, what should be done to prevent these betrayals and unhappy endings? Our answer? Set more realistic expectations, and be honest with each other.

This gets us back to that paradox that was mentioned earlier: For the best development and retention of your talent, you have to be willing to let your people go. In other words, employer and employee should recognize that we live in a Cell IV world, where careers are protean and no one can make long-term commitments.

What this means for the organization is that you have to be willing to give people highly autonomous, challenging assignments that will also give them visibility and contact with many organizations. These are the qualities that promote the growth of protean careers (Hall, 1996; Hall & Moss, 1998). These qualities in the international assignment will not only stimulate employees to develop their protean talents, but they will probably also contribute to success in their job performance, as we know that challenging assignments lead to success (Berlew & Hall, 1966; McCall et al., 1988). However, the visibility that comes from these high profile assignments will probably also lead the incumbents to appear on the "radar screen" of recruiters, who will make attractive competing job offers. This is how the protean labor market works.

But this is where the paradox comes in. Because of the short-term success that this international assignment has created for the person (as well as for the organization), the person will probably have high job satisfaction and a very positive attitude toward the company. We know that there is a positive, self-reinforcing commitment cycle, which goes like this (Hall, 1976; Hall & Foster, 1977):

CHALLENGE → SUCCESS → SATISFACTION →
IDENTITY GROWTH → INVOLVEMENT

Thus, the more you focus on loading the assignment with characteristics and expectations that promote short-term protean success, the more likely you are to reap long-term rewards of increased involvement and retention.

These positive effects of challenge and utilization are greatly enhanced if they are extended beyond the expatriate assignment to the repatriation experience. Again, even if no long-term promises are made – that is, even if the contract is clearly a protean one – if the person is given a stretching return assignment that truly taps the skills of this "new person" (the "returning hero") from abroad, the result will be a positive attitude toward the company and a step in developing a long-term relationship with the firm.

On the other hand, if the company tries too hard to hold on to the person (e.g. by a formal contract, by a no-compete agreement, by not letting the person participate in external executive development programs that might expose him or her to competitors), these actions could have the opposite effect. The person might feel so constrained and so mistrusted that he or she feels smothered – and then look for a way out. Thus, we see the paradox of commitment: People are most able to develop internal commitments and attachments when they have the free choice to leave and choose to stay. To paraphrase the late Fritz Perls: If you love someone, let them go. If they truly love you, they will return. And if they do not, it was not meant to be.

The power of this let-them-go mindset was demonstrated in an academic setting early in the first author's career. A junior colleague had just returned from another university, which had made him an attractive offer. When the department chair learned of this offer, the colleague, feeling guilty, attempted to assure the chair that he never would consider leaving. The chair's response was, "Of course you should consider leaving. And you should not feel guilty about it. The way I see it, as department chair, I have two goals related to your development. The first is to provide you with the assignments and resources for your career success so that you will always be receiving great offers from top competing schools. And the second is to make it so attractive here for you that you turn them down!" And, in fact, this colleague did stay and had a long-term relationship with the school, eventually receiving tenure there.

We can also approach this issue of employment freedom from another perspective. Most firms, in addition to making promotions from within, recruit executive talent from outside the firm. The intention in external recruiting is to attract individuals with fresh and rich experiences. If a firm sees value in having future leaders with cross-boundary, fresh experiences, this practice would send a strong signal to its own people that there is value in exploring external opportunities. If the firm behaves inconsistently and does not support outward-looking behavior by its employees, how attractive is it as an employer to potential employees? No employee wants to feel trapped. From this perspective, to help employees pursue advancement and protean development opportunities externally will soon be a new criterion used to evaluate a firm's effective management, at least human resources management. The worst scenario, in focusing too strongly on retention and an exclusive policy of promotion from within, is that the organization will end up keeping for too long those it doesn't really want, and shying away from those attracting those it really needs.

If the practice of "promotion from within" served well for motivation and development when workforce stability was a top concern, leadership development across firm boundaries becomes desirable, as creativity and adaptability are critical to business success. Thus, by being willing to let your talent go and by providing them with the protean development opportunities that will make them more employable and marketable inside and outside the present company, the more you likely you are to retain them (and to want to retain them). Also, adopting this protean mindset makes you more attractive to external talent that you may be trying to recruit. Thus, a policy of promotion from within and a policy of recruiting externally can be mutually reinforcing.

SUMMARY

To summarize, we have illustrated the flow or frame of our reasoning in the model in Fig. 3. In this figure, we hope to capture the following key points:

- There is no question of whether we need international assignments for global leadership development. The question is how to make them more effective.
- Organizational dilemmas or tensions exist between the importance of international assignments and how they are managed. How can they be managed in ways that will actually help people learn the lessons that these experiences offer them?
- Mismatches in the psychological contract often arise after the international assignment due to the nature of leadership and personal development in two dimensions: competencies and metacompetencies.
- Development in these two dimensions leads to a dilemma (1) of rewarding for development versus rewarding for performance (long-term vs. short-term success).
- Differing definitions of success result in a dilemma (2) of transactional contract versus relational contract (let-them-go or protean vs. hold-on attitudes).
- There is a feedback loop back to the initial assignment process. The implication of our analysis, based on a human capital argument is that to hold on to them, you have to be willing to let them go.

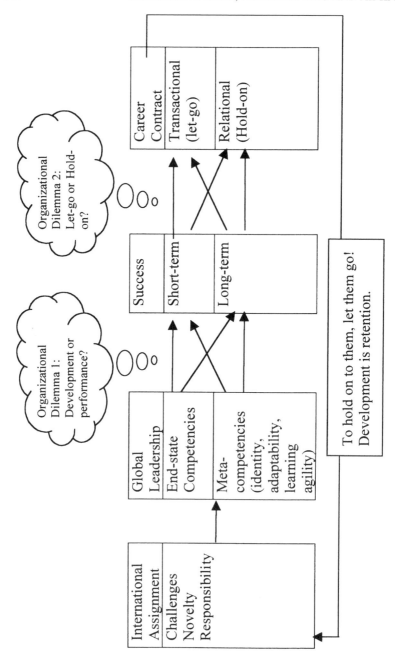

Fig. 3. Summarizing Key Elements in Managing International Assignments.

CONCLUSION

According to Michael Malone, co-author of the *Virtual Corporation,*

> We appear to be racing toward a protean, freelance economy in which a typical company will consist of a small core of long-term employees (to maintain the enduring relations with suppliers, distribution channels, and customers) surrounded by an ever-changing cloud of contractors, semi-permanent employees, and company-to-company relationships" (1995, pp. 40–54.).

This is the way it is in the global domain, where internationally seasoned leaders prefer growth and dynamic flexibility. The best way to hold on to these talented leaders is to help them to learn, even though this sometimes means helping them to leave.

The global competition landscape is changing, and so is the global leadership development mindset. The best way to lose people is to hold on too tightly. And the best way to keep talent is to be willing to let it go – and let it grow.

NOTES

1. Work on this paper was supported in part by the Executive Development Roundtable at the Boston University School of Management. The helpful comments of George Hollenbeck, Bill Mobley, and Morgan McCall on an earlier draft of this chapter are gratefully acknowledged.

2. The authors are indebted to our colleague Helen Long for introducing them to this way of describing this kind of humbling, identity-deflating role transition.

REFERENCES

Adler, N. J. (1991). *International Dimensions of Organizational Behavior.* Boston, MA: PWS-Kent.

Allard, L. A. (1996). Managing Global-Trotting Expatriates. *Management Review, 5,* 38–46.

Berlew, D. E., & Hall, D. T. (1966). The socialization of managers: Effects of expectations on performance. *Administrative Science Quarterly, 11*(2), 207–223.

Black, J. S., Gregersen, H. B., & Mendenhall, M. E. (1992). *Global Assignments.* San Francisco, CA: Jossey-Bass, Inc.

Bonnstetter, B. J. (2000). The DNA of global leadership competencies, *Thunderbird International Business Review, 42*(2), 131–144.

Business Week (2000). As leaders, women rule: New studies find that female managers outshine their male counterparts in almost every measure. November 20, 74–84.

Darling, J. R., & Box, T. M. (1999). Keys for success in the leadership of multinational corporations, 1990 through 1997, *Advanced Management Journal, 64*(4), 16–21.

Davids, M. (1995). Where style meets substance. *The Journal of Business Strategy, 16*(1), 48–59. Boston.

Fletcher, J. F. (1999). *Disappearing Acts: Gender, Power, and Relational Practice at Work.* Cambridge, MA: MIT Press.

Fortune (1999). Molding global leaders, October 11, page 270.

Global Relocation Survey (1999). *Global Relocational Trends 1999 Survey Report.* New York: Windham International, National Foreign Trade Council, Institute for International Resources.

Goleman, D. (1998). *Working With Emotional Intelligence.* New York: Bantam Books.

Halcrow, A. (1999) Expats: The squandered resource. *Workforce, 78*(4), 42–48.

Hall, D. T. (1976). *Careers in Organizations.* Glenview, IL: Scott, Foresman.

Hall, D. T. (1986a). Breaking career routines: Midcareer choice and identity development. In: D. T. Hall & Associates (Eds), *Career Development in Organizations* (pp. 120–159). San Francisco: Jossey-Bass.

Hall, D. T. (1986b). Dilemmas in linking succession planning to individual executive learning. *Human Resource Planning, 25*(2), 235–265.

Hall, D. T. (Ed.) (1996). *The Career Is Dead – Long Live the Career: A Relational Approach to Careers.* San Francisco: Jossey-Bass.

Hall, D. T., & Foster, L. W. (1977). A psychological success cycle and goal setting: Goals, performance, and attitudes. *Academy of Management Journal,* (June), 282–290.

Hall, D. T., & Moss, J. E. (1998). The new protean career contract: Helping organizations and employees adapt. *Organizational Dynamics,* (Winter).

Hart, S. L., & Quinn, R. E. (1993). Roles executives play: CEOs, behavioral complexity, and firm performance. *Human Relations, 46*(5), 543–574.

Harvard Business School (1987). United Parcel Service (B). Harvard Business School, case no. 9–488–017.

Hitt, M. A., Keats, B. W., & DeMarie, S. M. (1998). Navigating in the new competitive landscape: Building strategic flexibility and competitive advantage in the 21st century. *The Academy of Management Executive, 12*(4), 22–42.

Ireland, R. D., & Hitt, M. A. (1999). Achieving and maintaining strategic competitiveness in the 21st century: The role of strategic leadership. *The Academy of Management Executive, 13*(1), 43–57.

Kegan, R. (1980). *The Evolving Self: Problem and Process in Human Development.* Cambridge, MA: Harvard University Press.

Kegan, R, (1995). *In Over Our Heads: The Mental Demands of Modern Life.* Cambridge, MA: Harvard University Press.

Louis, M. R. (1980). Surprise and sense making: What newcomers experience in entering unfamiliar organizational settings. *Administrative Science Quarterly, 25*, 228–251.

McBer & Company (1995). *Mastering Global Leadership: Hay/McBer International CEO Leadership Study.* Hay/McBer Worldwide Resource Center, Boston, MA.

McCall, M. W., Jr., Lombardo, M. M., & Morrison, A. M. (1988). *The Lessons of Experience: How Successful Executives Develop on the Job.* New York: Lexington Books.

McCall, M. W., Jr. (1998). *High Flyers: Developing the Next Generation of Leaders.* Boston: Harvard Business School Publishing.

Mac Neill, I. R. (1985). Relational contracts: What we do and do not know. *Wisconsin Law Review,* 483–525.

Malone, M. (1995). The next 25: What Today's Leading CEOs, Management Gurus, and Futurists See Coming for Your Company, Your Job and Your Life Between 1995 and 2020. *Industry Week, 244*(15), 40–54.

Rosener, J. (1990). Ways women lead. *Harvard Business Review,* (November–December).

Rousseau, D. M. (1995). *Psychological Contracts in Organizations: Understanding Written and Unwritten Agreements*. Thousand Oaks, CA: Sage.

Seibert, K. W., Hall, D. T., & Kram, K. E. (1995). Strengthening the weak link in strategic executive development: Integrating individual development and global business strategy. *Human Resource Management, 34,*(4), 549–567.

Smith, A. (1937). *The Wealth of Nations*. New York: Modern Library.

Tung, R. L. (1988). *The New Expatriate*. Cambridge, MA: Ballinger.

Wall Street Journal (1989). *Going Global: The Chief Executives in Year 2000 Will Be Experienced Abroad*. Feb. 28, Section 1, Page 1, Column 1.

Yan, A., Zhu, G., & Hall, D. T. (2000). *International assignments for career building: Agency relationships and psychological contracts*. Working Paper. Boston: Boston University School of Management.

ADVANCES IN GLOBAL LEADERSHIP: THE WOMEN'S GLOBAL LEADERSHIP FORUM

Nancy J. Adler[1], Laura W. Brody and Joyce S. Osland

ABSTRACT

How prepared are CEOs to recognize that their global competitiveness depends on including the most talented people in the world on their executive team, women as well as men? As global competition intensifies, the opportunity cost of traditional male-dominated leadership patterns has escalated. The question is no longer, "Will the pattern of male-dominated leadership change?" but rather, "Which companies are taking advantage of new trends and which are falling behind? Which strategies are proving most effective in moving the best people – women and men – into senior leadership positions?" This chapter describes one major multinational's experience in creating an organizational change process, led by the CEO, designed to move the most talented women from around the world into the company's previously all-male senior executive positions. The overall goals for the organizational change process were to increase the company's global competitiveness; develop the global leadership skills of the company's most highly talented and senior women; create an internal network among the company's women leaders; and develop both global and local recommendations for enhancing the company's ability to support the career advancement and success of an increasing number of highly talented and senior women. The chapter describes the organizational change process leading up to the Women's

Advances in Global Leadership, Volume 2, pages 351–383.
2001 by Elsevier Science Ltd.
ISBN: 0-7623-0723-4

Global Leadership Forum (including the results of a company-wide survey), the design for the Women's Global Leadership Forum itself, the recommendations implemented by the company following the Forum, and the cross-cultural lessons learned in working with senior and highly talent women from around the world.

"Anytime you have a fiercely competitive, change-oriented growth business where results count and merit matters, women will rise to the top."

(Carly Fiorina, CEO, Hewlett Packard).

"For all practical purposes, all business today is global." (Mitroff, 1987: ix). As management scholar Ian Mitroff (1987: ix) aptly observes, "Those individual businesses, firms, industries and whole societies that clearly understand the new rules of doing business in a world economy will prosper; those that do not will perish." "Global competition has forced executives to recognize that if they and their organizations are to survive, let alone prosper, they will have to learn to manage and to think very differently." (Mitroff, 1987: x) How prepared are leaders of successful global corporations to think and to manage very differently?

WOMEN: INCREASINGLY IMPORTANT AS GLOBAL LEADERS

How prepared are CEOs to recognize that their global competitiveness depends on including the most talented people in the world on their executive teams, women as well as men? Based on history, many believe the answer to be *not very.* Women today hold less than 3% of the most senior management positions in major corporations in the United States (Wellington, 1996), and less than 2% of all senior management positions in Europe (Dwyer, Johnston & Lowry, 1996). In countries such as Italy, the proportion of women executives falls to a paltry 0.1% (Dwyer et al., 1996; also see International Labor Office, 1997).

Can companies – or countries – afford to continue their historic pattern of male-dominated leadership? As global competition intensifies, the opportunity cost of such traditional patterns escalates. Most leaders know that their companies can no longer afford to ignore potential talent "simply because it's wearing a skirt" or because it is holding the wrong passport (Fisher, 1992). As Harvard Professor Rosabeth Moss Kanter (1994: 89) emphasizes, in a global economy, "Meritocracy – letting talent rise to the top regardless of where it is found and whether it is male or female – has become essential to business success."

Careful observation reveals a rapidly increasing number of countries and companies moving away from the historic men-only pattern of senior leadership. For example, of the 47 women who have served in their country's highest political leadership position – either as president or prime minister – over 60% have come into office in just the last decade, and all but seven are the first woman her country has ever selected for such a position.[2] Similarly, among the current women CEOs leading major companies, almost all are the first woman whom her particular company has ever selected.[3] The question is no longer, "Is the pattern changing?" but rather, "Which companies will take advantage of the trend and which will fall behind?" "Which strategies will prove most effective in moving the best people – women and men – into senior leadership positions?" This chapter describes one major multinational's experience in creating an organizational change process, led by the CEO, designed to move the most talented women from around the world into the company's previously all-male senior executive positions.

ONE COMPANY'S ODYSSEY: GLOBAL LEADERSHIP AT BESTFOODS[4]

By any definition, Bestfoods, formerly CPC International Inc., had become one of the most internationally oriented food companies. Headquartered in Englewood Cliffs, New Jersey, it was among the largest U.S.-branded food companies, with annual sales in 1998 of $8.4 billion. Bestfoods' return on equity of 56% placed it in the top quartile of its peer group. The company earned 60% of its revenues from non-U.S. sources, operated in more than 60 countries and marketed products in 110 countries. The company forecasted future growth to continue to derive primarily from outside the mature markets of North America and Western Europe. Africa, Asia, Eastern Europe, Latin America, the Middle East, and the countries of the former Soviet Union were projected to lead increases in 21st century revenues.

Bestfoods has been best known for its most widely recognized product lines, including: *Hellmann's* and *Best Foods* mayonnaise and dressings; *Mazola* corn oil and margarine; *Skippy* peanut butter; *Knorr* soups, sauces, and bouillons; *Entenmann's* sweet baked products; *Thomas'* English muffins; *Arnold, Brownberry, Freihofer's and Oroweat* breads; *Boboli* pizza crusts; *Mueller's* pasta; and *Karo* syrup. Bestfoods' global *Knorr* brand comprises one of the world's most extensive lines of products. Bestfoods also had a catering division that was known as *Caterplan* in most global markets.

Bestfoods' leadership was as global as the company's operations. Almost half of the 20 corporate officers came from outside of the United States, with eight nationalities represented among them. Similarly, on the board of directors, five passports were represented among the 14 members. Two of the CEOs sitting on Bestfoods' board were women. Of the company's 44,000 employees, two-thirds worked outside of the United States.

Similar to many industries, consumer foods had become an increasingly competitive industry in which only the companies with top talent and top brands would survive. Moreover, whereas many consumer foods companies used to be able to operate as loose confederations of fairly autonomous individual country operations, global competition had begun currently forcing all members of the industry, including Bestfoods, to more closely coordinate their operations worldwide to an extent heretofore found unnecessary.

To succeed in such an environment, companies increasingly needed to attract and retain the best talent available worldwide, including both women and men from all nationalities. Bestfoods was no exception. Such global talent needs to operate effectively at both global and local levels. Moreover, with women making more than 80% of purchasing decisions for its products, Bestfoods knew that it would not survive if it failed to understand women's needs and priorities. Without women represented in both the most senior executive positions as well as broadly throughout management, neither Bestfoods nor any other company in this industry could hope to sustain a competitive advantage in the 21st century.

There is no question that Dick Shoemate, Bestfoods' CEO, fully understood this competitive necessity and its implications for his company's future. Shoemate had made explicit Bestfoods' commitment to actively attract, retain and develop the most highly talented women and men from all parts of the globe:

> We believe that one of Bestfoods' unique competitive strengths is a management team that delivers outstanding performance in the local marketplace and also works together to build the "Best International Food Company in the World." . . . We actively seek to identify and to develop high performing Bestfoods' managers throughout the company, including men and women from all countries and ethnic backgrounds.[5]

Moreover, the CEO recognized that words were not enough to institute the changes in thinking and behavior needed for 21st century success. By 1997, under Shoemate's leadership, the number of women in senior positions increased significantly, with women comprising 14% of the members of the board of directors, 16% of the corporate officers and 13% of directors and vice-presidents. Compared to many companies, these numbers were excellent. Shoemate, however, considered them insufficient to support the future he envisioned for Bestfoods. He therefore committed the company to making rapid progress in increasing the number of women from around the world in the company's senior management and leadership.

Of the many ways in which he could demonstrate his commitment, the CEO purposely chose the approach that the company used when addressing its other key strategic business issues and developing its top senior leadership. Together with the Corporate Strategy Council,[6] he announced that the company would hold its first Women's Global Leadership Forum as an off-site meeting at the Arrowwood Executive Conference Center outside New York City with participants from around the world. Because Bestfoods uses Arrowwood for its most important meetings and leadership development programs, choosing this location for the first Women's Global Leadership Forum symbolically communicated the importance and the urgency that the CEO attached to the issue and the meeting.

Shoemate further emphasized the urgency of the issue by announcing that Bestfoods would hold the forum within 90 days. The forum would differ from Bestfoods' other executive off-site meetings in that this time the primary participants would be exclusively women and the issue addressed would be how to assure Bestfoods' future competitiveness by attracting, developing and retaining the company's most talented women.

As announced, the Women's Global Leadership Forum was to be held for four-and-a-half-days under the direction of Laura Brody, Bestfoods' Director of Diversity and Development.[7] The CEO planned to invite 50 of the company's most talented and senior women from each region of the world and every function within the company. In addition, he invited both women members of the board of directors, all members of the Corporate Strategy Council, and the majority of other corporate officers to the opening of the forum as well as to other selected sessions. From the beginning, Shomate's intention was to integrate more women into the most senior levels of leadership, not to isolate them into a women-only event that could be perceived as tangential and, therefore, as unrelated to the company's core business strategy.

At no time did the CEO lose sight of the fact that the primary goal of this initiative was strategic – to increase his firm's global competitiveness. Reflecting this commitment, the company's explicitly stated goals for its first Women's Global Leadership Forum were to:

* **Increase the global competitiveness** of Bestfoods;
* **Develop the global leadership skills** of Bestfoods' most highly talented and senior women;

- **Create an internal network** among Bestfoods' women leaders to facilitate their global effectiveness; and
- **Develop both global and local recommendations** for enhancing Bestfoods' ability to support the career advancement and success of an increasing number of highly talented and senior women.

The Process Leading Up to the Forum: Creating an Environment for Change

To ensure the success of the broader initiative – increasing global business competitiveness – Shoemate and Brody embedded the Women's Global Leadership Forum into a larger process of organizational change and development. The initial step focused on identifying the company's most talented women and providing visibility for them, both as potential invitees to the forum and, more importantly, as part of the company's talent pool for its current and future leadership positions. To identify such women, Brody solicited nominations from all division presidents and personally reviewed all existing lists of the company's high potential and outstanding employees.

After Brody finalized the list of potential invitees, the CEO asked the six members of his Corporate Strategy Council to rank order the nominees from their divisions. Final selections maintained an equitable representation from each division and area of the world. Of the 50 women who were selected, more than half came from outside the United States.

During the selection process, some members of the Corporate Strategy Council expressed concern about potentially generating negative reactions to holding a global forum for women leaders. Contrary to their fears, the immediate response to the announcement was extremely favorable, with every division requesting additional spaces for women from their region. In response, the total number of invitations was increased to 60. Indications that the organizational change process was beginning to succeed quickly surfaced. One country manager, for example, in responding to the nomination process, revealed that he was pleasantly surprised to discover how many more high potential women worked in his affiliate than he had previously thought. In another case, the nominations review process led to the immediate promotion of one woman.

In the ensuing weeks, reactions varied among both the men and women. Some men reacted very positively, believing that such a forum was long overdue; others expressed skepticism. Still others responded negatively, believing that the very idea of a *women's* global leadership forum discriminated against men. Some of the most negative men informally began referring to the upcoming forum as "a coffee klatch" and "the girls' knitting club," and cautioned that the forum would turn into "a bitch session."

Many women in the company responded particularly positively to the announcement that Bestfoods would be holding a Women's Global Leadership Forum. They expressed their delight not only at Bestfoods holding the forum, but also that the CEO had invited them to take part in such a groundbreaking event. One senior woman sent a letter to the CEO expressing her amazement, "I never thought I would live to see the day that this company, or any company, would hold such a Forum. . . . Congratulations! I am 100% with you."

The women's reactions, similar to those of the men, also varied, with some more cautious or negative than the majority. A number of women expressed concern that in singling them out as women, the company was not recognizing their business accomplishments. As one senior European executive commented, "I am happy to attend the Forum if I'm being invited because of my business acumen as one of the top 100 people in this company; not simply because I am 'a girl.'" Other women expressed concerns about a possible male backlash as a result of the forum.

Gathering Outside Expertise: Going Beyond What We Know Well

The forum was not only a first for Bestfoods; it was one of the first in-company global leadership initiatives in the world to focus on women. Many, primarily American, companies offer women-in-management programs, but such programs are usually domestic in focus and rarely include women from around the world. Moreover, in most firms these domestically oriented programs target lower-level employees – often emphasizing entry-level personnel or managers rather than the company's most senior leaders (Adler, 1999a). Similarly, whereas many companies regularly hold global leadership programs for their senior executives, these programs rarely include many, if any, women. To make certain that Bestfoods had access to expertise beyond its own experience, Brody brought in Professor Nancy J. Adler, an expert on international management and women's global leadership, from Montreal's McGill University to help design both the overall organizational change process and the forum. After lengthy discussions, both women committed themselves to working together to help create something new, something few major companies had ever attempted. Brody later brought in Professor Joyce Osland, an expert on women executives in Latin America, from the University of Portland to help with the forum itself (see Osland, Snyder & Hunter, 1998).

Gathering Tacit Expertise: Making Explicit What We Implicitly Know

When trying to understand women and power, myths abound (see Adler, 1999b and 1994). To anchor the overall organizational change process and the Women's Global Leadership Forum in reality, Bestfoods designed a survey to differentiate between people's perceptions and the actual obstacles women and men encounter in achieving career success. The survey addressed many of the company's most pressing concerns about attracting, developing and retaining senior women.[8]

While generating an in-depth understanding of women's and men's perceptions and experiences within the company, the survey also constituted the second major initiative in the company's organizational change process. As such, Shoemate and Brody used the survey to more deeply involve Bestfoods' most senior men and women in the competitive challenges facing the company, and thus to build their support for implementing the recommendations that the forum would generate. The confidential survey was sent to all 20 corporate officers, the next 125 most senior executives – of whom 92% are men – and the 60 women whom the company had invited to attend the forum. Seventy percent of the men and women returned completed surveys.

The comprehensive survey contained more than 150 questions focused on a range of issues. It identified strategies that women and men had used to advance their own careers and identified barriers that each had faced. The survey also solicited recommendations as to what both the company and the women should do to increasingly attract, develop and retain the company's highest potential and most senior women. In addition, the survey sought to better document the potential benefits the company could gain from increasing the number of women in senior leadership positions.

While identifying some similarities among women and men's perceptions of reality and their respective recommendations for change, the survey revealed many highly significant differences. Most issues, concerns and gaps identified at Bestfoods are in no way unique to the company, but rather echo general patterns that are well documented in recent organizational research (see Ragins, Townsend & Mattis, 1998).

Moving Ahead: Career-Advancement Strategies
Women and men agreed on the three most important strategies for women's career success at Bestfoods:

• Consistently exceeding performance expectations
• Gaining line management experience
• Seeking difficult and high visibility assignments

Following these top three strategies, however, women and men saw the world quite differently. More than 10 times as many women as men, for example, believed that *developing-a-style-that-men-are-comfortable-with* is critical to women's career success.[9] Men, by contrast, believed that such a *make-men-comfortable* approach was almost the least important strategy that women could follow. Women and men also disagreed on the importance of having a mentor, with almost twice as many women as men believing that women needed to develop a relationship with an influential mentor in order to succeed.[10]

Whereas women consistently included both task-related and relationship-building competencies in their understanding of the requirements for senior management, men tended to focus more narrowly on task-related considerations. For example, in contrast to the women's recommendations to develop *a-style-that-men-are-comfortable-with* and *a-relationship-with-an-influential-mentor*, three times as many men as women stressed the importance of gaining international experience. If things did not work out well for them, none of the men reported considering changing companies to get ahead, while a noteworthy 14% of the women – all of whom had been labeled as high potential by the company – stated that they would seriously consider such a move.

When asked what the company should do to facilitate women's career advancement, women and men again agreed on the most important strategies:

- Give women more assignments that include managing people.
- Include more women on divisional and global strategic taskforces.
- Include more women in the Arrowwood Senior Management Development Programs.
- Hold managers more strictly accountable for identifying, developing and advancing high-potential women across all management levels.
- Ensure that succession plans include a higher proportion of women.

Women, however, consistently rated the importance of these and other company initiatives more highly than did men. For example, more than three-quarters of the women, but only half of the men, thought that it was important for the company to include women on divisional and global strategic task forces. Similarly, more than twice as many women as men reported that it was important for the company to send women to external development programs. Likewise, 60% of the women, and only 43% of the men, believed that it was critical to hold managers more accountable for developing and advancing high potential women – with three times as many women as men reporting that it was extremely important to use numerical targets. In addition, twice as many women as men thought that it was critically important to have flexible work policies.

Overall, women understand that it will take both corporate and individual strategies for women to move ahead. By contrast, male executives tend to de-emphasize what the company can do to foster women's development and advancement, while stressing what the women should do for themselves. Almost two-thirds of the men, but less than half of the women, explicitly stated that it was up to the women themselves to change to fit into the company's current corporate culture.

Failing to Move Ahead: Barriers to Career Advancement
Women and men agree on what are not barriers. Almost 90% recognized that women are equally as well prepared for senior leadership positions as their male counterparts, and that women have what it takes to get to the top. Additionally, more than three-quarters of both men and women agreed that women exhibit effective leadership styles, along with possessing the technical and educational credentials needed to succeed in senior management positions.

A very interesting pattern, however, emerged from the similarities and differences among men and women's perceptions of the most critical barriers to women's career success. Women agreed with the top five barriers identified by men:

• Women's lack of general management and line experience
• Women not having been in the pipeline long enough
• Women's lack of mobility to take international assignments
• Limitations imposed by the husband's career
• Women's unwillingness to sacrifice personal and family life to follow a traditional corporate career path

The women, however, reported an additional set of barriers that they experience as being even more critical to their advancement than all five of the top barriers (listed above) that the men identified. Approximately three-quarters of the women, yet only a third of the men, considered the removal of the following barriers to be a crucial first step prior to women progressing into senior-level positions:

• Senior men being uncomfortable with ambitious women
• Senior men's negative stereotyping and preconceptions of women
• Senior men's difficulty in reporting to a woman

These additional barriers faced by women appear to be largely invisible to most men. Women at Bestfoods clearly faced more barriers in their career advancement than did men, but more importantly, the types of barriers they faced differed. All barriers men recognize are framed primarily as women's own responsibility (e.g. women's lack of mobility, lack of line experience, and lack of time-in-the-pipeline). Women did not disagree that the barriers the men identified exist. However, they saw the most important barriers to their career progress as being the negative perceptions men hold about senior and high-potential women (e.g. men being uncomfortable with ambitious women, men negatively stereotyping senior women, and men feeling uncomfortable reporting to a female boss).

Given these marked differences in perception, the next step in the organizational change effort was to assist both women and men in better understanding each other's reality. The survey results indicated that both men and women would need to change for Bestfoods to succeed in meeting its strategic goals. As in other companies, the problem was neither singularly women's behavior nor men's attitudes; rather it was for both to learn to see organizational reality more clearly and to begin to work together in new ways. The survey results thus reinforced the need for the forum as a place where women and senior male executives could better understand each other's reality, and where the women could generate reality-based, rather than myth-based, recommendations to guide Bestfoods' future.

The Women's Global Leadership Forum: A Major Catalyst for Change

The third major initiative in the organizational change process was the Women's Global Leadership Forum itself. The forum convened on a Sunday evening to begin meetings that would last through the following Thursday. Fifty-five participants came from 25 countries and represented every function within the company.[11] The average woman participating in the forum was 41 years old, married and had at least one teen-aged child. The diversity among the women, however, was significant. There was a 29-year gap between the oldest and the youngest participant, with families ranging from those with grown-up children to toddlers, to single women without any children. The average participant had had at least 15 years of professional experience and 10 years of experience at Bestfoods; however, one woman had 26 years of experience and another had only joined Bestfoods in the past year. The women were highly educated. Most held a bachelor's degree, with almost half having earned a master's or doctorate degree. The typical participant spoke at least two languages, with some Europeans speaking as many as five languages. The majority of Americans were monolingual. A quarter of the women had worked outside their home country – some having lived and worked in as many as five countries. Fewer participants from the United States than elsewhere had benefited from such international or expatriate experience.

While at the forum attendees participated in plenary sessions involving all of the women, many of the company's senior male executives and one woman board member. They also deliberated in global teams that included small groups of women from around the world. Facilitators for the global teams, who themselves represented a wide range of cultures, received training prior to the forum to enhance their cross-cultural team-building, communication and facilitation skills.

The forum itself had a three-fold objective that simultaneously focused on the individual, the network and the overall organization:

• Enhancing individual participants' global leadership skills
• Creating a network of women leaders within the company
• Enhancing the company's strategic business capability

Forum activities were designed to further all three objectives, with some activities focusing more on the individual level, some on the group or network level and some on the organizational level.

Developing the Individual: Enhancing Global Leadership Skills

Global leadership is not the same as domestic leadership (see Adler 1997b; Bartlett & Ghoshal, 1989; Dorfman, 1996). In going beyond any one country or region and seeking to address all human beings, global leadership has been "... the most important, but rarest and most elusive, variety of leadership" (Gardner, 1995: 20). As CEO Shoemate appreciated, the "rarest leadership" of yesteryear had become today's competitive necessity. One of his goals for the forum, therefore, was to develop the global leadership skills of Bestfoods' most highly talented and senior women. As CEO, he recognized that the company's current and future senior leadership needed to replace their previously effective domestic and multi-domestic approaches with globally integrated, cross-culturally interactive competencies that would allow them to lead in the 21st century. Shoemate fully understood that, unlike their 20th century counterparts, leaders in the 21st century would need to be able to articulate a globally-encompassing vision and communicate that vision to people around the world in ways that would inspire them to work together to achieve individual, organizational and societal goals (Adler, 1997b; see also Bartlett & Ghoshal, 1989; Gregerson, Morrison & Black, 1998; Prahalad & Hamel, 1991; among others).

Woven throughout the forum, therefore, was a series of lectures, discussions, exercises and team meetings designed to enhance each participant's global leadership competencies. For example, forum activities focused on developing participants' skills at using a full range of types of power and influence, including *power to, power over, power with* and *power within*. Both cross-cultural and women's research suggests that this broader range of types and uses of power will be even more critical for success in the 21st century's flatter and more networked organizations than in the 20th century's more hierarchical organizations.

Power to. To enhance the women leaders' skills at creating a globally encompassing vision – that is, to enhance their *power to* skills – each woman presented a vision statement in the form of a CNN documentary scheduled for worldwide broadcast. Following the presentation, the women received feedback on their content and delivery from colleagues from around the world. Would the message be meaningful to Latin Americans? Would it inspire Europeans? Would it motivate Asians? Would North Americans consider it worthwhile? Would Middle Easterners find it respectful?

Power with. In the past, well-run organizations were described as those having a unitary command structure. Today, as organizations flatten into global networks, the relevant metaphor has shifted from single-leader models to the *leader-full* organization. In a global context, enhancing *power with* skills means increasing leaders' abilities to work closely with people from around the world in situations only minimally defined by hierarchy. Successfully using *power with* skills means being able to work effectively in the geographically dispersed and flattened organizational structures and project teams inherent to 21st century business dynamics. *Power with* skills include communicating, negotiating, team building, mentoring and leading across multiple cultures. A series of forum activities focused on enhancing the women's skills at working with colleagues from around the world, the most central of which were the daily facilitated global team meetings. Other opportunities to enhance cross-cultural *power with* skills included a global team-building exercise, a cross-cultural negotiating session, two mentoring panels and a closing session in which each woman received cross-cultural feedback on her overall effectiveness at the forum from Asian, European, Middle Eastern and North and South American colleagues.

Power within. *Power within* derives from leaders' more profound under-standing of themselves and their deeply held personal and spiritual values, beliefs and commitments. Leaders foster *power within* skills by setting aside daily time for reflection (Gardner, 1995). Specific sessions at the forum encouraged participants to reflect on the relationship between their career aspirations and leadership approaches and their most deeply held values, beliefs and commitments. Each day, for example, time was set aside for participants to reflect on their personal reactions and feelings and to record them in a personal *Global Wisdom and Insight Journal.* Time in the early morning and late afternoon, entitled *Healthy Breaks,* was set aside for personal exercise and/or additional private reflection. In another *power within* session, entitled *Herstory: The Roots of Global Leadership,* participants clarified the sources of their leadership role models by identifying women whose leadership they wished to emulate. The women discussed how they planned to incorporate their role models' approaches into their own leadership goals and style. The *Herstory* session allowed participants to examine more closely the ways in which women exercise power currently and have done so in the past.[12]

Increasing Effectiveness: Developing a Network of Women Leaders

The second goal of the Forum was to create a network among the Bestfoods women leaders to facilitate the company's and the women's global effectiveness. Bringing together 55 of the company's most senior and highest potential women at the Forum was the first step in achieving this goal. Most Forum activities were designed to strengthen the network initially by allowing the women to meet and to get to know each other, including learning about each other's national, regional and cultural backgrounds. In the opening session, entitled *Who Are We?,* for example, each woman introduced herself by describing either one way in which being a woman had helped her professionally or one funny professional experience that had occurred because she is a woman. Such stories allowed participants to more fully understand the professional impact of being a woman – including, contrary to the popular mythology that being a woman is always a disadvantage, when it is an advantage – and to more clearly appreciate the worldwide commonality among women's positive professional experiences. While each woman recounted her personal story, a picture of her accompanied by name, title, country and cultural affiliation were projected, thus ensuring that everyone would immediately recognize their fellow network members.

Among other network-building activities, a *How well do you know your international colleagues?* lunch session was held that paired women from various parts of the world in conversations about themselves, their countries and their leadership styles. The goal was not simply to increase understanding of each other's countries, but rather to create opportunities for cultural synergy – that is, to begin to combine unique cultural perspectives for the benefit of the individual women, the network, the company and society (Adler, 1997c).

Throughout the forum, the women exhibited increasingly high levels of energy and commitment. The teambuilding and networking aspects of the design worked well and resulted in numerous business and idea-sharing discussions. By the end of the forum, the women created a *Global Women's Network* and committed to staying in touch electronically and in person. Following the forum, the women quickly began using the *Network* for coaching, professional support and notifying each other of career, organizational development, and business opportunities and strategies.

Developing the Organization: Retaining and Developing Leadership Talent

Two of the most important goals of the forum focused on organizational development:

- Increasing Bestfoods' global competitiveness
- Enhancing Bestfoods' support for the career advancement and success of an increasing number of highly talented and senior women

Numerous aspects of the forum were designed to achieve these two organizational goals. First, rather than having the women meet only among themselves, the CEO invited all corporate officers and members of the board to participate in various aspects of the forum. Their presence represented a highly significant commitment of senior executive time. The CEO himself joined the forum on three of the four days.

To immediately focus attention on the organizational goals, Brody presented the survey results on the first morning of the forum. Following her presentation, the global teams met to begin developing recommendations for increasing women's chances of succeeding in the company.

Continuing the focus on the organization, a lecture given the second morning on *Competitive Frontiers: Women Managers in a Global Economy* outlined the experiences of companies worldwide in sending women abroad on global assignments. Following the lecture, the women identified the conditions needed for Bestfoods to successfully send both single and married women – either with or without children – abroad on shorter- and longer-term assignments (see Adler, 1994, 2000). They recommended the types of conditions and benefits the company would need to provide, as well as the kinds of preparation each woman and her family would need to undertake for global assignments to succeed. This discussion was particularly important, since most companies still design their expatriate philosophies, policies and benefits packages primarily for married men with stay-at-home wives – not for the type of women represented at the forum (see Adler, 1997c; Osland, 1995).

The third morning, a lecture on *Global Leadership: A Dialogue with Future History* was planned that highlighted the increasing number of women leading global companies and countries and their unique paths to power (see Adler, 1997a). The discussion was designed to give participants access to a wide range of role models of successful women from around the world who have become leaders in global organizations – women whose career paths rarely replicate those of the men who have traditionally led most major corporations.[13]

Organizational Change: It Doesn't Have to Take That Long

On the final morning of the forum, the women recommended to the CEO that the organization make changes in three major areas:

- *Diversity* – increasing women's representation in senior and high level positions
- *Career Development* – enhancing career opportunities
- *Work/Life Balance* – enabling women to perform to their highest level

To craft an immediate response, the CEO separated the recommendations into three response categories:

- **Current company initiatives.** Activities already underway whose progress the company needed to accelerate and to better communicate
- **New corporate-wide initiatives** with potentially high impact
- **New "local" initiatives** best addressed within specific countries, regions or divisions

Current Company Initiatives
Recommendations in this first category included activities that the company was already involved in, such as equitable job posting, performance enhancement, and career development. While still at the forum, the CEO committed to accelerating the company's efforts in these areas and to more effectively communicating the results achieved.

New Corporate-Wide Recommendations
Also, while still at the forum, Shoemate agreed to place the entire set of new corporate-wide recommendations the women had generated on the agenda at the next Corporate Strategy Council (CSC) meeting. The list included recommending that the company should:

- **Establish senior management accountability** for retaining and developing high-performing women by linking goal attainment to the annual incentive program

- **Increase women's participation** in high-visibility assignments and task-forces – especially those with a global focus
- **Create flexible global assignments** of shorter duration as an alternative to traditional expatriate assignments
- **Define the "work-day" and "work-place" more flexibly** to avoid the "all or nothing" ("work or stay home") choice managers currently face when attempting to balance professional commitments with extraordinary private life demands
- **Expand membership on the Diversity Advisory Council** to reflect global concerns by including participants from outside of the United States

Less than two months after the forum, the Corporate Strategy Council not only approved all the women's corporate-wide recommendations, but also endorsed two additional initiatives. The Corporate Strategy Council agreed to take responsibility for oversight of the company's global diversity strategy, thus inextricably linking the company's business and diversity strategies. To more effectively address the many regional and country-level issues, the Corporate Strategy Council members, as division presidents, committed to replicating the corporate diversity council architecture in each of their respective businesses. In addition, the Corporate Strategy Council initiated a company-wide strategy for communicating the results of the forum to all organizational units, including corporate objectives and commitments for advancing and retaining women. One month after the Corporate Strategy Council meeting, at the WorldTeam Meeting (the biannual meeting of the company's 145 most senior executives), Brody formally presented the forum results and the next steps that Bestfoods would be taking. She announced Bestfoods' new strategic performance goal: to increase the number of high potential women by 10% within the next seven years.

New "Local" Initiatives

The newly created division councils formulated their own local initiatives, with many forum participants helping to guide, influence and implement their division's strategy. In Latin America, for example, not only did Argentina, Brazil, Colombia and Mexico form country-level councils, but each country also started benchmarking itself against the diversity initiatives of other multinationals operating in the region.

Just three months after the forum, Argentina mirrored the corporate model and conducted an Argentine Women's Forum for their highest-potential and most senior women. Mexico soon followed. Asia and corporate headquarters similarly began to more actively use their executive education programs and senior-level positions to improve retention and development of high-performing women. Aided by the division president's visible commitment, Europe's newly formed diversity council likewise crafted a regional strategy for increasing the number of women and enhancing their development opportunities. To increase their effectiveness, all council representatives attended a senior executive program on *Managing Inclusion*.

The Forum in Retrospect: Taking a Global Perspective

As the forum ended, everyone agreed that it had been a success. The CEO stated that the forum had exceeded his already high expectations and expressed his belief that it would make a difference in the company's future. The women participants echoed the same positive sentiments. Reactions included one woman who exclaimed, "I had no idea that there were so many talented and outstanding women in this company!" Another woman, who leads a $400 million business, addressed the CEO at the closing session, saying, "At first I was hesitant about coming to a company forum just for women. Yet this has been a wonderful experience. Mr. Shoemate, this is a group of outstanding business colleagues, each of whom just happens to be a woman." The women's surprise at the breadth and depth of talented women within the company indicates the extent to which talented women tend to be invisible in most of today's major corporations.

Global Challenges

Brody and the consultants similarly concluded that the forum had been a success. Nevertheless, an analysis of the Women's Global Leadership Forum reveals the unique challenges of bringing together women from around the world to address major organizational issues while simultaneously focusing on enhancing individuals' global leadership capabilities. Inadvertently, the dual organizational- and individual-level agenda raised the question of who was primarily to blame for the under-representation of women leaders within the company. Was it the company – thus implying that the organizational change initiatives should take precedence – or was it some perceived deficiency in the women themselves, thus implying that the leadership development initiatives should take precedence?[14] Given both the women's and the company's appreciation of the systemic issues, many women's first priority focused on recommending ways in which the organizational culture could be changed. Consequently, some women viewed the personal leadership development aspects of the agenda as secondary, and, at times, as taking them away from their primary goal of changing the organization. Perhaps the lesson to be learned regarding first meetings of this sort is that participants – especially those as sophisticated in understanding organizational dynamics as the women attending the forum – may initially view sessions aimed at individual leadership development as superfluous or even as counterproductive (as taking time away from their primary objective, which is to change the organization). Designers must take care to ensure that individual leadership development and organizational change goals complement, rather than compete, with each other. This balance is particularly important today as corporate strategy shifts from a multi-domestic to a global focus, and all managers, whether male or female and whether from Asia, Africa, Europe or the Americas, need to upgrade their global leadership skills.

The second major challenge emerged from the implicit expectation – common at meetings such the forum – that the women attending would have had similar experiences and therefore would share similar points of view on most important professional issues, simply because they are women. Given that many women's experiences and perspectives are not identical to those of men – as the survey results had clearly documented – it is understandable that some women arrived at the forum expecting, consciously or otherwise, that they would finally be among a community of professionals who saw the world as they did. Yet, exactly as is true among men, women come from diverse backgrounds and career experiences. As the forum progressed, the company and the participants learned – not without considerable frustration – to accept that differences in the women's cultural background, age, tenure, rank and personal experience meant that the group could not, and should not, come to a consensus on a uniform "women's" perspective or position. The women expressed markedly divergent opinions, for example, on the existence, or lack thereof, of a *glass ceiling*. Some of the most senior women, a disproportionate number of whom had begun their professional lives as trailblazers in a very different social climate than that of the late 1990s, now saw their careers as having plateaued, albeit at a very senior level, below a very real *glass ceiling*. These senior women held attitudes and objectives very different from those of many younger women whom the company had only recently identified as fast trackers, and for whom the *glass ceiling* held no personal meaning. Moreover, so as not to dampen the optimism of their younger colleagues, the most senior women chose not to describe their most negative experiences in front of their junior colleagues. This choice made it easy for some younger women to blame their senior colleagues for not having progressed further and faster, rather than appreciating the systemic barriers these trail-blazing women had faced. Just as one would not expect a group of male executives to have had identical experiences or to hold identical opinions, a uniform "women's point of view" seldom exists, and neither companies nor women should expect one.

As highlighted in the forum, helping people appreciate different realities – not just between women and men, but among the women themselves – is a crucial step in allowing them to move beyond the need to reach consensus on either "the state of women" or attributions about why women do or do not make it to the top of major multinational corporations. A lack of consensus, however, neither indicates that companies have no systemic issues nor that there is no need for corporate action. Developing an understanding of the range of experiences and explanations makes it more likely that companies can achieve real organizational change.

The third set of challenges involved the impact of cross-cultural differences on forum dialogue and dynamics. The dynamics of global meetings differ from those of domestic meetings for both men and women (see Adler, 1997c). Over the course of the forum, communication and behavioral styles varied across cultures and significantly influenced the group's dynamics and learning climate. In many cases, the cross-cultural differences among participants were larger and became more important to the success of the meeting than many of the differences usually attributed to gender. Designers of global meetings for women, as well as the women participants themselves, need to guard against exaggerating the salience of the all-women nature of the group and erroneously assuming a level of homogeneity that simply does not exist.

Occurrences of cross-cultural differences were prevalent. Following the cultural pattern that is typical of people from the United States and Canada, for example, many North American women preferred to use a more inductive approach to resolving issues and formulating recommendations. In other words, they wanted to start with the specifics of their own and other's personal experience and later arrive at overall generalizations. Following the opposite cultural pattern, women from many other regions preferred to take a more deductive approach. They chose to begin with a general understanding and broad concepts and then work down toward the specifics of their own and others' lives. Both approaches ultimately arrive at an integration of the general and specific. The processes for arriving at integration, however, are culturally defined, opposite, and, if not made explicit, often difficult to bridge. Global leaders need to be able to use the strengths of both inductive and deductive approaches, rather than merely negating one in favor of the other.

Another cross-cultural difference that multinational groups frequently experience relates to what anthropologists call the source of truth – how a group seeks the "right" answer, or in the case of the forum, the "right" recommendations. Is truth believed to come primarily from scientific research, legal precedent, the opinion of experts, tradition, personal experience or trial-and-error experimentation? Participants' varied reactions to changing the forum agenda reflected this cultural difference regarding the source of truth. On the third morning, the organizers changed the agenda to give participants more time to work in teams on organizational development issues. When they announced the change, some Asian and Latin American women expressed disappointment because the new agenda left less time for the originally planned presentations by experts. While clearly reflecting their more deductive approach, the Asians' and Latin Americans' reaction also reflected the higher value they place on expert input. Adding to the cross-cultural complexity, the Asians' and Latin Americans' reaction may also have reflected the higher value they place on respect for authority, position and hierarchical status – what the anthropologists and cross-cultural management scholars refer to as high power distance (see Hofstede, 1980a, b; Hofstede & Bond, 1988). By contrast, most Americans welcomed the change in agenda, believing that it would give them more time to do what they saw as most important – developing recommendations based on their own personal experience. Typical of lower power-distance cultures, the Americans were placing less importance on expert input and hierarchical status. Which approach is correct? Neither – they simply differ. Global leadership involves bridging and integrating diverse approaches, not labeling one culture's approach as superior to that of other cultures.

Some Asian, European, and Latin American participants found that many of the North American women expressed themselves too bluntly and directly – taking charge and attempting to solve problems too quickly and without sufficient consultation or reflection. At one particularly frustrating point in the process, some Asian and Latin American women confidentially disclosed to the external consultant that they now realized that they would never want to work in the United States because they did not want to work with American women. Why would these very bright, highly effective professionals make such a strong statement (especially in a company headquartered in the United States)? And why did they express their opinion in this particular way? As is usually true in such situations, a number of cross-cultural influences were operating simultaneously, and, for the most part, below the level of conscious awareness of most of the people involved. Reflecting on the cross-cultural dynamics reveals that the women differed in their culturally-based orientations toward direct versus indirect communication, group versus individual decision-making, faster- versus slower-paced problem solving, and the proclivity to accept versus to attempt to change situations.

From the opposite cultural point of view, some Americans expressed annoyance with the more formal respect and deference that women from outside the United States frequently demonstrated to senior management. At times, the Americans interpreted their colleagues' reticence to challenge the hierarchy as tantamount to heresy. Were some of the women from outside the United States accepting, whether implicitly or explicitly, that women's status was somewhat lower in stature, knowledge and influence? The formality and reserved nature of many women from outside the United States contrasted dramatically with the behavior of the highly verbal Americans. Similarly, the strong emphasis that many non-Anglo Saxon cultures place on relationship building and on putting the needs of the group ahead of any one individual's opinion or needs (including one's own), also contrasts with the behavior of the more individualistic Americans. The difference is not so much in the level of respect each culture shows, but rather in the way that respect is communicated.

Alerting participants to potential cross-cultural differences increases their ability to manage the impact of culture. It does not, however, mitigate the differences themselves. When differences are made explicit, the inevitable discovery of differing cultural and value-based norms regarding appropriate behavior and communication styles can become a source of potential synergy, rather than merely a source of frustration, misleading interpretations and inappropriate evaluations.

THE CHALLENGES OF FOCUSING ON WOMEN LEADERS

As companies increasingly select their executives from among the best women and men worldwide, rather than restricting candidates almost exclusively to men – as has been done so often in the past – an inevitable question arises: How different are women executives, if at all, from their male counterparts? Advocates of the two seemingly opposing positions – "Women and men executives are exactly the same" and "Women and men are distinctly different" – often tenaciously adhere to their own point of view and respond incredulously or even with hostility to proponents of perspectives other than their own. Not surprisingly, this crucial similar-or-different dilemma surfaced numerous times at Bestfoods, both prior to and during the forum. Unfortunately, given the paucity of research on global women leaders, existing studies cannot, as yet, resolve the dilemma (Powell, 1999; Yeager, 1999).[15]

Given the inherent ambiguity, global executives need to understand the similarity-versus-difference controversy in such a way that it facilitates, rather than undermines, organizational effectiveness (Thomas & Ely, 1996). The first step toward such constructive framing is to recognize that, whether similar or different, increasing the number of women in the executive ranks will increase competitiveness. Why? Because whether women executives lead in similar or different ways to those of male executives, drawing from both groups increases the pool of potential talent. As basic statistics make clear, if you draw from a larger population, on average you will select better leaders.

Given the transparent advantage inherent in drawing from a larger pool of candidates – one that includes both women and men – why do so many people continue to get sidetracked by the similar-versus-different controversy? The explanation at Bestfoods, as well as at most organizations, lies in the fact that the controversy cannot be discussed, let alone resolved, by simply answering a single question. Rather, as highlighted in Table 1, the assumptions one makes relative to three distinct, albeit related, issues define both the confusion and the complexity. The first question is, "Do women lead in similar ways to men?" The second related question is, "If women and men lead differently, whose leadership style is more effective?" And third, if women and men are seen to differ, "Are the differences in leadership style an advantage or a disadvantage to the organization?"

Inherent in the three questions, and adding to the complexity of any global leadership initiative, is the confusion caused by alternatively appreciating difference as simply "difference" versus judging it to represent the inferiority or superiority of one side or the other. On this appreciation-versus-judgement spectrum, the three questions differ markedly. The first question, "Do women lead in similar ways to men?" is strictly descriptive. It simply asks if one observes differences in the ways women and men lead. Such differences are not judged to be either good or bad. Unlike the second and third questions, the first question is appreciative (or descriptive), not evaluative. In contrast, both the

Table 1. Global Leadership: The Nature of the Questions.

Fundamental: Questions	Types of Question	Treatment of Difference	Underlying Dilemma
Do women lead in Similar ways to men?	Descriptive	Appreciative of difference	Similarity vs. Difference
Do men or women lead more effectively?	Evaluative	Judgmental	Superiority vs. Inferiority
Is diversity an advantage or a disadvantage to the organization?	Evaluative	Judgmental	Advantage vs. Disadvantage

second and third questions – "If women and men differ, whose leadership style is more effective?" and "Are the differences an advantage or a disadvantage to the organization?" – are evaluative. Depending on their perspective, people judge either men or women's ways of leading to be superior. Similarly, depending on one's perspective, differences in leadership styles are judged to be either good or bad for the organization.

At Bestfoods, as in most organizations, the full range of the similar-versus-different, superior-versus-inferior and advantage-versus-disadvantage assumptions were made, believed, expressed and argued about. It is important, therefore, to understand how the various arguments influenced the forum and, more importantly, how they will influence any process that attempts to achieve a more balanced representation of women and men from all regions of the world in the executive ranks.

As shown in Table 2, alternative attitudes toward difference – as expressed in people's responses to the three questions – lead to four very different approaches to increasing the number of women in leadership positions and to

Table 2. Global Leadership: Approaches to Difference.

Approaches: Synergy	Denying Differences	Identifying with men	Identifying with women	Creating Synergy
Assumptions: Do women lead in similar ways to men?	Similar	Different	Different	Different
Do men or women lead more effectively?	Neither	Men	Women	Neither
Is diversity an advantage or a disadvantage to the organization?	Disadvantage	Disadvantage	Disadvantage	Advantage
What is valued?	Culture of Sameness	Conformity to Men's Ways	Conformity to Women's Ways	Integrating & Leveraging Diversity
Cross-Cultural Equivalent:	Parochial	Ethnocentric (Pro-men)	Ethnocentric (Pro-women)	Cultural Synergy

valuing, or not valuing, their potential contributions to the organization.[16] The four approaches are:

- Denying differences
- Identifying with men's leadership styles
- Identifying with women's leadership styles
- Creating synergy – integrating and leveraging and women's leadership styles

In the first approach, people deny the possibility of differences. In the next two approaches, by contrast, people acknowledge differences, but see them as negative. The second approach assumes men's ways of leading as better and the third approach assumes women's ways as better. The fourth approach acknowledges differences without judging either men or women's ways to be superior. While people can operate using any of the four approaches, the cultural synergy approach, by integrating and leveraging the various styles into complementary approaches, is most conducive to long-term organizational effectiveness (Adler, 1997; Thomas & Ely, 1996). Each of the four approaches, with its respective underlying assumptions, is described below.

Denying differences. The first approach to dealing with cultural or male/female differences is often denial – choosing to assume that no salient differences exist. In this approach, rather than judging women's leadership styles to be inferior (as is done in the second approach) or superior (as is done in the third approach), both men and women simply assume that there is only one way to lead. Talking about a men or women's style of leading, therefore, is meaningless, as is any consideration of diversity's value to the organization.

On a cultural level, denial is most similar to parochialism: "Because I am most familiar with my own culture, I believe that it is the only culture." Because people are most familiar with men's leadership styles, they simply assume, often implicitly, that men's approaches provide the only possible model for success. Women who deny differences believe that, as professionals, they are just like the men who have always led major corporations. Men who deny differences often compliment women for managing or leading "just like a man." Denying differences leads to a *culture of sameness* in how the organization treats its male and female professionals as well as in how it treats people from Asia, Africa, Europe, the Americas and the Middle East. Given the *culture of sameness,* organizations attempt to foster effectiveness by treating everyone identically.

Both men and women at Bestfoods, on occasion, denied differences. The women who expressed resentment at being invited to the forum because they were women, for example, were exhibiting denial. They rejected the idea that they differed from their male colleagues in any ways that would make it necessary to hold a forum just for women. Similarly, the male executives who questioned the CEO's decision to convene a separate Women's Forum denied the possibility that male and female professionals might differ. Similarly, the women who questioned whether the leadership training approaches used during the forum were identical to those used with male executives were also exhibiting denial. In all cases, those who deny differences prefer that everyone be treated the same.

Identifying with men's leadership styles. Unlike denial, the second approach accepts that differences exist, but judges men's ways to be superior. Men are seen as displaying certain characteristics that have historically allowed them to lead effectively, including: "...an ability to be impersonal, self-interested, efficient, hierarchical, tough minded, and assertive; an interest in taking charge, control, and domination; a capacity to ignore personal, emotional considerations in order to succeed; a proclivity to rely on standardized or 'objective' codes for judgment and evaluation of others; and a heroic orientation toward task accomplishment (Fondas, 1997: p. 184 based on Brod & Kaufman, 1994; Gilligan, 1982; Glennon, 1979; Grace, 1995; Kanter, 1977; Seidler, 1994)."[17] Whereas the specific characteristics vary somewhat from organization to organization, and culture to culture, the overall pattern in the second approach is to identify with men's, rather than women's, ways of leading.

Identifying with the masculine echoes the same cultural dynamics as classic ethnocentrism. In male/female terms, such ethnocentrism could be labeled as male chauvinism. Whereas women are seen as differing from men, all such differences are believed to diminish organizational effectiveness. From this perspective, it is inconceivable that women's ways of leading might benefit the organization. Both men and women, therefore, attempt to minimize the differences between their own approaches and the male norm. Seeing men's ways as superior, women attempt to think like, act like and lead like their most successful male colleagues. Similarly, men who see women's approaches as counterproductive attempt to minimize the differences by coaching high-potential women to act like men, and complimenting them when they succeed. Women who identify with men generally believe that they will only be promoted into executive positions if they lead in exactly the same ways as men. Such women admit that, in general, women differ from men but they see themselves as the exception. They see themselves as fitting men's typical pattern, not that of the majority of women (see Hampden-Turner, 1993).

Similar to many of their male colleagues, these women see the typical female pattern as incompatible with executive success.

At Bestfoods, on occasion both men and women made comments characteristic of identifying with the masculine approach. For example, the men who derisively described the upcoming forum alternatively as "a coffee klatch" and the "girls' knitting club," and cautioned that the meeting would likely turn into "a bitch session," were expressing their belief that women differed from men and that the difference would not help the company. Similarly, one woman's comment that "Men make better bosses" and another's question – "How could this meeting be important if only women are being invited?" – reflect the same pattern. In documenting that the majority of women believed that they needed to *develop-a-style-that-men-are-comfortable-with,* the survey revealed women's pervasive assumption that they had to adapt to the male norm to succeed. The historic pattern of promoting primarily men into the organization's most senior leadership positions reflects the company's overall tendency to value men's ways of leading above those of women. From this perspective, women's conformity with the male pattern is neither surprising nor illogical.

Identifying with women's leadership styles. Similar to the second approach, the third approach accepts that women and men differ. However, unlike the second approach, it judges women's – not men's – leadership styles to be superior, especially for the 21st century's more networked, less hierarchical, global organizations. Labeled as the *feminine advantage*, women's greater tendency to use more democratic, inclusive, participative, interactional and relational styles of leading is highly valued by the organization (Fondas, 1997: 259, based on Chodorow, 1978; Helgesen, 1990; Lippman-Blumen, 1983; Marshall, 1984; and Rosener, 1990, among others).[18] All managers are therefore encouraged to incorporate a more feminine approach into their leadership style.

Echoing the dynamics of the prior approach, identification with women's styles of leading could be seen as a type of reverse chauvinism, and is, in fact, a variant of traditional ethnocentrism. Similar to both the first and second approaches, managers perceive diversity to be a disadvantage to the organization.

At Bestfoods, the belief that women's ways of leading are superior was not expressed frequently, but was stated on occasion. The assumption, for example, that women executives could better understand and work with women clients reflects a belief in the *feminine advantage*. Similarly, including the *Herstory* exercise in the forum – in which participants focused on the female roots of their leadership style – also highlighted the value of a woman-based approach. The women's recommendation that Bestfoods adopt more flexible scheduling for expatriate assignments for all employees, rather than just for women, also embraced the superiority of an approach for everyone based primarily on women's needs and experience. As is clear from these examples, in identifying with the feminine, women are seen, and see themselves, as better than men at doing certain things that the organization requires.

Creating synergy – Integrating and leveraging men and women's leadership styles. The fourth approach, similar to the second and third approaches, accepts differences; women and men are not seen to lead identically. However, unlike the prior approaches, it does not judge either women or men's styles of leading to be superior. Rather, the organization values each style as contributing uniquely and synergistically to the whole. Benefits come primarily from the potential for combining and leveraging men and women's different styles of leading. Using a synergy approach, the organization benefits not just from combining men and women's styles of leading, but also those of people from a wide range of world cultures and countries.

At Bestfoods, the very act of the CEO convening a forum just for women reflects his acceptance of differences. The fact that he integrated a strategic business goal – increasing global competitiveness – with an all-women event shows that the CEO accepted women as different without, in any way, equating that difference with inferiority. On the contrary, he premised the forum on the possibility that combining men's and women's contributions would lead to a more competitive organization and, therefore, a more successful company. Similarly, the CEO's commitment to include both men and women from around the world on his executive team, so that each could contribute from his or her unique perspective, also reflects his fundamental appreciation of integration and synergy.

THE MEANING OF SUCCESS

In convening the Women's Global Leadership Forum, the CEO invited the most senior and highest-potential women in the company to contribute in ways that had been absent in the past. The organizational change process, the forum itself, and the outcomes proved that neither the company nor the women themselves knew the extent to which they could, should or would collectively contribute. As with all companies in highly competitive industries, Bestfoods' future success depended on the leadership of both women and men from around the world – on contributions from both feminine and masculine perspectives. The Women's Global Leadership Forum was an experiment in amplifying women's voices. Not only the success of individual companies, but also the success of 21st century society, depends on such voices being amplified and heard.[19]

NOTES

1. Nancy J. Adler is Professor of Management at McGill University in Montreal, Canada. Laura W. Brody is Director of Diversity and Development at Bestfoods in Englewood Cliffs, New Jersey. Joyce Osland is Associate Professor of Management at the University of Portland in Oregon. For further information, contact Adler at McGill University – (Tel) 514–398–4031, (Fax) 514–398–3876, (e-mail) adler@ management.mcgill.ca.

2. For a more in-depth discussion of women political leaders, see Adler's "Global Women Political Leaders: An Invisible History, An Increasingly Important Future" (1996), "Global Leaders: A Dialogue with Future History" (1997a), "Did You Hear? Global Leadership in Charity's World" (1998a), and "Societal Leadership: The Wisdom of Peace" (1998c).

3. For a more in-depth discussion of global women business leaders, see Adler's "Global Leaders: A Dialogue with Future History" (1997a), "Global Leadership: Women Leaders" (1997b), "Global Leaders: Women of Influence" (1999a), "Global Leaders, Women Entrepreneurs: The Myths of History" (1998b), and "Twenty-first Century Leadership: Reality Beyond the Myths" (1999b).

4. For a discussion of the planning process and the initial outcomes from Bestfoods' initiative, see Adler, Brody, and Osland's "The Women's Global Leadership Forum: Enhancing One Company's Global Leadership Capability" (2000).

5. CEO's statement is from Bestfoods' World Team Management Development Philosophy.

6. Bestfoods' Corporate Strategy Council is composed of the six most senior corporate officers, who are responsible for the four geographic divisions, the baking business, and the corporate staff. All six senior corporate officers are men.

7. See "Women and Global Leadership at Bestfoods" (Osland & Adler, 2001) for an in-depth discussion of the major role Laura Brody played in managing the organizational change effort and in leading the Women's Global Leadership Forum, with the support of her boss, Dick Bergeman, Senior VP of Human Resources.

8. The survey was loosely based on Catalyst's report, "Women in Corporate Leadership: Progress & Prospects" (1996).

9. Forty-four percent of women and yet only 4.8% of men believed that *developing-a-style-that-men-are-comfortable-with* was critical to women's career advancement.

10. Thirty-six percent of women, and yet only 19% of men, believed that having a mentor was important for women's career success. It should be noted that men may believe that such "mentorship" happens naturally and informally, whereas women – primarily due to their scarcity in senior management – may believe that such mentor relationships need to be more formal, and, at the minimum, organizationally sanctioned.

11. Whereas the CEO invited 60 women, only 55 were able to attend on the dates set for the Forum. Given the strict selection process, the company chose not to substitute other women for the five who could not attend.

12. For a discussion of the roots of women's power and the fact that this generation of women does not have to invent all aspects of leadership, even if many of them are firsts, see Cokie Roberts' *We Are Our Mothers' Daughters* (1998).

13. The agenda, however, was changed in response to some participants' desire for more time to work on their recommendations for changing the organization.

14. For a discussion of the history of attributions on why there are so few women in management worldwide, see Adler and Izraeli (1994).

15. While there has been very little research on women leaders, especially from a cross-cultural perspective, research has been conducted on differences between women and men in general, and between male and female managers. Although unanimity on the actual existence or effect of such differences has yet to be reached, there is agreement that male and female managers are perceived differently (Maccoby & Jacklin, 1974). Most U.S. research contends that both men and women describe successful managers as more like men than women (Schein, 1975; Powell & Butterfield, 1979), with the exception of Schein's follow-up study (Schein, Mueller & Jacobson, 1989) in which men, but not women, persisted in sex-typing managers.

16. The four-approach model is based on combining the work of Milton and Janet Bennett and Maureen Murdock. The Bennetts developed a six-phase model to understand people's ability to learn about cultures (see M. Bennett, 1993; J. Bennett, 1993; and J. Bennett, 1999). Based on the work of Joseph Campbell, Murdock (1990) developed a multiphase model for understanding women's personal and professional development vis-à-vis the masculine and feminine aspects of their personality.

17. Whereas the sex-trait stereotype for U.S. men – as aggressive, independent, unemotional, objective, dominant, active, competitive, logical, worldly, skilled in business, adventurous, self-confident, and ambitious – supports the image of men as leaders, the stereotype for women – talkative, gentle, tactful, religious, quiet, empathetic, aesthetic, submissive, and expressive – does not support the image of women as managers or as leaders (Ashmore, Del Boca, & Wohlers, 1986; Broverman et al., 1972; Harriman, 1996; and Williams & Bennett, 1975).

18. In one of the few cross-cultural studies on leaders, Gibson (1995) found that women in four countries were more likely than men to focus on interaction facilitation than men, who placed more emphasis on goal setting. Several studies from the United States and other countries found that women prefer a more participative style than men (Bayes, 1991; Eagly & Johnson, 1990; Soutar & Savery, 1991).

19. In 2000, as this chapter went into publication, Unilever bought Bestfoods. Only in the years ahead will it be possible to assess the impact of the Women's Global Leadership Forum on the now much larger human resource system of the two combined companies.

REFERENCES

Adler, N. J. (2000). Coaching Global Executives: Women Succeeding in a World Beyond Here. In: M. Goldsmith, L. Lyons & A. Freas (Eds), *Coaching for Leadership* (pp. 359–368). San Francisco: Jossey-Bass.

Adler, N. J. (1994). Competitive Frontiers: Women managing across borders. In: N. J. Adler & D. N. Izraeli (Eds), *Competitive Frontiers: Women Managers in a Global Economy* (pp. 22–40). Cambridge, Mass.: Blackwell.

Adler, N. J. (1998a). Did You Hear? Global Leadership in Charity's World. *Journal of Management Inquiry*, *7*(2), 21–33.

Adler, N. J. (1999a). Global Entrepreneurs: Women, Myths, and History. *Global Focus*, *1*(4), 125–134.

Adler, N. J. (1997a). Global Leaders: A Dialogue with Future History. *International Management*, *1*(2), 21–33.

Adler, N. J. (1999b). Global Leaders: Women of Influence. In: G. Powell (Ed.), *Handbook of Gender in Organizations* (pp. 239–261). Thousand Oaks, Calif.: Sage.

Adler, N. J. (1997b). Global Leadership: Women Leaders. *Management International Review*, *37* (Special Issue 1), 135–143.

Adler, N. J. (1996). Global Women Political Leaders: An Invisible History, An Increasingly Important Future. *Leadership Quarterly*, *7*(1), 133–161.

Adler, N. J. (1997c). *International Dimensions of Organizational Behavior* (3rd ed.). Cincinnati, Ohio: SouthWestern Press.

Adler, N. J. (1998b). Societal Leadership: The Wisdom of Peace. In: S Srivastva (Ed.), *Executive Wisdom and Organizational Change* (pp. 243–337). San Francisco: Josse-Bass.

Adler, N. J. (1999c). Twenty-first Century Leadership: Reality Beyond the Myths. In: A. M. Rugman (Series Ed.) & Richard Wright (Volume Ed.), *Research in Global Strategic Management* (Vol. 7, pp. 173–190: International Entrepreneurship: Globalization of Emerging Business). Greenwich, Connecticut: JAI Press.

Adler, N. J.; Brody, L. W., & Osland, J. S. (2000). The Women's Global Leadership Forum: Enhancing One Company's Global Leadership Capability. *Human Resource Management*, *39*(2 and 3), 209–225.

Ashmore, R., Del Boca, F., & Wohlers, A. (1986). Gender Stereotypes. In: R. D. Ashmore & F. D. Del Boca (Eds), *The Social Psychology of Female-Male Relations: A Critical Analysis of Central Concepts*. Orlando, FL: Academic Press.

Bartlett, C. A., & Ghoshal, S. (1989). *Managing Across Borders: The Transnational Solution*. Boston: Harvard Business School Press.

Bayes, J. (Ed.) (1991). Women and Public Administration: International Perspectives. *Women & Politics*, *11*(4), 111–131.

Bennett, J. M. (1993). Cultural marginality: Identity issues in intercultural training. In: R. M. Paige (Ed.), *Education for Intercultural Experience*. Yarmouth, Maine: Intercultural Press.

Bennett, J. M. (1999). *Turning frogs into interculturalists: A student-centered developmental approach to teaching intercultural competence.* Paper presented the Cross-Cultural Colloquium, June 11. Los Angeles: UCLA. (as published by J. M. Bennett & M. J. Bennett, The Intercultural Communication Institute, Portland, Oregon).

Bennett, M. J. (1993). Towards a developmental model of intercultural sensitivity. In: R. M. Paige (Ed.), *Education for Intercultural Experience*. Yarmouth, Maine: Intercultural Press.

Brod, H., & Kaufman, M. (Eds) (1994). *Theorizing Masculinities*. Thousand Oaks, Calif.: Sage.

Broverman, I., Broverman, D., Clarkson, F., Rosenkrantz, P., & Vogel, S. (1970). Sex Role Stereotypes and Clinical Judgements of Mental Health. *Journal of Consulting and Clinical Psychology*, *34*, 1–7.

Chodorow, N. (1978). *The reproduction of mothering*. Berkeley: University of California Press.

Dickinson, E. (1951). We never know how high we are. In: T. H. Johnson (Ed.), *The Poems of Emily Dickinson*. Cambridge, Mass.: Belknap Press of Harvard University Press.

Dorfman, P. W. (1996). International and cross-cultural leadership. In: B. J. Punnett & Oded Shenkar (Eds), *Handbook for International Management Research* (pp. 267–349). Cambridge, Mass.: Blackwell.

Dwyer, P., Johnston, M., & Lowry (1996). Europe's Corporate Women. *Business Week*, (April 15), 40–42.

Eagly, A. H., & Johnson, B. T. (1990). Gender and leadership style: A meta-analysis. *Psychological Bulletin, 108*(2), 233–256.

Fiorina, C. (1998). Anytime you have a fiercely competitive business. *Nortel World*, (November), 8.

Fisher, A. B. (1992). When will women get to the top? *Fortune*, (September 21st), 44–56.

Fondas, N. (1997). The origins of feminization. *Academy of Management Review, 22*, 257–282.

Gardner, H. (1995). *Leading Minds: An Anatomy of Leadership*. New York City: Basic Books.

Gibson, C. (1995). An Investigation of Gender Differences in Leadership Across Four Countries. *Journal of International Business Studies, 26*(2), 255–279.

Gilligan, C. (1982). *In a different voice: Psychological theory and women's development*. Cambridge, Mass.: Harvard University Press.

Glennon, L. M. (1979). *Women and dualism*. New York: Longman.

Grace, N. M. (1995). *The feminized male character in twentieth-century literature*. Lewiston, NY: Edwin Millen Press.

Gregersen, H. B., Morrison, A. J., & Black, J. S. (1998). Developing Leaders for the Global Frontier. *Sloan Management Review, 40*(1), 21–33.

Hambrick, D. C., Korn, L. B., Frederickson, J. W., & Ferry, R. M. (1989). *21st Century Report: Reinventing the CEO*. New York: Korn/Ferry and Columbia University's Graduate School of Business, pp. 1–94.

Hampden-Turner, C. (1993). *The structure of entrapment: Dilemmas standing in the way of women managers and strategies to resolve these*. Paper presented at the Global Business Network Meeting, New York, December 9–10.

Harriman, A. (1996). *Women/Men/Management*. Westport, CT: Praeger.

Helgesen, S. (1990). *The female advantage: Women's ways of leadership*. New York: Doubleday.

Hill, C. W. L. (1998). *International Business: Competing in the Global Marketplace* (2nd ed.). Whitney, STATE: Irwin/McGraw Hill.

Himelstein, L. (1996). Shatterproof Glass Ceiling. *Business Week*, (October 28th), 55.

Hofstede, G. (1980a). *Culture's Consequences: International Differences in Work-Related Values*. Sage: Beverly Hills.

Hofstede, G. (1980b). Motivation, leadership and organization: Do American theories apply abroad? *Organizational Dynamics, 9*(1), 42–63.

Hofstede, G., & Bond, M. (1988). The Confucius Connection: From Cultural Roots to Economic Growth. *Organizational Dynamics, 16*(4), 4–21.

International Labor Office (1997). *Breaking Through the Glass Ceiling: Women in Management*. Geneva: International Labor Office.

Kanter, R. M. (1994). *Comments on Nancy A. Nichols' Reach for the Top: Women and the Changing Facts of Work Life*. Boston: Harvard Business School Press, as cited in the book review by J. R. Hook in *The Academy of Management Executive, 8*(2), 87–89.

Kanter, R. M. (1977). *Men and women of the corporation*. New York: Basic Books.

Lipman-Blumen, J. (1983). Emerging patterns of female leadership in formal organizations. In: M. Horner, C. C. Nadelson, & M. T. Notman (Eds), *The Challenge of Change* (pp. 61–91). New York: Plenum Press.

Maccoby, E., & Jacklin, C. (1974). *The Psychology of Sex Differences*. Stanford, CA: Stanford University Press.

Marshall, J. (1984). *Women managers: Travellers in a male world*. New York: Wiley.

Mitroff, I. (1987). *Business Not As Usual*. San Francisco: Jossey-Bass.

Murdock, M. (1990). *The Heroine's Journey.* Boston: Shambhala.

Murdock, M. (1998). *The Heroine's Journey Workbook.* Boston: Shambhala.

Osland, J. S. (1995). *The Adventure of Working Abroad: Hero Tales from the Global Frontier.* San Francisco, CA: Jossey-Bass.

Osland, J. S., & Adler, N. J. (2001). Women and Global Leadership at Bestfoods. In: J. S. Osland, D. Kolb & I. Rubin (Eds), *Organizational Behavior: An Experiential Approach* (pp. 533–555). Upper Saddle River, NJ: Prentice-Hall.

Osland, J. S., Snyder, M. M., & Hunter, L. (1998). A comparative study of managerial styles among female executives in Nicaragua and Costa Rica. *International Studies of Management and Organization, 28*(2), 54–73.

Powell, G. (Ed.) (1999). *Handbook of Gender in Organizations.* Thousand Oaks, Calif.: Sage.

Ragins, B. R., Townsend, B., & Mattis, M. (1998). Gender gap in the executive suite: CEOs and female executives report on breaking the glass ceiling. *Academy of Management Executive, 12*(1), 28–42.

Roberts, C. (1998). *We Are Our Mothers' Daughters.* New York: William Morrow and Company.

Rosner, J. (1990). Ways women lead. *Harvard Business Review, 68*(6), 119–125.

Schein, V. (1975). The Relationship Between Sex Role Stereotypes and Requisite Management Characteristics. *Journal of Applied Psychology, 60*(3), 340–344.

Schein, V., Muller, R., & Jacobson, C. (1989). The Relationship Between Structured and Requisite Management Characteristics Among College Students. *Sex-Roles, 20*(1–2), 103–110.

Seidler, V. J. (1994). *Unreasonable men: Masculinity and social theory.* London: Routledge.

Soutar, G., & Savery, L. (1991). Who Should Decide? Key Areas for Participation. *Leadership & Organizational Development Journal, 12*(5), 8–11.

Thomas, D. A., & Ely, R. J. (1996). Making differences matter: A new paradigm for managing diversity. *Harvard Business Review,* (September–October), 79–90.

Wellington, S. W. (1996). *Women in Corporate Leadership: Progress and Prospects.* New York City: Catalyst.

Williams, J., & Bennett, S. (1975). The Definition of Sex Stereotypes Via the Adjective Check List. *Sex Roles, 1,* 327–337.

Yeager, M. A. (1999). *Women in Business* (Vols 1, 2, & 3). Cheltenham, U.K.: Elger Reference Collection.

CONCLUSIONS

William H. Mobley and Morgan W. McCall, Jr.

The thing to do, to get us through the short run, the years just ahead, is to celebrate our ignorance. Instead of presenting the body of human knowledge as a mountainous structure of coherent information capable of explaining everything about everything if we could only master the details, we should be acknowledging that it is, in real life, still a very modest mound of puzzlements that do not fit together at all.

Lewis Thomas (1983)

The title of this book is *Advances in Global Leadership*, and the first word is certainly appropriate. We don't see here "breakthrough" or "great leap forward." Instead we see the halting, sometimes retrograde, but steady movement of science. The terms global and international do not appear in the index to Stogdill's original *Handbook of Leadership* published in 1974. By 1990 "Leadership in Different Countries and Cultures" had worked its way up to one of 37 chapters in Bass's *Bass & Stogdill's Handbook of Leadership* (though neither "global" nor "international" appear in its index either – "internationalization" has a single page reference). That manifesto of U.S. culture, *The Complete Idiot's Guide to Leadership*, (DuBrin, 1998) devotes a full 10 pages to becoming a "multicultural leader," providing such insights as "to be a multicultural leader, you must be able to work well with people from several cultures" (108).

From those humble beginnings we see signs of movement. In this volume, dedicated entirely to international and global leadership, are authors from many different countries, multiple methodologies, multiple perspectives, and yes, the terms "global" and "international" both appear in the index.

Advances in Global Leadership, Volume 2, pages 385–389.
ISBN: 0-7623-0723-4

We began the introduction of this volume with the Publilius Syrus quote that "Anyone can steer the ship when the sea is calm." The speed of technological change and globalization of business across borders and cultures have assured that the seas are not calm and unlikely to become calm in the foreseeable future. Steering the ship is not to be vested in just anyone. The question is, who and how should the ship be steered in global seas; and how to develop such persons? The vignettes we offered in the introduction framed some of the real time "who and how" issues facing organizations and leaders operating across multiple national and cultural boundaries. The chapters in this volume offer some insights into some of these issues, but as each contributing author noted, much remains to be learned, much remains to be integrated, much needs to be further specified.

As we review these chapters and the literature upon which they are based, what are some of the major insights to be gleaned or reinforced by some of these "*advances*?" At the risk of being too parsimonious or presumptuous of the authors or readers, here are some of the spots on the leopard we observed in these chapters.

- There is no universal set of global leadership competencies (Hollenbeck; Crabtree).
- "Global mindset" provides a convenient way to capture the critical competencies of global leaders (Hollenbeck).
- Information processing models provide a way to look at perceptions of leadership based on both inferences about performance and recognition based on matching of leader characteristics and behavior to prototypes. The matching process is a universal but the content of the prototype varies by culture (Dickson, Hanges & Lord).
- Effectiveness of leadership style depends on stage of organizational development, and this may be more important than country culture as the homogenization/socialization of global business erodes cultural differences (Crabtree).
- Changes in individual status in transforming economies can drive the decision making of leaders in those economies (Pearce, Ramiriz & Branyiczki).
- Perceptual distance between leader and team differentially influence team cohesion and outcomes in different cultural contexts (Gibson, Conger & Cooper).
- Creating a hybrid, blended or third-culture in multicultural organizations is an important leadership challenge (Kiely).

- Effective virtual or distance leadership and teaming requires balancing face-to-face interaction at early and other key stages of development on certain tasks, including intense negotiating; overcoming loss of creativity from informal face-to-face interaction; establishing and maintaining trust across cultural differences; and building in communication checks and balances (Kiely; Eyring).
- A broader field to play in – Hollenbeck takes us lots of new places to look.
- Questioning assumptions – Crabtree suggests that culture may not be the important variable.
- Relationship between Cultural Revolution and effective leadership – Chen and Fahr show how two Chinas evolved.
- Deeper look at relationships – Tjosvold and Hui find some common ground amidst seemingly vast differences.
- Higher sights – Pearce et al. give us a way of looking at macroeconomic and social transformation effects on leaders.
- New perspectives on where the early training of leaders may come from – Isabella and Spekman.
- Integration of the pieces – Corace builds a global leader pipeline.
- Using experience to develop leaders and managing the repatriation dilemma – concrete counterintuitive suggestions from Hall et al.
- Men and women have similarities and differences with regard to career development opportunities and barriers – Adler et al.

But for all the advances, much remains to be done. Crucial issues call for more research and gaps still exist. One of the largest ones is the increasing gap between the interests of traditional leadership researchers plying their variables and methods across cultures and the concerns of the practitioners facing the problems of leadership on a daily basis. Other than using the same words – global leadership – there seems to be little in common between the two groups. Our academic colleagues addressed relatively few of the real time vignettes described in the introduction, and few of our corporate colleagues reference the work of our academic colleagues. Are we looking for the same leopard in the same woods?

We have used the metaphor of the spots on the leopard to characterize our knowledge of multinational and global leadership. The leopard is camouflaged in deep woods, is moving and is growing. Dickson, Hanges & Lord reminded us that "Perhaps the greatest cultural difference is the limiting effects of the researcher's host culture on the on the types of leadership theories developed." Yet, we must try to lift our own cultural blinders as we examine leadership in a global context. Dickson et al. also reminded us that culture is not geographic,

WILLIAM H. MOBLEY AND MORGAN W. MCCALL, JR.

but that reference groups have shared values and a given country can have multiple reference groups.

Where do we go from here? It is clear that individual differences; organizational strategy, structure, practices and cultures; and country cultures have to be measured more effectively and considered concurrently to effectively capture the determinants and consequences of effective international and global leadership. It is long established that performance is a function of both individual and situation. But individuals and situations are changing, neither is static, and the set of individual, organizational and cultural variables worthy of examination is expanding.

Understanding effective leadership in international settings requires more specificity about individual differences than a set of static competencies. We know that cognitive complexity, perceptual and information processing, relationship competency, ability and willingness to learn and adapt from experience are particularly important in international settings. But we also know that the importance of various other competencies are related to the organization's strategy, stage of development and maturity, the markets and cultures involved, and the level at which leadership is being exercised. The call for more multivariate, multilevel research is not new, but nowhere is the need for such research more compelling than in the area of international and global research. The high level of confounding and lack of generalizability in narrowly conceived leadership research is amply evident. We may learn something from each bit of data, no matter what method or design, but we will accelerate learning through seeking to unravel the complexity rather than by ignoring it.

We also would encourage our colleagues to consider framing their research models and hypotheses in terms of some of the issues and challenges faced by global organizations and global leaders rather than by narrowly confined individual, cultural or organizational variables. Further, longitudinal studies that capture the socialization (Chen & Fahr), economic transformation (Pearce et al.), and homogenization (Crabtree) processes discussed in several chapters will be increasingly important as globalization of business continues.

The leopard is still in the woods, is moving, growing, adapting and reproducing. Many dots remain to be seen, connected and fully mapped. But some new dots have been focused, some new connections made, some speculative images offered, and some future ideas suggested. While the hunt continues, we hope both those engaged in the hunt for better understanding of the global leadership leopard as well as those making real time global leadership and leader development decisions will have garnered some useful insights from this volume.

REFERENCES

Bass, B. (1990). *Bass and Stogdill's Handbook of Leadership* (3rd ed.). New York: Free Press.

DuBrin, A. (1998). *The Complete Idiot's Guide to Leadership*. New York: Alpha Books.

Stogdill, R. (1974). *Handbook of Leadership*. New York: Free Press.

Thomas, L. (1983). *Late Night Thoughts on Listening to Mahler's Ninth Symphony*. New York: Viking.

ABOUT THE EDITORS

William H. (Bill) Mobley, Ph.D. is president and managing director of PDI Global Research Consortia Ltd. (GRC) with offices in Hong Kong, Dallas and London. For the past six years his primary residence has been in Hong Kong. GRC is a group of multinational companies – including IBM, H-P, Honeywell, Coca-Cola, Motorola, BP-Amoco, MCI Worldcom, Caltex and Shell, among others – that sponsor multinational organizational research on such topics as cross-cultural leadership, multinational joint venture effectiveness, global-virtual leadership and team effectiveness, and acceleration of the development of leadership in emerging markets. Refer to the GRC web-site (www.grcl.com) for more detail.

Born and raised in Ohio, Mobley earned his B. A. degree in psychology and economics from Denison University in Ohio and his Ph.D. degree in industrial-organizational psychology from the University of Maryland, College Park. His Ph.D. dissertation on employee motivation was recognized as the outstanding applied psychology dissertation in the U.S. He also has been awarded honorary degrees from the University of the Americas in Pueblo Mexico and the University of Akron. He has served as a Senior Fulbright Professor at National Taiwan University, visiting professor at Hong Kong University of Science and Technology and The University of Hong Kong and as a visiting fellow at Cornell University. He is a fellow in the American Psychological Society, American Psychological Society, Society for Industrial Organizational Psychologists and is a registered industrial-organizational psychologist in Hong Kong.

Mobley is best known for his work on international leadership development; executive coaching; management selection, development, motivation and turnover; international and strategic human resources management, and cross-cultural joint venture management. He is author of multiple publications including *Employee Turnover: Causes, Consequences and Control* (Addison Wesley) and is executive editor of *Advances in Global Leadership* (JAI Press, 1999, 2001).

Previous roles include manager of HR research and planning for PPG Industries, Dean of the College of Business Administration at Texas A&M University and president and chancellor of Texas A&M University. In 1999, he was named President Emeritus of Texas A&M University. He currently serves on the boards of directors for Concept Technologies Limited (Hong Kong) and Medici Medical Corporation (USA); as well as the boards of trustees of the AMMA Foundation, the Society of Industrial Organizational Psychology Foundation, and Denison University. He also is a U.S. representative on the Pacific Economic Cooperation Council (PECC).

Morgan W. McCall, Jr. is a professor of management and organization in the Marshall School of Business at the University of Southern California. In addition to his faculty responsibilities, he works with the Office of Executive Development in the design and delivery of executive programs, teaches in the International Business Education and Research (IBEAR) program, and is affiliated with the Center for Effective Organizations. Prior to joining U.S.C, McCall was director of research and a senior behavioral scientist at the Center for Creative Leadership in Greensboro, North Carolina.

Executive leadership, especially early identification, assessment, development, and derailment of executives, is the primary focus of McCall's research and writing. He is the author of *High Flyers: Developing the Next Generation of Leaders* published by Harvard Business School Press (and winner of the 1998 Athena Award for Excellence in Mentoring). He co-authored *The Lessons of Experience*, a book on how executives develop that won the "New Perspectives on Executive Leadership Award" and was a MacMillan Book Club and "Fast Track" selection. He is co-author of *Whatever it Takes: The Realities of Managerial Decision Making* (now in its second edition), *Leadership: Where Else can We Go?*, and *Key Events in Executives' Lives.* He has two new books in preparation, *Frequent Flyers: Developing Global Executives* (with George Hollenbeck) and, co-edited with Mobley, *Advances in Global Leadership* (Volume II). His career contributions were honored recently when he received the Marion Gislason award for "Leadership in Executive Development" from the Executive Development Roundtable at Boston University.

An active speaker and consultant, McCall has worked with a variety of organizations including Amgen, Boeing, British Airways, Cisco Systems, Royal Bank of Canada, Ford Motor Company, Hewlett-Packard, Johnson & Johnson, San Miguel Corporation, Sun Microsystems, and Toyota Motor Sales. He is on the faculty of SunU and the University of Toyota. In addition to conducting workshops and seminars on executive leadership, he works with senior executives to develop corporate strategies and systems for executive succession and development. He led the team that created *Looking Glass, Inc.*, a simulation of managerial work widely used in corporate management development. More recently he (along with Gretchen Spreitzer and Jay Mahoney) developed a multi-rater instrument to assess "openness to learning" based on a study of the early identification of global executives.

After receiving a B.S. with honors from Yale University, McCall earned his Ph.D. from the New York State School of Industrial and Labor Relations at Cornell. He is a Fellow of the American Psychological Association, the American Psychological Society, and the Society for Industrial and Organizational Psychology. He has served on numerous editorial boards, including the *Academy of Management Review*, the *Academy of Management Executive*, *Human Resource Development Quarterly*, and *Executive Development Journal*.

ABOUT THE CONTRIBUTORS

George P. Hollenbeck is an organizational psychologist specializing in executive leadership development. His career includes positions at Merrill Lynch as vice president-human pesources, at Fidelity Investments as vice president organization planning, and at the Harvard Business School as senior director, executive education. After receiving his Ph.D. from the University of Wisconsin, Hollenbeck worked at IBM and The Psychological Corporation, and he was a post-doctoral fellow at the University of California, Berkeley prior to joining Merrill Lynch. As a senior executive at Merrill, he attended Harvard Business School's Advanced Management Program. He is a Diplomate of the American Board of Professional Psychology, and a licensed psychologist in New York and Massachusetts.

Hollenbeck consults, teaches and writes about leadership. His consulting focuses on business leadership at all levels, working individually with a wide range of executives to augment their development. His teaching includes executives and MBA students at Boston University and doctoral students at Texas A&M University. At the Center for Creative Leadership he has taught in the program "Tools for Developing Successful Executives."

Hollenbeck has authored and co-authored articles and books in the areas of executive coaching, selection and leadership development. With co-author Morgan McCall, he is currently writing a book on developing global executives, based on data from interviews with a worldwide group of outstanding international executives, to be published by Harvard Business Press in 2001.

Howard Crabtree is vice president organization and human resources with Minerals Technologies Inc., a global producer and marketer of mineral, mineral-based and synthetic mineral products. He is a member of the company's Corporate Management Committee. Mr. Crabtree received a BSc (First Class Honors) in chemistry from the University of Sheffield in the United Kingdom in 1966 and achieved membership of the U.K. Institute of Personnel Management by examination in 1974. He has had firsthand experience in the management of manufacturing, information technology and human resources and has consulted on organizational processes and structures in many countries. Prior to joining his current company he worked for Pfizer Inc. for more than 20 years, located in places as diverse as Sandwich, U.K.; Nairobi, Kenya; and New York. He has also lived and worked in the Netherlands. This is his first published writing on a business subject although writing about similar subjects for internal company consumption has always been a passion. The writings are based on his observations of leaders in action at all levels and in a variety of companies in all parts of the world.

Marcus W. Dickson is assistant professor of Industrial/Organizational Psychology at Wayne State University in Detroit, Michigan. He was a charter member of the Global Leadership and Organizational Behavior Effectiveness (GLOBE) Research Project, a member of the GLOBE Coordinating Team for six years, and he served as co-principal investigator on that project for two years. He received his Ph.D. in I/O Psychology from the University of Maryland in 1997. His research interests include cross-cultural organizational culture analysis, organizational climate (especially ethical climate and climate for innovation) and computer-mediated communication in organizations. He currently serves as a member of the editorial board of the *Journal of Organizational Behavior*, and his work has appeared in *Leadership Quarterly*, *Applied Psychology: An International Review*, and *The Handbook of Organizational Culture and Climate*, among others.

Paul J. Hanges has been a co-principal investigator of the Global Leadership and Organizational Behavior Effectiveness (GLOBE) Research Project since its inception, and has primarily responsible for the quantitative data analysis on that project. He received his Ph.D. in Industrial/Organizational Psychology from the University of Akron. He is an associate editor for *Leadership Quarterly*, and a member of the Society for Organizational Behavior. In addition to leadership issues, other research interests include personnel selection, managerial/leadership performance, and research methodology. He is currently associate professor of Industrial/Organizational Psychology at the University of Maryland.

Robert G. Lord received his Ph.D. in Organizational Psychology from Carnegie-Mellon University in 1975. He has been at the University of Akron since that time and is currently a professor and chair of the Department of Psychology. He is a fellow of the Society for Industrial and Organizational Psychology and a founding fellow of the American Psychological Society. He has published extensively on topics related to motivation, self-regulation, social cognition, leadership processes, leadership perceptions and information processing. He co-authored *Leadership and Information Processing: Linking Perceptions and Performance*, (Routledge, 1991) with Karen J. Maher. He also served as associate editor of the *Journal of Applied Psychology* and is currently editing the Jossey-Bass Frontiers series book *Emotions at Work* along with Rich Klimoski and Ruth Kanfer.

Dr. Xiao-Ping Chen is an assistant professor in the Department of Management and Organization at University of Washington. She has received her Ph.D. in Social and Organizational Psychology in 1995 from University of Illinois. She had been a faculty member at Indiana University and the Hong Kong University of Science and Technology. Her current research interests include group dynamics, decision-making, conflict management, leadership, employee turnover and cross-cultural management. Her research has been published in academic journals such as *Organizational Behavior and Human Decision Processes, Academy of Management Review, Journal of Applied Psychology, Management Science, Journal of Cross-Cultural Psychology* and *Journal of Personality and Social Psychology*. Her teaching interest includes Organizational Behavior, Human Resource Management, Business Negotiation and Cross-Cultural Management.

Dr. Jiing-Lih Fahr is a professor and head of the Department of Management of Organizations at the School of Business and Management at the Hong Kong University of Science and Technology, Clear Water Bay, Kowloon, Hong Kong (e-mail: mnlfarh@ust.hk). His current research interests include *guanxi* and managerial networking, paternalistic leadership, organizational justice, organizational citizenship behavior and values and business ethics in Chinese societies. His articles have appeared in *Administrative Science Quarterly, Academy of Management Journal, Organization Science, Journal of Applied Psychology, Personnel Psychology, Journal of International Business Studies, Journal of Management, Journal of Vocational Behavior* and *Organizational Behavior and Human Decision Processes*. He is currently on the editorial boards of *Academy of Management Journal, Journal of Management, Personnel Psychology, Human Relations, Leadership Quarterly* and *Indigenous Psychological Research in Chinese Societies*. He has received his Ph.D. in business administration from Indiana University at Bloomington in 1983.

Dean Tjosvold earned his masters degree in history and his Ph.D. in the social psychology of organizations at the University of Minnesota, both in 1972. He has published over 150 articles and 15 books on managing conflict, cooperation and competition, decision-making, power, and other management issues. He has served on several editorial boards, including the *Academy of Management Review, Journal of Organizational Behavior* and *Small Group Research*. He has taught at Pennsylvania State University, Simon Fraser University, the National University of Singapore, the State University of Groningen, The Netherlands, Hong Kong University of Science and Technology and City University of Hong Kong. He is now chair professor and head of management, Lingnan University in Hong Kong. He is a partner in his family health care business, which has 600 employees and is based in Minnesota.

Chun Hui received both his M.A. in social psychology and his Ph.D. in organizational behavior/human resources management from Indiana University at Bloomington. His research interests include leadership, conflict management, selection, performance appraisal, comparative management and Chinese management. He has published in the *Journal of Applied Psychology, Organizational Behavior and Human Decision Processes*, and other top management and social psychology journals and books. He is an associate professor at the Department of International Business, the Chinese University of Hong Kong and before that he taught at the Hong Kong University of Science and Technology.

Jone L. Pearce is professor of organizational behavior at the Graduate School of Management, University of California, Irvine. She studies social processes and participants' expectations, attitudes and behavior in and across organizations, with particular attention to how they are affected by management and governmental practices. She received her Ph.D. from Yale University and has taught at Carnegie-Mellon University, the International Management Center (Budapest, Hungary) and Budapest University of Economic Sciences.

Raul R. Ramirez is currently a doctoral student in Organizational Behavior and Strategy in the Graduate School of Management at the University of California Irvine. His research interests include status, organizational change and human resources. He has worked in human resources management for Merck and Frito-Lay.

Imre Branyiczki is Director of Human Resources Management at Takarékbank and adjunct associate professor in the Faculty of Business Administration at Budapest University of Economic Sciences. His research interests center on organizational learning and change and the effects of human resources management practices. He received his doctorate from Budapest University of Economic Sciences and Ph.D. from the Hungarian Academy of Sciences, and has been a visiting scholar at the business schools of Harvard and Carnegie-Mellon universities and has taught at the University of California, Irvine.

Lynn A. Isabella is Associate Professor of Business Administration, Darden Graduate School of Business, University of Virginia, Charlottesville. She earned her B.S. from Tufts University in mathematics, an Ed.M. from Harvard University in Organization Development, and a D.B.A. and M.B.A. from Boston University. Before joining the faculty at Darden, Dr. Isabella was on the faculty at the Edwin L. Cox School of Business, Southern Methodist University in Dallas, Texas, and has taught at the Harvard Business School. Prior to her academic career, Dr. Isabella was a computer programmer on the first Apollo moon launch. Dr. Isabella's areas of expertise include leadership, team building, organizational change, and strategic alliances and partnerships. Dr. Isabella is co-author of a book on strategic alliances, Building Alliance Competence, Maximizing the Value of Your Partnerships. Numerous articles and management briefings have appeared in *Harvard Business Review*, *Academy of Management Journal*, *Organizational Dynamics*, *Journal of Organizational Behavior*, *Journal of Vocational Behavior*, *Journal of Management*, *Business Horizons*, and *Personnel*. As a management and organizational consultant, Dr. Isabella has worked extensively with private and public sector companies throughout the world. Recent clients include Continental AG, Bacardi-Martini Ltd., Lufthansa, Brown Forman, Petroles de Venezuela, S. A., and AT&T.

Robert E. Spekman is the Taylor Murphy Professor of Business Administration at The Darden School. He was formerly Professor of Marketing and Associate Director of the Center for Telecommunications at the University of Southern California. He is an internationally recognized authority on business-to-business marketing and strategic alliances. His consulting experiences range from marketing research and competitive analysis, to strategic market planning, supply chain management, channels of distribution design and implementation, and strategic partnering. Professor Spekman has taught in a number of executive programs in the U.S., Canada, Latin America, Asia and Europe. His executive program experience includes general marketing strategy, sales force management, channels strategy, creating strategic alliances and business-to-business marketing strategy, and a number of single company and senior executive management programs. He has edited/written seven books and has authored (co-authored) over 80 articles and papers. Professor Spekman also serves as a reviewer for a number of marketing and management journals as well as for the National Science Foundation. Prior to joining the faculty at U.S.C, Professor Spekman taught in the College of Business at the University of Maryland, College Park. During his tenure at Maryland, he was granted the Most Distinguished Faculty Award by the MBA students on three separate occasions. Among his clients are AT&T, Ameritech, Ameron, Bell Atlantic, Banc One, Bell Communications Research, BellSouth, Caterpillar, FMC, GTE, Hewlett Packard, Milliken, Monsanto, Nortel, NYNEX, Pacific Telephone, PDVSA, Phillips Petroleum, Procter & Gamble, Southern New England Telephone, Siemens, Scott Paper, Southwestern Bell, TRW, Weyerhaeuser, and Xerox. Spekman also serves on the board of directors of Comdial.

Laree Kiely, president of K/C Associates, Inc. – Organizational Change Consultants, also teaches managerial behavior in the Executive MBA, executive education and facilitator and trainer programs. She has 20 years' experience consulting, facilitating, and teaching organizational behavior in the U.S., Canada, Australia, the Czech Republic, and the People's Republic of China. She received her B.A. and M.A. from the University of Colorado and her Ph.D. from the University of Southern California. Her current work includes measuring the effects of "soft-skill" training, Ideamining, group processes and decision-making, negotiation, leadership, influence and persuasion, and intercultural issues. Dr. Kiely is the recipient of several teaching awards, including the U.S.C Marshall School of Business "Golden Apple" Award for Teaching Excellence and the "Teacher of the Year" Award from the U.S.C Food Industry Management Program. Her distance learning course called "Leading the Global Workforce" was awarded the Best Distance Learning Program of 1996 by the International Distance Learning Association. In 1997, she was given the "Most Significant Contribution by an Individual to Distance Learning" award by IDLCON. In 1998, she was awarded the overall "Excellence in Distance Learning Teaching" IDLCON, and in 1999, her course on "Negotiation: Plays, Ploys, and Pitfalls" was granted the Best Distance Learning Program for Corporate Development from IDLCON.

In addition to several papers and articles on communication issues, Dr. Kiely is the author of *Business Communication: Tools for Leadership*; and co-author of Taking Charge: A Guide to Personal Productivity, (Addison-Wesley, 1991), *Everything's Negotiable*, Amacom Press, 1994. You can see her award-winning program Business Communication: Tools for Leadership, regularly on PBS/ETV.

Cristina B. Gibson, Ph.D., is currently assistant research professor at the Center for Effective Organizations, University of Southern California. Her research interests include communication, interaction and effectiveness in teams, the impact of culture and gender on work behavior, social cognition and international management. In her work with teams in multinational organizations, Dr. Gibson strives to increase performance, longevity and quality of work life for team members from various cultures. She is co-author with P. Christopher Earley of the forthcoming book New Perspectives on Multinational Teams (Lawrence Earlbaum Associates, Inc.) and has contributed to numerous books on human resource theory and practice. Her research has appeared in the *Academy of Management Journal, Journal of Management, Journal of International Business Studies, Journal of Cross-cultural Psychology, International Executive, Advances in International Comparative Management,* and *Journal of Managerial Issues.* Dr. Gibson is also the recipient of numerous awards recognizing her research. In 1996 she was awarded comprehensive funding from the National Science Foundation to investigate the implementation of teams in multinational corporations. Together with colleague Susan Cohen, she received a second four-year research grant from the National Science Foundation in 1999 to investigate creating conditions for effective geographically dispersed and virtual teams.

Jay Conger is professor of organizational behavior at the London Business School and Senior Research Scientist at the Center for Effective Organizations at the University of Southern California. He studies leadership, corporate boards, empowerment, management development and innovation. He has published nine books and over 70 articles and chapters on the subject of leadership. Dr. Conger's 1998 co-authored book *Charismatic Leadership in Organizations* (Sage) won the Choice Book Award for its contribution to the management literature. He has served on the faculties of the Harvard Business School, INSEAD, McGill University and the University of Southern California. From 1995 to 1999, Dr. Conger was the executive director of the Leadership Institute, a research think-tank and educational center at the University of Southern California.

Cecily Cooper is currently a doctoral candidate specializing in organizational behavior in the Department of Management & Organization at the University of Southern California. Cecily's research interests include humor in the workplace, perception and misperception in social interactions, telecommuting, organizational dress and emotion (felt and expressed). She has presented her research at the Academy of Management and Southern Management Association annual meetings.

Alison Eyring is president of Organisation Solutions Pte Ltd., an international organization design, development, and change solutions company based in Singapore. Her professional experience includes work in the U.S., Latin America and Asia as an internal and external organization development consultant, corporate manager, and executive. Her work has focused in areas of strategy, organization and people development, and IT/internet design and implementation.

Eyring currently serves as a senior fellow (part-time) at the National University of Singapore where she has taught graduate level courses in organization development and change enablement. Her current research includes a consortium study on organizational practices that increase brand value in Asia, and a study of practices that promote effective performance in distributed work groups in Asia. Eyring's work has been published in academic journals such as the *Journal of Vocational Behaviour, Journal of Business Ethics* and the *Journal of Occupational and Organizational Psychology*. She also has presented her work at the Society of Industrial/Organisational Psychologists and the Academy of Management. Eyring received her Ph.D. and MA in Industrial/Organizational Psychology from the University of Houston in Texas. Her BA (hons) was in International Business from the University of Tennessee and the Universidad Autonoma de Madrid (Spain).

Charles J. Corace, director management education and development, for Johnson & Johnson, has responsibility for corporate-wide executive development products and services. In this role, he and his organization work closely with the senior management of Johnson & Johnson to define and implement experiences, which support the development of global business leaders. Prior to this assignment, he held the position of regional director, learning services. This organization was created as a shared service within Johnson & Johnson and provided organizational consulting support to the operating companies within North America. Over the past 15 years with Johnson & Johnson, Corace has held positions in the areas of human resources and quality management as well. He is a member of the Executive Leadership Development Network and the Human Capital Forum. He has graduate and undergraduate degrees from LaSalle University.

Douglas T. Hall is a Professor of Organizational Behavior in the School of Management at Boston University. He is also the Director of the Executive Development Roundtable and a core faculty member of the Human Resources Policy Institute. He has also served as acting dean and associate dean of faculty development and faculty director for masters programs at the School of

Management. He received his BS degree from Yale University and his MS and Ph.D. from the Sloan School of Management at Massachusetts Institute of Technology. He has held faculty positions at Yale, York, Michigan State and Northwestern universities, as well as visiting positions at Columbia and the U.S. Military Academy at West Point. At Northwestern he held the Earl Dean Howard Chair in Organizational Behavior and served as department chair.

Hall is the author of *Careers in Organizations* and co-author of *The Career Is Dead – Long Live the Career, Organizational Climates and Careers, The Two-Career Couple, Experiences in Management and Organizational Behavior, Career Development in Organizations, Human Resource Management: Strategy Design and Implementation,* and *Handbook of Career Theory.* He is a recipient of the American Psychological Association's James McKeen Cattell Award (now called the Ghiselli Award) for research design. He also received the Walter Storey Professional Practice Award from the American Society for Training and Development (ASTD). He is a Fellow of the American Psychological Association and a Fellow of the Academy of Management, where he served on the board of governors. He was also a member of the board of governors of the Center for Creative Leadership. He has served on the editorial boards of nine scholarly journals.

Hall's research and consulting activities have dealt with career development, women's careers, career plateauing, work/family balance and executive succession. He has served as a consultant to organizations such as Sears, AT&T, American Hospital Supply, General Electric, Borg-Warner, Price Waterhouse, Monsanto, Honeywell, Ford Motor Company, Eli Lilly, and the World Bank.

Guorong Zhu is a doctoral candidate in organizational behavior at the School of Management, Boston University. Her dissertation study is on psychological contract alignment and repatriation success. Her research is in international human resources management, with a focus on expatriation, repatriation and global leadership development.

Aimin Yan is associate professor of organizational behavior, faculty director of the International Management Program-China, and research director of the Human Resources Policy Institute of the School of Management of Boston University. He is a core faculty member of the Executive Development Roundtable, an honorary advisory professor of the Shanghai University for Science and Technology and an honorable visiting professor of the Dong Hua University of China. Yan received his Ph.D. in business administration from Pennsylvania State University and graduated from the Bachelor of Engineering and MBA programs at the Shanghai Institute of Mechanical Engineering.

Yan's primary research interests are in the areas of negotiation, control and management of inter-firm strategic alliances/joint ventures, organizations in transforming economies, organizational restructuring, and executive development in the international setting. His study of U.S.-China manufacturing joint ventures won him the Barry M. Richman Award for Best Dissertation of 1994 in International Management from the Academy of Management. He is also the winner of the School of Management's 1994–1995 Broderick Prize for Research.

Yan is the author of *International Joint Ventures: Theory and Practice*, and about 20 articles published in journals such as the Academy of Management Journal, *Journal of Applied Behavioral Science, Global Focus, Human Relations, Journal of International Business Studies*, and *Journal of Management Studies*. He teaches international/global management and organization design/theory at the undergraduate, MBA and doctoral levels; teaches in Boston University's International Management Programs in Japan and in China; and he teaches executive programs.

Nancy J. Adler is a Professor of Management at McGill University in Montreal, Canada. Dr. Adler consults with global companies and government organizations on projects in Asia, Europe, North and South America and the Middle East. She conducts research on strategic international human resource management, global leadership and global women leaders. She has authored more than 100 articles and produced the film, *A Portable Life*. Her books include *International Dimensions of Organizational Behavior* (with over 100,000 copies in print), *Women in Management Worldwide*, and *Competitive Frontiers: Women Managers in a Global Economy*. Professor Adler is a Fellow of both the Academy of Management and the Academy of International Business.

Laura W. Brody is currently the Director of Diversity and Development for Bestfoods. Over the past three years she has been responsible for a variety of workforce diversity initiatives including: Culture Connections – an employee driven education and awareness program, Sponsoring Our Success – a peer coaching and mentoring program for new hires, The Women's Global Leadership Forum – a worldwide career development and leadership program, as well as serving the facilitator for the Diversity Advisory Council, which is chaired by the CEO.

Joyce S. Osland is Associate Professor of Organizational Behavior at the University of Portland, Oregon. She lived and worked overseas in seven countries, primarily in West Africa and Latin America for 14 years, working as a manager, researcher, consultant and professor. Dr. Osland's current research and consulting focus includes expatriates, cultural sense making, Latin American management and global leadership. She is the author of *The Adventure of Working Abroad: Hero Tales from the Global Frontier* (Jossey-Bass, 1995) and co-author of *Organizational Behavior: An Experiential Approach and The Organizational Behavior Reader* (Prentice Hall, 2000).

TABLE OF CONTENTS FROM VOLUME 1

BASEMENT